Praise for

Flee North

"This book is a treasure. Weaving together three unforgettable characters, Scott Shane transforms the origins of the underground railroad from a romantic nickname into a full-scale human drama of tears, triumph, and laughter."   —Taylor Branch, Pulitzer Prize–winning
author of *Parting the Waters: America in the King Years, 1954–63*

"Scott Shane has unearthed an extraordinary tale. His fast-paced story is not just inspiring, but also offers the satisfying spectacle of seeing exasperated slaveholders who had lost their human property get publicly taunted by one of the brave pair who helped smuggle these men, women, and children to freedom."

—Adam Hochschild, award-winning historian and
author of *American Midnight* and many other books

"The tremendous achievements of the man who coined the term 'underground railroad' are given their full due in the former *New York Times* journalist Scott Shane's *Flee North*."   —*The New York Times*

"Written in an engaging, dynamic style, *Flee North* will captivate readers who want to know how people like Smallwood succeeded in duping countless enslavers. The fascinating tale of a swashbuckling abolitionist and his white activist companion will make readers wish for a film adaptation. This book is a tale of triumph in the face of unspeakable adversity. Highly recommended for both public and academic libraries."

—*Booklist* (starred review)

"A forgotten chapter in abolitionist history is restored to history in a lively, readable narrative."   —*Kirkus Reviews*

T0370120

Flee North

A Forgotten
Hero and the
Fight for Freedom
in Slavery's
Borderland

Scott Shane

CELADON
BOOKS

NEW YORK

www.celadonbooks.com

Designed by Michelle McMillian

The Library of Congress has cataloged the hardcover edition as follows:

Names: Shane, Scott, 1954– author.
Title: Flee north : a forgotten hero and the fight for freedom in slavery's borderland /
  Scott Shane.
Other titles: Forgotten hero and the fight for freedom in slavery's borderland
Description: First edition. | New York : Celadon Books, 2023. | Includes bibliographical
  references and index.
Identifiers: LCCN 2023012436 | ISBN 9781250843210 (hardcover) | ISBN 9781250843227
  (ebook)
Subjects: LCSH: Smallwood, Thomas, 1801–1883 (Main entry to be updated & alt. id) |
  African American abolitionists—Biography. | Abolitionists—United States—Biography. |
  Underground Railroad. | Torrey, Charles T. (Charles Turner), 1813–1846. | Slatter,
  Hope H. (Hope Hull), 1790–1853. | Slave trade—United States—History—19th century. |
  Fugitive slaves—United States—History—19th century. | Toronto (Ont.)—Biography.
Classification: LCC E450.S59 S53 2023 | DDC 973.7/115092 [B]—dc23/eng/20230425
LC record available at https://lccn.loc.gov/2023012436

ISBN 978-1-250-84323-4 (trade paperback)

Our books may be purchased in bulk for promotional, educational,
or business use. Please contact your local bookseller or the Macmillan Corporate
and Premium Sales Department at 1-800-221-7945, extension 5442,
or by email at MacmillanSpecialMarkets@macmillan.com.

First Celadon Books Paperback Edition: 2024

10 9 8 7 6 5 4 3 2 1

For Francie, my whole-souled partner in all things

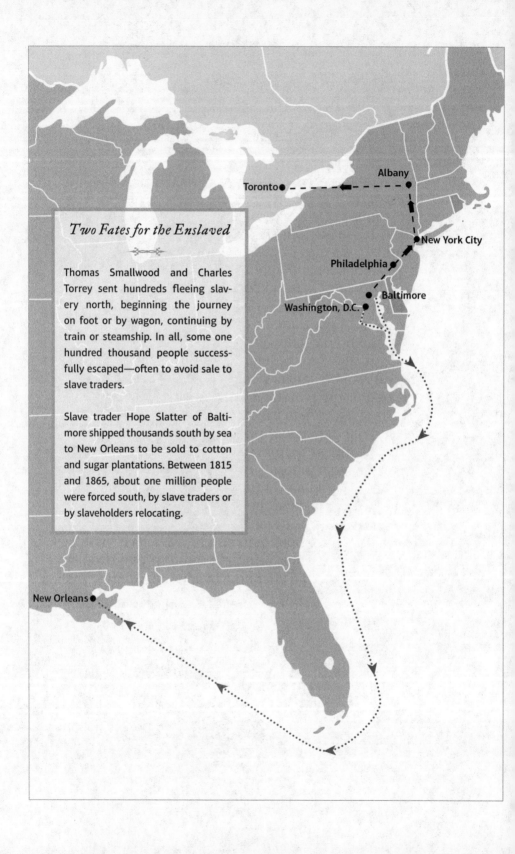

Two Fates for the Enslaved

Thomas Smallwood and Charles Torrey sent hundreds fleeing slavery north, beginning the journey on foot or by wagon, continuing by train or steamship. In all, some one hundred thousand people successfully escaped—often to avoid sale to slave traders.

Slave trader Hope Slatter of Baltimore shipped thousands south by sea to New Orleans to be sold to cotton and sugar plantations. Between 1815 and 1865, about one million people were forced south, by slave traders or by slaveholders relocating.

Toronto

Albany

New York City

Philadelphia

Baltimore

Washington, D.C.

New Orleans

Contents

Contents

Flee North

Prologue

There were a hundred details for Thomas Smallwood to worry about as he organized yet another mass escape from slavery in the nation's capital. But when he wrote about this particular episode years later, he paused to savor one especially satisfying memory: a half dozen pampered Washington slaveholders awakening to discover that something had gone drastically wrong. Prosperous people accustomed to thinking of themselves as masters and mistresses found themselves, quite literally, at a loss:

> Morning arrived, and with it a terrible uproar. One had no one to get breakfast: Ann had absconded taking with her all her children; another had no one to black the boots, to set the table, and to wait breakfast—Bill had taken French leave, and gone about his business; and a third, had no one to drive the coach to church; others were also in as bad a fix.

At the urging of Smallwood, a Black shoemaker who had bought his own freedom and was now engineering escapes from bondage on an unprecedented scale, some fifteen enslaved people had slipped away from their slaveholders' houses on a sweltering August night in 1842—taking what Smallwood called "French leave," a sardonically elegant term for skipping work. One of the fleeing families had to overcome a poignant obstacle: a daughter, only five years old, had been assigned the job of staying up all night, every night, in her enslavers' bedroom, beside the baby's cradle. Should the infant stir she was required to instantly rock the cradle "to prevent it from disturbing their slumbers."

The cradle rocker's enslaved mother managed to spirit her daughter from the bedroom without waking the baby or its parents, "as if by special providence of the Lord," Smallwood wrote. All fifteen people managed to gather as planned that night, but their liberators had run into trouble procuring the getaway wagon and the horses to pull it. So the uneasy fugitives had to hide for an extra day with Smallwood's help, scattered around the city in the homes or sheds of trusted friends, keeping an eye out for their angry enslavers and the bounty-hunting police who prowled for runaways.

On the second night, Smallwood handed off this latest band of freedom seekers to his white partner, Charles Torrey, a devout young New Englander—"that most excellent and whole-souled Abolitionist," in Smallwood's words—and the group took off, with Torrey driving the wagon. A tense overnight journey brought them to a safe house in Baltimore, where the fugitives again had to be on the lookout for police constables and slave catchers looking for runaways. Another day's travel would bring them to the Susquehanna River and the Pennsylvania line, with its promise of liberty.

As the suddenly bereft slaveholders realized what had happened, there was pandemonium. The wagonload of enslaved people had a value on the auction block of some $200,000 in today's dollars. They had vanished simultaneously from households all over Washington—a heist on the scale of a major bank robbery, if the bank held human deposits. The slaveholders organized a pursuit, assuming the fugitives had departed the first night, but were puzzled to find no trace of them on the roads and rough trails north of Baltimore. The next day the baffled search party turned back—and headed south on the very road that Torrey's delayed wagon was now taking north. The fugitives' escape seemed doomed.

But they got a remarkable break—in this case, no metaphor. An axle snapped on the overloaded wagon, and Torrey, a bookish Yale graduate not entirely accustomed to such driving, steered it off the highway into the thick woods of northeastern Maryland to try to make repairs. There, from the shelter of trees, the fugitives watched their pursuers pass south on the way back to Washington.

A week later, from the Hudson River town of Troy, New York, Torrey wrote to Smallwood, mocking the enslavers' bloodless language about their "property," a standing joke between the two men.

"I have arrived at Troy safe, with the chattels," he wrote, "and am now shipping them on board of a canal boat for Canada."

Did Smallwood, taking satisfaction in their clandestine success, choose to keep quiet about it? Far from it. He celebrated the runaways and mocked their oppressors in the column he wrote for an abolitionist newspaper in Albany, where Torrey was shortly to take over as editor. Smallwood's lengthy dispatch ran under a headline lampooning the pro-verbial claims of slaveholders about the supposed contentment of their enslaved workforce.

"More Fleeing from Happiness," it read.

In the distinctive satirical writing style he was developing, Smallwood addressed by name the enslavers who had just suffered such a painful loss—and also named those who had fled to freedom in the north, most of them to Canada. To the aggrieved slaveholders, he offered his mock sympathy, "paying my respects to the large number who have recently been afflicted by the loss of their beloved servants!" And he went on to bare the slaveholders' secrets—secrets those they had held in bondage knew only too well. He exposed one who had been raping, or attempting to rape, a young woman who had fled. Another he denounced for his brutal whippings of those he enslaved. Of two others, who were known to be smarting from their losses, he reported with pleasure that they had been overheard vowing never to buy another slave. He addressed several of them sternly, including a doctor, William H. Gunnell—the man who had required the little enslaved girl to rock his infant's cradle:

On reflection, don't you think it was cruel, Dr. Gunnell, to make that little child, only five years old, lie on your chamber floor, and keep awake to tend your own *white* baby, while you and your wife slept?

But if the slaveholders saw intimate details of their lives revealed, they did not learn who had the audacity to expose them. Smallwood signed his dispatch to the Albany paper with his usual pseudonym, borrowed from a favorite writer, Charles Dickens. Samivel, or Samuel, Weller was a comic character in Dickens's bestselling *Pickwick Papers,* and Smallwood posed as Weller's son, Sam Weller Jr. And to make sure his stinging missives hit their mark, he asked his editors to mail a copy of the appropriate issue of the newspaper, the *Tocsin of Liberty*, to the slaveholders he had identified. Finding themselves taunted and humiliated in print, they could only wonder just which of their neighbors this Sam Weller might be.

It was the latest triumph in a rocky and risky business. Smallwood and Torrey had begun to describe their spiriting away of people from bondage with a new term, one Smallwood was the first to use in print: "under ground rail-road." Smallwood used it initially to ridicule the slaveholders' wide-eyed bafflement that the people they enslaved, whom they often derided as incapable of planning anything or even looking after themselves, somehow managed to disappear overnight without a trace. He fashioned this mythical transport system into a trope of Black empowerment and a lash for the enslavers and their hired hands, the slave-catching police. The name caught on.

The goal of the two swashbuckling abolitionists was not just to help people by the score escape from slavery and start a new life in the north. They hoped their tactics might add up to a strategy: that by stealing the human assets of the enslavers, they might destroy the slaveholders' faith in the profitability of treating people as property. Disillusioned by their losses, Smallwood and Torrey imagined, enslavers would conclude that actually paying people for their labor might be a safer and cheaper bet. And then, they imagined, the malevolent institution on which the American economy had been built just might begin to crumble.

⊷═◉═⊶

A daring activist and searing writer, self-taught and selflessly motivated, Thomas Smallwood was a striking figure in the American antislavery movement who has largely been lost to history, either mentioned in passing as a Black sidekick to Torrey or overlooked altogether. He deserves much more.

Having acquired his own freedom, Smallwood risked it again and again for the sake of others still in bondage. With Torrey, he forged an escape network that became a model for radical action up to the Civil War, operating a decade before the far-better-known Harriet Tubman. A man of wonderful wit, Smallwood not only gave the underground railroad its name (picking up the phrase from a casual remark by a frustrated slave-catching constable). He also left a short, fascinating memoir. And in his pseudonymous newspaper dispatches, he crafted unique, real-time accounts of escapes from slavery that add up to a satirical masterpiece, Dickensian in style and rich in detail. In his blunt, shrewd, often sardonic analysis of American racism as the enduring plague that underlay slavery, he was far ahead of his time.

But the man who called himself, with a wink, the "general agent of all the branches of the National Underground Railroad, Steam Packet, Canal and Foot-it Company" would fade into oblivion. His bold white partner, Torrey, would get a much-deserved monument and two biographies. Smallwood, whose achievements were by many measures greater, would receive no such attention. Until recently, his remarkable newspaper columns lay moldering and forgotten in a Boston Public Library warehouse.

The unusual partnership of the older Black man and the younger white man commands attention, too. They forged an enterprise that was breathtakingly audacious. They worked courageously together to liberate people in Washington, Baltimore, and beyond, helping them to flee north. When the two men could they tried to do it wholesale—not in ones or twos, but whole families and carriage loads at a time. They did not passively wait until enslaved people decided on their own to run—

they actively encouraged them to flee. In shifting their efforts from theoretical debates about the fate of the enslaved to practical action, and in their merciless ridicule of the enslavers whose human property was vanishing, they hoped to erode the very institution of slavery. For a time, their operation was a blazing success.

Yet despite the pose of ostentatious celebration and carefree glee that Smallwood cultivated in his newspaper columns, he and Torrey knew they were engaged in a deadly serious enterprise, one that was making dangerous enemies. Organizing escapes was hazardous enough for a white man like Torrey, as events would prove. But even nominally free African Americans in the 1840s in the mid-Atlantic lived in a separate reality, under the tyranny of white leaders who reserved full freedom for their own kind. Smallwood, who had freed himself but still walked the legal tightrope reserved for free Black Americans, knew he was working against a relentless clock. Soon enough, the blows Smallwood and Torrey struck for liberty would rebound against both men, with dire consequences.

Their adversaries included not only the slaveholders Smallwood portrayed as hapless and degraded and the police officers paid to do the enslavers' bidding but also, perhaps most perilously, the slave traders who operated from Washington's mall and Baltimore's harbor. These human traffickers were directly competing with them for Black bodies—every person who successfully fled north was one more who could not be sold south. Even as Smallwood and Torrey were discreetly collecting enslaved people to lead to freedom, Hope H. Slatter, the region's leading slave trader and this book's third major character, had agents combing the towns and countryside, buying and carting away in shackles those the slaveholders deemed excess labor or a source of easy cash.

On October 21, 1842, the day before Smallwood sent his latest rollicking satire to Albany's *Tocsin of Liberty*, Slatter, whose "Cash for Negroes!" advertisements ran daily in *The Baltimore Sun* and other newspapers, signed the paperwork for his latest shipment south: seventy-seven men, women, and children, ages one to forty, who had been locked in Slatter's private slave jail near Baltimore's waterfront until he had accumulated a cost-efficient shipload. They were forced aboard the ship

Burlington and departed on a cold, wet, fetid journey to New Orleans, to be sold to the highest bidder and dispatched to the cotton and sugar plantations of the Deep South, where the lives of the enslaved were often cut short by a labor regime of appalling brutality. Many had been torn from their wives, husbands, mothers, fathers, children; most were leaving behind, almost certainly forever, everyone and everything they had ever known.

Slatter saw the likes of Smallwood and Torrey as lethal enemies to his business, and they returned the favor. He was regularly featured in the pages of the Albany paper as the iconic human trafficker, a diabolical character wringing profits from human tragedy. But business was steady, and Slatter had rationalizations at the ready. His story would end far more happily than those of his adversaries.

Together, the stories of Smallwood and Torrey, on the one hand, and Slatter, on the other, capture the contrasting possible fates that awaited the men, women, and children held as property in slavery's mid-Atlantic borderland—slave states that were tantalizingly close to free states. They could try to flee north, with great difficulty and at huge risk to their lives and safety. Or they could take their chances and stay put, enduring whatever physical or sexual abuse their enslaver might perpetrate, and risk being sold south at his whim. It was a terrible, terrifying predicament, and the two desperate possibilities fed on one another, as Smallwood knew well.

"I frequently had lots of slaves concealed about in Washington," he wrote, "who had fled to me for safety when they got wind that their masters were about to sell them to the slave traders."

But there was an excruciating irony: if the enslaved were caught trying to escape to avoid the hazard of being sold south, their punishment would often be exactly that. Their owner, no longer trusting that his property was secure, would drop the would-be runaway at Slatter's jail to await the next ship to New Orleans. This intertwining of the domestic slave trade and the underground railroad would continue to the Civil War. It is a stirring, agonizing chapter in the story of a foundational American crime, one whose consequences continue to haunt us every single day.

Thas Smallwood

Thomas Smallwood's signature in 1842, twelve years after he purchased his freedom and as he began organizing mass escapes from slavery, was a mark of his self-education and self-creation. No image exists of Smallwood, who would soon become a writer of extraordinary insight and style. [*Smallwood v. Coale*, National Archives]

The Most Inhuman System That Ever Blackened the Pages of History

A memory that would stay with Thomas Smallwood all his long life mixed pride with wry wonderment. As a young boy he was taught to read by the couple who enslaved him, a skill that distinguished him not just from other enslaved children but from most Black adults as well. In their rural community of Bladensburg, just east of the District of Columbia boundary, he became a sort of neighborhood spectacle, asked repeatedly to perform for the friends and neighbors of his owner.

> They were amazed at the fact that a black or colored person could learn the Alphabet, yea, learn to spell in two syllables. I appeared to be a walking curiosity in the village where I then lived, and when passing about the village I would be called into houses, and the neighbors collected around to hear me say the Alphabet and to spell baker and cider, to their great surprise, (which were the first two words in the two syllables of Webster's Spelling Book.)

It is an affecting scene—the cute Black prodigy wowing his white and Black neighbors with his mastery of the leading primer of the day. The passage presages Smallwood's dual identity in adulthood, as a Black man but one whose literacy, wide learning, and political consciousness would set him apart, first in slavery and later in freedom. He would develop the power to operate behind enemy lines in a slave society, studying the enslavers and their allies while rarely attracting notice.

Yet years later, as he wrote his memoir, Smallwood did not linger for long on the sentimental appeal of his childhood skill at spelling. Characteristically, he went straight to the larger context and its bitter significance in politics and power. He knew his boyish feats were seen as extraordinary only because he was Black and enslaved:

> This may afford the reader a glimpse into the abyss of intellectual darkness into which the African race in America has been so long purposely confined, to serve the avarice and ends of their tyrannical oppressors.

This poignant childhood memory and Smallwood's brutally clear-eyed adult understanding of it capture a critical fact about Smallwood's early life. He was born into slavery, but unlike the vast majority of people in bondage, he benefited from unusual enslavers who helped him educate himself and obtain his freedom. His "slave narrative," as his memoir has sometimes been labeled by the few scholars to take notice of it, is no catalog of the horrors he suffered. Instead, he devotes only a few paragraphs to the thirty years he spent in slavery, lingering mainly on his luck in the owners he got by virtue of a will and a wedding.

Smallwood was born on February 22, 1801, in Prince George's County, a Maryland jurisdiction of tobacco plantations and small farms bordered to the west by Washington, D.C. When he sat down decades later to write his memoir, he said not a word about his parents, a curious omission that may have signaled lingering personal pain. It is quite possible that Smallwood, like so many enslaved children, was separated permanently from his parents in very early childhood, either because they were dispatched to different farms by the dictates of an estate settlement or because his parents were sold to a slave trader who shipped them to the Deep South.

Archival records shed no light, but Smallwood would later write fiercely of the domestic slave trade: "Who can calculate the amount of suffering occasioned by the sudden snapping of conjugal and parental ties, among those poor creatures, by an unrighteous law?"

What is known is that as small children Thomas and his sister, Catharine, called Kitty, were inherited by a Prince George's County woman, Sarah Ferguson, and her children. In 1808, Sarah Ferguson married a cousin, John Bell Ferguson. It turned out to be a stroke of luck for Thomas, then seven. John Ferguson was a Methodist minister who frowned upon slavery, but by Smallwood's account he was constrained by the terms of his wife's inheritance:

> Myself and Sister had been bequeathed to the Lady whom he married and to her children. Although by the terms of the will he could not dispose of us, at pleasure, yet by paying the amount at which we were valued he could do so by mutual agreement with those interested. That he did (for he was no friend to slavery) by paying $500 for me, but with the amount he paid for my sister I never became acquainted.

For both John and Sarah, it was a second marriage, and both brought children to the match. Because Thomas and Kitty had been bequeathed jointly to Sarah and her children, Ferguson was obligated to buy them from his new wife and stepchildren. Having spent the considerable sum of $500 (a very high price for a child at the time, some $15,000 today), he chose not to immediately grant Thomas his freedom. Instead, Ferguson told young Thomas that he would have to go to work and gradually pay off the $500 debt, not an unusual arrangement at the time.

Unlike many slaveholders, though, Ferguson put legal weight behind his promise of eventual emancipation. He went to the Prince George's County courthouse and filed a document in 1815, when Thomas was fourteen, pledging to free him when he turned thirty. Ferguson may have intended his deed of manumission, witnessed by his neighbor Thomas

Bowie, to reassure Smallwood that the promise of freedom was sincere and irrevocable. He might also have wanted the scheduled emancipation placed on the record in case Ferguson should die in the meantime, to preempt any move by Sarah or her children to ignore the arrangement and try to reenslave Thomas Smallwood for life.

"To all whom it may concern," Ferguson wrote in the wordy, official style of such documents, he had "released from slavery liberated manumitted and set free and by these presents do hereby release from slavery manumit and set free my Negro Boy Thomas." The deed incorrectly makes Thomas a year older than he was, saying he was fifteen "and able to work and gain a sufficient livelihood and maintenance."

Given the treatment of most enslaved people at the time, Smallwood appears to have found the arrangement fair. He later spoke fondly of Ferguson. Though he reached the end of his term of enslavement in 1830 with a small debt to Ferguson remaining, Smallwood insisted on carrying out his end of the bargain to the letter: "Hence it left me in debt at the end of my service $60, which I subsequently paid to the last farthing." His gratitude to Ferguson was surely due in part to John and Sarah's decision to teach the enslaved boy to read—a legal but highly unusual step in Maryland. "What little I know of the letter," Smallwood would write, referring to literacy, "was obtained in the following manner, for I never had a day's schooling. The gentleman before mentioned, as my master, and his wife, learned me the English alphabet, and to spell in two syllables."

Smallwood's earliest years showed him how random events and decisions in the world of white people could determine the fate of the enslaved. Perhaps because of those early lessons, he would later take particular satisfaction when the actions of enslaved people—taken with his own determined help—turned the tables and upset the plans and comfort of their enslavers. But in his case, the lottery of white power happened to break in his favor. The sense that he was the beneficiary of rare good fortune seems to stand behind his later decision to act so boldly on behalf of those still in slavery.

❖═◉═❖

One feature of the despicable treatment of enslaved African Americans was to leave them out of official records except when their existence was noted in a legal accounting of a slaveholder's possessions. It's not quite right to say they were erased from history—in many cases, there was no record that could be erased. They were "chattels," the chilling word (often used ironically by Torrey and Smallwood) that meant movable property and came to be applied routinely to people in slavery, stripping them of humanity and character. The United States Census collected only the sex and age of enslaved people in a household, not bothering with their names. Other official records were just as sketchy, and newspapers took little note of people in bondage except when they ran away or were accused of a crime. To trace the early life of a man like Smallwood requires looking for places to glimpse his reflection, however distorted or imperfect, in the lives of his owner and employers and in the events that shaped his time and place.

We know, for example, that from early childhood Smallwood lived with the Fergusons in Bladensburg, a modest river town about six miles northeast of the U.S. Capitol. In the early nineteenth century, Bladensburg was a significant port on what was then called the Eastern Branch of the Potomac River—today the Anacostia River. But by the time Smallwood was a teenager it had become clogged with silt and lost business to the wharves downriver in Washington, where he and his owner would eventually move. A momentous event when Thomas was thirteen, old enough to be paying attention, was the Battle of Bladensburg in the War of 1812. British troops overwhelmed a poorly organized American militia in August 1814, swept across the bridge over the Eastern Branch, and marched to the heart of the capital, where they famously burned the presidential mansion, later called the White House. The Americans' helter-skelter retreat was memorialized in newspaper sarcasm as the "Bladensburg Races."

One striking element of the invasion surely reached young Thomas Smallwood by word of mouth: fighting with the British force under Major General Robert Ross in Bladensburg and Washington were units of the Corps of Colonial Marines, composed of Black troops recruited from among thousands of enslaved Americans who had responded to a British promise of freedom for those who joined their fight. Men who looked like him were dressed in splendid uniforms, armed with muskets and swords—and marching to victory. In addition to those who had joined the Colonial Marines, hundreds of African Americans who had fled slavery in the Chesapeake region tagged along with British forces to avoid reenslavement.

"A great number of negroes, delighted at the unhoped-for freedom our expedition had placed within their reach, followed the army," one British officer recalled, declaring that some of the enslaved who joined the invaders "possessed infinitely more sense and judgment than their late owners gave them credit for." Some of the Black men who fought for the British, like others who had joined the British side in the American Revolution, were subsequently given land grants in the British colonial territory of Canada, homesteading there years in advance of the thousands who would flee American slavery and settle there in the ensuing decades.

Three weeks after the rout at Bladensburg, a Washington lawyer named Francis Scott Key, watching from a ship off Baltimore as the British bombarded Fort McHenry, penned the poem that would become the national anthem. Few Americans know that its rarely sung third stanza appears to denigrate those who fled enslavement by crossing over to the British side: "No refuge could save the hireling and slave / From the terror of flight or the gloom of the grave." But the villains of Key's rhyme may have been heroes to an impressionable young Black man. Such were some of the complex contradictions of freedom and bondage, loyalty to country or to principle, that might have reached the young Smallwood, who would himself, much later, acclaim and enjoy liberty on Canadian soil.

The fact that hundreds of his neighbors were willing to abandon their homes to fight or flee with an enemy army must have left an impression.

By his teenage years, Smallwood would have had a visceral understanding of the cruelty, violence, and bedrock unfairness of slavery—if not always from his own experience, then from the experience of those around him. Just a year after the Battle of Bladensburg came a horrifying episode that would become an oft-cited example of slavery's particular atrocities. An enslaved woman from Bladensburg named Anna Williams, twenty-four, was sold to a slave trader and locked with her two children in a room above a tavern on F Street in Washington. They had been forcibly taken away from her husband, whom their owner happened not to want to sell at the time. Frantic with despair, Williams threw herself out the window and landed in the street below, breaking her back and both arms.

When an antislavery activist heard the terrible story and visited her, Williams told him she had come to regret leaping—not because of her injuries, but because the slave trader had sold both of her children. "I was so confused and 'istracted, that I didn't know hardly what I was about," Williams said, "but I didn't want to go, and I jumped out of the window;—but I am sorry now that I did it;—they have carried my children off with 'em to Carolina." She did not know, and would likely never find out, where exactly they had been taken. Both events, the woman's leap and her children's forced removal, were the talk of Bladensburg and surely reached fourteen-year-old Smallwood.

The activist who recorded Williams's story, Jesse Torrey (no relation to Charles Torrey), learned that such wrenching episodes, and worse, were anything but rare in the daily life of a slave society. In the months before his visit, a woman sold in Bladensburg cut the throat of her child, and then her own throat, in the wagon taking them to a trader in Washington. Another woman, sold in nearby Georgetown, had cut her own throat as she was carted off to a slave trader in Alexandria, Virginia. It was just a tiny sampling of the horrors of slavery that rarely made the newspapers but were a daily conversation in the community of the enslaved.

What was the impact on young Thomas Smallwood of such horrific stories, some of them involving his neighbors? He surely had heard adults whisper about whipping, torture, rape, kidnapping, suicide, and the rest of the brutal baggage of the slave system. Some of the atrocities he had undoubtedly witnessed with his own eyes. Some terrible things had happened to people he had known all his life. The experiences would shape his growing understanding of the society in which he had been born and drive his grappling with what he might do about it.

⸺◉⸺

By the time Smallwood was in his early twenties, John Ferguson and his family had moved a few miles from Bladensburg to settle in southeast Washington. Ferguson would become a respected figure in town, sometimes serving as a clergyman but mainly earning a living working at a lumberyard on the wharves along the Eastern Branch. He seems to have been a public-spirited man, inclined to charity. Licensed by the city as a "wood corder," he was qualified to fairly certify an honest cord of wood. He was the chaplain at the city's penitentiary, served on the board of health, and helped oversee the Guardians of the Poor.

In a second stroke of good fortune, Smallwood would credit a Scottish immigrant in the same southeast neighborhood with having an influence on his life nearly as great as Ferguson's. He spent several years, he later recounted, working as a household servant for John McLeod, who had become one of Washington's leading educators:

> But for my advancement from two syllables to the little I now possess I owe a deep debt of gratitude to a family of that people who are proverbial for their love of learning and imparting it to others, viz. Mr. John McLeod a Scotch gentleman in whose excellent family I lived several years as servant. He had a large family of sons and daughters, these young gentlemen and ladies not only took great pleasure in learning me, but all the other servants about the house, who would take their teaching, for they were all colored, and hired help notwithstanding. He employed many servants about his house, he hired all; for be it said to his credit and humanity, he would own no slaves, although living in a slaveholding country.

In his later writing, despite the pose of modesty ("the little I now possess"), Smallwood would flaunt his impressive learning, quoting classical philosophers and contemporary British and American poets. His advance from mere literacy to deep learning and wide reading came at McLeod's house. McLeod, who had started his first school in Washington in 1808 with just four students and the motto "Order is Heaven's first law," would go on over nearly four decades to found and operate a series of institutions: the Eastern Academy, the Central Academy, the Female Central Academy, the Columbian Academy. He occasionally feuded with rival schoolmasters and at times struggled to collect the tuition parents owed him, but he appears to have been widely admired. He served as president of the Washington Relief Society, which sought to help the poor, and, as Smallwood noted, he opposed slavery—he loaned his schoolhouse on F Street for meetings of Washington's Abolition Society. One featured speaker was Francis Scott Key, whose record on slavery as an attorney was checkered but who had represented a number of Black people in freedom suits challenging their enslaved status.

From McLeod's school advertisements, and others' comments about him, it is easy to form an impression of Smallwood's boss and mentor: a stern, old-fashioned pedagogue with affection for his students and a very dry wit who took full advantage of his location in the capital. At some school gatherings, the Marine Band, based at the Navy Yard nearby, performed for the parents and students. In June 1838, none other than the vice president of the United States, Richard M. Johnson, stopped by graduation ceremonies to hand out medals to top pupils. McLeod required students to start class at dawn and once denounced vacations in a deadpan newspaper notice that would find an echo in Smallwood's future satirical prose:

Columbian Academy—The subscriber informs the public that no vacation will be given in this establishment this year. He has not given vacations for many years past. When he formerly gave a few days in August, he found that the practice did much harm and no good. For many days before the vacation it was impossible to make the children study—the girls tormenting their parents for dresses to visit their relations; the boys planning how they should spend their time in swimming, robbing the neighboring orchards, &c.

Once, placing a "situation wanted" notice on behalf of a veteran teacher looking for a job as a principal or private tutor, McLeod began the item:

A Gentleman, a graduate of a respectable University, who I will not say pretends to teach, but who actually can teach, the English and French languages grammatically, the Latin and Greek languages well, Geometry and Algebra.

During some years, McLeod took in boarders in his own home, where he also conducted classes. There is no evidence that McLeod allowed Smallwood to attend them, but there is every indication that the educator and his adult children pitched in to help the young man with his self-education. The qualities of Smallwood's adult character—his devotion to broad learning, his impatience with laziness, his delight in an ironic style of writing, even his penchant for feuds and ferocious sense of right and wrong—surely had some roots in McLeod's household.

＊⟶⟩◯⟨⟵＊

Inevitably, as a curious young man whose personal situation had put him on a long road from slavery to freedom, Smallwood began to take an interest in the politics boiling around the institution of slavery. In his twenties he became a supporter of a movement that was drawing significant backing from prominent white men and some educated Black people. It was called "colonization," and it would introduce him to the complications of racial politics and become his first intellectual battleground.

For Black supporters like Smallwood, the underlying notion was simple: only by cutting ties with the racist United States and starting anew in another country could African Americans escape not just the scourge of slavery but the deep-seated prejudice that constrained the lives of free Black people. It's easy to imagine Smallwood, an ambitious young man with a steadily more sophisticated view of the world, getting caught up in the promise of such an adventure. For decades there had been scattered examples of enslaved or free people leaving behind America for a fresh beginning in Haiti or British Guiana in South America or Sierra Leone in West Africa or somewhere else where, they hoped, Black people would not be a despised underclass. As Smallwood came to adulthood, powerful white men had created the American Colonization Society (ACS) to push for the organized, wholesale emigration of African Americans, especially to the new colony of Liberia that the society founded in West Africa.

Even as he experienced relative kindness from the Fergusons and the McLeods, Smallwood knew well the horrors of slavery, and he was surely beginning to grasp the indignities faced by free African Americans. It was no wonder that he took an active interest in colonization, which attracted some white people who were critical of slavery. Like many other Black Americans, he was drawn to the notion that he might do better, or at least avoid the terrors and humiliation of slavery, somewhere outside the United States. And at least at first, he thought the colonization movement might simultaneously work for the eventual eradication of slavery inside the United States.

> If my memory be not at fault, I was from the year 1822 or 23, up to about 1830, an advocate of African Colonization, because I thought the object of that Society was the entire abolition of slavery in the United States; and which I thought would lead to its final extinction every where else. Thus placing my race, together with all others, in an elevated position.

Through his attendance at colonization meetings, Smallwood met other educated and politically engaged Black people and made some close friends. James E. Brown was training as a pharmacist with the support of the American Colonization Society and would start an apothecary business in Liberia. Samuel Ford McGill came from a leading family of Black colonizationists and had grown up partly in Liberia. He would return to the United States and become the first Black medical school graduate in America, completing his training at Dartmouth College in 1839. For the self-educated Smallwood, their friendship must have been a flattering form of approval.

But by the late 1820s, even as his friends Brown and McGill remained deeply committed to emigration as the best option for a dignified life for Black Americans, Smallwood began to develop deep misgivings. When individual Black people had decided on their own to strike out for a new land, that was one thing. But it gradually became clear to Smallwood that the American Colonization Society was funded by white people, including many slaveholders, who feared the emergence of a growing class of free Black people in the United States. White leaders saw the colonization movement as an ideal solution to both the problem of slavery and the threat of a growing free Black population: enslaved people could be emancipated on the condition they sail for Liberia. America's race problem would be solved—because there would be no Black people, or at least no free Black people, left in the United States.

A pamphlet published by the American Colonization Society in 1830, just as Smallwood gained his freedom and broke with the movement, was worded tactfully, but its import was clear. Eleven states, it said, had directed their congressional representatives to devise "measures for removing such free persons of color, as are desirous of emigrating to Africa." The movement, the pamphlet said, "has shown how manumissions may be effected without injury to any class of Society"—clearly implying that freeing Black people would somehow "injure" the interests of whites. The following year, white backing for Black emigration got a huge boost when the slave rebellion led by Nat Turner in Virginia left more than fifty white people dead. Many slaveholders decided Black people needed to be either chained in slavery and watched carefully—or put on the first boat out of the country. Colonization amounted to a long-term strategy of ethnic cleansing. As a Black man just trying out life outside slavery,

Smallwood began to understand that the encouragement to emigrate was an insult to him and those like him.

Smallwood's friend Brown worked as a pharmacist and doctor in Liberia, returning periodically to give lectures encouraging Black Americans to move to the colony. Such a life might reasonably be viewed as enterprising and public-spirited. But Smallwood ended their friendship. He had come to believe that Brown had sold out to white colonizationists and that he himself had been temporarily fooled by the American Colonization Society:

> I was grievously deceived. The object and policy of that Society proved to be, under the mask of philanthropy, the draining of the free colored population from among the slave population by inducing them to emigrate to Africa; for the doctrine of its leaders was that the free population contaminated the slave population with a spirit of freedom, which made them uneasy in their bonds, and made it very difficult for their oppressors to hold them. But said they, if we can get rid of the free negro population we can put a stop to any further emancipations, and thus have perpetual slavery without danger.

Smallwood understood how the system worked, he later wrote, because the ACS leaders had tried to use the promise of riches to lure him, too, into what he called their "African colonization trap":

> My humble self happened to be among the number to whom inducements were held out. And for the sake of my influence in that direction, I could have become a merchant in the Liberia trade, backed with the aid and influence of that Society. But I preferred to live in indigent circumstances, and enjoy my morsel with a good conscience, rather than be possessed with wealth and a burning conscience, with a recollection that I had come into possession of these through treachery to my afflicted race.

＊━◉━＊

Smallwood seems to have come of age politically in the battle against colonization, and many of his friends and neighbors experienced the same change of heart. He very likely attended a public meeting of African Americans in Washington in April 1831 that took a strong stance for staying and fighting for rights in the United States:

> Resolved, that this meeting view with distrust the efforts made by the Colonization Society to cause the free people of color of these United States to emigrate to Liberia, on the coast of Africa, or elsewhere.
>
> Resolved, that it is the declared opinion of the members of this meeting, that the soil which gave them birth is their only true and veritable home.

In Baltimore, home to the largest free Black population in the country, a gathering of opponents took an even tougher stand, declaring with a snarl: "When *we* desire to remove, we will apprise the public in due season."

Smallwood's turnaround on colonization was influenced by a sensational pamphlet published in 1829 that sheds some light on his growing political radicalism. Its author, David Walker, became for Smallwood a hero and role model, though they never met. The uncompromising and vitriolic language of Walker's *Appeal to the Colored Citizens of the World* became the subject of excitement and debate in the Black community and touched off fear and fury among southern whites. Black people in Charleston and New Orleans were jailed for trying to hand out the pamphlet. While Walker touched on many aspects of slavery and racism— famously declaring African Americans "the most degraded, wretched, and abject set of beings that ever lived since the world began"—he reserved special venom for the ACS.

Do they think to drive us from our country and homes, after
having enriched it with our blood and tears, and keep back millions of our dear brethren, sunk in the most barbarous wretch-
edness, to dig up gold and silver for them and their children? . . .
Tell us now no more about colonization, for America is as much
our country, as it is yours.—Treat us like men, and there is no
danger but we will all live in peace and happiness together.

Smallwood felt huge admiration for the firebrand Walker, a North
Carolina–born Bostonian in the clothing business whose radicalism was
widely criticized by abolitionists of both races in 1829 but whose influence would last. Many years later, when Smallwood wrote his own
memoir, he would include a short biography of Walker and quote him.
Perhaps emboldened by Walker's outspoken example, Smallwood did
not hide his changed opinion of colonization. He denounced it so ve-
hemently that few people in his circle of Black Washingtonians were
willing to express support:

I determined to do something in the matter, therefore I directed my efforts, first, against the influence of the Colonization Society, among colored people, and by the assistance of
the Lord I was in them successful, for where I lived, not one in
a hundred could be induced to go to Africa.

From the shards of information that remain from his first thirty years,
it is possible to roughly reconstruct the political education of Thomas
Smallwood: his boyhood immersed in the pitiless world that slavery created, his glimpse of Black soldiers who freed themselves to fight for the
British, his increasing command of literacy and literature, his embrace of
and then rejection of colonization as a solution to the existential problem of being Black in America, his inspiration at the courageous public
stance of David Walker. It was a set of influences that held the seeds of
future political engagement.

Amid all his passionate political agitation, Smallwood prepared to forge a new life in freedom. He married a free Black woman originally from Virginia, Elizabeth Anderson, who would become a dedicated ally in his underground railroad work. While the marriage was officially recorded in court records in 1836, Smallwood in his memoir dates their union to a decade earlier, in 1826. Because he was still in slavery at the time, Thomas and Elizabeth, who were about twenty-five and fifteen, respectively, might not have sought to, or might not have been permitted to, register their marriage officially. The first of their five children, named Thomas after his father, was born in 1831, months after Smallwood had officially become free.

In the 1830s, Smallwood started a shoemaking and shoe-repair business in his southeast Washington neighborhood near the Navy Yard, Washington's major military installation and a bustling center of ship repair and ordnance production on the Eastern Branch waterfront. Acquaintances began to refer to him as "Smallwood of the Yard," an impressive moniker considering that surviving records do not show him directly employed by the navy. Perhaps Smallwood worked from his house, a stone's throw from the Navy Yard gates. Or possibly he located his shoe business at or just outside the yard, taking advantage of the heavy workday traffic and using that prime location as an advertising gambit.

Smallwood's neighborhood at the time was a village within the small town of Washington. Famously built on swampy territory by a mostly enslaved workforce, the nation's capital had been situated there not for any charms of the landscape but as a compromise between northern and southern politicians. With few impressive buildings along unpaved roads and a comically sparse population, it fell so far short of European capitals as to shock and amuse foreign visitors. Charles Dickens, the leading novelist of the day, visited in 1842 and described the bleak view from his hotel, which he said "looks like a small piece of country that has taken to drinking, and has quite lost itself." Dickens noted how far the city fell short of the grand plans devised half a century earlier by Pierre Charles L'Enfant, its French designer:

> It is sometimes called the City of Magnificent Distances, but it might with greater propriety be termed the City of Mag nificent Intentions; for it is only on taking a bird's-eye view of it from the top of the Capitol, that one can at all comprehend the vast designs of its projector, an aspiring Frenchman. Spacious avenues, that begin in nothing, and lead nowhere; streets, mile-long, that only want houses, roads and inhabitants; public buildings that need but a public to be complete; and ornaments of great thoroughfares, which only lack great thoroughfares to ornament—are its leading features. One might fancy the season over, and most of the houses gone out of town for ever with their masters.

It's not hard to understand Dickens's derision. His capital city of London had two million inhabitants. Smallwood's Washington City had only 23,364 people in 1840; it was smaller than Albany. That included 16,843 white people and 4,808 free African Americans, who easily outnumbered the 1,713 enslaved African Americans. But the slave traders plying their business around the city, from private jails or hotel barrooms, meant that the shadow of slavery was inescapable. (The separate jurisdictions of Georgetown and Alexandria were included with Washington City in the District of Columbia, which had a total population of 43,712.)

Apart from the few imposing government buildings and a handful of major roads, Washington had a decidedly backwater feel, with unpaved lanes and modest wood houses. Smallwood seems to have known everyone in his neighborhood around the Navy Yard and the Eastern Branch wharves, which was not especially racially segregated by modern standards. Prosperous and working-class whites, free and enslaved Black people shared the same streets. Smallwood lived in 1834 on the

east side of Fourth Street S.E., between L and M Streets, according to a
city directory, where the inclusion of his name (albeit labeled "col'd") was
a mark of his status, modest but real, as a longtime resident. But the rules
of social position and racial hierarchy were strictly enforced, including by
the police or bands of vigilantes when necessary.

The point is illustrated by the history of another Smallwood, this one
white and incomparably more powerful, who lived a few blocks from
Thomas and Elizabeth at Second and N Streets. He had been notably responsible for enlarging the chasm between the rights and status of white
people and free Black people.

Samuel N. Smallwood had served as Washington's mayor and owned
Smallwood's Wharf on the Eastern Branch, where John Ferguson
worked. Samuel Smallwood, like most of the Smallwoods in Maryland,
both white and Black, had roots in Charles County, southeast of Washington. His first job after arriving in Washington in 1795 had been as
overseer of the enslaved workers building the Capitol. In 1821, during
his first mayoral term, the city had responded to white nervousness about
Black emancipation by imposing draconian requirements on the growing free Black population: attestations of good character from mayors or
justices of the peace at previous places of residence, certificates of good
conduct signed by three white citizens, financial bonds to guarantee the
"quiet, peaceable and orderly behavior" of their children, and more.

Clearly, the establishment represented by Mayor Smallwood, who signed
the measures, was determined to curtail any possibility of political power
or social standing for emancipated African Americans. Yet given the history of white men impregnating the women they enslaved, and despite
the vast differences in their wealth and power, it is entirely possible that
Samuel the former mayor and Thomas the shoemaker were related.

Despite the unjust laws and the hostile atmosphere, Black tradesmen
and laborers found work, many on the waterfront. The dominant feature
of Smallwood's neighborhood was the Eastern Branch, the waterway
that served both the Navy Yard and the commercial wharves up and
down the river that were the area's biggest employers. Some people, in

fact, called the neighborhood "the Island." But the rest of Washington was hardly far off: Smallwood could have reached the Capitol, which the British had partially burned in 1814 and did not yet have the grand central dome, in a brisk fifteen-minute walk. A half hour on foot would get him to the president's house, covered with the lime-based whitewash that would give it its official name decades later.

As a small businessman and activist, Smallwood would have had occasion to meet hundreds of Washingtonians, white and Black, and at least to observe the politicians and government officials, famous preachers and acclaimed physicians drawn to the capital. When he began to reach out to enslaved people who wanted to escape, he was often talking to his friends and acquaintances. When he mocked their enslavers, he was often talking about his white neighbors, whom he observed closely even as they ignored him.

Some Washingtonians, white and Black, he knew from church. He was active in local Methodist churches, probably first at Ebenezer Methodist Episcopal Church, where his enslaver John Ferguson worshipped. It was a biracial congregation for many years until 1827, when African Americans, who were confined to an overcrowded balcony and resented their second-class status, formed a separate congregation, known as Little Ebenezer. Smallwood likely was one of those walking out in 1827, but he did not drop out of Ebenezer's adult education program: a class register at Ebenezer for 1836 lists him as a student. (Interestingly, Smallwood's owner, Ferguson, perhaps inspired by the African American walkout the year before, helped lead his own exodus from the church, this time of white worshippers in 1828, to start the city's first Methodist Protestant Church.)

◆═◎═◆

The name of a female fellow student in Smallwood's class at Ebenezer church suggests how the legal and human drama over slavery simmered constantly around him long after he had obtained his own freedom. Phillis Shiner was the wife of Michael Shiner, a Navy Yard worker remembered today for a diary he kept of ordinary and extraordinary events in the city and his family's life. In March 1833, when the Smallwoods and the Shiners were neighbors and almost certainly friends, Phillis Shiner and the couple's three children were caught up in the legal squabbles that followed their owner's death. They "wher snacht away from me and sold," Shiner wrote in his diary—seized by slave dealers armed with clubs and knives and locked in a slave trader's jail. They were released a few weeks later after filing a freedom petition—with the help of none other than Francis Scott Key.

Another Navy Yard worker whom Smallwood surely knew experienced his own disastrous encounters with the legal complications of the slave system. Daniel Bell, a blacksmith, had been born into slavery in Prince George's County a year after Smallwood. When his wife's enslaver died, his wife, Mary, was supposed to be freed under the terms of her owner's will; their six children were to be freed when they reached adulthood. But as often happened, the owner's widow challenged the will, claiming her dying husband had not been in his right mind when he signed it. A court battle ensued. Meanwhile, Bell's owner had him delivered to a slave trader for sale south, and Bell, too, managed to mount a successful legal fight for freedom in local courts.

As he followed his friends' experiences, Smallwood witnessed the blurred line between slavery and freedom when courts were hardly colorblind, and any white person could tie up a manumission with legal maneuvering. And if the courts could be hostile, so could the streets. In August 1835, a roaming white mob made clear that many white residents of Washington saw both free and enslaved Black workers as a competitive threat. The so-called Snow Riot targeted, among others, a thriving restaurant owned and operated by a free African American entrepreneur, Beverly Snow, whose Epicurean Eating House was patronized by many well-to-do whites. Touched off by white fears that an urban version of Nat Turner's bloody rebellion in Virginia might be afoot in Washington, the disorder quickly became an excuse for white rioters to attack Black businesses and intimidate Black citizens.

Smallwood had special reason to be aggrieved by the violence. The mob running through the streets was led by white Navy Yard workers, then on strike because of a series of complaints, among them their resentment of competition from Black coworkers. Such a display of open racial animosity and violence in his own backyard was surely unsettling. And at the same time Francis Scott Key, who had become the district attorney, chose to mount a prosecution of a white physician named Reuben Crandall, who had received from the north a large quantity of abolitionist pamphlets as part of a national campaign to spread antislavery ideas. Crandall was accused of "seditious libel and inciting slaves and free blacks to revolt," though the material in question simply attacked the slave system. White fury at any advance toward Black freedom and equality seemed to hold sway not just in the streets but in the prosecutor's office as well.

As if to prove its bias, the city council responded to the rioting by banning gatherings after dark—not of the white laborers who had run wild for days but of African Americans. The restaurateur Snow had shown Smallwood and others how a talented Black businessman could break racial barriers and thrive. Now, the loss of his restaurant and his brush with death made it clear that racist whites could not tolerate such shows of Black success. Snow was forced to flee town to escape a lynch mob and didn't stop until he had left the country. In far-off Toronto, he re-created his success as a restaurant owner and caterer—this time on British territory, where slavery had recently been banned. Smallwood had reason to be quite aware of Canada as a refuge—perhaps from learning about African American neighbors in Bladensburg who had joined the British side in the War of 1812 and ended up free on Canadian soil, and now with Snow's successful new start in Toronto.

Inside Washington's small free Black community, threatened as it was by the oppressive majority, there was by no means always peace and comity. In 1833, Smallwood had been a founder of the Wesley Metropolitan African Methodist Episcopal Zion Church on West D Street— the Wesley African Society for short. But in early 1841 he clashed with Abraham Cole, the founding minister of the church, denouncing him at a church leaders' meeting for sexual impropriety and a passive attitude toward the slavery issue. Their dispute divided the congregation and led to the expulsion of Smallwood and an ally, Israel Wallace, in March 1841, that was chronicled in tit-for-tat letters to the newspapers. That December Smallwood filed suit against Cole, accusing him of slander and a deliberate attempt to undermine his shoemaking business. It was a bitter intramural struggle, but it grew in part out of consequential differences over how to confront slavery. The dispute with Cole eventually would have serious repercussions, even endangering Smallwood's freedom.

This personal battle, the rioting of hostile white laborers, the persecution of abolitionists, and the excruciating experiences of friends fighting for their freedom made for a tumultuous backdrop to Smallwood's life as he sought to earn a decent living, raise his family, and make his way in the world. Together, all these experiences may be a clue to the seeming paradox of Smallwood's life: How did a man whose personal experience with slavery was, by his own account, relatively benign come to devote himself at huge risk to obtaining freedom for others who were not so fortunate?

The answer seems to be that Thomas Smallwood, while expressing no rancor, only gratitude, toward his own former enslaver, was a thoughtful, principled, and sometimes pugnacious man who had closely observed the abuse of African Americans. He had seen many free acquaintances suffer, and he understood that full freedom was not available even to those Black Americans who were given their manumission papers. But he also knew that any fight for rights had to begin with the humiliating, brutal, arbitrary, and cruel nature of slavery; he had seen how its tentacles continued to grasp even his neighbors who managed to get to court to insist upon their freedom.

He had participated in heated debates over the morality of slavery; he had seen through the machinations of white promoters of Black emigration; he had heard abolitionists of various stripes denounce what was beginning to be called "the slave power." He had read widely, and by the end of the 1830s he had concluded that the practice of bondage in America was, as he put it later, "the most inhuman system that ever blackened the pages of history."

Smallwood turned forty in February 1841, perhaps a goad to reflect on what he had done in his life so far and what he still wanted to accomplish. He had acquired for himself an extraordinary, if piecemeal, education, from John McLeod's bookshelves to the overheated meeting halls of summertime Washington. He was, perhaps, a little fed up with endless debate. His family life and business were in reasonable order. He was ready to wage his own personal war on slavery.

Charles Torrey's portrait and signature, from the posthumous
memoir compiled by Joseph C. Lovejoy, 1847.

2

Until No Slave Should Be Found in Our Land

Charles Torrey sat in the decrepit Annapolis jail in January 1842, eagerly questioning members of the two African American families who were his fellow inmates. For a while, the aspiring abolitionist reporter forgot his own predicament. He heard how the death of a Maryland slaveholder, John D. Hutton, had thrown the lives of these thirteen men, women, and children into turmoil and uncertainty. Hutton had freed them toward the end of his life, but he had died in debt, and now his creditors were trying to seize them as valuable property. Already, they had been jailed and released twice and then arrested once more as the complex probate case made its way through the courts. Now they were awaiting possible sale south, to be converted to cash to pay Hutton's debts, which would likely mean their separation to suit the whims and needs of new enslavers.

The keen attention of Torrey, twenty-eight, a slender, frail, and hyperactive white man, must have surprised them. Torrey was a New Englander who had long condemned slavery from afar but was now on his first extended visit to the south. He had been jailed partly at the demand of and partly for protection against a mob of slaveholders who didn't like the inquisitive northerner who had showed up at their convention. In his newspaper dispatches, Torrey was given to dramatizing his own situation, as if he were simultaneously speaking and watching himself speak. But this time he had stumbled into a drama of genuine pathos and consequence.

"I could not help weeping as I looked at the two little infants about a year old, in their mother's arms, smiling in sweet unconsciousness of the bitter doom their parents were anticipating, a sale to the trader," he wrote to *The Emancipator,* the newspaper whose longtime editor was Torrey's friend Joshua Leavitt.

So Torrey made a vow to return to the same jail cell—to mark what he hoped would be the abolition of slavery in less than a decade:

> After listening to the history of their career, I sat down and wrote, and signed and prayed over a solemn re-consecration of myself to the work of freeing the slaves until no slave should be found in our land. May God help me to be faithful to that *pledge made in Annapolis jail.* In that cell, God helping me, if it stands, I will celebrate the emancipation of the slaves of Maryland, before ten years more roll away.

There was something self-regarding about this young white man and his brash pledge, which he so obviously hoped would prove historic. Was his vow really about enslaved African Americans, or was it more about their self-appointed savior, who had already failed quite spectacularly at two professions and was searching for a new way to make his mark? Despite his self-centered pose, Torrey would soon prove himself deadly serious about the antislavery cause, risking everything to pursue the goal he had set.

⋄⇒◉⇐⋄

Torrey had moved to Thomas Smallwood's Washington just a month earlier. After receiving an education as prestigious as any available to an American at the time, the pious young man had tried his hand at teaching and preaching, but both efforts had ended badly. Then he had been drawn into the burgeoning campaign to abolish slavery, which was centered in his native New England, far from those on whose behalf the abolitionists were fighting. Now, leaving behind his wife and two children in Massachusetts, he had relocated quite deliberately inside the belly of the beast. Using his connections, he had arranged to become a correspondent for abolitionist newspapers, reporting on the debates in Congress—and also acting as a firsthand witness of the slave system he so stridently opposed.

Suddenly the evil he had preached and lectured about from a distance was all around him. Settling into Mrs. Padgett's boardinghouse on Thirteenth Street N.W.—where it happened that Elizabeth Smallwood did the laundry—Torrey was shocked to see slave traders operating openly on the Mall between the Capitol and the White House. He called on the few radical abolitionist members of Congress, introducing himself and asking for their help with his reporting. And he began to visit Black churches, including Smallwood's Wesley African Society, where in the same month—December 1841—the feud between Smallwood and Abraham Cole had grown into a lawsuit. Torrey attended a class, not a service, but found himself deeply moved, as he wrote to his wife:

> I have not enjoyed the "communion of saints," so much, for a long time, as when mingling with that little band of despised colored people, partly slaves; and, when one of the poor women, nearly white, spoke of the "persecution" she endured, with sobs, I felt my heart filled with new energy to make war upon that hateful institution that so crushes the disciples of the Lord to the earth.

There was condescension in Torrey's earnest description; surely not all of the free, proud members of this Black church class would have welcomed being called a "little band of despised colored people." Torrey's attention to the skin tone of enslaved people and the euphemistic reference to a woman's rape by her enslaver were standard in abolitionist writing. But his introduction to the racial dramas that were playing out daily in the nation's capital was clearly thrilling for him, and he seemed to use every encounter to renew his vow to battle slavery.

And then, almost before he had a chance to write his first dispatch, he stumbled onto some news—a highly unusual event called the Slaveholders' Convention was scheduled to start January 12 just thirty-five miles away in the courthouse in Annapolis, Maryland's capital. With the license of a newspaper correspondent, he thought he could safely eavesdrop on the enemy, reporting to his readers on the perfidious plans of the owners of human property in Maryland. He hastened to the scene.

It was the first such gathering in Maryland, and it reflected the swelling anxiety among slaveholders about what they perceived as threats to their economic and political position. Most were wealthy men with large acreages planted in tobacco and the newer grain crops. They were a formidable power in the Maryland General Assembly and faced few truly powerful opponents. But they were worried nonetheless about the growing free Black population in the state, which they feared might infect their enslaved workers with dangerous ideas and someday swamp the white population. They were also worried about the increasing problem of runaways. And they were concerned that the rise of the abolitionist movement in the north over the previous decade might erode their advantage in both the Maryland legislature and in Congress.

Torrey's reports from the convention captured the anxious tone and extreme demands of some speakers. A slaveholder from Prince George's County, where Smallwood had been born, declared that "he took it to be an axiom, that two races that could not be mingled, could never be happy in the same community." Another speaker noted that the state's branch of the American Colonization Society had for years been receiving $10,000 a year in state money to, in his words, "remove the free colored population." But in fact, he complained, since the payments had begun, the number of free African Americans in Maryland had actually increased by thirty thousand!

One of the planters proposed that the state should "pay a high reward for the arrest and conviction of any person who aids a runaway slave."

Another demanded that police should be "appointed to watch the arrival and departure of all steamers, railroad cars, etc., to prevent runaway slaves from traveling in them." Children of free Black people should be taken from their parents at age eight, another speaker proposed, and forced to work for white people until age eighteen for women and age twenty-one for men—at which point they would be "induced" to leave their native state, never to return. Negroes should never be allowed to hold meetings after dark or to own firearms. Should they somehow acquire any real estate, it should be sold by law at the time of their death. These ideas were the slaveholders' notion of life, liberty, and the pursuit of happiness for their Black fellow Americans.

⊷⇒⊜⇐⊶

Torrey duly took notes on what he called "such a system of diabolical propositions." Though he was by no means a well-known figure, some in attendance became suspicious of the slight man with the moustache scribbling so furiously as plantation magnates took their turns at the lectern. Others may have been warned by friends in Washington to be on the lookout for a troublemaking journalist. A doorkeeper demanded to know whether Torrey was a delegate, and asked him to leave the meeting room when he said he was not.

Rather than joining the other reporters waiting in the lobby, Torrey climbed to the gallery and kept on writing. The doorkeeper returned and escorted him to the floor of the meeting, where "a Babel-like confusion of opinions was uttered as to what should be done" with this interloper. What Torrey described as "the mobocratic part" of the crowd began to threaten violence, and he was ushered out by more civil delegates, who urged him to leave town. He returned to the tavern where he was staying and retrieved some books he needed to return to the editor of the Annapolis paper. But when he reappeared on the street, the mob, by now a collection of the more militant convention delegates and ruffians drawn to the unrest, confronted him again:

They were now at a loss what to do. Some urged to take me
five miles out of town and let me go. Others were for hanging,
tar and feathering, etc., but too many respectable Annapolis
people had now gathered around to allow this, and I believe
the perfect composure I was enabled to maintain calmed them.

Despite his "perfect composure," more rowdies showed up, out for
blood, so a "kind and worthy, but timid magistrate" wrote up an arrest
warrant and escorted Torrey to jail, with a crowd of two or three hundred
screaming men and boys following. It was in the "old and ruinous" jail,
where "a jackknife would free any prisoner in two hours," that Torrey met
and was so taken with the two Black families who seemed likely to be
sold south at any moment.

Torrey's lively, sometimes witty account shows how the unexpected
turn in his first major reporting venture left a huge and lasting impression. He had arrived in Washington a few weeks before, a virtual unknown. Now he had managed single-handedly to disrupt and throw into
confusion a large gathering of slaveholders. Despite the excitement of the
crowd and the shouted threats, he didn't seem to be seriously frightened;
as an educated white man, he may have assumed, rightly or wrongly, that
the mob would not dare harm him. It is hard to avoid the impression that
he was enjoying the adventure, jail and all. He was decidedly the hero of
his own story.

A volunteer legal team was assembled to defend Torrey—though
against what charges remained unclear. The judge overseeing Torrey's
case, after listening to a contradictory collection of witnesses, decided
to have him held over the weekend. Meanwhile, the Massachusetts congressional delegation, having heard of the jailing of a journalist with deep
roots in their state, asked a prominent Boston lawyer who happened to
be visiting Washington to take on his defense, and by Sunday David A.
Simmons had joined the defense team. By Wednesday the judge had
"found no cause to detain me, not one of all the allegations and suspicions having even a plausible or *any* proof whatever to sustain them."

Torrey was thrilled to hear one delegate to the Slaveholders' Convention grumble that the hoopla surrounding his detention and court appearances, and the associated antislavery agitation, "would destroy all the effect of the Convention." Indeed, newspapers around the country had picked up the story of the brave abolitionist reporter who had dared go into the lion's den and who had been jailed in retaliation. "GREAT EXCITEMENT," said the headline in the *Boston Daily Mail.* "Arrest of an Abolitionist Reporter," cried the *Newark Daily Advertiser.*

"I can only say, that if my imprisonment has such an effect," Torrey wrote, relishing the attention, "I shall devoutly thank God for it."

The Annapolis escapade had lit a fire under his embryonic journalism career, but, more important, it had given him a taste for action. In the drama to come, Torrey would opt for being a participant rather than a mere chronicler.

⋆═◉═⋆

When Charles Torrey was a child—one already orphaned—he had a strange and striking dream that he would long remember, feeding a compelling sense of religious mission in a world of haunting moral conflict:

> In my childhood, when about seven years old, I dreamed I was dead and in hell! It seemed not unlike the scenery of our world. Its devil, not unlike a smiling man! He offered to the lost, beautiful and fragrant fruits, that turned to bitter ashes in the mouth; and still he smiled! There seemed no restraint on men's motions, or intercourse. Their sufferings were in their hearts. Full of anguish at being shut up with the wicked, I approached the low wall that seemed to divide the place from heaven. Child as I was, I could see over it; but had no power to climb it.

When he wrote about the dream more than twenty years later, it had lost none of its emotional power. He recalled seeing his grandparents on the other side of the wall and calling for their help, but "they only looked at me mournfully, and passed on." The seven-year-old Charles had to find his own way out of the predicament, and he formed a lifelong habit:

> For the first time in my life, I knelt, and tried to pray, *not* to be saved from hell; for it never had, in all my life, any terror to my mind; but to be reserved from such a *just* punishment. The habit of secret prayer then formed, was never wholly lost, through long years of youthful folly and sin.

If the young Charles Torrey was obsessed with religious faith and hyperfocused on judging his own conduct and state of mind, he came by his extreme Christianity honestly. He was descended from the Puritans, who believed God had chosen them for a special covenant and who had fled England to settle on the rocky Massachusetts coast. His early childhood was a series of losses to tuberculosis: his father, when he was about two; his infant sister, the following year; and his mother, the year after that. His memories of that time have an authentic feel:

> I think I remember playing with my little sister; remember my glee at the "pleasant ride" I thought we had when she was buried; my father's great coat, which hung in a particular place; my mother's sick bed; aunt Amanda's parching corn for her; my playing about father's house, near a board fence.

At three years old, he was taken in by his maternal grandparents, who raised him in Scituate, a fishing, shipbuilding, and farming town south of Boston where four rivers meander toward the stormy Atlantic. His entire upbringing, just up the coast from where the Pilgrims had landed at Plymouth Rock, coincided with the Second Great Awakening, a religious revival marked by camp meetings, saved souls, and the anti-alcohol fervor of the temperance movement. His Torrey ancestors traced back to the town's founding, and his grandfather Charles Turner Jr. was finishing two terms in Congress when the orphaned boy came to live with him. Turner had been postmaster and town moderator and served in the

Massachusetts legislature as Charles was growing up, providing the boy with a model of public service and political engagement. At some point Charles was given his grandfather's family name as a middle name.

Torrey's education could hardly have been more different from Smallwood's. His grandparents sent the bookish Charles Turner Torrey to the prestigious Phillips Exeter Academy, over the New Hampshire line north of Boston, and at the age of seventeen he entered Yale as a sophomore. He kept a journal that largely survives; his younger years are as thoroughly described as Smallwood's are sparsely documented. Despite his reference to "long years of youthful folly and sin," he seemed to be measuring himself by a preposterously puritanical standard. At Yale, he makes constant references to prayer meetings, missionary circles, and word of spiritual revivals from other cities. He fantasized that Yale students might take on the religious conversion of all of "China with its 350 millions"; in his diary entry for November 21, 1831, his eighteenth birthday, he wrote not about friends and parties but about God:

> O may I not, any more, dishonor God by neglecting him as I have done. I have deeply offended him; prayer I have often, especially lately, neglected. I have not studied the Bible as I should. I think very little of my duty to him; very little of his love.

He could be comically disapproving of the most ordinary laziness:

> Sabbath, August 5, 1832.—Sat up late last evening, studying and washing myself. Hence I laid till nearly eight this morning, a very bad practice, which I do now resolve to break off at once; I must retire earlier, lesson or no lesson.

But Torrey also showed a lively and curious mind, enjoying the discovery of philosophers and poets, and even displaying interest in meeting girls—though the conquests he reports seem to be focused more on their souls than their bodies. In 1833, as Smallwood was experiencing his third year as a free man, Torrey graduated from Yale, fretting that he was in debt, in part because he had bought so many books.

◂━◉━▸

Just nineteen years old, he started hunting for the only job for which he might be remotely qualified: teaching even younger people. He found a position in a sort of provisional school in West Brookfield, some sixty miles west of Boston, and noted the start of his pedagogy in October 1833 with ample exclamation points: "In the forenoon, about 10, commenced school with *five*! pupils!!!!! Courage! afternoon, six!" By January 1834, he had twenty budding scholars and things seemed to be going well, though he admitted he had not yet "secured the affection of all the pupils."

Then his journal entries grew darker. "In truth, I have been, for some time past, quite discouraged, having no rational prospects of better times," he wrote. By late winter, not quite four months into his teaching career, he was down to five students, all boys, and he was struggling to control their "roguish" behavior. His paltry pay had not kept up with his spending, and he was deeper in debt than ever. In March 1834, he gave up the job and left West Brookfield, a decision he portrayed as his own. But he had clearly failed to draw a sufficient number of students to support himself. At twenty, he was again at loose ends.

Having evidently concluded that he could not instruct or inspire children, Torrey seems to have decided he would try his hand at ministering to adults. He entered the Andover Theological Seminary at Andover, Massachusetts, intent on studying for the ministry. He did well in his studies and was introduced to the antislavery movement, then drawing fervent support from aspiring northern clergymen. But only a year later, he was forced to leave because of the precarious state of his health. He had discovered that he was infected with tuberculosis, possibly dating to earliest childhood, when the disease killed his parents and sister. The infection was often latent, allowing him reasonable health, but when it became active, it would sap his strength, racking his slender body with a cough, fever, and weight loss. The bacterial disease, incurable at the time, was then known as consumption for its wasting effects.

He spent a year resting and walking and gradually recovered his health, though the chronic infection remained. When he resumed his studies in 1835, it was in private tutorials with a series of respected clergymen, notably the Reverend Jacob Ide of West Medway, Massachusetts, southwest of Boston. Ide was a community leader, involved in local schools and the town library, and he had been a founding member of the American Anti-Slavery Society in 1833.

By late 1836, Torrey, twenty-two, was writing to Mary Ide, the minister's nineteen-year-old daughter, as "my beloved Mary." He began looking for a ministerial post, since an income would be necessary if he and Mary were to wed. He'd already tried his hand at preaching, on one occasion addressing at Boston's Odeon lecture and concert hall a congregation of eleven or twelve hundred people who, by his account, remained "very attentive" during what he admitted was his "rather long sermon."

"The Lord will send me somewhere, if he has anything for me to do for him, as a minister of Christ," he told Mary. And evidently the Lord found an opening: in March 1837, he was ordained at a Congregational church in Providence, Rhode Island, with Jacob Ide preaching at the ordination, and he and Mary were married a week later. He got a job on the ministerial staff of the Providence church, though he fretted that his strong antislavery views might offend some conservative worshippers.

Whether because of his increasingly outspoken abolitionism or for some other reason, he left the Providence church just seven months later. Two Massachusetts churches, one in Randolph and one in Salem, then expressed interest in his services, and he soon settled as a pastor in Salem. But some parishioners were unimpressed with his sermons—one called him a "miserable preacher"—and it was becoming clear that his animating interest lay not in the ministry but in the battle against slavery. After eighteen months, he was asked to leave the Salem church. One can only imagine what Jacob Ide, a highly successful clergyman, thought of his son-in-law's professional and financial struggles, even if he shared the younger man's views on slavery.

✦⟹⟸✦

Between the time Torrey started at Yale in 1830 and the time he left the job in Salem in 1838, abolitionism had grown into a powerful and divisive force in American politics, with local antislavery societies popping up all over the north. Torrey had closely followed the movement, while on occasion also discovering that plenty of northerners had no objection to slavery—particularly if the alternative was accepting Black people as equals. He had been in New Haven in 1831 when—days after the shocking news from Virginia of Nat Turner's rebellion—a plan for a vocational college for African Americans next to the Yale campus set off two nights of rioting that targeted abolitionists and Black neighborhoods. But Torrey was not put off by the prospect of political struggle. At the Andover seminary in 1835 he had served as president of the Andover Anti-Slavery Society, reporting to an activist clergyman named Amos A. Phelps, who was an "agent" for the Massachusetts Anti-Slavery Society. The friendship between Torrey and Phelps, a fellow Yale graduate who was eight years older, would have a profound influence on the younger man.

As the newly emancipated Thomas Smallwood broke with his Black colonizationist friends in Washington, Torrey was battling white support for colonization in New England. In the tumultuous summer of 1835, northern abolitionists organized a massive postal campaign, sending antislavery pamphlets to the south, and the Snow Riot destroyed Black businesses in the nation's capital. Amid the national tumult, Torrey wrote to Phelps to report on shifting public opinion on slavery and race at his seminary and among the citizens of Andover.

He said too many students and town residents, confronted with the debate over slavery, retreated to "their Idols, apathy & colonization." But he wrote that Phelps's book *Lectures on Slavery and Its Remedy*, published the previous year, was winning support for the abolitionist cause.

Meanwhile, a senior seminary professor, regretting the "coming storm" over slavery, had sternly advised Torrey and his fellow activists that they "need not make war with the Colonization Society."

"You see how the wind blows," Torrey told Phelps.

By this time Torrey had given up on full-time preaching, which he had found no more rewarding or satisfying than teaching. He and Mary had married and seen the birth of their first child, a boy they named Charles. Now Torrey, with Phelps's encouragement, turned his full attention to the antislavery cause and the debate over how best to pursue it.

The dominant figure in the abolition movement was William Lloyd Garrison, eight years older than Torrey and already widely known by the impressive triple-barreled name that would go down in history. There were superficial resemblances between the two Massachusetts men: Torrey would make his first splash with his jailing in Annapolis; Garrison had first drawn public attention in 1830 when he was jailed in Baltimore for forty-nine days for defaming a ship owner by accusing him of shipping enslaved people south. (The charge was true, but the young activist was convicted anyway.) Garrison had committed himself completely to the antislavery cause, just as Torrey was doing. And with his demand for immediate abolition and his take-no-prisoners rhetoric, Garrison presented himself as a radical, which initially appealed to Torrey.

But as he came to understand the debates inside the abolitionist camp, Torrey learned that Garrison had embraced an oddly self-defeating strategy that rejected conventional politics and government as too corrupted by slavery to be used in combating it. Garrison even opposed voting, which required participating in what he saw as an immoral system. A frustrated Massachusetts opponent once publicly confronted him, asking, "Mr. Garrison! do you or do you not believe it is a sin to go to the polls?" Garrison replied: "Sin for me." He advocated instead a hearts-and-minds strategy known as "moral suasion"—a fervent appeal to the consciences of enslavers to see the error of their ways.

Torrey, Phelps, and some other abolitionists found it preposterous to accept that slavery should continue until the slaveholders gave in to the arguments of Garrison and his friends, who also preached "nonresistance," or nonviolence, and were generally hostile to clergymen (which Phelps and Torrey had both trained to be). They regarded Garrison as an overbearing absolutist and thought that, no matter what his merits as a pioneer of the movement, he had become an obstacle. The resulting rift in the Massachusetts Anti-Slavery Society came to a head at a January 1839 meeting in Boston, where Torrey, Phelps, and their allies sought to oust Garrison from his leadership post—a brazen attempt at a coup d'état.

Garrison outmaneuvered them, however, mobilizing the votes of African Americans who were personally loyal to him and of women, since he was an avowed supporter of women's rights. So he remained in charge of the Massachusetts Anti-Slavery Society and the dissidents broke off and formed their own organization, the Massachusetts Abolition Society, with its own newspaper, *The Massachusetts Abolitionist,* as an alternative to Garrison's *The Liberator.* The "old organization" and the "new organization," as they were called, then engaged in a ferocious competition for supporters and funders—often expending as much energy battling each other as they did fighting slavery. Energized by the intramural combat, Torrey (in Salem) and Phelps (in Boston) discussed tactics in their regular letters, sometimes consisting of a series of numbered points.

"We must force them on the horrors of perfectionism, nonresistance and recreancy [cowardice] about political action," Torrey wrote to Phelps in March 1839. "What say you brother plotter?" Torrey had picked up the epithet "Lloyd Garrulous" from the press and now began referring privately to Garrison's newspaper, *The Liberator,* as "The Lyingberator" for its attacks on the dissidents of the new organization.

"I know how hard it is to my own spirit to keep still," he wrote to Phelps, "and be the object of attack in the Lyingberator, from week to week, without the power to reply. But yet our battery must be mounted with *5000* guns before one is loaded, or a shot fired."

Torrey sometimes demonstrated an ability to think beyond the feud with Garrison. Notably, at the very first gathering of the new Massachusetts Abolition Society, in May 1839, he committed the new organization not just to warring against the slave system but to the "improvement of the free people of color, in this their native country." He hired one of those free Black people, Jehiel C. Beman, to work for the society on projects involving "colored youth." Like Smallwood, Torrey had grasped that while the abolition of slavery might be the activists' preeminent goal, it would not be nearly enough to ensure justice and equality for African Americans.

⊷══◑══⊷

Torrey's inevitable departure from his minister's job in Salem—for months he had worked almost exclusively on antislavery activities—became formal in July 1839, and he proposed to Phelps that he embark on a lecture tour as a paid agent of the Massachusetts Abolition Society. He said his financial position would no longer allow him to work as a volunteer. "I am so much in debt, that I have no room to be disinterested in the matter," he wrote. Phelps agreed to Torrey's proposed salary of $1,000 a year plus expenses, and for the first time Torrey was being paid to pursue what had become his passion and his mission.

But abolitionist lecturers did not always get a warm welcome. Though the enslaved African American population was in the south, slavery was a critical part of the American economy, and many northerners knew their livelihoods depended on it. Cotton picked in the south was often woven into cloth in northern mills. That self-interest fed a widespread populist view that abolitionists were radicals and troublemakers, an offensive clique of elitists and extremists. As Torrey traveled on behalf of the Abolition Society, he repeatedly ran into hostile crowds. If they were not exactly well-informed advocates of the slave system, the white hooligans knew they didn't like these earnest antislavery speakers who inexplicably seemed to favor Black people. In extreme cases, the harassment could turn lethal. In the Mississippi River town of Alton, Illinois, in 1837, the abolitionist editor Elijah P. Lovejoy had been shot to death defending his printing press from a proslavery mob.

In the western Massachusetts town of Pittsfield, one of Torrey's early stops as a paid agent, he spoke repeatedly to large and small groups and gathered donations to support the abolition efforts. But even here, a thousand miles from the plantation labor camps of the slave south, he ran into trouble. "A few symptoms of mobocracy have disgraced this beautiful village," he wrote to Phelps. "Last evening some mill youth, a few of them southerners, shouted & yelled around the house and blowed a horn to supply us with music." The next night, he added, "one of them showed his love for the cause of scoundrelism in a new form, by throwing cents at me, as I stood in the pulpit." He pocketed the coins, thanked the young rowdy, and "promised that, by God's blessing, these coppers should not be lost to the cause of humanity. I would willingly be pelted till doomsday for the cause of the poor." It was mild harassment by the standards of the thugs and arsonists who were attacking Black businesses and neighborhoods farther south, but it gave Torrey a taste of battle.

Because Torrey and his allies had split with Garrison first of all over his refusal to engage with the political system, they moved swiftly to consider whether to form an abolitionist political party. There were differences over timing and tactics, but they were more or less settled when Gerrit Smith, an immensely wealthy heir to a fortune from real estate and the fur business, lent his support to the idea. On April 1, 1840, at a convention amid a spring snowstorm in Albany, delegates voted to create the Liberty Party—an avowedly abolitionist alternative to the two national parties, the proslavery Democrats and the equivocating Whigs. Garrison ridiculed the gathering as "April Fools" and would keep up a steady stream of vilification, but the Liberty Party gave opponents of slavery a formal political home.

Torrey threw himself into traveling and lecturing on behalf of the Liberty Party in Massachusetts and Maine, probably with financial support from Smith, who was becoming a crucial friend and backer. Torrey even bought a parcel of land in Maine at this time, as his biographer E. Fuller Torrey notes, a rare moment when he had more than enough money to scrape by—and a possible sign that he was considering a quieter future life with his family than the one he was living.

But if Torrey had believed the new political party would catch fire and quickly give the major parties a run for their money, he was disappointed.

The Liberty Party managed to nominate a presidential candidate in 1840, James G. Birney, a lawyer who had been born into a slaveholding family in Kentucky but had embraced first colonization and then abolitionism. Birney got just 7,453 votes, not quite a third of 1 percent, an irrelevance in the victory of William Henry Harrison, the Whig candidate, over Martin Van Buren, the Democrat. In some later contests, the Liberty Party would make a slightly better showing, but it would never approach becoming a real force in American politics.

Torrey remained loyal to the new party, but he was an impatient man—his constant awareness that tuberculosis endangered his health made him eager for swift progress. He had broken with Garrison and moral suasion with the reasonable belief that slavery must be fought in the political realm. But the early experience of the Liberty Party suggested that the political route, if it ever led to emancipation, might be a long one. If Garrison's approach was a dead end, and if the Liberty Party was not going to produce rapid results, then where might Torrey direct his burning ambition for both personal accomplishment and victories over slavery?

In Boston in mid-1841, while still working for the Liberty Party, Torrey heard about the moving plight of a man named John Torrance. Here was a new fight to capture his imagination—not over the tactics of the abolition movement but over the fate of a particular man and his family. Torrance, about thirty, had been enslaved in North Carolina and had carefully planned his family's emancipation. He had saved the money to purchase the freedom of his wife and child, who traveled to Philadelphia. Then, desperate to join his family in freedom, Torrance hid aboard a ship bound to Boston, only to be discovered en route. Though the captain wanted to put him off in slave country, in Virginia, the crew insisted that he be allowed to stay aboard. Arriving in Boston, Torrance managed to leap overboard, but he was picked up by a passing boat and returned to the ship. Now he was shackled aboard the schooner *Wellington* in Boston harbor, with every prospect of being hauled south again and returned to his enslaver. The Fugitive Slave Act of 1793, after all, required federal judges and magistrates in the north to help slaveholders recapture fugitives from slavery, prescribing a $500 fine for anyone who interfered.

Torrey went into action. He went to Boston's police court and filed kidnapping charges against the ship's captain and first mate, saying that they "with force and arms, did forcibly seize and confine" Torrance with the intent to return him to North Carolina. Torrey recruited an abolitionist lawyer, Richard H. Dana Jr., who had just published a gripping account of sailors' lives aboard a merchant ship, *Two Years Before the Mast*. Torrey also made sure the press was informed, and a *Boston Daily Mail* correspondent duly turned up to cover the court proceedings—and to describe Torrey with some hyperbole as "a leading abolitionist in this city."

But even in New England, Torrey's kidnapping charge against the captain and mate—both from the Boston area—seems to have been viewed as extreme. The *Boston Daily Mail* reporter referred to the role of "agitators" in the case. A letter to *The Boston Morning Post* complained that it had suggested no such charge was justified because the man "forcibly held in irons was a runaway slave," as if that settled the matter. The grand jury declined to indict the seamen. The decision prompted a scathing public letter from Torrey addressed to the twenty-three grand jurors by name and saying they had "disregarded the law and the facts."

"What would you say," he asked the grand jurors, "if you were compelled to buy your wives and children from the slave driver's hands, and separate them from your society to preserve their liberty and chastity?" He called their decision "Monstrous!" and suggested it betrayed Massachusetts's proud moral superiority over the slave south.

"Has Massachusetts, has Boston, have the merchants engaged in trade with the South, sunk so low?" he asked. The decision, he wrote, "says that whenever *southern slavery* and *northern* FREEDOM conflict, the latter must bow down in slavish subjection."

Torrance was taken south again, where his enslaver very possibly sold him to slave traders, the usual punishment for those who tried to flee. For Torrey, the case seems to have had a profound effect. Despite the outcome, he took satisfaction in his central role in the case, the acclaim from fellow abolitionists, and the jeremiad he had published. Yet he was frustrated that the courts had denied what he saw as simple justice.

Within a few months he had conceived a new plan. He would not move his family to Maine in search of stability and peace. He would no longer travel New England lecturing on behalf of the Liberty Party. Instead, this New Englander was going south for the first time in his life. He reached out to abolitionist newspaper editors in his latest attempt at a career, offering to send them dispatches from Washington. He would leave his family behind for the time being and move to the nation's capital, seeing firsthand a place where slavery reigned—and where there was a government with the power to do something about it.

Within a few weeks of his arrival in Washington, Torrey's decision to move south had been powerfully vindicated by his unexpected adventure in Annapolis. The jailhouse encounter with the two Black families awaiting sale south, his thrilling confrontation with slaveholders, his turn in the press spotlight as a hero of abolition—all of it persuaded him he was on the right course. The only question was whether he would now be satisfied with the relative drudgery of sitting in Congress and sending stories north. He had had a taste of intoxicating action.

In his busy life as a shoemaker at the Navy Yard, and as a church leader and activist, Thomas Smallwood kept close track of the news. When he heard about the northern newcomer, courageous or crazy or a little of both, who had dared challenge Maryland's slaveholders at their own convention, he was intrigued. The Baltimore and Washington papers had been full of the tale, lambasting Torrey as a provocateur or deriding the slaveholders for overreacting to the note-taking troublemaker.

The Baltimore Sun reported, with dark insinuation, that Torrey just might be an abolitionist, though it didn't deign to use the word: "a strong suspicion exists of his being an emissary of an association of those unhappy and misguided zealots who have endeavored by illegal means to interfere with our domestic institutions." *The Cecil Whig,* northeast of

Baltimore, complained about meddling "Northern fanatics" like "a person calling himself the Rev. Charles T. Torrey," as if the editor could not be sure Torrey was who he said he was. "There is little doubt that the Torrey case will prove a perfect Windfall for the abolitionists," harrumphed *The Georgetown Advocate,* criticizing the decision to jail him. "A dignified contempt for their malignant industry would have been infinitely the wiser course."

All this outrage must have impressed Smallwood. Anyone so despised by the proslavery editors must be a man of interesting conviction. Smallwood likely had also heard about, if he hadn't witnessed, Torrey's recent visits to Black churches, including his own. Most important, he had heard about Torrey from his wife, Elizabeth, who did the laundry at Torrey's boardinghouse. He wanted to meet this pot stirrer. As Smallwood wrote:

> I had heard of his arrest and trial at Annapolis, the seat of the Maryland government, to which place he had gone to take notes of the proceedings of the slaveholders then assembled in convention, at that City, and I myself watched its progress with great anxiety. Although I was not at that time personally acquainted with him, yet immediately after his acquittal and return to Washington, the seat of the government of that Union, I formed an acquaintance, with him through the agency of my wife, who took washing out of the house in which he then boarded; through her, I sought and obtained an interview with him.

Runaway ads for six of the people Thomas Smallwood and his allies helped to escape slavery——the four described here and two who had "absconded" earlier, *Daily National Intelligencer* of Washington, D.C., November 1, 1842. [Courtesy of American Antiquarian Society and Genealogy Bank]

3

That Mock Metropolis of Freedom

In many ways, Torrey and Smallwood made for an odd couple, two men who met across a chasm of race, privilege, and age. Torrey was just twenty-eight, and despite his flailing experience at teaching and preaching, he had the arrogance of a white Yale graduate, along with an extra helping of religious grandiosity. Smallwood, about to turn forty-one, was smoldering but steely, a hardworking father whose tenuous status as a free Black man made him tread carefully. He might have been expected to look askance at Torrey's pretensions and bravado. But their differences of social station, experience, style, and personality were set aside when they discovered that they shared a burning purpose: to combat slavery in the most urgent, practical way.

As they met and talked, in fact, they may have found they had a surprising amount in common. Both men had broad literary educations with a heavy religious emphasis, though Torrey had received his in elite institutions and Smallwood had seized his informally at every opportunity. Both had spent years in antislavery circles, if largely confined to their respective races, and both had come to reject colonization as a pernicious and fundamentally racist movement. Both had seen up close that when enslaved people turned to the courts to seek their freedom, they were often rebuffed, and that any legal progress took months or years. Smallwood had followed the struggles of his Navy Yard neighbors, the Shiners and the Bells. Torrey had battled unsuccessfully for John Torrance and interviewed the families awaiting their fate in the Annapolis jail.

Inside their separate enclaves in the antislavery camp, they had watched the endless debates over tactics and witnessed the bitter rivalries, sometimes becoming combatants themselves. They had seen no sign whatsoever that Garrison's moral suasion was undermining southern confidence in slavery. Quite the contrary—whatever Garrison or any other abolitionist said was treated by southerners as vile and dangerous propaganda. Southern defenses of slavery were becoming bolder: it was no longer a necessary evil but "the highest toned, the purest, best organization of society that has ever existed on the face of the earth," as the South Carolina congressman James Henry Hammond said in an 1836 speech.

Their frustration with the state of abolitionism was shared by others. As Garrison and Amos Phelps, Torrey's friend and mentor, remained mired for months in the dispute about the role of politics in battling slavery, John Greenleaf Whittier, a popular and prominent Quaker poet with abolitionist convictions, expressed his impatience with what he called "this everlasting dingdong." He jocularly called for "a regular set of fist-icuffs" between the two men to settle their dispute. Ultimately, he broke with Garrison and took Phelps and Torrey's view—that the political system should be fully engaged in the fight against slavery.

◆⇒◯⇐◆

But Torrey and Smallwood had little hope that political abolitionism, which Torrey championed, offered any immediate hope of emancipation. So now they agreed that it was time to move beyond politics. They may well have been influenced by an extraordinary speech, delivered and reported in the newspapers around the time of their first meeting, by Gerrit Smith, the wealthy Upstate New York businessman who had helped finance the Liberty Party and probably paid for Torrey's political lecturing. At the Liberty Party convention at Smith's mansion in Peterboro, New York, on January 19, 1842, Smith delivered what he framed as "An

Address to the Slaves of the United States of America" that proposed a radical shift of tactics.

Smith noted that abolitionists had long focused their attention on slaveholders—haranguing them, threatening them, or pleading with them to change their ways (surely a reference to Garrison and moral suasion, though Smith did not say so explicitly). He now spoke not to slaveholders but directly to the men and women they held in bondage. Violent rebellion might be morally justified, he said, but would certainly fail. Instead, he advised the enslaved to flee their enslavers: "We . . . call on every slave, who has the reasonable prospect of being able to run away from slavery, to make the experiment," Smith said, estimating that the number of "escapes from the house of bondage" was now one thousand a year, or more than five times what it had been a decade earlier. The growing number, he suggested, resulted in part from a major shift in public opinion in the northern border states, like Pennsylvania and Ohio, where he asserted that nineteen out of twenty citizens, influenced by the abolitionists, now thought escape was justified and were willing to assist the runaways on their way north.

Smith said it was up to those escaping slavery to choose for themselves whether to resettle in the free states or continue on to Canada, where they had less to fear from the kidnappers and slave catchers who would return them to bondage. "If he prefers the latter"—crossing into Canada—"we will gladly furnish him with facilities for realizing his preference. The abolitionist knows no more grateful employment than that of carrying the dog- and rifle-hunted slave to Canada." And, he told the enslaved, they should not hesitate to grab whatever they needed of the slaveholder's property to ensure a successful flight—"the horse, the boat, the food, the clothing"—feeling no more hesitation "than does the drowning man for possessing himself of the plank, that floats in his way."

Back in 1829, David Walker's *Appeal to the Colored Citizens of the World* had encouraged Smallwood to abandon colonization and stand up for his rights as an about-to-be free man. Now, thirteen years later, Smith's "Address to the Slaves" was a clarion call for self-liberation, copies of which Smith set about reprinting and smuggling south to friendly whites and to those enslaved people who could read.

Smith's brazen and straightforward message, which set off howls of outrage in southern newspapers, coincided with what Torrey and Smallwood were already thinking. They hoped to sabotage the very institution of slavery, destroying its financial foundation. If banks were robbed every week, Smallwood and Torrey calculated, would anyone keep their savings at a bank? Given that the value of an average enslaved worker was close to that of the average house at the time, would slaveholders tolerate their workers repeatedly disappearing? Might they not decide at some point that simply hiring free people and paying them wages was a more efficient and sensible system?

People held in slavery in every land and in every era had, of course, tried to escape when the opportunity presented itself, and some had found sympathetic helpers along the way. By the early nineteenth century, along the Ohio River and the Mason-Dixon Line and other major boundaries between slave states and free states, stories of African Americans traveling north by night were already familiar. But in 1842, when Gerrit Smith openly called on the 2.5 million African Americans held in bondage to make a run for it, and Smallwood and Torrey began plotting how to assist them, a major shift was in the works. The numbers willing to risk the flight from slavery were growing, and their supporters were getting more organized.

Smallwood later suggested that his efforts to aid escapes had been limited until his alliance with Torrey, in part because the enslaved were so understandably wary:

> It is extremely hazardous to undertake to do any thing for the slaves, but I do not blame them; it is just the way they are tutored in their raising. It is one of the grand policies of the slaveholders to keep up a continual lack of confidence on the part of the colored people toward each other, whether they be free or bond, by inspiring them with jealousy and envy against each

other in order to keep down that sympathy and mutuality which is so necessary among people having a common interest at stake.

As a result of such difficulties, Smallwood wrote, "much could not be done in the way of the underground railroad until 1842," when Torrey, "that most excellent and whole-souled Abolitionist . . . made his appearance in Washington." The two men saw Washington as an ideal ground for what Smith called the "experiment" of escape. It provided, on the floor of Congress, the one place in the country where outspoken abolitionists could face off against fanatical defenders of slavery, even though a "gag rule" pushed by southern congressmen severely limited open debate on slavery. It had a vigorous press to take note of the flight of the enslaved. And while journalists reported escapes with little sympathy, an act of self-liberation that elsewhere would be hardly noticed beyond the enslaver's family might have political resonance, unnerving the enslavers and even influencing the national debate over slavery.

In Washington, where a stroll from the Capitol to the president's house took one past the premises of a major slave dealer, the clash between the founding principles of the nation—"all men are created equal"—and the reality on the streets made the hypocrisy of the American creed especially hard to miss. The city was what Smallwood would call, in a memorably scathing phrase, "that mock metropolis of freedom, and sink of iniquity." It was in the uniquely charged atmosphere of the capital that Smallwood and Torrey started brainstorming their next steps.

As they began to think aloud about an unusual biracial partnership, they would quickly have grasped the striking advantages it would offer. A longtime resident, Smallwood knew the roads, alleys, wharves, and railroads of Washington and had important allies to the north, in the much larger city of Baltimore. He knew the police officers by name and reputation, which local officials were malicious and which were kindly, who was openly hostile to Black people and who might be sympathetic. He knew Washington's Black community, both free and enslaved, quite intimately, including who might have access to a storeroom or attic where a family might be hidden temporarily. He knew the stories of escapes, successful and unsuccessful, that amounted to a do-and-don't guide for prospective runaways.

His color, while imposing a stamp of vulnerability in a white-dominated society, allowed him easy, frequent, discreet, unremarked access to other Black people. He would have no trouble devising an excuse to visit or stage an encounter with an enslaved person in the course of an ordinary day, chatting about church or taking orders for new shoes. He could consult or recruit or advise or arrange while drawing little notice from white people. His race, usually a cloak of inferiority, conferred a kind of superpower—invisibility. He would use it in astonishing ways.

Torrey, meanwhile, brought his own capabilities to the enterprise. As an educated white man, he could enter homes and institutions that were off limits to Smallwood—including the offices of certain congressmen. He had ties to many in the abolitionist world—at least to those he hadn't denounced or offended—including deep-pocketed figures like Gerrit Smith, who, after all, had just endorsed flight from slavery as the most promising tactic. He had former colleagues and friendly acquaintances in towns from Philadelphia to Boston. He had connections to newspaper editors and correspondents. He had traveled far more than Smallwood, and so would have at least limited knowledge of promising escape routes. Yet Torrey also had an openness to the African American community that was rare in a white man of the era, as he had shown in his forays into Black churches.

Just a few weeks earlier, on December 8, 1841, Torrey had written yet another deferential letter to the speaker of the House of Representatives, pleading for a correspondent's desk on the House floor and explaining that he would write for several abolitionist newspapers. His earlier letters had failed to win what amounted to accreditation to cover Congress, so now he listed the newspapers: *The Massachusetts Spy, The New York Watchman, The American Citizen, The New-York Evangelist, The Christian Freeman,* and *The People's Advocate.* He claimed that the six papers together sold twenty-five thousand copies and "humbly" noted that some correspondents with desks represented tiny papers with circulations of as little as thirty-five hundred, adding a fulsome sign-off: "With entire respect, your obt. Servant, Charles T. Torrey."

This time, the House Speaker, John D. White, a Kentucky slaveholder who may not have felt warmly toward the antislavery press, finally scribbled "Granted" on Torrey's missive. But Torrey's Annapolis adventure and his meetings with Smallwood had dramatically changed the picture. He would indeed cover Congress, if sometimes perfunctorily. But he had a more exciting project in mind. The man who had dreamed in childhood that he was in hell was proposing a joint enterprise to the man who had impressed the neighbors with his two-syllable spellings. As Smallwood later recounted:

> At our first interview he informed me of a scheme he had in view, and requested my assistance, to which I readily assented. The scheme had for its object the rescue of a family of slaves, consisting of a man, his wife, and several children, who were owned by Mr. Badger of North Carolina, a Cabinet Minister, then living at Washington, and whose price for them was fifteen hundred dollars. I was dispatched to see the woman and apprise her of the scheme, her husband being away North at the time begging money to pay for them.

Torrey had chosen for their first target not just any slave owner, but a member of a special class: the prominent southerners who had come to Washington to serve in the government. George Edmund Badger, then forty-six, was a North Carolinian who had arrived the previous spring to serve as secretary of the navy. Badger made a tempting target. He had brought with him to Washington his enslaved household staff. As a cabinet member (the navy secretary was in the cabinet until the creation of the defense secretary's post), his personal troubles might attract press attention and he seemed a stronger symbol of the slaveholding south than the average Washington slaveholder.

Torrey and Smallwood worked on the details of this first escape, deciding what responsibilities each would take on in their new venture, scouting routes, and recruiting allies. What they were proposing to do was both quite novel and extremely hazardous. One of the few local men who had attempted to organize escapes was a free Black hackman, a sort of taxi driver, named Leonard Grimes, who had tried to use his hackney, or carriage, as cover for helping people flee. In December 1839, two years before Torrey and Smallwood met, he was jailed for driving an enslaved woman named Patty and her six children from Virginia to Washington, where they departed for Canada.

Testimonials to his good character reduced his sentence, but Grimes still spent two years in prison. Maryland law, which then also applied in the District of Columbia, set a maximum penalty of six years in prison for anyone who "enticed, persuaded or assisted" an enslaved person to run for freedom. The possibility of prison presumed that Smallwood or Torrey would survive to face trial; the slaveholders and their hired guns would not hesitate to use lethal force to retrieve their "property." And for a free African American like Smallwood, there was yet another dire possibility: that he would be unable to pay the large fines that might be imposed and would be sold into slavery, for a term or for life, to cover the debt.

In this case, Badger, who was planning to return to North Carolina, had already allowed the father of the enslaved family, Waller Freeman, to buy his freedom for $800. But now Badger was demanding another $1,500 for the rest of the family: Freeman's wife, Eliza, and their three sons and three daughters, ranging in age from two to fifteen years. If Badger didn't get the money from Freeman, he planned to sell Eliza and the six children south, where they might never see their husband and father again. Freeman, Smallwood would later write, thought the payment demands unfair:

> That good man thought that Mr. Badger had already got more of their labor than he was justly entitled to, according to the law of God; he therefore resolved if possible to deprive him of any pecuniary consideration for their liberty, in addition to the

value of the labor he had already robbed them of. Besides, he was not in favor of paying slaveholders for any of their slaves that could be otherwise rescued from their grasp.

Word had reached Torrey of the family's predicament, and he decided that escape was the answer. But by then Freeman was already making the rounds of northern abolitionists in a desperate effort to raise the necessary cash. The story circulated in multiple newspapers, and Freeman managed to collect the $1,500 and liberate his family, making an escape unnecessary.

Smallwood and Torrey were clearly frustrated, because they agreed with Freeman that it was a gross injustice to pay Badger for human beings they believed he had no moral right to claim. Smallwood suspected that Freeman had been "induced" to choose purchase over escape "through the influence of Colonizationists, and others in the North, who are always very anxious to recognize and acknowledge a right of property by man in man."

It was a shame, Smallwood said, because he and Torrey could have financed the escape of dozens more with the $1,500 that went into Badger's pocket. In the view of the new partners, depriving a slaveholder of his enslaved workers was clearly justified as payback for years of unpaid labor. Many less bold abolitionists wanted to make sure no law was broken and no property taken without compensation—and they were wrong, Smallwood wrote:

> But they should also remember that justice has two sides, or in other words, a black side as well as a white side. And if it is just for slaveholders to compel men and women to work for them without pay, because they are black, and they have the power to do so; then it is equally just for them, or their friends, to deprive their masters of such labor without pay.

The Badger-Freeman episode had given Torrey and Smallwood a chance for a dry run and shown them the risk of involving other abolitionists in engineering escapes. Many still wanted to work within the system and obey the laws even of slave states, supporting a less dangerous, more incremental effort to purchase the freedom of the enslaved. Gerrit Smith's call on the enslaved to "make the experiment" of fleeing north was still a radical stance. Smallwood and Torrey—who quite consciously planned to, in the words of Maryland law, "entice, persuade, and assist" as many people as they could to escape slavery—were out on the militant edge.

The Badger case reinforced a terrible truth about their mission: the more robust the slave trade, the greater the number of people who would dare to, or could be persuaded to, attempt an escape. Waller Freeman had been motivated to raise a small fortune to buy his wife and children because the alternative was too horrible to contemplate: they could be sold away and he would never see them again. Smallwood, of course, had lived with the terrors of the trade for many years, back to the stories of the local women who chose suicide over sale. Torrey had lost the battle to save John Torrance, the Boston stowaway, who, he knew, had likely been sold and separated from his family as punishment for running away. Torrey had also discussed the dark prospect of sale and separation with the thirteen people, pawns in an estate dispute, who had been jailed with him in Annapolis.

As Smallwood put the word out discreetly in the Black community about what they were planning, he and Torrey soon realized that it was the fear of being sold to the distant south that was driving many people their way.

CASH FOR NEGROES.—The subscriber has built a large and extensive establishment and private jail, for the keeping of SLAVES, in PRATT-ST., one door from Howard-st. opposite the Circus or Repository.

The building having been erected under his own in, spection, without regard to price; planned and arrang ed upon the most approved principle, with an eye to comfort and convenience, not surpassed by any establishment of the kind in the United States, is now ready to receive SLAVES. The male and female apartments are completely separate—the rooms for both are large, light and airy, and all above ground, with a fine large yard for exercise, with pure delightful water within doors. In erecting and planning this edifice, the subscriber had an eye to the health and cleanliness of the slaves, as well as the many other necessary conveniences. Having a wish to accommodate my Southern friends and others in the trade, I am determined to keep them on the lowest possible terms, at *twenty-five cents per head a day*, and furnish them with plenty of good and wholesome provisions. Such security and confidence I have in my building, that I hold myself bound to make good all jail breaking, or escapes from my establishment. I also will receive, ship, or forward to any place, at the request of the owner, and give it my personal attention.

N. B.—Cash and the highest prices will at all times be given for likely slaves of both sexes, with good and sufficient titles. Persons having such property to dispose of, would do well to see me before they sell, as I am always purchasing for the New Orleans market — I, or my agent can at all times be found at my office, in the basement story of my new building.

j9-tf   HOPE H. SLATTER.

Hope Slatter's ad in *The Baltimore Sun*, August 4, 1838. Variations would run almost daily during Slatter's years in Baltimore. [Courtesy of Newspapers .com]

4

The Flesh-Mongers

In his advertising copy, Hope Hull Slatter sought to ease the consciences of his many customers. "CASH FOR NEGROES," the headline declared. He had built a capacious private jail for his slave-trading business steps away from Baltimore's harbor, and his ubiquitous marketing read as if he were promoting an elegant new hotel and spa:

> The building having been erected under his own inspection, without regard to price; planned and arranged upon the most approved principle, with an eye to comfort and convenience, not surpassed by any establishment of the kind in the United States, is now ready to receive SLAVES. The male and female apartments are completely separate—the rooms for both are large, light and airy, and all above ground, with a fine large yard for exercise, with pure delightful water within doors.

He had designed it all, Slatter wrote in the 1838 ad, with a focus on "the health and cleanliness of the slaves," and he provided "good and wholesome provisions." Such ads, with variations, were printed almost daily for a decade in *The Baltimore Sun* and other city papers, and regularly in the weeklies of the eastern and southern parts of Maryland where the forced-labor camps known as plantations predominated.

After all the boasting about convenience and well-being, Slatter got down to business. Despite the charms of the premises, some guests evidently were not fully satisfied—so "I hold myself bound to make good all jail-breaking, or escapes from my establishment." And his offer to Maryland slaveholders was pure lucre: "Cash and the highest prices will be given at all times for likely [i.e., promising] slaves of both sexes, with good and sufficient titles. Persons having such property to dispose of, would do well to see me before they sell, as I am always purchasing for the New Orleans market."

Slatter, son of a Georgia planter, incongruously named Hope for a Methodist preacher, had served as a small-town sheriff in his thirties. He had learned the human-trafficking business in several southern cities, but in 1835, at age forty-five, he had decided he was ready for the big time and moved to Baltimore, with its thriving market and easy access to waterways. Within a few years he dominated the Chesapeake trade, taking the crown from Franklin & Armfield in Alexandria, Virginia, shipping hundreds of people south each year and building a personal fortune.

But in his appeals to the general public, he attempted a tricky balancing act, as his ads reflected. As the abolitionists' campaign to vilify slavery steadily gathered support, Slatter did his best to dress up his grim business for outsiders. Anxious for social acceptance among Baltimore's well-to-do, he regularly received visitors, including antislavery activists, and presented his operation as a kinder and gentler variety of the flesh traffic—a regrettable necessity, he said, in this perfectly legal business of slavery.

Slatter, described by a sightseer from Philadelphia as "a tall, well-formed and good-looking man, and withal quite gentlemanly in his manners," liked to regale visitors with assurances of his fine character. He told them he had started in the business with $4,000 borrowed from his mother, a devout Methodist, he said, and he too was a regular churchgoer. He never swore or committed any immoral act, he assured them. When John Greenleaf Whittier, the abolitionist poet, visited Slatter's jail with a British Quaker friend in 1841, "The proprietor received us with great courtesy," the friend, Joseph Sturge, wrote, and Slatter told his visitors that "he should be as willing as any one to have the system abolished, if the State would grant them compensation for their property." They were impressed with the "cleanliness and order" of the place. Most important, Slatter assured them that "he never parted families."

It was claptrap, concocted for the gullible. Like the other traders, Slatter regularly sold children south without their parents, husbands without their wives—whatever proved profitable. After leaving his jail, his innocent 1841 visitors happened to hear a story that showed they had been deceived: a desperate free Black man had visited Slatter days before, offering to indenture himself to raise $800 to buy the freedom of his wife and child, who had been sold to the trader. He was rebuffed, and the man's family disappeared on the next ship.

A few years earlier, Ethan A. Andrews, a professor from Connecticut, had stopped by Slatter's place, concealing his antislavery views and posing as a potential buyer. On that occasion, Slatter had spoken not of his mother's religious devotion or his own humane ways but of the special virtues of one particular human being on offer: "a little girl—bright mulatto—seven years old, whom he will be glad to sell; as fine a servant as he ever saw; quick and handy."

Anyone strolling around Baltimore's busy harbor or walking from the Capitol to the White House would spot the traders' jails. To many whites, it was just another form of legal commerce, perhaps a bit seedy but quite ordinary. To African Americans, who often had both enslaved and free people in their family, the traders stood for something terrifying and intractable: the constant threat that their loved ones could simply vanish into the maw of distant cotton and sugar plantations in the Deep South.

Far less understood today than the Middle Passage that first brought enslaved Africans to the colonies in the seventeenth century, the domestic slave trade that evolved two hundred years later was something quite different. From 1815 to 1865, an estimated one million enslaved African Americans were forcibly moved many hundreds of miles south, mostly from the mid-Atlantic and usually with the involvement of middlemen like Slatter. To put that one million in context, it is worth considering that the entire enslaved population in 1850 was 3.2 million. It was one of the largest forced migrations in human history, and it permanently separated families. For decades after the Civil War, Black families would place newspaper notices seeking lost relatives, desperately trying to restore kinship networks that the traffickers had torn asunder.

The business that would make Slatter wealthy had its origin in the United States Constitution. Southern planters, notably those from South Carolina, wanted to keep importing captives from Africa indefinitely. Northern opponents wanted the international slave trade stopped. They struck a compromise: the African slave trade would not be tampered with for twenty years, until 1808. And indeed, Congress outlawed the African trade, effective January 1, 1808, the first day such a ban was permitted. But by then, the measure was not just a concession to antislavery opinion. In 1808 the political coalition supporting an end to the international slave trade was more complex. Those representing the Chesapeake region knew that a prohibition of the African trade would make the enslaved workers they owned and their future offspring far more valuable, creating a strong pecuniary interest among slaveholders in the measure.

Thomas Smallwood shrewdly remarked on this hidden motive: "They abolished the external or African slave trade, in 1808, the effect of which gave an impetus to the infamous traffic of slave breeding and trading among themselves; and perhaps it was one of the main objects they had in view, the protection of their slave breeders and traders."

Slatter's booming business also benefited from two agricultural trends that had started in the early nineteenth century. The first was the decline of tobacco farming in the mid-Atlantic states. Tobacco had been the foundation of early Maryland's economy, not just a commercial product but almost a currency, used for barter; the fines imposed for crimes were sometimes set in pounds of tobacco. "Tobacco, as our staple, is our all, and indeed leaves no room for anything else," wrote Benedict Leonard Calvert, a colonial governor of Maryland, in 1729.

But by the 1800s the soil in many places was growing exhausted from tobacco monoculture, prices were declining, and many growers were shifting to wheat, corn, and livestock. This meant a huge downsizing of the workforce: tobacco was by far the most labor-intensive crop, and planters had purchased enslaved workers to cope with the laborious planting, pruning, picking, and drying of the big leaves. The shift to grain crops meant that many planters found themselves with more workers than they needed—but they could not simply be laid off. Because they were the planters' valuable property, they had to be fed and housed.

This economic dilemma might have sapped the strength of the slave system in the Chesapeake; as unneeded workers became a burden, they might simply have been freed. But the second trend discouraged such a development. The invention of the mechanical cotton gin by Eli Whitney in 1793 had automated the tedious process of separating the cotton fibers from their seeds and made cotton growing far more profitable. This new technology and the steady movement of Americans from crowded eastern cities to the frontier led to an astonishing boom in cotton production, from 73,000 bales in 1800 to 2.1 million five decades later. Prices stayed strong, because European demand for cotton seemed inexhaustible—and 87 percent of the 1850 crop was exported. This lucrative explosion in cotton production required a colossal workforce, because cotton, like tobacco, required many hands for harvest.

So just as the mid-Atlantic was experiencing a labor surplus, the Deep South needed huge numbers of new workers, and few were coming from Africa. It was true that some illegal Atlantic slavers kept operating in defiance of the 1808 law—often using the speedy sailing schooner called the Baltimore clipper, which could outrun the authorities. An 1840 report on the transatlantic slave trade found that eleven of twenty-one American vessels caught engaging in the illegal trade the previous year had been Baltimore-built, and federal authorities sometimes seized ships at the city's harbor they believed were fitted to carry captives from Africa. But the ban nearly choked off the supply of newly enslaved Africans.

Had domestic slave trading also been banned, it is possible to imagine an alternative history, in which cotton and sugar planters might gradually have been forced to shift to paid labor, while unneeded workers in the upper south might have been emancipated.

Instead, a completely legal domestic slave trade came to the rescue of slavery across the south. The payoff for white planters everywhere was substantial: in Maryland, Virginia, and the upper south, excess workers could be sold to traders like Slatter for ready cash; an enslaved woman's children, or "increase," as official documents called them, became not a burden but a source of future wealth—hence Smallwood's reference to "slave breeders." Speaking in England in 1846, Frederick Douglass would explain this strange and horrifying situation:

> We have in the United States slave-breeding states. The very state from which the minister from our court to yours comes, is one of these states—Maryland, where men, women, and children are reared for the market, just as horses, sheep, and swine are raised for the market. Slave-rearing is there looked upon as a legitimate trade; the law sanctions it, public opinion upholds it, the church does not condemn it. It goes on in all its bloody horrors, sustained by the auctioneer's block.

In Mississippi and Louisiana and the rest of the Deep South, meanwhile, the critical demand for more workers could be met by those uprooted from the Chesapeake region. A slave trader like Slatter served many purposes in this gruesome commerce. He or his agent could show up at a plantation or a small farm or a city house and simply fill out a bill of sale, hand over cash, shackle the unwanted workers, and cart them away. From the slaveholder's perspective, it was an easy and rapid transaction, without prolonged, painful scenes of pleading and parting. From the slave trader's perspective, it was a straightforward, profitable matter of buying a person for $500 in Maryland or Washington or Virginia, going south, and selling him or her for $800.

But for enslaved Black families, the trade was a generations-long catastrophe. Those held in bondage were "chattels," movable property, who could be sold at the whim or convenience of the slaveholder—even when it meant that a man was sold away from his wife or a wife from her husband, children taken from parents, siblings separated forever. While the slave-labor camps of Maryland could be cruel, many of the enslaved worked in less dire situations: on small family farms, in Baltimore homes as servants, or hired out for all kinds of work.

In the Deep South, by contrast, the cotton plantations were brutal factory farms, and work on sugar plantations, the second-largest user of enslaved labor, regularly proved lethal. So for African Americans in the mid-Atlantic, the arrival of the "Georgia man" or "Georgia trader"—a commonplace term that was largely out of date, though it happened that Slatter really was from Georgia—meant separation, despair, and death. A Methodist preacher traveling in Maryland recorded a mournful song he heard enslaved farm workers singing:

> *William Rino sold Henry Silvers*
> *Hilo! Hilo!*
> *Sold him to de Gorgy Trader*
> *Hilo! Hilo!*
> *His wife she cried and children bawled*
> *Hilo! Hilo!*
> *Sold him to de Gorgy Trader*
> *Hilo! Hilo!*

One day in 1842, a group of people who had fled Maryland—likely with Smallwood and Torrey's help—were standing together in Albany and a sympathetic local man asked about the domestic slave trade. "Do they often sell slaves away from their relations?" the man asked. A dozen fugitives—eyewitnesses from the south—kicked the question around for the benefit of their northern listeners, naming Slatter as the prototypical trader. One listener took notes on the encounter:

"Oh yes, some out of every family gets sold. I've had a mother and two brothers sold!" "I've had a father and a sister," said a second. "All my family were sold!" gasped a third. And so it was with the others. Said one, "why they sells us for every thing. If master wants a new carriage he takes a slave down to Slatter's (the principal trader in Baltimore) and sells him. If he wants some grain for seed, sell a slave! If the ladies want to go a plea-suring, sell another, and so on."

James Watkins, who was born into slavery north of Baltimore, re-called accompanying his mother on an awful mission to Slatter's jail to try to say a final goodbye to his two brothers, sister, and cousin, whom their owner had decided to sell south. The owner agreed to allow the visit only "after ridiculing the idea of black people having any feelings"—a common racist rationalization. "My mother and I were only allowed about half an hour to take leave of those whom we were about to lose for ever," Watkins wrote. "I shall never forget the parting as long as I live."

Like survivors of a merciless war, every family had a story of loss and despair.

-•➝═◉═⬅•-

The world Hope Slatter had been born into in 1790 in rural Warren County, Georgia, took slavery, the slave trade, and the associated suffer-ing entirely for granted. His father, Solomon, grew up in North Caro-lina, served in the Revolutionary War as a teenager, and later moved to Georgia, becoming a farmer and slaveholder, raising a large family, and serving in the state senate. Solomon died in 1812, leaving his widow, Nancy Flewellen Slatter, to live nearly three more decades, which may explain Hope's frequent references to his mother's supposed religious influence on him. "She was a member of the Methodist E. Church about 52 years," says the inscription on her gravestone in Clinton Cemetery in Georgia, referring to the Methodist Episcopal Church, and "lived the life of a Christian and died a most triumphant death."

From early adulthood, Hope Slatter showed up in Georgia public records as a small-time lender and mortgage holder in local real estate transactions that gave him plenty of exposure to the sale of human beings. In 1821, he was advertising for sale "Twenty nine Negroes" as part of a foreclosure. Two years later he was selling "15 likely negroes" who had belonged to a deceased relative. In 1825, he was offering a toast at a public dinner for a visiting retired general—one known for having brutally suppressed a slave insurrection in Florida a decade earlier. By 1826, Slatter was serving as the sheriff of Jones County, Georgia, where one of the largest businesses was a factory making cotton gins. Like other southern sheriffs, he routinely oversaw the sale of enslaved people from estates or legal disputes. His long exposure to such sales may have persuaded him—belatedly, at about forty years of age—to seek his fortune in full-time slave trading.

It's worth pausing for a moment to consider our main characters and their pursuits in 1830. Thomas Smallwood was finally completing the purchase of his freedom. Charles Torrey was starting his studies at Yale. And Hope Slatter, a decade older than Smallwood and more than two decades older than Torrey, was roaming the south in search of people to buy and sell. In 1831, he was working from a tavern in Fayetteville, North Carolina, making deals to buy enslaved people. By 1834, he had rented a house for a year in Charleston, South Carolina, and was placing daily "Negroes Wanted" notices in the local papers. Soon he moved on to Baltimore, an even more profitable market than the Carolinas, and one that allowed him to settle in the largest city in the slaveholding south. (His family had an earlier connection; his younger brother, John Jefferson Slatter, had been born in Baltimore during an 1802 stay, when Hope was twelve.) Slatter worked out of taverns and hotels for a few years, but by 1837 he had applied to Baltimore authorities for permission to build a house, a slave jail, and a compound near the corner of Pratt and Howard Streets, just west of the harbor. The next year he married a Baltimore woman, Emma Clackner, his third wife; he had been widowed twice before. He would father eight children, at least one of whom would die in childhood.

The Baltimore Hope Slatter settled in was the nation's second most populous city after New York and was a sophisticated and prosperous mercantile port with an 1840 population of 102,313—four times as big as the self-important village of Washington. Ships arrived from all over the world, carrying goods from Asia and immigrants from Europe. With plentiful coach, rail, and steamship connections to the nation's capital, Baltimore was the business and shopping center used by well-off Washingtonians. Baltimore pioneered gas lighting, opened the world's first dental college, and was the recipient of Samuel Morse's first-ever telegram. When the national political parties held their conventions, Baltimore was a natural choice: it hosted the Democrats in 1840 and both Democrats and Whigs in 1844.

At the very beginning of the interstate slave trade in 1810, as traffickers settled in Baltimore, a report from the local grand jury had expressed horror and alarm. The grand jurors described "an evil for which in the present state of our laws there seems to be no adequate remedy. To Wit the Evil which necessarily attaches itself to the Slave Trade or to the transportation of Slaves from this, to other states." The report described horrendous conditions in the traders' slave jails: "the slaves being crowded together, male and female in one common dungeon, there being loaded with irons, confined in their filth together with being subjected to various species of Cruelty and Tyranny from their Keepers, presents a scene at once abhorrent to every principle of humanity and in our opinion disgraceful to any civilized community."

Coming two years after the ban on the African trade, the grand jury report was a remarkable document. It was clear-sighted and principled, written in language that might have come verbatim from the abolitionists two decades later. But capitalism trumped human rights. The exposé did nothing to curb the rapid growth of the domestic trade as demand for labor in the Deep South grew insatiable. By 1840, after thirty years, the kind of good white citizens who had authored the grand jury report had learned to ignore or rationalize the slave trade, which was everywhere around them. Traders like Slatter had learned to dress up their business in euphemisms, the kind that appeared daily in his *Sun* ads.

Slatter's compound on Pratt Street was directly opposite the city's Repository, a large public arena that hosted traveling circuses and commercial exhibits. C. H. Bacon's circus, boasting of "astonishing feats, which to be credited must be seen," opened just as Slatter was completing his jail. When "Wild Beasts and Birds" were on display, "colored persons" were admitted on Saturdays only, except as servants for white families—a marker of the deeply inferior treatment of Black residents in the largest free Black community in the country.

About one in five Baltimoreans was Black in 1840, and 85 percent of them were free, negotiating the difficult middle ground between enslavement and full citizenship. The city had an official enslaved population of 3,199—but hundreds more enslaved people in the city at any given time were only passing through. They were being held in the slave jails, or slave pens as they were also called, of Slatter and his smaller competitors, awaiting a forced journey south.

Slatter and his family occupied a brick house on Pratt Street, with his office in a smaller side building marked by a sign: HOPE H. SLATTER, FROM CLINTON, GEORGIA. (Perhaps the mention of Slatter's hometown was a polite way to suggest the nature of his business without any explicit mention of slavery.) In the back was an open courtyard about seventy-five feet by forty feet and a separate brick building with barred windows containing the cells for his prisoners—or "apartments," in the language of Slatter's advertising—which one of Slatter's assistants described as "hot as a little hell" in the long Baltimore summer. The whole compound was hidden from the street by twenty-foot brick walls. When a tax inspector visited Slatter's home and business in the early 1840s, he assessed the land and buildings at about $17,000 (around $500,000 today), plus $3,000 in furniture ($90,000) and hundreds of dollars more in horses, carriages, wagons, and "three gold watches."

But the most valuable single category of Slatter's property, worth more than the land or the buildings, was what the tax inspector called "stock in trade": the thirty-nine enslaved people whom the slave trader happened to be holding on that day, ranging in age from nine (William) to forty (Nancy), in value from $200 (for the youngest and oldest) to $525 for men in their twenties.

Ahead of them was a weeks-long journey south. Some traders took people south on foot, a grueling overland trip with the men shackled together and women and children following behind. The traders or their employees usually traveled alongside on horseback and were armed to prevent any attempt at escape. Such "coffles," as these strings of enslaved people were called, were a common sight for travelers in the south and even in Washington. But most people sold south from Baltimore went by sea.

Slatter would accumulate a shipload in his jail, making most of his purchases after the annual harvest, when labor was in less demand. Then, operating late at night, when wailing and pleading families were less likely to be a nuisance, he would march his captives across town to a wharf where a ship lay waiting or where the prisoners could be rowed out to a ship at anchor. Before Frederick Douglass escaped slavery in the city in 1838, dressed as a sailor and with borrowed freedom papers, he spent several years of his childhood living in Baltimore, including in a house in the waterfront neighborhood of Fells Point. He later recalled awakening in the middle of the night to hear the chilling sound of enslaved people passing on their way to the wharves:

> The flesh-mongers gather up their victims by dozens, and drive them, chained, to the general depot at Baltimore. When a sufficient number have been collected here, a ship is chartered, for the purpose of conveying the forlorn crew to Mobile or to New Orleans. From the slave-prison to the ship, they are usually driven in the darkness of night; for since the anti-slavery agitation a certain caution is observed. In the deep, still darkness of midnight, I have been often aroused by the dead, heavy footsteps and the piteous cries of the chained gangs that passed our door.

The menace of the slave trade at times came still closer to Douglass. When he was fourteen, his sister Sarah was sold to a Mississippi planter, one of fifteen relatives sold south during his childhood. And Douglass himself, like many rebellious enslaved people, was repeatedly threatened with sale.

⋅⟶⊚⟵⋅

This was Slatter's trade, and he made an excellent living, almost exclusively in the Baltimore–to–New Orleans coastwise traffic, as it was called. In early 1842, as Smallwood and Torrey were plotting their first trips north, a 444-ton ship called the *Tippecanoe* left Baltimore carrying south sixty-seven men, women, boys, girls, and infants for Slatter, who had bought them over the previous weeks across Maryland with the help of his agents.

By the 1840s this traffic was so routine that it went on without particular public notice, except for the paperwork required by federal law. Dozens of enslaved people were crammed into a ship's fetid hold, filling whatever space was left between the crates and bundles of cargo and small herds of livestock being carried south. The first week or two of the trip could be brutally cold, since the slave traders moved their captives generally between October and April. The ship would pass through the Bahamas, round the Florida Keys, and be pulled by a steamboat on the treacherous last leg up the Mississippi River to the wharves. The entire journey generally took three to four weeks, by which time the enslaved were often weak and ailing. Some died of disease en route, sometimes prompting the trader to sue a slaveholder for misrepresenting the health of the enslaved; a few, despairing over separation from family left behind, committed suicide by leaping into the sea. The overriding tragedy of the trade, family separation, is illustrated by the fact that two of every three people shipped south from Baltimore shared a last name with no one else on board, the historian Jennie K. Williams has found.

After a frigid seventeen-day journey, the forced migrants of the

Tippecanoe arrived in New Orleans on February 4, 1842, and were taken to Slatter's southern hub, a slave jail usually operated by Slatter's son Henry and brother Shadrack at Esplanade Avenue and Moreau (now Chartres) Street at the edge of the French Quarter. The traders allowed them to wash, fed them on heavy rations for a few days, and then had their bodies greased to give potential buyers an impression of health and muscularity. Transactions in New Orleans were recorded by notaries, and the city's notarial archives give just a hint of what happened to those forced south from Baltimore.

An enslaved woman named Ruthy, about twenty-four, was sold in early 1842 to James M. Wolfe for $700 as a sort of gift to his son, George. Hope Slatter's brother Shadrack was the seller of record, and he signed an oath that the young woman was "fully guaranteed against all the vices and maladies" listed in the law. A few months later, Shadrack sold James Cook, twenty-seven, a skilled carpenter, to Valery Gaudet for the very high price of $1,500, along with a bricklayer named Joe for another $1,000. Gaudet was a major sugar planter; a few years earlier, he had been compensated $300 by the state of Louisiana after the execution of a man he enslaved, who had been convicted of murder. Multiply such voyages by the scores, and sales by the thousands, and you have Slatter's slave-trading career.

As was standard in the trade, Slatter shipped no one south during the warm months after the *Tippecanoe* sailed, as Maryland slaveholders needed hands for spring planting and summer crops. But by October, he had accumulated another large shipment—the seventy-seven people who, as noted in the prologue, were dispatched south on a twenty-one-day trip to New Orleans aboard the *Burlington*. In November he shipped eighteen more people south aboard a smaller vessel called a barque, the *Peres*. In December, another forty-four people were sent aboard another barque, the *Irad Ferry*.

In January 1843, another thirty-two people were torn from their relatives and sent to New Orleans. In February, forty-nine more. In March, thirty-one more. As the trade flourished and Baltimore reclaimed the title of busiest Chesapeake slave port, which it had temporarily lost to

Alexandria, the manifests carefully recorded the names and numbers of people shipped south, leaving to the imagination the suffering of those dispatched to plantations in Louisiana or Mississippi or elsewhere and the family members they left behind.

Top of a manifest Hope Slatter was required to file for every shipload of enslaved people he sent south. This manifest lists the eighty-eight captives shipped from Baltimore to New Orleans on November 1, 1843, aboard the ship *Superb*. [Courtesy of the National Archives]

Abolitionists hammered away at the domestic slave trade, which they understood to be the most flagrantly cruel and callous part of the slave system. Some southern politicians and grandees dubiously claimed a paternal fondness for their human property, arguing that the people they enslaved were actually better off than if they had been free and on their own. But slave traders could not make even that threadbare claim. So antislavery advocates repeatedly highlighted a seeming contradiction in American law: If the African trade was so reprehensible that it had to be banned, how could the all-American trade, which was hardly less despicable, carry on with government's blessing? Charles Torrey, perhaps with not the most nuanced notion of Africans, wrote that Baltimore had a *daily traffic* in the persons of men, women, and children, which is as much more atrocious than the African slave trade, as the people are more enlightened than the savages of the dark coasts of that wretched continent. There, a savage, maddened by liquor, sells to a white stranger, captives taken in war from hostile tribes. Here, native citizens sell American husbands, wives, sons and daughters, in cool blood, as a part of the *regular traffic* of this Christian city. The traders in souls ride in their carriages; their families mingle in its social circles, and own pews in its churches, and are very respectable men.

In his writings, Torrey repeatedly singled out Slatter, an obvious and worthy target, for special scorn. Here he noted that Slatter had recently purchased a pew—a common way to finance church construction at the time—"in the splendid new Methodist church in Charles street, much to the annoyance of many of the worshippers." In this aside, Torrey put his finger on a striking grievance of the region's dominant human trafficker: Slatter resented the fact that his wealth had not won him automatic admission to the most prestigious social circles, even those dominated by slaveholders. It was as if the slave trade put a permanent asterisk next to his social status, and he was always looking for ways to prove his respectability.

Joseph Sturge, the British Quaker who visited Slatter in 1841 with the poet Whittier, was fascinated by this contradiction. Slatter had argued that if the slave trader was a sinner, the slaveholder was equally a sinner, because the second relied regularly on the former. Sturge tended to agree, writing of Slatter:

I subsequently learned that this person, though living in considerable style, was not generally received in respectable society, and that a lady whom he had lately married, was shunned by her former acquaintance. Such is the testimony of the slaveholders of Baltimore against slave dealing, by which they condemn themselves in the sight of God and man, and add the guilt of hypocrisy to their own sin.

When the Methodists held a grand meeting in Baltimore, Slatter gave some of the visitors a tour of his compound. "Gentlemen, I suppose this looks strange to you, coming from the North as you do," one of the visitors recalled him saying. "I live in a slave State, where the laws fix these matters. These people are with me a short time, I feed and clothe them well, and consider that I do not make their condition any worse than it was before."

What the church officials thought was not recorded. Clearly Slatter had hoped to launder his reputation by his purchase of an expensive pew in the fashionable new church, an imposing neoclassical building in the heart of downtown that one Marylander said was built by wealthy Methodists "to gratify the aristocracy, nabobery, and fashionable ladies among that once plain and praying people." But it was not to be. A northern-born man living in Baltimore wrote to a New England friend that "a slave trader here is regarded exactly as we at the North regard a grogseller"—a disreputable peddler of liquor. Slatter had "bid off the most expensive" of the pews, the writer said, adding:

> Another gentleman, a wealthy member of the church, without knowing who were to be his neighbors, bid off the one next behind. The next Sabbath, on taking his seat, the latter found that the notorious slave-dealer was seated with his family, next before him; and was to be the object on which his eyes were henceforth constantly to rest, during divine service. On leaving the church, he at once declared that he would never sit in his own seat again, while the one before him was thus occupied.

◆──◉◉──◆

Such social shunning seems to have motivated not only the language of Slatter's ads about his "light and airy" jail with the "pure delightful water" but also his willingness to allow visits to the premises. Many of the surviving accounts of his jail were written by antislavery activists engaging in what might be called slavery tourism, a politicized and publicly demonstrative kind of travel quite popular at the time. Slavery tourists sought out the most horrifying (but safe) settings to witness the crimes of the slave system, often writing about their visits and declaring their renewed devotion to the abolitionist cause.

A popular singing group, the Hutchinsons, stopped by Slatter's place in 1840, for instance, and often spoke about it at subsequent concerts. "Our hearts sickened," John Hutchinson later declared of what they saw in the slave trader's jail. "We inwardly cursed such an institution and re-resolved to do everything in our power to ameliorate the slaves' conditions and wash from our escutcheons the bloody stain." Some distinguished foreign tourists were so fascinated by slavery that they were determined to see it for themselves. Alexis de Tocqueville, the French aristocrat who would write the celebrated *Democracy in America*, visited Baltimore and left memorable notes on a man seemingly unhinged by fear of a slave trader:

> Today, 4th of November, we saw in an Alms-house a Negro whose madness is extraordinary; there is at Baltimore a slave-trader who, it seems, is much feared by the black population. The Negro of whom I speak imagines that this man sticks close to him day and night and snatches away bits of his flesh. When we came into his cell, he was lying on the floor, rolled up in the blanket which was his only clothing. His eyes rolled in their orbits and his face expressed both terror and fury. From time to time he threw off his blanket, and raised himself on his hands shouting: "Get out, get out, don't come near me." It was a terrible sight. This man is one of the most beautiful Negroes I have ever seen, and he is in the prime of life.

Charles Dickens, on his American tour, stopped in Baltimore in 1842 and was shaken to realize the people serving him at his hotel were enslaved. He found himself uncomfortable with "the sensation of exacting any service from human creatures who are bought and sold ... though I was, with respect to it, an innocent man, its presence filled me with a sense of shame and self-reproach." He was horrified by the "Cash for Negroes" ads that he saw in every newspaper.

Aboard the train to Richmond—not long after having viewed the original of the Declaration of Independence in Washington—Dickens glimpsed firsthand the consequences of the domestic slave trade:

> In the negro car belonging to the train in which we made this journey, were a mother and her children who had just been purchased; the husband and father being left behind with their old owner. The children cried the whole way, and the mother was misery's picture. The champion of Life, Liberty, and the Pursuit of Happiness, who had bought them, rode in the same train; and, every time we stopped, got down to see that they were safe.

Another visitor the following year, a few months before Smallwood and Torrey first met, was a Vermont abolitionist, an acolyte of William Lloyd Garrison named Oliver Johnson. Johnson had come to Baltimore chiefly hoping to visit the cell in the city jail where his hero Garrison had been held for forty-nine days a decade earlier. But this pilgrimage was thwarted when jail officials would not admit him. So he went instead to Slatter's business on Pratt Street and wrote a full account of what he saw, which was soon published in several abolitionist newspapers.

Inside, by Johnson's account, he was quickly surrounded by "nearly a hundred human beings of all ages and both sexes, locked up like so many wild beasts," awaiting shipment south. Once he announced to the prisoners his fervent antislavery views, Johnson wrote, those around him exclaimed "God bless you!" while "tears of gratitude filled their eyes." He heard about families torn apart: "Among the group were several mothers, with infants in their arms, who told me, with deep emotion, that they had been sold away from husbands and children, whom they never expected to see again in this world." He was particularly horrified by the story told by two sisters from the western Maryland town of Frederick—"nearly white," he noted, with the era's reflexive attention to racial mixture. They told him they had fled their owner—who was also their biological father. They had been recaptured and now, in retribution, had been turned over to Slatter for sale. "For the crime of running away," Johnson wrote, "they were sold *by their own father*, for the New-Orleans market!"

Hope Slatter was away that September day, but Johnson had a sharp exchange with Slatter's brother Shadrack, visiting from New Orleans, who had let him inside but now became infuriated: "D—n you! You've been taking notes." The brother defended the business and lectured Johnson at length on the subject: "Slavery is according to Christianity, and justified by the ablest divines in this country, at the North as well as the South. I treat my niggers in the kindest manner. . . . why, d—n it, there is not a happier set of laborers on God's earth than the niggers of the south."

By his account, Johnson departed for New England "with a firmer resolution than ever to wage a war of extermination against the nefarious and bloody system" of enslavement. But it is hard to escape the impression that his Baltimore visit had been as much about him as it was about the enslaved captives who were the subjects of his pity and outrage. Abolitionism, like other social movements, was rife with rivalry and division, plagued by egotism and self-promotion, admirable in its goals but frustrating in its entangling self-regard. Abolitionists were clearly on the side of right, as they would be the first to tell you. But the compelling moral issue of the era could be all but lost in endless proclamations and exhausting infighting. Anyone who joined the cause looking for rapid results, for practical impact on the lives of the enslaved, could lose patience. A few, like the shoemaker and the correspondent who had connected in Washington, were driven to radical action.

In the newspapers of Maryland, Washington, and Virginia, two possible fates for the enslaved—sale south or escape north—often appeared in adjacent ads, like these in the *Daily National Intelligencer* of Washington in 1842. [Courtesy of American Antiquarian Society and Genealogy Bank]

5

Slavery's Borderland

There was a reason why Charles Torrey had been drawn south, and Hope Slatter north, to the Chesapeake region where Thomas Smallwood had spent his life. The mid-Atlantic was a boiling cauldron where all the disparate categories of Americans met and all the elements of racial, political, and legal conflict simmered like nowhere else. Few New Orleans residents ever saw a radical abolitionist. Few Bostonians ever met a slave trader. But in the Chesapeake, the combatants were thrown together.

Years before, a drama on the streets of Baltimore had captured the warring parties in one of their early encounters. A precursor to Torrey and Smallwood, an abolitionist firebrand named Benjamin Lundy, faced off against Austin Woolfolk, Slatter's predecessor and Baltimore's first leading slave trader, who was, like him, a son of Georgia. Lundy had chosen the city as the place to publish his pioneering newspaper, *The Genius of Universal Emancipation*. He later recruited the twenty-three-year-old William Lloyd Garrison to be his assistant, hoping to speed their publication schedule. Lundy often focused his fire on the slave trade—and on Woolfolk in particular.

In 1826, an enslaved man named William Bowser was being shipped south by Woolfolk on the ship *Decatur* when he and others managed to revolt, took control of the vessel, and threw the captain and first mate overboard to their deaths. When the *Decatur* was captured, Bowser was charged with the murder of the men thrown off the ship and sentenced to hang. In his newspaper, Lundy recounted the drama and essentially blamed the deaths of the captain, the first mate, and Bowser entirely on Woolfolk's greed, claiming as well that the slave trader had traveled to New York to ghoulishly witness Bowser's execution. Lundy declared Woolfolk "a monster in human shape" and advised Baltimoreans: "Hereafter let no man speak of the humanity of Woolfolk."

Woolfolk, who denied that he had attended the hanging, did not take the insults well. Some days later, he encountered Lundy as the editor walked to the post office, accosted the smaller man, and, by Lundy's account, "With a brutal ferocity that is perfectly in character with his business, he choked me until my very breath was nearly gone, and stamped me in the head and face, with the fury of a very demon."

So Lundy spent two days in bed recovering from the thrashing and then filed assault charges against the slave trader. Woolfolk pleaded guilty—there were plenty of witnesses, after all. But when Woolfolk's lawyers read Lundy's published vituperation in court, Judge Nicholas Brice declared that "he had never seen a case in which the provocation for a battery was greater" and that Lundy "had received no more than a merited chastisement." What's more, the judge said, Woolfolk was working in a "beneficial" trade that "removed a great many rogues and vagabonds who were a nuisance in the state." Brice said he would impose a punishment only because state law required one. He fined Woolfolk a token one dollar.

⋆⇒◯⇐⋆

Early in the nineteenth century, wealthy, well-connected Quaker businessmen in the Chesapeake who opposed slavery as their religion required had held considerable sway. For instance, Elisha Tyson, a rich Baltimore Quaker who owned mills and banks, once faced down a pistol-packing Woolfolk, who had ordered his men to drag a Black woman down the street to his jail. When Tyson intervened, Woolfolk pulled his gun, pointed it at him, and threatened to "send him to hell for interfering with his *property*." Tyson, so the story went, stood coolly in front of the barrel and told Woolfolk "he was in hell already, though he did not know it." Woolfolk didn't fire; an investigation showed the woman was legally free; and Tyson went on to finance freedom suits for people challenging their enslavement until his death in 1824.

But that kind of bracing moral victory was increasingly the exception as the nineteenth century went on. As the judge's hostility to Lundy and lenient attitude toward Woolfolk show, an overwhelming share of political and legal clout lay with the proslavery establishment—what abolitionists had started to label with that apt phrase "the slave power." Lundy would leave Baltimore, moving his small paper multiple times, and die, deeply in debt, in 1839. Woolfolk would retire to Louisiana with a fortune earned in the slave trade. Brice would serve as chief judge of Baltimore's criminal court from 1817 to his death in 1851. The judge, born into a prominent slave-owning family in Anne Arundel County, south of Baltimore, was a leader in the Maryland State Colonization Society, and his remarks in court made quite clear why. He supported sending Maryland African Americans to Liberia for the same reason he found the domestic slave trade "beneficial": it would rid the state of the "nuisance" of Black people.

Brice's comments suggested another fact about the slave power: though its principals controlled most of what happened in the region, they felt deeply insecure. Torrey's eventful visit to the Slaveholders' Convention in Annapolis in January 1842 had exposed the anxieties of this ruling class. Its members felt threatened because their slaves were running away, and they worried that the growing free Black population was undermining the slave system. The same concerns gave rise to broad white support for a colonization movement motivated, as Smallwood came to understand, not by empathy but by fear.

This paradox of power and insecurity is explained in part by population trends. Slavery's borderland—the northern tier of the slave states—encompassed first of all Maryland, politically divided but very much in the grip of the slave power. There was the larger and more culturally southern state of Virginia, farther from the free states and with a far larger enslaved population—36 percent of the population in 1840, versus

19 percent in Maryland. And there were the much smaller jurisdictions of Delaware and the federal government seat of the District of Columbia, which roughly mirrored trends in Maryland.

The defining trend across the region was a steady increase in the free Black population, which deeply unsettled slaveholders. In Maryland in 1840, the number of free African Americans had passed sixty-two thousand and was growing fast, compared to about ninety thousand enslaved Black people, a number in steady decline. In Baltimore, the free African American population had long since outpaced the enslaved population. The response of slaveholders was to rush to reactionary and paranoid measures, often with a totalitarian feel. In March 1842, just as Smallwood and Torrey began inciting escapes, the Maryland General Assembly passed a law imposing a sentence of ten to twenty years on any free Black person caught in possession of abolitionist literature.

Another law prohibited Black people from joining any secret society, and a free person convicted of a second offense could be sold into slavery—with proceeds split between the state and the "informer." These were but two in a parade of so-called Black laws designed to erode the rights and presence of free African Americans. Even in Baltimore, where most African Americans were free, a curfew was imposed in 1838 on all Black people, who were required to be in their homes by 10 p.m.

But perhaps the biggest cause of the growing unease among slaveholders was simple geography: the Mason-Dixon Line, the border between Maryland and Pennsylvania, was also the boundary separating slavery from freedom. In Pennsylvania, with a powerful Quaker influence, slavery had practically disappeared as a result of the Gradual Abolition Act of 1780, which declared that children born to enslaved women would be free from the age of twenty-eight. By 1840, census takers counted only sixty-four enslaved people in the entire state, presumably traveling with their enslavers—compared with the ninety thousand people enslaved in neighboring Maryland.

Smallwood called the proximity of the border the "foundation" of his and Torrey's operation to lead people to freedom. People fleeing slavery in Washington and environs could be in Pennsylvania the third night after they ran; those departing Baltimore and the surrounding counties could often cross the Mason-Dixon Line the second night. While that didn't make the journey safe or easy, it made it feasible in a way that it was not for people enslaved in Georgia or Mississippi. Maryland laws and customs were designed to counter that feasibility, threatening those who tried to flee with being sold south and prescribing severe punishment for anyone who helped with an escape.

Maryland officials repeatedly clashed with Pennsylvania officials over the status of fugitives. The archives of both states are replete with demanding letters: Maryland insisting on the prompt return of an enslaved person who had fled to Pennsylvania; Pennsylvania protesting the incursion of slave catchers across the Mason-Dixon Line in search of runaways. The long-running confrontation came to a head in a Supreme Court ruling handed down on March 1, 1842, just as Torrey and Smallwood were engineering their first escapes.

Five years earlier, Edward Prigg, a lawyer, and three other men had traveled into Pennsylvania to seize Margaret Morgan on behalf of a Maryland woman who claimed Morgan belonged to her and had run away in 1832. A local grand jury in Pennsylvania indicted Prigg and his three companions for kidnapping, saying they had taken Morgan and her children south illegally. The Pennsylvania governor sought the four men's extradition, and after extensive negotiations Maryland's governor sent the four back for trial. Their appeal of their convictions reached the Supreme Court, which ruled in *Prigg v. Pennsylvania* that Pennsylvania's anti-slave-catching law was unconstitutional and that, under the Fugitive Slave Act of 1793, states could not interfere in slaveholders' attempts to retrieve runaways. It was a victory for Maryland and slavery, which Torrey and Smallwood denounced in the Albany newspaper. But the contest between the two states would go on.

⊷══◉══⊶

Here was the cauldron bubbling in slavery's borderland: a volatile mix of slaveholders and slave traders, colonizationists and abolitionists, free and enslaved African Americans, plus a growing number of European immigrants, mostly Irish and German arrivals who found themselves in direct economic competition with Black workers. But the dramatis personae did not stop there.

The phenomenon of flight from slavery—people with prices on their heads—created a profession of slave catchers who traveled the counties north and south of the Mason-Dixon Line on the lookout for fugitives who might be captured for the substantial rewards slaveholders offered. Such bounty hunting spawned a new class of criminals, kidnappers who captured free Black people, dragged them south to unscrupulous slave traders, and sold them into slavery. In 1841, months before Smallwood and Torrey began their collaboration, scoundrels tricked a farmer and fiddle player named Solomon Northup into traveling from his home in New York to Washington, supposedly for a lucrative musical gig. Instead, they sold him to a trader for $650. He was locked in William Williams's slave jail—"within the very shadow of the Capitol!" Northup later wrote—and began a long odyssey through the plantation south.

But what was most unusual about Northup, whose memoir *Twelve Years a Slave* would be made into a hit movie in 2013, was not his ordeal but the network of sympathizers who managed to win his freedom, by persuading his ostensible enslaver that he could prove his freedom in court. The kidnapping of free African Americans and their sale into slavery happened regularly in cities north and south. It was especially frequent in the borderland, where the regular passage of actual runaways made a kidnapper's claim to have caught a fugitive more credible. The historian Richard Bell, who wrote a riveting account of the kidnapping of five free Black boys in Philadelphia, proposed a striking name for the kidnapping phenomenon: the reverse underground railroad.

The kidnapper was a terrifying figure in Black communities. Frederick Douglass feared capture and reenslavement even after writing his famous and bestselling first autobiography. He was so "tormented with the liability of losing my liberty" that he left for a long stay in Ireland and England and did not return until British abolitionists had raised the money to officially buy his freedom. Perhaps the most famous of the kidnappers was the Delaware-based gang led by a woman named Patty Cannon, whose sensational story took on the status of legend. Though Cannon shared responsibility for the gang's depredations with other family members, her gender made her the focus of many embellished tales, especially after her jailhouse death while awaiting trial for murder in 1829.

What was true was that, for many years, her gang staged kidnapping raids on Baltimore and Philadelphia, chained their captives in an attic for days or weeks, and then marched them south or put them aboard boats to slave dealers or slave markets to cash in. The abductions continued long after Cannon's death. In 1840, *The Sun* reported on a free boy named Brinkley, who had been offered for sale in Baltimore. But "the boy being very intelligent, made known to the proper authorities that he was a free boy, and had been stolen from the State of Delaware." The boy had been purchased and sold multiple times, and the original kidnapper was apparently never punished. Hope Slatter regularly got entangled in legal battles over claims that he had purchased kidnapping victims. Though he denied that he had known the people he purchased were free, he had a reputation, like other dealers, for not always inquiring too closely about the status of the men and women he bought and sold.

Torrey recounted a particularly devious kidnapping ring. Two white men in Maryland employed a Black man, dressed in tattered clothing, to pose as a runaway. When free Black people offered to help him, he would set them up for abduction by the two white kidnappers. Smallwood had witnessed or heard in detail about multiple kidnapping cases in Washington. One involved a free Black man he knew named Henry Chubb, who worked on the docks loading and unloading ships. One day, Chubb went ashore and left his two sons aboard a ship to finish some work. "In the meantime the captain set sail, and carried the two sons into slavery, to the unspeakable grief of their parents, who were both free born!" Smallwood wrote. "Similar acts have often been done, and are still doing, in this metropolis of free and Christian America."

For free African Americans in the Chesapeake region, the fear of trans-
gressing the punitive racial laws, or worse, falling into the clutches of
kidnappers, was a daily anxiety. In Baltimore, sheer numbers offered a
bit of comfort: the city's 17,967 free Black residents created a vibrant
and politically active community, rivaled only by Philadelphia's. The
debate around colonization was heated and unceasing, reflecting deep
dissatisfaction with the status of free African Americans in the United
States. The local leader of the anticolonization faction, which Smallwood
had joined, was a remarkable minister, schoolmaster, and political leader
named William Watkins.

A stunning exchange in 1820 had revealed much about slavery in
Maryland. Watkins had approached James Carroll, a member of the
state's most famous and powerful family, seeking to buy the freedom of
his wife, Rebecca, and her son Henry for $150. Carroll, later a judge and
congressman, agreed to the sale—but not to their freedom. He set conditions, insisting that Rebecca remain enslaved for five years and Henry
for twenty-six years—with Watkins as the slaveholder for his own wife
and stepson. Carroll wanted to uphold the institution of slavery even as
he was being paid to allow two people to exit it. He prepared the legal
documents, and Watkins, with little choice, signed them.

Watkins became known for his erudite and passionate letters to Benjamin Lundy's *The Genius of Universal Emancipation* and William Lloyd
Garrison's *The Liberator*, signing not with his name but as "A Colored
Baltimorean." His main enemy was the colonization movement, and for
more than a decade he battled both the American and Maryland colonization societies. The white ministers who promoted the idea of departing
for Liberia, Watkins wrote, seemed to be part of an effort "to make us
miserable here, that we may emigrate to Africa with our own consent."

That was a widely held view throughout the 1830s. But the outra-
geous discrimination endured by free families was so unrelenting that
the appeal of emigration never entirely faded. Those who decided to leave

the United States but did not trust the Liberian experiment often departed for the British colonies of Trinidad in the Caribbean and British Guiana on the north coast of South America. Planters often paid the passage of free African Americans who had agreed to join the agricultural workforce in the two colonies. An 1839 notice in *The Baltimore Clipper* addressed to "free, industrious persons of color" promised "passage in a first-class ship" to Trinidad as well as "ample provisions" and "high wages" on arrival. In 1840, the brig *Porpoise* sailed from Baltimore for British Guiana with seventy emigrants, who *The Sun* said "seemed buoyant with the highest anticipations of the good fortunes that awaited them in their new home."

One of the free Baltimoreans who boarded the *Porpoise* would become a close ally of Smallwood—but not until he had tried out emigration. Jacob R. Gibbs worked as a housepainter and whitewasher in the city, but he was so captivated by the encouraging reports from British Guiana that he decided to make an exploratory trip. Several weeks after his arrival, on June 20, 1840, he sent three letters to acquaintances that were so positive they were given by promoters of emigration to *The Sun* for publication. "I am highly pleased with this place, and am certain that I can make it my home," he wrote to one friend.

What happened in the subsequent months is unclear, but Gibbs changed his mind about his new country, as did many who tested the prospects abroad. Like many free Black people who emigrated, Gibbs had taken the trouble to apply to Baltimore authorities for a travel permit before departing; a demeaning Maryland law prohibited free African Americans, including lifelong Marylanders, from returning to the state unless they had such a document. Gibbs was back in Baltimore by December 1840 and resumed his old life—with a difference: he would soon become a crucial part of Smallwood's escape network.

⁙

If free Black Marylanders always lived with the fear of punitive racial laws and kidnappers, their worries paled beside those of people still in bondage. The enslaved lived their lives between two possibilities, one horrific, the other tantalizing. They faced every day the chance that they could be sold south—converted to cash at the whim of their enslaver. Yet they were close enough to the powerful magnet of Pennsylvania to imagine escape, if they found the right opportunity, made the right connections, or got hold of the necessary information.

And as Smallwood understood, these two possibilities were deeply interdependent. Running for freedom was a bold and dangerous act in the best of circumstances—because failure often meant being sold south. Yet it was precisely fear of being sold south, whether because of a slaveholder's debt or legal squabble or death, that gave people the motivation to dare running north. The two phenomena fed on each other: as more people fled slavery, more slaveholders were driven to sell their remaining human assets for fear they, too, might disappear. "A vicious circle developed as slaveholders sold slaves south to prevent escape and slaves escaped to prevent sale south," wrote Stanley Harrold, one of the shrewdest chroniclers of the borderland. If not for the dire threat posed by the slave traders, many in slavery might never have dared to flee north. This strange equation put Smallwood and Torrey in a kind of competition with Slatter, as the enslaved frantically considered their options.

"The fear of being sold South had more influence in inducing me to leave than any other thing," William Johnson told Benjamin Drew, who in 1856 published interviews with many of the formerly enslaved who had crossed the Canadian border in search of safety. "Master used to say, that if we didn't suit him, he would put us in his pocket quick—meaning he would sell us."

For George Ross, who fled Hagerstown in western Maryland with his wife and children and made it to Ontario, the deciding factor was clear: "I came away because I was standing in fear of being separated from my wife and children."

There was an irony: fleeing slavery often meant leaving family behind, at least temporarily. Rather than wait for some imaginary alignment of the stars that would allow an entire family to depart together, many people voluntarily ran without family members. But in such a case, the runaway knew where his or her spouse and children were and could still try to help them with advice or money to make their own escape and reunite the family. A person sold south essentially disappeared.

Every escape attempt required a hugely risky decision. Even with the Mason-Dixon Line nearby, anyone choosing flight could be betrayed by an acquaintance, a police constable, a professional slave catcher, a suspicious storekeeper, or a meddlesome white citizen. Most fled alone, grabbing what few possessions and meager food they could carry. Many ran without maps, without money, and with only the sketchiest notion of where they were going. It is no wonder that while most enslaved people certainly contemplated the possibility of fleeing north, many didn't try it until they were frightened into action by the looming possibility of something even worse.

Or until they heard about some audacious characters who might help them beat the odds, evade the slave catchers, foil the kidnappers, and reach freedom alive and well.

☞ **Special Notice.** ☜

350 SLAVES TURNED FREEMEN!!!
$175,000 SAVED FROM KIDNAPPERS!

The "Albany Vigilance Committee" have done a great work the past season. They have aided in their flight from slavery 350 men, women, and children, at an expense of more than $1,000. And even during this inclement season, these children of sorrow still come. Two have arrived within the last twenty-four hours, and a man-thief from Baltimore is here, offering a reward of $50 to any one who will aid him in securing a girl named Emeline. Under these circumstances, we appeal to the public for aid; and that our wants may be fully known, we have secured the services of Rev. A. Brown, of this city, who will, in company with *at least two colored persons who have for about forty years been slaves*, and as many more as we can conveniently convey, attend meetings (with the leave of Divine Providence,) in the following places.

Notice in the *Albany Weekly Patriot*, previously known as *Tocsin of Liberty*, March 23, 1843, when Charles Torrey was editor, claiming to have aided in the escape of 350 people, many from Thomas Smallwood's operation in Washington and Baltimore and the surrounding counties. [Courtesy of Boston Public Library]

6

Safe from the Fangs of Robert Gilmor

Elizabeth Castle was a young Baltimore seamstress, the married mother of a little girl, when she discovered in early 1842 that she was pregnant again. Her reaction combined joy with apprehension, because, like her, her daughter and unborn child were considered property, always subject to sale. Baltimore's slave trade was a constant topic of anxious conversation among the enslaved, and Castle was terrified that at any moment her children might be swept away to a trader's jail, to disappear on a ship south. According to someone who spoke with her a few months later:

> The birth of her first child convinced her that her master regarded her as of more value, as every child she bore increased his wealth and caused him to watch her closer than ever. She found to her sorrow that not only herself but also her children were considered to be mere articles of merchandise, and would in all probability be sold from her as soon as the market would warrant a profitable sale. She resolved, therefore, to flee.

Castle had reason to be aware of her enslaver's close eye on profit. He was a merchant—and not just any merchant. At sixty-eight, Robert Gilmor Jr. was one of Baltimore's wealthiest and most distinguished citizens. With his brother William he had turned their father's firm, which specialized in the import of wine, into a lucrative enterprise—he was worth an estimated $600,000 in the mid-1830s, equal to about $20 million today. He was chairman of the board of both the fast-growing Baltimore and Ohio Railroad Company and the respected Bank of the United States of Pennsylvania, the state-chartered continuation of the country's first central bank.

Gilmor's real passion, however, was not commerce but collecting. He was one of America's most avid and knowledgeable collectors of paintings, minerals, gems, and valuable documents. He owned Greek vases, Roman coins, letters of Washington and Jefferson—even the papers of the surveyors Mason and Dixon who had delineated the border between Maryland and Pennsylvania. He caused a sensation when he ordered from Paris one of the earliest daguerreotypes. His art and artifacts would be scattered after his death to the Smithsonian Institution and leading art museums around the country. This combination of prosperous enterprise and cultural sophistication made Gilmor an attractive public figure, and he got glowing coverage from the local press. When Daniel Webster, days after stepping down as secretary of state, was honored at a Baltimore dinner, it was Gilmor who organized the occasion and led the toasts—and was himself toasted as "a merchant whose books are without a blot—a man whose life is without a stain."

Well, not exactly without a stain, at least not for those who considered human bondage to be a loathsome blot on a man's character. This paragon, like most of his class, had no qualms about slavery. His wife, Sarah, was a South Carolina plantation belle and the granddaughter of a slave trader whom he had met in his early thirties on a tour of the south. During that journey, on one South Carolina plantation, "Colonel" James Chesnut—an honorific common among planters—impressed young Gilmor with an explanation of how the cotton gin was producing a cotton boom. "This of course renders negroes valuable," Gilmor wrote in his journal. "A planter is valued here in proportion to the number of negroes he owns." Whether he understood it at the time or not, his trip south in 1806 and 1807 gave him an early glimpse of the trends that were just then creating a slave trade in his own city.

Elizabeth Castle lived in or behind Robert Gilmor's mansion on Water Street in Baltimore, just north of the harbor where his casks of wine arrived from Europe. Slatter's jail was a five-minute walk away— one block south and three west—and she would have been keenly aware of his business and its implications. In the spring of 1842, the pregnant mother somehow connected with the Smallwood-Torrey network, just then taking shape. The most likely scenario is that word of mouth led her to none other than Jacob Gibbs, the housepainter who less than two years earlier had tried out life in British Guiana before returning to Baltimore after deciding that his destiny lay with battling the scourge of slavery and not running from it. Gibbs would become Smallwood's linchpin in the city, both helping fugitives on their way north from Washington and recruiting local people who feared sale south and hungered for freedom. His help was critical in expanding Smallwood and Torrey's efforts beyond the Washington area to Baltimore, the largest city in the slaveholding south. "Friend G.," as Smallwood would discreetly call him in his memoir, had mapped out the route north and one day would lead Smallwood himself on an emergency run.

Castle must have quietly spread the word about her flight plan inside Gilmor's household, because soon two more of his enslaved women, by the names of Polly (also called Minerva Polly) and Marianna, had joined the escape plan. So had two men also held in slavery by Gilmor, John Weston and Charles Stewart. Together the five probably made up most of Gilmor's household staff, and they represented a considerable investment even for such a prosperous man. And one night in the spring of 1842, they were all suddenly gone.

How the public came to learn about the mass escape from Gilmor is a crucial part of the story, perhaps the Smallwood operation's greatest innovation. The encouragement, planning, and execution of escapes from Washington, Baltimore, and the surrounding counties was, of course, the core of the enterprise. But telling the world about those escapes was very much part of the plan—and quite a daring move for clandestine operators. It wasn't mere boasting. Smallwood and Torrey hoped a steady drumbeat of news about the escapes, and mockery of the slaveholders, would undermine their morale. One of the abolitionist newspapers that had agreed to publish Torrey's dispatches about Congress was the Liberty Party outlet based in Albany. It went by the name *Tocsin of Liberty*, "tocsin" being a poetic word for "bell."

Albany, the New York state capital, along with the nearby town Troy, would become an important hub for the Smallwood-Torrey escape operation. One pillar of Albany's support was fundraising. Torrey had traveled to Albany in April 1842 to attend the annual meeting of the Eastern New York Anti-Slavery Society, persuading the society to "collect and disburse funds for the purpose of aiding fugitive slaves." Another crucial contribution from Albany was public relations: Torrey and Smallwood would use the Albany paper to document, amplify, and celebrate the escapes. But the escape of Elizabeth Castle and her companions came before Smallwood began sending his columns, and the sardonic report about them in the *Tocsin of Liberty* was written by Abel Brown, a young antislavery preacher who became a key ally in Albany for the Smallwood-Torrey operation. Brown had helped organize Albany's Vigilance Committee, whose sole purpose was to aid and protect people fleeing slavery, and he was a virtuoso of the ironic style.

Brown's letter to the editor of the *Tocsin of Liberty* asked that word be passed to a number of Chesapeake slaveholders who, in the letter's pose, were presumed to be deeply concerned about the welfare of the people they had enslaved. It is among the first of what might be called the laughingstock letters, designed to ridicule the slaveholders and their allies in a genre that Smallwood would bring to perfection. This missive singled out Gilmor for special attention:

> *Please also inform* Robert Gilmore, of Baltimore, that he need not give himself further trouble about his very intelligent and noble slaves, Marianna, Polly, Elizabeth Castle, and her fine little girl, for they have got safe over the great Ontario, where

such men as his honor, would not look very well placing their feet for the purpose of kidnapping. Tell him also, that his slave John Weston left here more than a week since, at full speed, in a fine carriage drawn by fleet horses. . . . I am quite sure that Marianna, Elizabeth and John, and the little girl, have had a joyful thanksgiving in the other land. I hope Robert will not envy them their happiness.

Brown, who added an *e* to Gilmor, a common mistake, signed this piece and many others with a barbed reference to his role in the escape network: "Abel Brown, Forwarding Merchant, Albany."

⊷⊜⊶

By mid-1842, word of the escape operation was spreading quietly in Washington's antislavery community, even attracting a few collaborators in high places. The story of the Douglass brothers, three Washingtonians who went north with Smallwood's help, showed how.

Ann Sprigg ran a boardinghouse adjacent to the Capitol, one of dozens that advertised rooms and meals for the members of Congress who traveled to Washington from distant points. Naturally, congressmen tended to cluster by party and opinion, and "Mrs. Sprigg's" became known as Abolition House for hosting the fiercest congressional opponents of slavery. In 1842, Mrs. Sprigg's boarders included two congressmen, Joshua Giddings of Ohio, who would be censured and resign at the demand of proslavery lawmakers—only to be quickly returned to Congress by his state's voters—and Seth Gates, a former teacher and lawyer from New York. In residence as well was the noted antislavery journalist and minister Joshua Leavitt, a friend of Torrey's. Torrey, who boarded across town with Mrs. Padgett near the White House, was a regular visitor to the rival Sprigg establishment.

Despite her customers' views, Mrs. Sprigg, like Mrs. Padgett, followed local custom and employed enslaved people, "hired out" by their enslavers, who pocketed most of their wages. Among such workers was a waiter named John Douglass, who was a living, breathing reminder of the institution of human bondage every time the abolitionist congressmen sat down for a meal. In the fall of 1842, Douglass learned that his enslaver, John Harry, planned to sell him away from his wife and two children. Seth Gates, who felt particularly grateful to Douglass for nursing him through a serious illness, discreetly connected him with Torrey, who introduced him to Smallwood. "He went to Smallwood of the Navy Yard & told him his distress," Gates wrote later in a letter to his sometime housemate Giddings, a rare account by an outsider of the Smallwood operation. Within days, John Douglass, as well as his younger brother Lewis, had joined an impressive caravan of eighteen people sent north by Smallwood.

"They came most of the way in a body on foot past Philadelphia, & then were boldly taken on board the cars"—in other words, the train, Gates wrote. John Douglass went to Canada, where he would stay for eighteen months before recrossing the border into Upstate New York.

Just a few weeks after John and Lewis Douglass had departed, another Douglass brother, Robert, learned that his enslaver, a Mrs. Harrington, had decided to sell him south. He went to Smallwood, who hid him in the house of Joseph Bradley, a lawyer who Smallwood knew was away from Washington for several weeks. "He took John's brother there & hid him in Bradley's garrett 3 weeks, till another gang were ready to start north, and he got safely thro," Gates recounted.

Smallwood weighed in with a pseudonymous newspaper account of the escape of the first two brothers. The "boarders at Mrs. Sprigg's, last session," he wrote, referring to the congressional term, "will not be sorry to learn that their favorite waiter, John Douglass, and his younger brother Lewis, have escaped from 'Massa Harry's' grasp, and are free!" Smallwood added a wry reference to the lawmakers living at Abolition House, widely seen as radicals and surely despised by a slaveholder like John Harry: "The pleasure of gratifying so many good men, must be a comfort to Mr. Harry, under his losses."

❖══◉══❖

So how did Elizabeth Castle, the three Douglass brothers, and their many fellow fugitives make their getaway? Many of the details were closely held at the time, for obvious reasons. But from the writings of Small-wood, Torrey, and their allies, it is possible to reconstruct their route, the means they used, and the hazards faced by those who followed them on this Chesapeake-to-Ontario journey.

From the beginning of their enterprise, one of the essential notions driving Smallwood and Torrey was the idea of mass escapes—that when-ever feasible it was better to help people north not one at a time but by the wagonload. The more people in a single journey, the greater the blow to the slave power and the more efficient the operation. But they did not have at their disposal a barnful of horses and carriages, so they generally had to rent or purchase their transportation.

Castle and her companions, who knew the habits and bedtimes of the Gilmor household, would have agreed with Jacob Gibbs on a night, time, and place to gather. They would have slipped out of the house and made their way stealthily through the dark streets of downtown Balti-more. They probably walked separately, since any group of Black people would have drawn greater suspicion from white passersby. They may have tried to beat the city's 10 p.m. curfew for African Americans, imposed by a city ordinance four years earlier, or they may have decided to take their chances by waiting till the quiet middle of the night. Gibbs would have had a wagon or carriage ready at the meeting spot, and they would have sped away into the darkness on a route chosen to minimize the risk of witnesses.

When the journeys began in Washington, Smallwood wrote, "we had two places of deposit between Washington and Mason's and Dixon's line." Though he did not name the exact spots of these safe houses, he gave quite exact distances—thirty-seven miles to the first stop, which would have reached from Smallwood's southeast corner of Washington

to downtown Baltimore, presumably to Jacob Gibbs's home or some
other safe spot designated by him. Then, Smallwood said, it was another
forty miles to the second "place of deposit"—which would have carried
the fugitives to the broad Susquehanna River, just above where it flows
into the Chesapeake Bay, near the river town of Port Deposit.

The Susquehanna was a formidable natural barrier, and the bridge at
Port Deposit was a choke point that posed a particular danger from lurking slave catchers. Smallwood and Gibbs had recruited a woman named
Turner who lived just south of the bridge. Her job was to harbor fugitives
while they awaited a local man who would ferry them across. The ferry-
man, whom Smallwood called only "Mr. P.," would accompany them on
the north side of the river as far as the Pennsylvania line, where he could
"deliver them into the hands of the Quakers." The antislavery Quakers
were active in helping fugitives throughout Pennsylvania, and some had
been drafted by Smallwood, Torrey, and Gibbs to help.

Smallwood said that the first seventy-seven miles, from Washington
to the Susquehanna, "our passengers generally travelled in two nights,
and the third night they cross the line, and accomplish a distance of nine
miles into Pennsylvania, to another place of deposit." He suggested that
if only a man or two were traveling, they might go by foot, but:

> If we had women and children to convey, we had to hire con-
> veyances at the rate of from fifteen to fifty dollars to the first
> place of deposit; the prices varied according to the numbers we
> had to convey. We had to pay teamsters a very high price in or-
> der to induce them to risk themselves and teams in so danger-
> ous an enterprise. Besides, there was great difficulty in meeting
> with teamsters to whom we could make propositions of that
> kind. We have paid for the conveyance of one person fifteen
> dollars, for the conveyance of three twenty-five, and for eight
> or nine fifty dollars, for a distance of only thirty-seven miles.

These were considerable costs; fifty dollars then would be about fifteen
hundred today. Smallwood does not fill in the details of travel north from

Pennsylvania, and different escaping groups probably took different routes, depending on the shifting availability of allies, sleeping quarters, and intelligence about slave catchers on the prowl. But odds are that most of the fugitives, like the Douglass brothers, traveled through Philadelphia, a center of abolitionism where Torrey and Smallwood had reliable friends. From there, money permitting, they most likely traveled on major routes, by rail or steamboat, to New York, then up the Hudson by boat to Albany or Troy, where they could count on a friendly reception and beds, food, and cash for onward travel. Abel Brown and others associated with the *Tocsin of Liberty* and the Liberty Party, who had formed the Albany Vigilance Committee in May, would often meet the travelers, advise them, and help with their costs.

Brown, in particular, embraced the cause of the freedom seekers. A fierce advocate with a rapier wit, he was born in Massachusetts three years before Torrey, developed a similar devotion to Christianity and morality, and studied for the ministry at Hamilton College when Torrey was at Yale. As a young Baptist minister he joined both the temperance and abolitionist causes with a similar radical passion, and like Torrey he eventually gave up church jobs to work full-time against slavery. In Albany he was a well-known, even notorious public figure. While northern New York was not exactly a hotbed of proslavery sentiment, Brown was on multiple occasions attacked by mobs, burned in effigy, and once charged with criminal libel for a poster attacking Henry Clay, the Whig senator from Kentucky and presidential candidate. Brown and his first wife, Mary Ann, opened their home to fugitives, and he tirelessly toured New York State, often accompanied by one or more people who could recount their own lives in slavery. A regular co-lecturer was Lewis Washington, who had spent four decades in slavery in Maryland before escaping with the help of Smallwood's ring and had earned a reputation as a spellbinding speaker with a "living, burning eloquence."

When runaways reached Albany and Abel Brown's territory, they were at a crossroads that was hotly debated inside the fractious antislavery movement. Some abolitionists urged those fleeing slavery to settle in the northern states, arguing that growing free communities could become both a haven for freedom seekers and a political force against the slave power. Others, including Smallwood, and at times Torrey and Brown, believed that it was foolhardy to stay inside the United States, where slave catchers and kidnappers posed a genuine threat even in the relatively friendly territories of New England and Upstate New York. Smallwood regarded Canada, where British authorities had abolished slavery in 1833, as the far better option. It offered freedom that was guarded by an international border and backed up by the British monarchy. He wrote with some impatience:

> I would be greatly annoyed when with great danger to my own freedom I had got off slaves and advised them to go to Canada, to hear when they had got north, they had been induced by the abolitionists not to go to Canada; that they told them the most absurd stories about it imaginable, and promised them perfect freedom and safety in the Northern States;—whereas they knew they could do no such thing.

If the freedom seekers were continuing to Canada West, as Ontario was called at the time, there were multiple rail, boat, or wagon possibilities from Albany, including routes into Vermont and up Lake Champlain or past Buffalo, up the Niagara River, and around the famous falls. The last leg was often across "the great Ontario," as Lake Ontario was called, to Toronto or St. Catharines or Hamilton, all lakeside cities with significant Black communities.

The route north from Pennsylvania for runaways, in other words, often belied the familiar image of families running through the woods. Many used their savings or the charity of allies to take advantage of the latest modes of transportation, which promised speed, comfort, and relative safety. "The cars," or trains, sometimes were fast enough to allow the fugitives to reach Canada before their pursuers got to New York, since it generally took a day or two for a slaveholder to decide to hire a bounty hunter and for the bounty hunter to decide what route to follow. Frederick Douglass had famously borrowed a Black mariner's credentials and boldly caught a northbound train in Baltimore in 1838. But traveling in the open could also make runaways more vulnerable to being sighted or grabbed by slave catchers sent north after them—or by kidnappers spotting vulnerable Black travelers. When such a danger loomed, a shift to rougher travel on foot or by wagon, usually by night, could offer greater security.

All this travel ran up considerable costs. As Smallwood described, there was the price of renting or buying horses and a carriage or a wagon for the first legs of the journey. Then there were multiple train and steamboat fares and often the costs of food and simple lodging. Torrey and his New York allies were constantly raising money to fund the operation, and discreet donations probably came from Gerrit Smith, the wealthy New York businessman who had financed Torrey's Liberty Party lecturing and whose "Address to the Slaves" had urged all who were able to "make the experiment" of escape.

But Smallwood sometimes asked the people he was helping—some of whom were "hired out" by their enslavers and were able to keep some of their earnings—to make a contribution. Not surprisingly, nearly destitute people were wary when their helpers asked them to pitch in, accusing those arranging their passage north of "taking an undue amount of money from them," as Smallwood later recalled. The contrast with the slave trade was stark: if Slatter's forced shipment of enslaved people south generated immense revenue, Smallwood's operation always struggled to pay its modest costs.

⊷≡◑⊂≡⊷

Elizabeth Castle, the seamstress, made it safely to Canada, took in sewing work, and eventually opened a dressmaking business. She asked those who had helped her north to try to do the same for her husband, who was still enslaved by Robert Gilmor in Baltimore. It's unclear why he had not joined the original escape—perhaps by ostentatiously remaining at his post he had distracted Gilmor from the flight of his wife and child. In any case, Abel Brown in his next published report toned down his mockery a few notches, if not his moral indignation, and made a public appeal to Gilmor on Castle's behalf. He wrote that he had visited a town in Canada where some of those who had fled north had settled—he calls it "D—M—," probably Dalhousie Mills, a town north of Lake Ontario. He had spoken with the escaped Minerva Polly, who told him that she was earning decent wages in her new country and that "as for slavery, she had had enough of it already; that even Mr. Gilmore's slavery was not desirable."

Brown may have been flattering Gilmor with that "even," but it was a common and reasonable sentiment among people who fled the Chesapeake, and its cities in particular: they did not always complain of ill treatment; they simply wanted to be free. Elizabeth Castle's young daughter evidently had picked up the talk she heard around her: "The little girl talks of liberty, and hates slavery." Brown explained that "My great object in writing this letter, is to appeal to the philanthropy of Mr. Robert Gilmore," asking him to free Elizabeth's husband. She would soon give birth to her second child and needed his support, he wrote Gilmor via the *Tocsin of Liberty*:

> Suppose, friend Robert, yourself and wife were prisoners in this province [in Canada]—unlawfully detained—and your wife should find herself about to become the mother of an infant child, and rather than have it born a slave, should flee to the U. States? Do you not think she would like to have the father of the child with her during her sickness, and would you not think that man a monster, who would detain her under such circumstances? . . . If you think the sacrifice too great, come up and see the joyful meeting of the family here in this free land. I am sure you would go home and free all your slaves.

Even if that assertion was sincere, Brown could not entirely suppress his sarcasm. He added that Gilmor's two former bondsmen John Weston and Charles Stewart were safe—and "I believe they intend to call the place where they will permanently reside, 'Gilmore's Settlement,' out of respect to their never to be forgotten master." He quipped that perhaps Castle would name her newborn "Robert Gilmore Jr."

Brown's alternately lukewarm and ice-cold attitude toward Gilmor may be explained in part by the wealthy merchant's reaction to the escape. Gilmor did not, as was standard practice, place ads in the Baltimore newspapers offering a reward for the return of the five adults and the child. Among the city's moneyed elite, the decision of one's household staff to risk everything to flee might reflect poorly on the slaveholder. Instead, Gilmor dispatched a slave-catching police constable on the trail north. Brown later said the constable was lucky to have missed the escaping men—because they had six loaded pistols among them.

It appears that Gilmor did not—at least immediately—liberate Castle's husband. By the time Brown was writing, or helping write, the annual report of the Albany Vigilance Committee, he no longer was in a mood to mince words. Castle, he wrote, was "delighted in looking upon her free born infant, safe from the fangs of Robert Gilmore, who sent the constable of Baltimore to seize it, even before it was born."

⊷⇒◖⇐⊷

In the months after the well-documented escape of Castle and her companions, Smallwood and Torrey, with the help of Gibbs, Brown, and others along the route, sent one group after another on the road north. Smallwood later claimed that between March and November 1842, from Washington alone, some 150 people had been assisted in escaping to the north. At an average value of $500 each, he noted, that would mean a loss of $75,000 to the slaveholders—well over $2 million today. He called it a "tax," and hoped it would grow and prove crippling to the slave system: "In any other form, such a tax would make a rebellion! I mean to tax them twice that, next year!"

Is the suspiciously round number 150 reliable? Just 62 people who had fled slavery in those months were named, along with their enslavers, in dispatches by Brown and Smallwood for the *Tocsin of Liberty*. But given the necessity of secrecy, the informal arrangements, and the late-night departures, it seems likely that Smallwood would not have written about every runaway he helped; he may not even have always known their full names. Abel Brown had stated in a public talk in August that 100 fugitives had passed through Albany since May, a figure that roughly fits with Smallwood's total of 150 when the autumn escapes are added. (Brown later claimed, possibly with some exaggeration, that the Albany Vigilance Committee had assisted 350 fugitives between March and December; obviously, some would have fled places other than the Washington-Baltimore area, but that number is hard to square with the total of 100 he had given in August.)

Smallwood's claimed total of 150 travelers over nine months would be a pace of more than 16 a month, though departures were likely concentrated in the warmer months. Smallwood and Torrey sometimes put 15 or more people in a single wagonload, so it seems a feasible tempo. Certainly, many other people escaped slavery during those months without the activists' help—self-liberated, as the abolitionists called it—though it's hard to make a realistic estimate.

By comparison, Hope Slatter shipped some 208 people south from Baltimore during 1842, and his competitors in Washington and Alexandria, Virginia, probably sent at least that many more. If this were a contest—and in a very real sense it was a contest, for human lives and futures—the slave traders were ahead. The traders were operating a legal, well-capitalized, well-staffed, government-regulated business that ran up big profits. Smallwood, Torrey, Gibbs, Brown, and those like them were breaking the law every time they so much as chatted with an enslaved person about the possibility of flight. They survived on modest donations; they had few trusted partners; they were defying the government's laws and had to hide from the police at every turn. It was no surprise that more people were being shipped south than were escaping north.

Even as the pace of escapes accelerated, the Smallwood-Torrey partnership underwent a dramatic change. In August 1842, after accompanying a large group of runaways to northern New York—the episode when the broken wagon axle may have prevented their capture—Torrey did not return. By October, he had settled in Albany and taken the job of editor of the *Tocsin of Liberty*. He was still absolutely committed to trying to liberate as many people from slavery as possible, and he did what he could to help Smallwood from 350 miles away, raising funds and assisting those who reached the New York state capital.

But just eight months after the pair had first met, Smallwood was left largely on his own in Washington. He found himself operating a high-stress, high-risk secret enterprise with the help of his wife, Elizabeth, and his network of allies along the way. He also made time to write up his activities for Torrey and the *Tocsin of Liberty*. His dispatches soon became a favorite of the newspaper's antislavery readers. Eventually they would add up to an astonishing literary feat.

A TRUE LIBERTY MAN.

"Sir," said an old man, to one of the publishers of the Tocsin, "I have not been able to take a liberty paper, but I don't know how to get along without one any longer, and I have made up my mind that I must have the Tocsin, and will do without using tobacco in order to enable me to pay for it. I have seen several copies of it and am so deeply interested with Samuel Weller, Jr.'s letters respecting the Underground Rail Road, that I had rather give up my tobacco than lose the pleasure I derive from reading them."

Tocsin of Liberty.

THURSDAY, DECEMBER 15, 1842.

CHARLES T. TORREY, *Editor*

A promotion in the *Tocsin of Liberty* for the popular satirical letters written by Thomas Smallwood under the pen name Sam Weller. [Courtesy of Boston Public Library]

7

The Laughingstock Letters

I t was early August 1842, and Thomas Smallwood, in his ebullient Dickensian guise as "Samivel Weller Jr.," was as usual lambasting and mocking the slaveholders whose property he had recently helped liberate. In his latest dispatch to the *Tocsin of Liberty* in Albany, he explained to Thomas A. Scott of Washington just why the man he had enslaved, Henry Hawkins, had headed north:

> It was your cruelty to him that made him disappear by that same "under ground rail-road" or "steam balloon," about which one of your city constables was swearing so bitterly a few weeks ago, when complaining that the "d—d rascals" got off so, and that no trace of them could be found!

Smallwood's letter, published on August 10, 1842, marked a signal moment in the history of both the American battle against slavery and the American language. Judging from an extensive search of newspaper archives, it was the first time anyone had used the term "underground rail-road" in print to refer to the way Black Americans escaped slavery. The discovery of Smallwood's pioneering role, made possible today by the existence of vast digital newspaper collections, solves a historical mystery that has been the subject of legend and speculation for a century and a half.

It is worth pausing to dissect Smallwood's early uses of "underground railroad," a rolling gag at first, just another comic stick with which to beat the slaveholders. Within a few months, his metaphor would be picked up nationwide and become shorthand for any escape route used by people fleeing slavery. Over the following century it would be draped in legend, becoming a comforting way for Americans—white Americans in particular—to talk about the unpleasant subject of slavery. Its stories, often apocryphal, often featured good-hearted white people helping Black people to freedom.

But here at its origin, Smallwood treated this imaginary "underground railroad" as mainly a fantastic joke—a patently absurd notion deployed to ridicule the slaveholders who could not fathom how enslaved people were getting away in such large numbers, undetected, and so quickly that the slave hunters sent after them could not catch them. Naturally, the escapes, much discussed in Washington and Baltimore at the time, were extremely frustrating to the police constables who doubled as slave catchers. In another letter published two weeks after this first reference, Smallwood credited John Zell, a notorious Baltimore constable who was often hired by slaveholders to pursue runaways, as the first to use the phrase. He said that Zell, in ranting about all the disappearances, had made a bitter joke that they must somehow be escaping on a "steam balloon" or aboard a subterranean railroad. Those were technologies that were then futuristic, almost imaginary, as we might say today that the escapees must have been abducted by aliens or teleported to a northern state. In 1842, tinkers were trying to build steam balloons—an Alexandria newspaper that year advertised a twenty-five-cent pamphlet with instructions for building "Pennington's Steam Balloon"—and while there were already trains running through tunnels, the first true subway was still two decades away.

Whatever the term's genesis, Smallwood picked it up and used it with relish. It was a way to underscore just how elegantly the antislavery forces were fleecing the slaveholders and fooling the slave catchers. Over the next few weeks, in his Sam Weller letters, he reeled off multiple variations on this fictional mode of transportation, turning it into an empowering metaphor. In his August 24 dispatch, he told a Washington physician named James G. Coombes that, alas, he would not be able to reveal just what had happened to two men Coombes had advertised as runaways. Chiding Coombes for trying to get information on the escape from police and from a poor African American woman he had been badgering, Smallwood offered what would much later be called an inside-the-Beltway joke.

> I hope he won't take any offense at my bluntness! I would just hint to him, by way of caution, that the secret of the "underground rail-road," has never been communicated to any but the PRESIDENT and his CABINET: so that a few constables and an ignorant woman who knew nothing about it, won't help him very much!

Soon Smallwood was puckishly advising slaveholders "to apply at the office of the underground railroad" in Washington for information on their missing property. After Torrey's departure, Smallwood noted the continuing flow of enslaved people to the north and declared triumphantly: "Here am I, Samuel Weller, jun., still in the city to scourge and mock at them and defy all their puny efforts to discover me or the 'underground railroad.'" At the Albany paper, the editors quickly caught on to the joke. An unsigned piece published a few weeks after Smallwood introduced the concept praised "Sam Weller" for his activities: "Sam invented and constructed the 'underground railroad.' It commences in the city of Washington and terminates in Canada."

Smallwood's grand joke spread fast in antislavery circles. Just days after Smallwood's first published use of the term, Joshua Giddings, the Ohio congressman who lived at Abolition House, wrote with obvious sarcasm to his twenty-year-old son about how enslaved people just somehow kept vanishing from the nation's capital. "Some swear that there is a Subterranean rail road by which they travel under ground. Men, women & children all go—whole families disappear," Giddings wrote, adding a quotation from Shakespeare's *The Tempest*: "Like the baseless fabric of a vision & leave not a rack behind."

—◦═◦═◦—

Thomas Smallwood's letters constituted a unique satirical attack on slavery, one that was all the more extraordinary because the letters were written by a self-educated, formerly enslaved shoemaker with no known previous history of writing for publication. He created a rare contemporaneous record of escapes from slavery, a running madcap chronicle that continued for nearly two years, dealing a flurry of literary blows against some of the ideological pillars on which the institution rested.

It's worth remembering that Smallwood carved out this new vocation as a writer when he had much else going on. He was the father of four children, whom he was trying to support with his shoemaking business. He was devoting every moment he could spare from work and household duties to recruiting for and organizing escapes. Yet he found time every couple of weeks to pause and craft dispatches for the Albany paper reporting on the latest departures—how the "walking property walked off," as he once put it—and to lampoon the slave system and its defenders.

And Smallwood did it all in an engaging style that hugely appealed to his antislavery audience, a style utterly unlike that of the long-winded, humorless treatises common in the abolitionist press. His was a story of a clever David triumphing again and again over the Goliath of the slave power; he was a trickster in the African and African American Br'er Rabbit tradition. "The poor manstealers and their watchdogs are greatly at a loss to know how their victims escape," he wrote. "All this shows that they would give a plum to know where the under-ground Rail Road begins!"

Where did Smallwood get the idea and the style? Abel Brown's earlier handful of taunting articles in the *Tocsin of Liberty* offering insincere sympathy to the slaveholders for their losses were surely an inspiration. Torrey may have had a hand in a few of the Sam Weller letters that were published in the summer of 1842 before he left Washington and took over as editor of *Tocsin*. But a more exalted influence is hinted at in the nom de plume, Samivel Weller Jr., that Smallwood lifted from Charles Dickens's bestselling *Pickwick Papers*.

As Smallwood was purchasing his freedom and improving his literary knowledge in the employ of John McLeod, the Scottish schoolmaster, Charles Dickens was a struggling London journalist with a keen eye for the city's absurdities. He had collected his vivid tales in 1836 in his first book, *Sketches by Boz* (Dickens's family nickname). By then, he was already serializing his first novel, *The Posthumous Papers of the Pickwick Club*, better known as *The Pickwick Papers*, which soon became a publishing phenomenon around the world. These loosely connected yarns sold modestly until Dickens introduced Samivel Weller (the spelling reflecting Weller's Cockney conflation of *w* and *v* sounds), a bootblack hired by Mr. Pickwick as his valet. Sales of the installments shot up from four hundred copies to forty thousand, and in book form *Pickwick* would sell 1.6 million copies during Dickens's lifetime. The quotation of "Wellerisms"—the sometimes mangled, often insightful, always comical sayings of Sam Weller—became a staple of the press. The spin-off products were comparable to what a Disney hit might spawn today: there were cigars and playing cards with the Pickwick brand, as well as puzzles, boot polish, and taxicabs named for Sam Weller.

So it was natural enough for Smallwood, looking around for a pseudonym in 1842, to grab that one. But there was more to it. The original Weller was a bootblack—so Smallwood the shoemaker, who kept his identity as the author of letters to the *Tocsin of Liberty* so carefully hidden, may have been toying with the enemies who were trying desperately to identify him. Dickens's exuberant style, rooted in close observation of the people around him and his jaundiced eye on their words and actions, became a model for Smallwood. Just as importantly, Smallwood was offering a sort of literary tribute to Dickens's ferocious opposition to slavery, which the novelist had first witnessed during his travels around the United States in the first half of 1842, with stops in Baltimore and Washington.

Dickens's *American Notes* was published in November 1842, and Torrey excerpted the book in the *Tocsin of Liberty*. In the passage Torrey chose, Dickens denounced "owners, breeders, users, buyers and sellers of slaves, who will, until the bloody chapter has a bloody end, own, breed, use, buy and sell them at all hazards; who doggedly deny the horrors of the system . . . ; who when they speak of Freedom, mean the Freedom to oppress their kind, and to be savage, merciless and cruel." Dickens's antislavery views were known by the time of his American travels, and his visit to Washington would have been of special interest to Smallwood.

This brings up a fascinating mystery, because Sam Weller, in one of Smallwood's letters to the Albany paper, would describe how he had met the great author in person in Washington. In a long parenthetical digression following his flaunting of his knowledge of Latin phrases, "Weller" declared:

> You never heard how I learned Latin, did you? One day Boz Dickens and I were walking down to see Williams' *Slave Pen*, right in front of the President's House. Boz, after turning up his nose, in his very curious way, at the flag, on the Capitol, began to quote some Latin stuff about hypocrisy and republican despotism, as he said. And I thought I would learn it, *to use in cursing slavery with!* And it comes very convenient sometimes, when I'm at a slave auction, or looking at a whipping, or visiting the slaves, in connection with our operation, to vent my feelings in a language the woman-whippers don't understand. A surly slave-catcher actually took off his hat to me, when I denounced him as a *"monstrum horrendum."*

The passage is a lovely example of Smallwood's style, but it also raises a tantalizing question: Could Thomas Smallwood have led Charles Dickens to the premises of William Williams, Washington's most notorious slave trader? The answer is yes, he could have, though it is impossible to prove. Dickens visited Washington in mid-March 1842, when Smallwood and Torrey were in town and had started organizing escapes, and the English author paid particular attention to the slave trade, though he did not specifically describe a visit to Williams's slave jail. Dickens was by the time of his visit a major celebrity, and everywhere he went in Washington he was followed by a crowd. When he visited the White House for tea with President John Tyler (a slaveholder, like twelve of the first eighteen presidents), one reporter wrote that "the fifteen hundred or two thousand people present went in pursuit of him like hounds, horses and riders in pursuit of a fox in the chase." Smallwood, as a big Dickens fan, may well have been in the crowds accompanying the author around town. So it seems plausible, if not provable, that Smallwood might have called out, "Come this way, Mr. Dickens, to see a slave trader's jail!" Or, at the least, that Smallwood might have been present when Dickens stopped to stare at the spectacle of the slaver's operation in the midst of the capital of a country that prided itself on its embrace of freedom.

Or, of course, it could have been just another of Smallwood's bittersweet jokes.

⋯⇒◉⇐⋯

Like most nineteenth-century newspapers, the *Tocsin of Liberty,* which would merge with another paper in early 1843 and become *Albany Weekly Patriot,* with Torrey remaining as editor, made no attempt at nonpartisanship. It was a Liberty Party newspaper, avowedly antislavery and contemptuous of the institution and its supporters. But it also sought to be a general-interest paper, offering a grab bag of information and entertainment, from the shocking news of the slaughter of thousands of British troops as the British army withdrew from "Cabool" in Afghanistan to the latest speeches of President Tyler and the political combat in Congress and the New York legislature.

There were steamboat fires and train wrecks, juicy divorces and gruesome murders, plus the trivial but captivating fodder of most popular media. "Money Digging" was one 1842 headline, reporting that "a demented old watchman" in Baltimore by the name of Hill had started digging for buried money ("$15,000 to $30,000") on the basis of three dreams; so far, he'd had no luck in finding the cash. A cow at the New York State Lunatic Asylum had produced a record 1,013 gallons of milk! The paper ran a list of the last living New York State veterans of the Revolutionary War—two dozen of them, ranging in age from 99 to 109.

There was a tip on removing grease from silk (powdered magnesia did the trick) and a skeptical notice about "mesmerism," a popular therapeutic method involving magnets and hypnotism—"the latest exposure of this humbug took place in Baltimore last week."

Tocsin was of course a business, or an attempt at a business, and Smallwood's dispatches from Washington were often wedged amid a captivating array of oddball advertisements. A specialist in producing dyes for clothing was a regular with the catchy slogan "I DYE to live, and live to DYE." There was "an improved plan for cleaning WOOLEN CLOTHES by STEAM." A variety store in Albany offered "Dr. Jayke's Vermifuge," guaranteed to cure worms in children. A bookseller featuring encyclopedias claimed they were "the cheapest works ever issued."

But none of it was enough to produce adequate revenue, and the situation only grew worse when Torrey made the principled but financially dubious decision that the renamed *Albany Weekly Patriot* would no long carry ads for "quack medicines," among other things. "Now be it known," Torrey wrote, that the *Patriot* would not run a lot of things: "any notices of Theaters, Circus, Grogshops, Porter Houses, Liquor sales, or any thing else, of a nature so offensive to good morals. . . . Rather let the Patriot sink!" And sink it almost did, repeatedly. The newspaper that chronicled and cheered on so many escapes from slavery and that gave Smallwood an outlet for his writings was a shoestring operation that was plagued by deadbeat subscribers. Torrey regularly harangued readers who failed to pay their bills, saying they were undermining the fight against slavery and his own family's well-being. "Your Editor and Printers *can't* work without prompt payment. We are determined to do what never was done yet: make an abolition paper *pay its own way*," Torrey wrote in early 1843 when subscribers owed $3,500 in back bills, a considerable sum.

When Smallwood's Sam Weller letters first made their appearance, before Torrey took over as editor, the newspaper seemed nervous about making room for his raillery. An abject apology under the heading "Sam Weller" in August 1842 declared: "We exceedingly regret that the last two articles over this signature found their way into our paper without the preliminary of 'the editorial shears.'" It was unclear what the "objectionable" content was in the previous two Weller letters. In one, true, he addressed a slaveholder as "you soft headed man-thief" and called slave catchers "man-hyenas" and ridiculed a Washington widow whose enslaved servants had headed north, but that was standard fare. In the other, he had noted that an enslaved boy named Henry Clay had fled and insinuated that the distinguished senator from Kentucky might well be his father. Who may have complained, and what internal debates took place, was not disclosed. But soon enough it became clear that the Weller letters were a big hit with the readers, and there were no more apologies. By the time Torrey was in charge, the Weller letters were being promoted regularly, once with the bold image of a finger in the margin pointing to the text: "Don't fail to read what SAM says." Just four months after Smallwood had introduced the underground railroad, the newspaper ran an advertisement attesting to what "Sam Weller Jr." had done for the paper:

> "Sir," said an old man, to one of the publishers of the Tocsin, "I have not been able to take a liberty paper but I don't know how to get along without one any longer, and I have made up my mind that I must have the Tocsin, and will do without using tobacco in order to enable me to pay for it. I have seen several copies of it and am so deeply interested with Samuel Weller, Jr.'s letters respecting the Underground Rail Road, that I had rather give up my tobacco than lose the pleasure I derive from reading them."

The first task Smallwood set himself in his Samivel Weller letters was to set down the facts: who had escaped from whom. This was extraordinary in its own right; while in the future there would be published compilations of escapes, they would generally come years after the fact. (*The Underground Railroad Records*, by the great African American activist William Still of Philadelphia, did not appear until 1872, long after emancipation.) Smallwood's reports were so timely that he often delayed sending a dispatch for a week or two until he could be sure the fugitives he was naming had reached Canada or some other safe haven.

Sometimes he just gave the basics. But often, like any good reporter, Smallwood had details to spin into an entertaining and enlightening drama. Peter Matthews, a twenty-seven-year-old man in Washington, worked as a dining room server and carriage driver for his enslaver, a Treasury Department chief clerk and real estate dealer named James Larned. The woman Matthews loved had fled to Canada a year earlier, and Matthews had tried to follow her, only to be caught by slave catchers paid by Larned to go after him. (Flaunting his inside knowledge, Smallwood scolded Larned for his loud swearing at the bank where he collected the hundred dollars he needed to pay the slave catchers.)

Larned decided to sell Matthews south, determined to cash him in before he could flee again. But Larned's wife persuaded him not to take such a cruel step. Then Matthews took off again—and this time, with Smallwood's help, he made it. Smallwood told the story with gusto and with his usual faux sympathy for the sufferings of the enslavers. "Peter, the graceless scoundrel! when his loving master got him back a few weeks ago, and went to such an expense about him, wouldn't stay at home, after all! So one day he passed to Canada by the 'under-ground rail-road.'" Smallwood mimicked the pronunciation of Dickens's Cockney character:

> It was wery cruel, wery, in Peter Matthews to run off to Canada, after his sweet, swearing master had paid $100 for catching him only 6 weeks before! Poor James Larned! Why did you listen to your tender hearted wife? Had you sold him when he first come back, your money would have been safe. But alas, there is no hope for you! Peter is in Toronto. He loved a certain bright eyed Sophy Jackson even better than his dear master; and Sophy you know, left Washington a year ago, on the grand tour! If you are really rich enough to pay the second cool hundred out of your salary as Clerk, it would only be fair to send it to Peter. . . . Will you do it?

The Treasury Department's chief clerk had gotten an expensive lesson in the hazards of Chesapeake slaveholding, thanks to Smallwood and his crew. And such lessons were very much the point. The Albany newspaper was not much read in Washington or Baltimore. So the editors made a point of spending a little extra cash from their minimal reserves on postage to mail to Chesapeake slaveholders any issue in which those slaveholders were named. Larned would thus have received a newspaper from Albany absolutely free of charge. His reaction is, alas, not recorded, though one can imagine that more swearing may have been involved.

⊶≡◉≡⊷

Smallwood was doing something else quite deliberately in his missives. He was flamboyantly treating the enslaved people as human beings, fully deserving of respect—and doing it in a newspaper, for all the world to see. Most important, he was naming them, almost always with a first and last name, defying the enslavers who preferred to refer to their "chattels" by first name only, to emphasize their inferior status. When slaveholders placed runaway ads in the newspaper, some would include a last name, presumably because they thought it might help them recover their property. But they snidely made it clear that they by no means accepted the notion that an enslaved person deserved a complete name. Smallwood took on the name issue explicitly in a letter published on December 1, 1842, that rattled off the latest fourteen people to escape and proudly declared, "They went by the Great National Underground Rail Road!" Slaveholder W. H. Edes, he noted, had placed an ad seeking the return of "Bill, *who calls himself* William Martin" and who had "gone off without the least provocation." Another enslaver, J. Y. Young, had lost "negro man William, who *calls himself* William Hall" (italicized emphasis very much Smallwood's). Smallwood bristled:

> What should they "call themselves"? Because *slaveholders* allow their victims *no family name*, in order to accustom the people to the denial of their *family relations*, is that any reason *they*

should unman themselves, and forget the ties of nature and of love? Oh how thoroughly the accursed system strikes at the root of every thing noble, just and humane!

Whenever he could, Smallwood wielded his satirical dagger to skewer the conceit of the slaveholders and ennoble the runaways. Sophy Jackson had fled slavery for Canada, but Smallwood worded it more wittily: she "left Washington a year ago, on the grand tour!" The grand tour was for prosperous white people, but Smallwood hijacked the language to proclaim that African Americans escaping slavery were making their own, quite grand travel plans. When Martha Lee fled Zaccheus Collins Lee, who happened to be the United States attorney for Baltimore, her enslaver placed a runaway ad saying she had "absconded." Smallwood wanted to make clear that the only crime involved was his, not hers. "She *scorns* the word 'absconded,'" Smallwood wrote. "No such thing! She went openly in the public vehicle as a member of your very respectable family ought to go. So take back your shabby word about one so *dear* to you."

Smallwood sometimes went further, turning the racist hierarchy of the slaveholders upside down. The enslavers' standard justification for owning their fellow human beings was a twisted claim of compassion: African Americans were lesser creatures, incapable of taking care of themselves, the argument went, so the white man's decision to work them and house them was a mercy, not a crime. In Sam Weller's telling, it was the other way around. The slaveholders were slow-witted, buffaloed, delusional. "Besides, a shrewd slave has *wit enough at any time* to get round a lazy, mole-eyed slaveholder," Smallwood declared. He took delight in informing Azariah Fuller, a Washington hotelkeeper, and his sons just how the ten-year-old boy they had enslaved, Henry Jefferson, had slipped their grasp. "The great blockheads cannot yet account for the mysterious disappearance of their man! Let me explain it to you, sweet sirs!" Smallwood taunted. They had sent the boy down a busy street on an errand, he wrote, but they had not watched carefully enough. "He slipped into one door of the apothecary's shop on 11th street, and out of the other, that opens on the back street!"

When he could, Smallwood quoted slaveholders' own assessments of the people who had run from them, to highlight the runaways' intellect and skills. When "John, who calls himself John More" fled J. Y. Young of Georgetown, Young's runaway ad offered an impressive $150 reward for the return of the twenty-eight-year-old man. Seemingly oblivious to the implications of the ad's description, Young wrote that More "*reads and writes well, and is a good mathematician*; is a sagacious, shrewd fellow, *a professor of religion, and an occasional exhorter*," or church evangelist. Smallwood did not even need to point out the absurdity of treating such a talented man as an inferior suited only to be property; to Young's own words, he merely added italics.

Smallwood made a show of pitying "the Patriarchs," as he called these self-absorbed, overprivileged characters who relied on unpaid laborers, for they seemed genuinely baffled that the people they enslaved would so ungratefully decide to run off. "There's a peck of trouble among the Patriarchs, in this city, since you left," he wrote in a Weller letter, addressing Torrey a few weeks after he had started the editor's job in Albany. "I want to comfort the dear souls a little, by assuring them that their absent friends have all reached Canada, in safety, having been seen in Toronto, and some of them having written back to me, in this city, that their relations might be assured of their health and good prospects."

Notley Maddox, a slaveholder outside Washington, advertised in the summer of 1842 that in addition to the people who had fled him in 1841 another man had now run away. "I have now five males and one female that have left me without cause known to me," Maddox wrote in the ad. Smallwood found this pose of baffled innocence provoking. He called Maddox a "booby" for advertising rewards for the return of runaways who had long ago settled in Canada. As for their motive: "I *must* say, Notley Maddox, if you insult the nation again, by pretending that your six slaves left you 'without any cause known to you,' that I shall be obliged to expose your *cruelty* to them; your robbing them of liberty and property, was quite bad enough. But it hurts my feelings to write about your violent temper, and tyrannical conduct and it *might hurt* yours to have it known."

Because Smallwood was working in Washington, the enslavers whose
workers he was helping to disappear were sometimes government officials, giving him inviting targets for his wit and scorn. "Mr. James Maher,
the public gardener, must regret to lose the company of Margaret Myers,"
he wrote in November 1842. "But Uncle Sam pays him so much money
for nothing, that he can afford the pecuniary loss, very well." Drawing on
his local knowledge, Smallwood also offered some devastating personal
history on this public servant: "Doubtless, Mr. Maher's conscience has
never been quite easy, since he killed that slave in his barn with the piece
of old cart tire. . . . I don't wonder Margaret wanted to leave him." As in
many of his reports, Smallwood was highlighting his intimate knowledge of the slaveholders and his eagerness to reveal it.

Playing up his status as an anonymous insider in small-town Washington, a spy walking undetected among the enslavers, was one of Smallwood's
most effective gambits. When a local newspaper, *The Georgetown Advocate*,
took "Sam Weller" to task for alleged mistakes in reporting escapes—a sort
of backhanded tribute, since it showed the editors were reading Smallwood's
columns—Torrey replied in *Albany Weekly Patriot* with a spirited warning.
Using another pointing finger in the margin for emphasis, he wrote: "A
word of advice to you, Mr. Advocate: Samivel Weller Jr. *is among you*, 'takin'
notes,' and if you provoke him, he will unfold the *secrets* of slavery in your
pleasant little city, in such a style, that many a man, now called 'respectable,'
will hang their heads for shame!" And unfold the secrets he did.

Sometimes Smallwood obtained his intelligence directly from the
people he was helping to escape, such as Lawrence Paine, who had fled
from Philip R. Fendall II, the successor to Francis Scott Key as the
United States attorney for the District of Columbia. "Lawrence Paine
begs leave to say to Esq. Fendall, that if he is smart enough to be district
attorney, he isn't quiet enough to catch a slave who wants his freedom!"
Smallwood wrote in late 1842. "And he has never forgotten or forgiven
the brutality that *branded* him on the hand, in 1840, with a red hot door

key, to *mark* him! Pretty fellow this Fendall is for a public officer, or for a lawyer to plead the cause of justice and mercy!"

In other cases, Smallwood had inside information simply from lurking on the streets of Washington and keeping his eyes and ears open. One telling example: Smallwood's repeated letters referring to Dr. William H. Gunnell, the enslaver of the five-year-old girl forced to stay awake all night to rock his baby's cradle.

Gunnell lived about ten blocks from Smallwood in southeast Washington. "How many times I've heard him boast that 'no nigger could ever get away from him!'" Smallwood wrote, after he had assisted on their way north several people the doctor had enslaved. Smallwood evidently witnessed how infuriated the physician was by the issue of the *Tocsin of Liberty* with the story of escapes from his house, mailed to him by the Albany editors. "Recently, Dr. Wm. H. Gunnell received a copy of your paper containing my poor attempts to comfort him under the weight of afflictions quite enough to break the heart of any Patriarch! He was, strange to say, quite furious with me. How I laughed at him, as I stood by his side, one day, and heard him sputter. . . . He was ready to eat up alive your humble servant, Sam Weller, jr. if he only knew who he was!" In the same *Tocsin*, Torrey, as editor, highlighted precisely this aspect of Smallwood's letters: "SAM speaks what *he knows*. He is ever in the secrets of those dark and dastardly conspirators against human liberty, the slaveholders of the District of Columbia."

What is most poignant about Smallwood's eavesdropping on the slaveholders of Washington is that he was exploiting one of the poisonous elements of racism that most galled him. Like other African Americans, he was often powerless and irrelevant in the eyes of his white fellow citizens, beneath their notice, virtually invisible. Thus they sometimes spoke within his earshot about the most sensitive matters. Smallwood had turned a grave and painful burden of racism into his secret superpower.

⊷═◉═⊷

These dual methods—interviewing the runaways and observing the slaveholders—Smallwood put to particular use to expose one of the most disturbing features of the slave system: sexual slavery. The rape of enslaved women by their enslavers was routine, though it was rarely spoken of. In their rants about miscegenation and the possible pollution of the white race, southern firebrand politicians somehow failed to notice that the ban on interracial sex applied only selectively—that thousands upon thousands of enslaved African Americans had white fathers, grandfathers, or great-grandfathers. Smallwood, like Torrey and many other abolitionists, often dwelled on this especially heinous element of the crime of slavery.

When a butcher named Philip Otterback—another neighbor of Smallwood's—advertised the sudden disappearance of three people he had enslaved, Smallwood focused on the story of Betsey Williams. She had been groomed from childhood by Otterback "for a certain purpose," Smallwood claimed, but after being pursued sexually by Otterback she had repulsed him, on one occasion jumping out the window to get away. "Happily, the vigilance of a wife and son will sometimes prevent the evil intended by the head of the family," Smallwood wrote. Betsey Williams was by then in Toronto, he said, and far out of Otterback's reach. Playing again on his ability to hide in plain sight, Smallwood declared that he repeatedly saw Otterback after Williams's disappearance: "It *was* sad to see how dejected he looked for weeks in the market." When the ten-year-old boy named Henry Clay ran from his enslaver in Washington, Smallwood highlighted the "very entertaining advertisement" that described him as "a light copper color" with "tolerably straight black hair," suggesting that the senator from Kentucky might well be the boy's father.

Later, Smallwood would write that the sexual exploitation of women by their enslavers was a key to "the demoralizing influence of slavery." "Their virtue is tampered with, trampled on, violated; and is entirely at the mercy and will of any and every debauchee who chooses to arm himself with the advantages he has over the poor colored female." As a result, enslaved men saw their own respect for women eroded, Smallwood argued: "For if one should chance to get a virtuous companion, her fidelity to him is almost sure to be destroyed by some white man." Smallwood attributed the debauchery and sexual violence that ran rampant in the slave states to "the easy and luxurious life of the Southerners, by means of slave labor."

Torrey, too, often remarked on sexual exploitation as a pillar of the slave system. Shortly after taking over the editorship of the *Tocsin,* he printed a report of a talk by Lewis Clark, formerly enslaved in Kentucky, who spoke candidly about what many were too embarrassed or ashamed to discuss. He noted that Black men were often executed on suspicion of rape, but white men experienced no such fear. "Just think for a minute," he told his majority-white audience in Brooklyn, New York, "how you would like to have *your* sisters, and *your* wives, and *your* daughters, completely, and altogether, in the power of a master." He described how his "pretty sister," when she turned sixteen, was first "sent for" by her enslaver. When she complained to her mother about the serial rapes, the man became angry and sold the teenager south to Louisiana. "We heard afterward that she died there of hard usage," Clark said.

⋯⋯

Smallwood's penning of regular reports on his highly illegal activities—and Torrey's enthusiastic publication of them—was controversial in abolitionist circles. Most clandestine operations do not have a public relations arm. It is uncertain whether Frederick Douglass, then just a few years from his escape from Baltimore, was following the Sam Weller reports. But when he wrote his first memoir in 1845, Douglass paused to complain about unnamed activists (he called them "western," probably meaning Ohio, which shared a long border with the slave state Kentucky) who insisted on speaking and writing openly about their escape efforts (and note his casual use of "underground railroad," common parlance by then, three years after Smallwood introduced it):

> I have never approved of the very public manner in which some
> of our western friends have conducted what they call the under-
> ground railroad, but which, I think, by their open declarations,
> has been made most emphatically the uppergound railroad.
> I honor those good men and women for their noble daring,
> and applaud them for willingly subjecting themselves to bloody

persecution, by openly avowing their participation in the escape of slaves. I, however, can see very little good resulting from
such a course, either to themselves or the slaves escaping; while,
upon the other hand, I see and feel assured that those open
declarations are a positive evil to the slaves remaining, who are
seeking to escape. They do nothing towards enlightening the
slave, whilst they do much towards enlightening the master.
They stimulate him to greater watchfulness, and enhance his
power to capture his slave.

Smallwood and Torrey disagreed with Douglass. They hoped that
pounding the public drum about escapes, and humiliating the slaveholders, might stimulate not watchfulness but discouragement. Occasionally
Smallwood was cheered to hear that a local slaveholder, relieved of enslaved laborers with his help, had vowed to use hired hands instead. In
any case, he appears to have so enjoyed penning his irreverent reports
that he may simply have preferred to ignore the cautious counsel of public silence.

But Smallwood stayed carefully hidden, and his relentless reporting
and writing through 1842 and 1843 led to a guessing game as to his
identity. "Those letters were a great annoyance to the slaveholders in
that section, and they would have been very glad to have got the writer,"
Smallwood would write in his memoir. When another abolitionist paper
in New York, *The Friend of Man*, speculated that "Sam Weller" must be
a member of the Albany Vigilance Committee, Smallwood enjoyed cor-
recting the record in his next letter: "Samivel Weller wishes to say to the
Friend of Man, and all that sort of people, that he is not a member of the
Albany Vigilance Committee, and don't live any where near that place.
In fact, he lives in no particular spot; but where humanity has work to
do, and the pay is *small*, he hopes to be found doing his small share of it."

A few weeks later he gleefully scolded the Washington hotelkeeper
Azariah Fuller (featured in a previous letter because his enslaved people,
too, had headed north) for threatening Charles Torrey with "beating, a
mob, and sundry other minor evils, because he mistook Mr. Torrey for

me, even me, Sam Weller, jr! The ignorant blunderhead! Is not *my* name carried to the world's end? Am I to be confounded with an obscure aboli-tionist, and *he* to be persecuted for my misdeeds?" He assured his readers that he and Torrey were "very, very different persons" in every way, in-cluding their "looks," he added, with a wink to their different races. He revealed nothing about himself, of course, and merely vowed to keep on writing: "I, Samivel Weller, jr. will continue to SCOFF at, *annoy*, and *ex-pose* the slaveholders, and their crooked ways, to their perfect mystification and great pain, during weeks and months to come! The poor ignoramuses! to think to catch *such* a weasel as I, asleep!"

All this jeering celebration, accompanying the steady departure of people from bondage, began to attract hostile attention. It had become

Meanwhile, lest Mr. Torrey should be troubled again by these hyenas on my ac-count, I beg you to assure them, that he and Samivel Weller, jr. are very, very different persons in their habits, views, feelings, characters, homes, names, looks, and every thing else! And farther, that while Mr. Torrey will, as heretofore, be occupied with more important matters, I, Samivel Weller, jr. will continue to SCOFF at, *annoy*, and *expose* the slaveholders, and their crooked ways, to their perfect mys-tification and great pain, during weeks and months to come! The poor ignora-muses! to think to catch *such* a weasel as I, asleep.

An excerpt from Smallwood's letter to the *Tocsin of Liberty* in September 1842, protesting that the identity of the pseudonymous Samivel Weller was not Charles Torrey and describing his own role as a satirist targeting slavery in his usual antic style. [Courtesy of Boston Public Library]

obvious that there was an organized effort to "entice" (in the words of the law) people in the Chesapeake to run north. The connection to Albany and its abolitionist newspaper had also become clear—the more so as slaveholders in Baltimore and Washington found in their mail Sam Weller's galling comments about them. In Albany, a letter arrived from Baltimore—postage due, no less—addressed to "The Abolitionist Brown" with a copy of an ad from *The Sun* in which slaveholder Walter Fernandis offered one hundred dollars for the return of "a Mulatto Man named Robert Hill," whom he had enslaved.

Fernandis evidently had guessed correctly. Abel Brown replied: "Mr. Fernandis: This is to inform you that the noble Robert Hill reached this city in safety, and was safely sent on his way rejoicing. We charge you $25 for the money paid him and services rendered, and 56 cents for the letter containing the advertisement. Please send a draft for the same." He signed it as usual, "Abel Brown, Forwarding Merchant," and added a cheeky P.S. to the beleaguered Fernandis: "The business is very good this year. Please inform the slaves that we are always on hand, ready to receive them."

By late 1842, Smallwood wrote, the aggrieved slaveholders of Washington were offering $2,000 "for the detection of the person or persons who were thus depriving them of their goods and chattels." In April 1843, some "gentlemen" in Baltimore, having studied the Albany connection, offered a bounty for three of the people they believed to be the guilty parties: Torrey, Brown, and an Albany portrait painter and hard-core abolitionist named E. W. Goodwin, who had preceded Torrey as editor of the *Tocsin of Liberty*. Smallwood's identity remained a secret. Who exactly put up the reward money? That was uncertain; the newspapers did not carry any signed announcements. The defenders of the slave system evidently preferred to work quietly, via the police and slave catchers. But Torrey, clearly flattered by the attention, replied publicly and in fine style:

> By the way, the gentlemen who made an offer, the other day,
> in Baltimore, to one of our city Constables, of $500 each for
> the following persons, viz: CHARLES T. TORREY, ABEL

BROWN, and E.W. GOODWIN, are informed that each and every one of them will go to Baltimore for half that sum, only deposit the money in a good bank, and send the certificate of deposit, or in any other sure way that the money will be paid. Suit yourselves, gentlemen. Any way, we are not particular, so that we get the money. We want funds to help the poor fugitives, who are escaping from your ungodly man-market, and your Sodomite villainies and barbarian oppressions.

It was a defiant riposte, perhaps worded so forcefully because the three men in Albany were in little danger from the constables and other enforcers from the Chesapeake. The same could not be said of Thomas Smallwood, aka Samivel Weller Jr., who ran terrifying risks every day but somehow managed to stay well hidden, continuing to help liberate the enslaved and then torment the slaveholders with his own gloating, searing brand of satire.

An 1846 newspaper ad for the southern end of Hope Slatter's business in New Orleans, where Slatter's brother Shadrack presided over a "showroom" of captives taken from the mid-Atlantic states and put on sale. [Courtesy of American Antiquarian Society and Genealogy Bank]

8

That Vile Wretch Slatter

If Hope Slatter, Baltimore's church-pew-purchasing, respect-craving king of Chesapeake slave traders, was among the "gentlemen" offering a reward in the spring of 1843 for the arrest of the three Albany agitators, he didn't come forward to say so. But if Slatter wasn't putting up the cash, he had every reason to cheer on those who were.

Charles Torrey and his newspaper repeatedly held up Slatter as the chief symbol and villain of the domestic slave trade, which they spotlighted as an especially grisly and inhuman part of the criminal institution of slavery. For Slatter, the attacks, sometimes reprinted in other newspapers, would have been not just personally wounding but an unwelcome hindrance to his campaign for respectable social status. A February 1842 report for the *Tocsin of Liberty* on the Annapolis Slaveholders' Convention, almost certainly written by Torrey, quoted a Slatter ad in its entirety, then accused the Baltimore trader of "heartless hypocrisy" and called him "the American Blanco," equating him to Pedro Blanco, a Spaniard infamous for his ruthless conduct in the African slave trade.

In November 1842, after becoming editor of the *Tocsin,* Torrey called Slatter "the great slave trader of Baltimore" and noted that a court had ruled that he had imprisoned a free African American woman. Slatter, with his usual eye to reputation, accepted the verdict and even covered the expenses of the woman's lawsuit. "There is a sort of *standard of respectability,* even in this horrible trade; and Slatter is one of the few traders who wish to rise to or above it," wrote a grudging Torrey, adding: "Yet no tongue can paint the horrors of his 'private prison.'"

Torrey, before he relocated to Albany, had set eyes on this baron of human trafficking, telling a friend that Slatter resembled Judas Iscariot as painted by Raphael, evidently associating the guilty, shifty look of the Judas figure with the slave trader who was so focused on nervously asserting, against all evidence, his own decency. "His pride is that he always requires and gives 'good titles' to the 'goods and chattels' he sells," wrote Torrey of the claims in Slatter's newspaper ads. "This gives him the confidence of purchasers! He professes to be very humane!" Torrey's sarcasm, and his acute assessment of the slave trader's anxiety about social status, surely would have annoyed Slatter.

Other abolitionists took their own shots at Slatter; a Boston physician and antislavery activist, Henry I. Bowditch, roundly attacked "this vile wretch Slatter" in Garrison's *The Liberator* in February 1843. But Torrey had a subtler understanding of his adversary. In April 1843, in the same *Albany Weekly Patriot* commentary in which he mocked the reward offered for his own arrest, Torrey lit into Slatter. Reproducing Slatter's latest "Negroes Wanted" ad in *The Sun,* Torrey wrote, "The great *Negro thief,* Hope H. Slatter, 'before Israel and the *Sun,*' unblushingly publishes his shame, and the shame of the whole man-stealing South, to the Christian world." The quoted phrase was from the Old Testament. Torrey, aware of Slatter's purchase of the church pew and his frequent references to his devout Methodist mother, had indeed found a way to enrage Slatter—as subsequent events would show.

Yet Torrey also remarked on how invisible the slave trade had become to white Baltimoreans by the 1840s, more than three decades after the grand jury report whose authors had been so outraged by the city's slave jails when they were new. For more than ten years, Slatter would send people south at an average rate of five a week; he was a relentless, terrifying presence for enslaved African Americans, who could never be sure they wouldn't be forced aboard the next ship. But by moving his captives at night and working to shape a benign image with his ads, Slatter managed to make his business fade into the daily life of the city. The grotesque continuing crime of families torn apart might have made for an endless supply of the heart-wrenching tales that nineteenth-century newspaper readers favored; after all, some years later, Harriet Beecher Stowe would sell millions of copies of her novel *Uncle Tom's Cabin,* whose plot was built around the domestic slave trade. But for now, in prosperous Baltimore, where white men of means were busy making money and sparring over politics, the slave trade drew little notice. In a letter written from Baltimore, Torrey recounted the reaction to news that an enslaved Maryland family, a couple and four children, had just been sold south:

> Such occurrences are by no means unusual here. Yet the CHRISTIANS of Baltimore never know anything about them, when you ask; in truth, it would be incredible news to nine-tenths of the better sort of people in this city, that from two to four thousand slaves are every year sold, in their midst, including at least five hundred members of the body of Christ, humble, prayerful, ignorant but sincere Christians. Such topics they do not inquire into. . . . Why? The victims are poor, black, or 'yellow,' and AMERICAN SLAVES; victims of the great American slave trade.

What would have been, in Torrey's words, "incredible news" to white Baltimoreans was an inescapable everyday tragedy for African Americans. Their concerns, however, rarely made the newspapers except on those few occasions when they bought advertisements to bring attention to developments white journalists had missed or ignored. So it was, in November 1842, when James Powell, a free Black Baltimorean, bought a small ad on the last page of *The Sun* to offer his gratitude:

TO THE FEELING AND HUMANE COMMUNITY.— JAMES POWELL begs leave to return his thanks to his friends for their liberality to him in aiding him to save MARIA BERRY, that was in the possession of Hope H. Slatter, and

was to be sold out of the State. I also return my sincere thanks
to Mr. Murray and his aid, and likewise to Mr. Richard Bradford and his choir, in aiding me with two Concerts, to helping
me who stood in need.

The ad does not explain Slatter's business, nor elaborate on Maria
Berry's plight—its African American audience understood such things
all too well. Richard Bradford's choir, whose concerts had evidently
raised money to buy Berry's freedom, was the brand-new First Colored
Union Musical Association of Baltimore. The city's Black community
was building its institutions and rallying where it could against the bar-
barities of the slave trade.

◂═◉═▸

If Torrey and Smallwood were, in effect, shouting from the rooftops
about the crimes of the slave traders, Slatter took pains to keep the grim
details of his business out of public view when he moved his captives to
a ship, eager to avoid the grieving, interfering relatives and friends of the
enslaved. While Smallwood and Torrey were using horse-drawn wagons
to help people escape to the north, Slatter used a horse-drawn omnibus,
a newfangled conveyance with shades over the windows, to avoid the
spectacle of men and women in shackles being marched through the city
streets to the wharves.

He may have gone to still greater lengths for discretion. In 1937, Baltimore utility workers digging to bury electrical conduits discovered a capacious tunnel that appeared to run between Slatter's slave jail on Pratt Street
and the closest point of the Basin, as the Inner Harbor was then called, on
Light Street. An elderly African American man named Rezin Williams,
interviewed in Baltimore the same year by the Federal Writers' Project,
lent credence to the idea that this was yet another means Slatter used to
hide his business. Williams claimed improbably to be 115 years old and
the son of a man enslaved by George Washington, though he had always
been free. But his detailed recollections offer some support for his claims.

Slatter had apparently purchased a large number of people, perhaps on Maryland's Eastern Shore, and moved them by ship to Baltimore. Williams recalled being paid to lead a group of thirty or forty enslaved men, women, and children "through a dark and dirty tunnel for a distance of several blocks" to a slave trader's jail. The tunnel would have been just as useful for later moving the captives to ships bound for New Orleans.

Williams recalled that "he was told to sort of pacify the black women who set up a wail when they were separated from their husbands and children. It was a pitiful sight to see them, half naked, some whipped into submission, cast into slave pens surmounted by iron bars," the interviewer wrote.

It was a scene Slatter never shared with his visiting antislavery tourists. Nor did Slatter call attention to the steady profit he made with the assistance of the city government. Some of the most distressing tales from the tragic tapestry of borderland slavery could be read, at least in outline, in the Runaway Docket of the Baltimore City Jail, where Slatter was the most regular customer.

Black people suspected of attempting to flee were routinely locked up in the city jail until their identities could be verified, their status as enslaved or free determined, and, if they were enslaved, their enslaver could be consulted. Most slaveholders, forewarned that their laborers desired to escape, would choose to cash them in. A note to Slatter's Pratt Street office would suffice. He or an associate would visit the city jail to take possession. It was one of innumerable ways in which local government aided and abetted the slave trade.

Richard Brown was a twenty-five-year-old man enslaved by Richard Selman, a Baltimore boat captain, when he was caught trying to run in July 1842. Selman contacted Slatter, they agreed on a price, and Slatter stopped by the city jail to pick up Brown, paying the jailers $5.69 for the cost of keeping Brown for eighteen days. Brown was then moved to Slatter's private jail, and in October he was among the seventy-seven people forced aboard the ship *Burlington* and transported to New Orleans, where he was sold to people he'd never met in a state he'd never seen for a life of unpaid labor far from his Maryland relatives.

The roll went on and on: Bill Smith, nineteen, had run from Edward Griffith but failed to make it to Pennsylvania; Griffith sold him off, and Slatter shipped him south aboard the *Tippecanoe*. Perry Tilghman, who was hired out by his enslaver to work aboard a steamboat, ran, was caught, and was redeemed by Slatter for $3.69 in jail fees plus another $2 for medical services from Dr. Dionysius Downes, the city jail's on-call physician. Tilghman, too, was sold by his enslaver and shipped south. So were Charles Lewis, Cornelius Brown, Evan Thomas—the list grew every week. For all of Slatter's years in Baltimore, the city jail fattened his bank account with a steady supply of prisoners.

What did Slatter think about such cases? Did he think about them at all? Unlike Thomas Smallwood, Slatter left no memoir to explain himself and his actions. If he wrote dutifully to his devout mother in Georgia and sent business and personal letters to his brother and son at his southern headquarters in New Orleans, the letters are not preserved, unlike much of Charles Torrey's correspondence. For anyone trying to understand Slatter's frame of mind about his business, his victims, and his enemies, the record is frustratingly scant, glimpsed through the occasional accounts of his visitors. Most of those who reported publicly on their visits were his antislavery opponents.

A Philadelphia abolitionist visiting in 1843 was appalled when Slatter introduced an enslaved boy of ten as "Jim Crow, jr." and "commanded" the boy to "jump Jim Crow"—to dance for the visitor. (The name of the minstrel-show character and his dance would be borrowed as a label for strict racial segregation.) "It was evidently done to draw off our attention from a contemplation of the real situation of these unhappy beings," the abolitionist wrote. If that was Slatter's purpose, however, he failed. The visitor continued: "In the fourth apartment, we beheld a heart-rending scene. A mother, with six little children clinging to her, the oldest, perhaps, not more than ten years of age, with a countenance expressive of more anxiety and despair than any I have ever looked upon. The fear of being separated from those dear objects of her love, seemed to drive her almost mad."

Hope Slatter paid her no notice. "Mr. Slatter looked upon the scene with as much indifference, as if they had been dumb beasts. How completely had his connection with the damning institution obliterated every spark of humanity from his heart!" Like so many others who encountered Slatter, this visitor was struck by his almost frantic quest for respect.

"Mr. Slatter was continually occupied in telling how comfortable and happy they were—how much enjoyment they derived from jumping, dancing, fiddling, gallanting, &c; and frequently remarked that they enjoyed more happiness than he or we did." Later in the tour, the abolitionist observed that "Mr. Slatter seemed very anxious to impress us with a sense of his kindness and humanity. 'Do you see any irons, or handcuffs, or instruments of torture here?'"

It was a low bar that Slatter had set for himself, and still his attempt to impress fell short. The abolitionist, who identified himself only as "S.D.H.," wrote that while he had heard and read much of the horrors of slavery, "the scene I witnessed in that prison, made me feel more than ever before the wickedness and the cruelty of the abominable system."

An unsympathetic northerner who toured Slatter's jail in 1844 found that his quest for social status was failing. The trader "has made himself very rich by his slave-trading, and makes a great display of wealth in the city," the visitor wrote. Naturally, "his money, like money everywhere, procures him some outward respect." But evidently not much. "I was gratified, however, to learn that he is regarded with contempt by all the respectable portion of the community. The slaveholders themselves despise his business; and were it not for his wealth, he would not find his way into any society but the lowest."

⊷═◉═⊶

Such censorious accounts of Slatter's business were exclusive to the abolitionist press. News clips in the major papers offer tantalizing but only fleeting glimpses of the man, treating him as just a Baltimore businessman of means and rarely mentioning how he earned his money.

Though Slatter does not seem to have been seriously interested in politics, he did take a sporting interest—he won a bet on the 1840 Pennsylvania governor's race and had to go to court to collect his $500. When the mangled body of a man Slatter enslaved, named Isaac, was found on the railroad tracks north of Baltimore, an inquest found that he had apparently fallen asleep on the tracks—possibly during an escape attempt—and was run over. Slatter got a little public notice when he bought the Repository, the exhibition and circus hall across the street from his jail, for $14,400, a sign that his profits were flowing nicely after a few years in Baltimore. In the summer of 1842, Slatter's "establishment," in *The Sun*'s polite locution, narrowly escaped destruction when a horse shed of the confectioner next door was engulfed in flames. Later that year, he advertised for "a genteel female of middle age" to "manage the affairs of a house"—was his wife ailing or planning to be away for an extended period? In the spring of 1844, a front wheel of his carriage fell off as he rode through downtown Baltimore, but fortunately the "ladies" riding inside were not injured.

Court records, in which Slatter's name regularly appeared, shed a little more light. Once, in an uncharacteristic breach of public decorum, he was spotted assaulting a Black woman in front of his jail on Pratt Street. He was forcing a man in shackles through the gate into his compound when the woman, perhaps a relative of the man, approached Slatter and challenged him. He made no reply, and the woman, evidently unwilling to give up on her intervention, spoke to Slatter's twenty-year-old daughter, Anne, who stood nearby.

The woman's persistence, and her daring in involving his daughter, enraged him. Two witnesses saw Slatter "come down the street, and strike the negro woman across the head and back several times"—the newspaper's trial report leaves uncertain whether he used a weapon or his hand, but he cut her head badly. A doctor was consulted and thought, from the volume of blood, that Slatter had cut an artery. The doctor summoned a "professor," a specialist, who managed to stanch the bleeding and dress the wound. Slatter was charged with assault, but at trial the judge seemed unmoved by his brutality. He asked Slatter whether he had paid compensation to the woman. He had not, so the judge gave him a suspended sentence on the condition that he pay her something.

On multiple occasions Slatter was found to have bought, and prepared to ship south, free African Americans who had been kidnapped and presented to him as enslaved. He always protested ignorance, and Baltimore newspapers often suggested that he, rather than the kidnapped person, was the swindlers' victim. In a few instances, friends of a person held in Slatter's jail managed to find an antislavery lawyer willing to pursue a freedom case, usually based on the peculiarities of state law.

For instance, Charles Stafford was enslaved in Delaware when his owner brought him to Baltimore to sell him to Slatter. But somehow Stafford managed to get a prominent lawyer, the nephew of the renowned local abolitionist Elisha Tyson, to intervene, arguing that Delaware law held that any enslaved person removed from the state automatically became free. The lawyer's argument prevailed, and what might have been a catastrophe for Stafford became a triumph.

On another occasion, a young woman named Charlotte Jane Strother was sold to Slatter by her enslaver in Winchester, Virginia, for $275 and brought to his Pratt Street jail. A Mississippi man, Dr. Thomas H. Buckner, stopped by, looking "to purchase a servant," and made a deal with Slatter: he would buy Charlotte Strother for $500, and sell the twelve-year-old girl he had brought from Mississippi, Dolly, to Slatter for $200. He paid Slatter the $300 difference and took Strother to his hotel. Strother somehow managed to contact lawyers willing to challenge her sale on the basis of an old Maryland law designed to discourage the import of African Americans: any enslaved person brought into Maryland from another state and sold in Maryland must be freed.

When the case ended up in court Slatter argued that Strother had been placed with Buckner only for a "trial"; any final sale would be completed only after she left with him for Mississippi. The jury deliberated for an impressive fifty-two hours, and then split 7–5 in favor of Slatter—Strother remained enslaved. At that point, Slatter's attorney made what sounded like a charitable proposal. Supporters of Charlotte Strother could raise the money to buy her freedom, the lawyer said, and Slatter himself would make the first contribution.

Upon closer inspection, of course, Slatter's proposal served his interest in multiple ways: he would be generously paid for Strother's freedom, pocketing a neat profit; he would avoid further legal wrangling; and his offer might even add a little burnish to his reputation. But Strother's lawyers rejected the idea, saying they planned to appeal the ruling. If the appeal was filed, Baltimore newspapers never reported it, and it seems likely that Strother went with Buckner to Mississippi.

And what about the fate of young Dolly? Of all the news reports on the Strother case, not one mentioned what became of this twelve-year-old girl, uprooted from any family she had in Mississippi, taken to a strange city, and turned over to Slatter. She had been imported to Maryland and sold, in evident violation of state law. Dolly is lost to history.

—◉—

A subtle insinuation lurked in the press coverage of Charlotte Jane Strother, who evidently lost her legal fight and ended up in Mississippi, the property of Thomas Buckner. She was described in one story as "an exceedingly bright mulatto" and in another as "*white,* or so nearly so that she would pass for *white,*" with a "fine figure" and "personal beauty." The suggestion, never explicitly stated, was that she was what was known as a "fancy girl," an attractive, often biracial young woman purchased not just for her labor but as a forced sexual partner. Smallwood and Torrey often called attention to such cases, and to the hypocrisy of white slaveholders who professed to be horrified by "miscegenation" while raping their captives and fathering biracial children. There is ample evidence that Slatter, like other traders, took full advantage of the demand for such young women.

In 1835, when Slatter was new in Baltimore and was operating from a local hotel, Owing's Globe Inn, he was quite explicit about his interest in purchasing "fancy girls": "N.B. I wish particularly to purchase several seamstresses and likely small fancy girls for nurses." The references to seamstresses and nurses were largely cover; the operative word was "fancy," as male slaveholders understood. In his 1931 book on the slave trade, Frederic Bancroft quoted a description of a sort of showroom for enslaved women advertised as "seamstresses" who were asked by the trader to stand and turn around when prospective buyers visited. "Do you wonder why the trader did not have them display their needle-work," Bancroft asked, "instead of their 'finely developed and graceful forms'?" The question was rhetorical.

In subsequent years, in keeping with his aspiration to be seen as a gentleman, Slatter toned down the ads. But there was little need to be indiscreet. Slaveholders knew they could get a premium when they sold an appealing young woman, and Slatter knew the markup in New Orleans would be substantial, often with a bidding war for the most beautiful. One especially tragic case was that of a fourteen-year-old girl named Mary Ellen Brooks, sold to Slatter's son Henry by a Baltimore woman for $400. Henry sold her to his father, and Hope Slatter sent her to New Orleans in February 1847 aboard a ship called *Zoe*. She was put on display in the showroom overseen by Slatter's brother Shadrack and then sold by a Slatter employee, James Blakeney, to a Louisianan for $600. A few weeks later she was dead of tuberculosis. The purchaser sued Slatter, claiming that Slatter should have known the teenager was ill and had defrauded him.

The lengthy legal battle over whether Slatter should refund the $600 was recorded in unusual detail in the archives of the Louisiana Supreme Court, and the picture that emerged from one hundred pages of testimony gradually complicated the case, making clear it was not merely a matter of an enslaved teenager who got a fatal illness. Mary Ellen Brooks, known as Nelly, was "a very pretty girl, a bright mulatto, with long curly hair and fine features," Slatter's agent Blakeney told the court. Under cross-examination by Slatter's attorney, he repeated the point: she "was a fancy girl: witness means by that a young handsome yellow girl of fourteen or fifteen with long curly hair." The purchaser, Buckner Payne, had taken the girl away for several hours, saying he wanted to show her to his wife and to a physician. And then the veil of euphemism was torn off and, with substantial money at stake, the brutal truth was stated outright: "Witness told Mr. Payne that her death had been hurried by improper intercourse between him and said girl, and that he had been so informed by the girl. Mr. Payne denied it, but the witness afterward ascertained that he, Payne, had no wife on the Plantation where he lived." When the Louisiana Supreme Court heard the case on appeal, the court avoided any mention of the allegation of rape. But it ruled against Payne, the purchaser, perhaps influenced by the evidence that he had bought the teenager as a sex slave.

Mary Ellen Brooks's story was an absolute horror—a girl of high school age, ailing and alone, sold from man to man and state to state, confined on a freezing ship in the coldest month of a year, put on display in a New Orleans showroom, and then purchased and immediately raped—before dying two weeks later. But word of her gruesome fate and the resulting lawsuit appears not to have reached the Baltimore newspapers, and Slatter, well protected from the consequences of his transaction by a troupe of lawyers, was not publicly tied to the death. Over the years, however, he could never entirely escape the moral taint of the "fancy girl" trade, one of the reasons he had such a struggle to attain the social station of a respectable businessman.

Two months after the death in New Orleans of Mary Ellen Brooks, President James K. Polk stopped in Baltimore for a day and a night on his way north to Philadelphia. Polk, a former House Speaker and Tennessee governor, was an absentee planter who before becoming president had moved his enslaved workers from his Tennessee plantation farther south to a new Mississippi plantation in part because too many people were escaping. While serving in the White House, he bought additional slaves, including thirteen children, arranging the purchases secretly so that the public would not learn that their president was responsible for separating children from their families.

Perhaps because of Polk's involvement in the slave trade, Slatter had gotten advance word of the president's travel plans and managed to insinuate himself into the event. The newspapers reported the next day that the president had been met at the rail station and transported from meeting to meeting with Baltimore's mayor and the United States attorney general in a horse-drawn carriage. The elegant transport had been provided by a citizen who wanted to do his part for his country, and perhaps for his reputation. "The President was conveyed in a magnificent carriage, owned by Mr. Hope H. Slatter," one newspaper reported, "and drawn by four richly caparisoned grays."

The slave power, in the person of Slatter, was cozying up to the government. But at a level far below that of the president, wherever police constables patrolled the streets, a cozy relationship between local authorities and the slave power was an old story.

POLICE AT WASHINGTON. — Robberies and fires abound, in Washington, more and more. Four house-breakings have occurred within ten days past. The Auxiliary Guard seem to have little effect in restraining crime. Doubtless our friend Samuel Weller, jr., was correct in saying that they were too busy in hunting *fugitives from crime*, to care for those who committed it.

Report in the *Albany Weekly Patriot*, April 20, 1843, probably written by Charles Torrey, confirming Thomas Smallwood's mockery [using his pen name] of Washington's Auxiliary Guard, a police unit, for ignoring crime and focusing on recapturing people fleeing slavery. [Courtesy of Boston Public Library]

9

Very Vigilant Officers!

The diary entry was a curious one. On June 4, 1842, Abel Brown, the antislavery preacher in Albany who had become Torrey and Smallwood's bold and steadfast ally, scribbled a few lines about his activities that day in neighboring Troy: "Went to Troy, to watch a constable from Baltimore, and aid the friends in Troy, in knowing and watching him."

We saw earlier how Robert Gilmor, the wealthy Baltimore merchant and wine seller, sent a police constable to try to track down and retrieve the enslaved members of his household staff who had headed north. But why would a police constable from Baltimore, a major city with plenty of crime, agree to travel 350 miles north to Troy at the behest of citizens, even rich ones? The answer sheds light on the dark early history of American policing: in both Washington and Baltimore, law enforcement was bound by the demand of slaveholders and slave traders that the government protect their investment in human property.

The "wretched constable" sent to retrieve a rich man's enslaved servants, Brown later reported, more than met his match when surrounded by abolitionists from Albany's Vigilance Committee. The constable, whom Brown does not name but derides as a "kidnapper," was trying to apprehend John Weston and the others who had fled Gilmor's mansion a couple of blocks north of Baltimore's harbor. But Brown and his associates turned the tables, gathering to heckle the constable and the local police officers helping him. The slave catcher ultimately had to return to Baltimore empty-handed, disappointing Gilmor and missing out on a generous reward.

But for Smallwood and Torrey, as well as for those they were trying to help, the police were a real and constant threat. In a region where slavery enjoyed the support of people with money and political clout, the police inevitably became the slaveholders' de facto agents, with many drawing a government salary for slave catching—and earning an additional cash reward from grateful slaveholders on the side.

The official rules for police officers were designed to protect slavery, and the harassment of Black people, free and enslaved, was built into daily routines. In Washington in 1808, for instance, police were required to break up any gathering of African Americans after 10 p.m., fining the participants. If the people rousted were enslaved, their enslavers would be fined—but the fines would be reimbursed, minus fifty cents, if the slaveholders gave police permission to whip the offenders. In 1818, Washington authorities approved the payment of half a dollar to any constable who whipped an enslaved person for violating city rules.

Such violence was built into the policing laws and rules all over Maryland as well. In Baltimore, the mayor's delineated duties from the early nineteenth century included "repaving and lighting the streets, lanes, and alleys," "regulat[ing] weights and measures"—and also "punish[ing] slaves corporeally for breaking of ordinances." In Prince George's County, where Smallwood was enslaved as a child, white men formed "slave patrols" to prevent escapes and enforce control, and the patrols gradually took on the formal powers and pay of policemen.

An 1831 court document in the Maryland State Archives bears the signatures of a dozen white slave patrollers who attest to the service of Alison F. Beale, who "hath discharged the duty of a constable, in patrolling and dispersing the tumultuous meetings of the negroes for the last twelve months." The very definition of "constable" appears to denote white men policing African Americans. An invoice given to the state of Maryland by a Prince George's constable, Daniel R. Dyer, for a year's service in 1842–43, as Smallwood was engineering escapes, covered a total of $62.66 for such items as "inflicting stripes" on "5 Negroes" and "bringing to jail six negro men committed as runaways."

Two officials signed the certification that Dyer "has acted as Constable with fidelity, patrolled, and dispersed tumultuous assemblages of negroes." The job seems to have entailed no enforcement of the law at all against white citizens.

As such documents suggest, when Smallwood and Torrey were working to send people north, they and those they were assisting had to be constantly on the alert for the police in every jurisdiction they passed through. Even as far away as Albany, fugitives were in danger of capture, as the enslaved people who had run from Baltimore's Gilmor discovered. It was in part because of this danger from slave catchers, whether police officers or private bounty hunters, that Smallwood urged the people he helped flee not to stop until they were in Canada, where laws that prohibited slavery generally guaranteed safety. Even so, Torrey reported in the Albany paper an unusual account of a Maryland policeman, unnamed, who had "gone to Canada to recover by stratagem several slaves and return them to their 'owners' in Maryland."

He and other antislavery editors had tried to warn fugitives in Canada about the agent from the south, and Torrey urged other newspapers to "sound the note of alarm, that the kidnapper may be foiled in his piratical attempts." It was a rare instance of an American police officer chasing the formerly enslaved beyond the country's borders, but it showed the well-compensated enthusiasm with which some constables pursued their prey.

⋅→═◑⬤◐═←⋅

In 1842, as Smallwood and Torrey were plotting escapes, policing in Washington took a major step toward expansion and professionalization. Vice President John Tyler had replaced the Whig president William

Henry Harrison, who had caught pneumonia and died just a month into his term, and crowds of disappointed Harrison supporters staged violent protests against the man they called "His Accidency" for the way he had gained the presidency. Some threw tar at the front of the president's house, and an intoxicated printer threw a stone at Tyler outside the mansion. Congress feared that things were getting out of hand, and in August voted "to establish an auxiliary watch for the protection of public and private property in the city of Washington."

The Auxiliary Guard, headed by a Rhode Islander and former city alderman named John H. Goddard, who will return in our story, became the new face of nighttime law enforcement in the city. Goddard was paid a handsome $1,000 a year and headed a force of fifteen men who worked overnight shifts for $30 or $35 a month. The new force, according to a colorful 1894 history of what would become D.C.'s Metropolitan Police, replaced their batons with a more formidable weapon: "Each officer carried a stick surmounted by an iron spear-head, intended originally to pry open doors in case of fire or when in pursuit of thieves. In the use of this instrument some of the officers became so proficient as to make it a formidable weapon either when used as a club or thrown as a javelin."

Though political rowdyism had led to the creation of the force, the Auxiliary Guard from the start focused its patrols intensively on both enslaved and free African Americans. It was headquartered in the city's Center Market off Pennsylvania Avenue, where the slave trade thrived. It enforced the 10 p.m. curfew for Black people, announced each night when the bell of the Perseverance Fire Company near the market was rung. "The ringing of the bell at 10 p.m. was of special importance to the colored people, as after that hour if out without a pass they were liable to arrest, fine, and flogging," the 1894 police history reported. The whippings were delivered either at the Auxiliary Guard's headquarters or at the whipping post at the city jail, a few blocks away on Judiciary Square.

The police history duly records the guard's earliest arrests, which make clear its intense focus on Washington's Black minority: "During the first two weeks the number of arrests was 46: 28 colored, 4 of whom were women; and 18 whites, of whom 4 were also females."

Smallwood watched the Auxiliary Guard take shape with deep skepticism and offered acid commentary in his Sam Weller dispatches. Whatever the guard's ostensible purpose, he repeatedly exposed its focus on the lucrative business of slave catching, which he suggested Congress had discreetly failed to list as an official purpose. In November 1842, just a few months after its creation, Smallwood called the guard "infamous" and noted that its statutory duty was "to protect this city from incendiaries and robbers, and to keep the public property safe, *and* for other—not named, purposes." These "not named" purposes had distracted it from its supposed goals, Smallwood wrote:

> There have been more stores broken open, and more incendiary attempts, since the Guard was established, than for many years before, in the same space of time! Do you ask why this is so? The answer is easy. The Guard, instead of doing their duty, have been prowling about, searching the houses of colored people in search of fugitive slaves, that they may get the reward offered for them! This fact they cannot deny. It is right that the people of the Free States should know for what purposes their Representatives have taxed them with the support of this infamous Guard, in the Nation's Capital.

Smallwood, as Sam Weller, named names. "The most active of this crew, are COX and LITTLE," he wrote, referring to police officers William Cox and John E. Little. He recounted the recent capture by Officer Cox of an Alexandria man who had fled his enslaver and hidden in a barn. Smallwood highlighted the financial incentives that distorted the priorities of the police officers. As a result of this single episode, Cox "will get $50 for his share of the reward, besides his $30 a month from the Government."

Smallwood also reported that the guard officers were seeking to profiteer off the nightly curfew for Black people, which could generate fines:

You are aware of the city law, requiring the watch to take up colored people who are found in the streets after 10 o'clock at night. The pale faced rowdies want the streets to themselves, after that hour! The colored people are so generally within doors, after that hour, that it is a matter of great regret, on the part of the watch, they lose their fees! So they talk of limiting the time of the colored people to 9 o'clock! No colored person can pass after 10 o'clock, no matter how respectable he is, unless he is a tool in their hands to betray his own color. This then, is a most important part of the duty of the Auxiliary Guard, which a *Whig Congress* imposed upon us, and to sustain which they tax the people $7500 a year!

Eight months later, Smallwood renewed his attack on the guard, which he said had developed "*a new branch of business*" by stationing officers outside Black churches during evening services, hoping to catch worshippers who had stayed late and broke the 10 p.m. curfew. "I wish to bestow a passing notice on the AUXILIARY GUARD," he wrote. "Don't let the people forget these scoundrels!" He pointed out a particular outrage in an ostensibly Christian town: if the evening church parishioners were enslaved, "they are whipped, for the CRIME *of attending on the public worship of* God, a few moments later than 10 o'clock!" He again named Officers Cox and Little as the most eager profiteers, getting very personal this time in his vituperation.

"Little is too lazy to support his family in any other way; and he is as famous for administering *discipline* to his wife! as he is for negro hunting! How long will the people of the North support these scoundrels?" Once again, Smallwood was hidden in plain sight in the center of Washington's grapevine, picking up the gossip, and perhaps more solid evidence, that exposed the perfidy of his enemies and publishing it for all to see.

From Albany, where he was working in his editor's post, Torrey added his own backing for Smallwood's attacks, reporting that robberies and arson fires were proliferating in Washington—including four house

break-ins in ten days. "Doubtless our friend, Samuel Weller jr. was correct in saying that they were too busy in hunting *fugitives from crime,* to
care for those who committed it," he wrote. Both Torrey and Smallwood
claimed that they, or their allies, had taken advantage of the corruption
of Auxiliary Guard officers by paying them to ignore escapes. "We have
bought up a few of the *Guard,*" Smallwood wrote. Torrey later wrote that
most members of the Auxiliary Guard "can be bribed to help people
off"—that is, help them escape slavery—"for $5 a head."

Torrey also asserted that nearly the entire guard had been recruited
from among "the *old professional slave* catchers of the District," whom he
called "this class of human monsters." Whether they really bribed members of the guard and whether most of its members had been slave catchers is hard to know for sure. The claims might have been propaganda
aimed at undermining the guard's morale and sowing suspicion inside
a police force that was among Torrey and Smallwood's chief adversaries. But they were certainly in a position to know which Washington
policemen were bribable and which had made a business of recapturing
fugitives in the past.

The chronicles of Baltimore's early policing tell essentially the same story
as the Washington accounts: a growing corps of night watchmen, under-
paid, regularly accused of corruption and devoted to the more lucrative
enterprise of slave catching. On a November morning in 1840, James
Ducket attempted a bold flight from Baltimore, where he was enslaved
by a woman named Mrs. Hanna. He followed the example of Frederick
Douglass—he boarded a train. But Ducket, who was about twenty-one,
was being watched closely by a white police officer named John Zell, who
had been surveilling the depot at Baltimore's Basin to spot anyone who
looked like they might be fleeing slavery. Zell, from whose exasperated
complaint Smallwood would later take the term "underground railroad,"
testified that he had seen a free Black man named John Robinson confer

with Ducket before approaching the ticket office and buying a ticket, which he then handed over to Ducket. Zell followed Ducket aboard the Philadelphia-bound train, arrested him at the next stop—and delivered him to Hope Slatter's jail.

John Robinson, who had dared to help a fellow Black man, was also arrested and charged with "enticing, persuading and assisting" an escape from slavery. A poignant detail at Robinson's trial was Ducket's attempt to return the favor Robinson had done him: on the stand, Ducket insisted that he had never seen Robinson before and that another man, whose name he did not know, had bought the ticket at his request. Robinson was nonetheless found guilty and sentenced to three years in prison for his generous act. As for Ducket, he was purchased by Slatter from Mrs. Hanna, who presumably concluded he might run away again. Slatter shipped James Ducket south on the *Ewarkee* as soon as the trial was over.

John Zell fared much better. He earned a glowing write-up in *The Sun*, which called the apprehension of Ducket and Robinson an "Important Arrest" and lavished praise on the constable and his partner, Archibald G. Ridgely, for taking on the growing problem of escapes by the enslaved. "Zell and Ridgely, most active and vigilant officers, becoming cognizant of this, determined to ascertain the mode of escape, and terminate the evil," wrote *The Sun*, as always reliably sympathetic to slaveholders. Though the newspaper didn't mention it, Zell surely collected from Mrs. Hanna a handsome reward for Ducket's capture; rewards at the time ran from $50 to $200 for the return of a healthy young man.

Torrey found that Baltimore police officers sometimes exploited the enslaved to wring extra money out of slaveholders. On Sundays, when enslaved people traveled into the city from neighboring counties to attend church and visit relatives, police officers would demand to see their "pass," signed by an enslaver, that permitted people in bondage to leave their immediate neighborhood. Anyone who had forgotten their pass would be locked in the city jail, or sometimes in a slave trader's jail, and the officer "says nothing about it till the master offers his reward;

and then Mr. Constable coolly pockets the reward of his knavery." On top of that, Torrey wrote, because the person locked up was now often considered a suspected runaway, he was "commonly sold to the traders at a low price, and the trader, out of pure gratitude (!) gives the officer another fee."

Perhaps even worse was another corrupt police practice—paying Black collaborators to "inveigle" enslaved people to run away and then give them a place to hide. But it was a trap set by police officers, who in a few days, Torrey said, "are ready, of course, to hand over the poor victim of their arts, and pocket the reward, besides getting praise as *very vigilant officers!*" Torrey even claimed he had exposed a spy, in the pay of the police, who had joined an antislavery "vigilance committee" in the north, presumably to feed information to slave catchers about fugitives and their whereabouts. "He is not *now* on the committee," Torrey wrote.

Such schemes were likely quite familiar to John Zell and his longtime partner Ridgely. Both were veterans of the night watch, but as they rose in seniority they began simultaneously to operate a private police agency to supplement their salaries, usually by tracking and capturing runaways. Zell in particular was the most prominent Baltimore constable and private investigator in the 1830s and 1840s, and was notorious—or "active and vigilant," in *The Sun*'s view—for chasing down fugitives from slavery.

Zell's grandfather, a Pennsylvania slaveholder, had fought in the American Revolution. His father had served in a militia that helped put down the Whiskey Rebellion, the 1794 tax revolt in western Pennsylvania. John, born in 1801, initially opted for less martial work: he followed other family members into the grocery business in Baltimore. But his store failed, and in 1833 he joined the city's night watch, where he appears to have made quite an impression, often starring in newspaper accounts that featured daring arrests and imaginative investigations of murder, arson, and robbery.

It is not hard to detect in such stories the familiar symbiosis of a cop eager to share tales of his heroism and reporters happy to get a good story. But Zell's dual role for more than a decade as city police constable and principal of a private detective agency left plenty of room for self-enrichment, and his integrity came repeatedly into question.

A month after he helped convict Robinson and send Ducket south, Zell was charged criminally with taking fifty dollars to let an accused pickpocket escape. Because the pickpocket had subsequently fled to Philadelphia and conveniently failed to show up for trial, Zell and colleagues with whom he had shared the bribe got off. But the rival constable who had made the original arrest, Madison Jeffers, wrote a blistering letter to *The Baltimore Clipper* making clear that he believed that justice had been miscarried and that Zell was thoroughly corrupt. In any case, Zell's energetic pursuit of fugitives sometimes strayed into collaborating with slave catchers who crossed the line into kidnapping, helping to seize African Americans in Pennsylvania who were free or whose legal status was in dispute.

⟡

In late 1842, the annual report of the Albany Vigilance Committee singled out Zell and Ridgely as essentially the leading police slave catchers of the Chesapeake-to-Canada escape route. It asserted that after antislavery crowds had repeatedly harassed and intimidated constables who had traveled to northern New York from Maryland in pursuit of fugitives, the slave catchers grew discouraged and came north less often. The report, likely written by Torrey and Abel Brown, claimed victory over the slave-catching police:

> The slave hunter has often been here, and in Troy, the past summer; but in every instance these villains have found the friends of freedom so determined, or public feeling so hostile to them, that any legal enforcement of their bloodhound claim was utterly hopeless; and they have given it up. Such is the state of feeling now in the free states generally, that the most experienced slave hunters, like Constables ZELL & RIDGELY of

Baltimore, have been known to say that it was in vain to pursue a slave that had 24 hours the start; for the abolitionists would protect him.

This boasting certainly reflected genuine victories, but the police had deep financial and political backing from the slave power. As Torrey would learn, it was far too soon to declare victory over the likes of Constable John Zell.

In a satirical dispatch to the *Albany Weekly Patriot*, June 15, 1843,
Smallwood, posing as Sam Weller, bestows on himself a grand title as
overseer of the mythical underground railroad he had named the previous year. [Courtesy of Boston Public Library]

10

◦•◦•◦

Between Two Fires

In mid-1843, judging from the jaunty pronouncements of Samivel Weller Jr. in the *Albany Weekly Patriot,* Thomas Smallwood was feeling extraordinarily confident about his personal war on slavery. And why not? For more than a year he had worked to deliver enslaved men, women, and children from bondage. He had evaded all the traps set by the slaveholders and defied a $2,000 reward for his exposure and capture. He had spied on the aggrieved and bewildered white slave-owning citizens of the nation's capital, Baltimore, and nearby counties as they puzzled over their losses. He had fired off letter after letter to Albany cheerfully chronicling the escapes, celebrating the escapees, and ridiculing their (suddenly former) enslavers. He had given the urgent passage north its name, already spreading through newspapers across the country: the underground railroad.

As it would turn out, his bravado was an act, a performance, a willed projection of cockiness. But what an act!

In his latest letter from Washington to the *Albany Weekly Patriot,* published on June 15, 1843, Smallwood celebrated the latest escapes and bestowed on himself a wonderfully fanciful title:

> Mr. Printer—Here I am, back to my post, as general agent of
> all the branches of the National Underground Railroad, Steam

Packet, Canal and Foot-it Company. Business begins to be
very brisk. I have sent off no less than nine passengers, from
this city, in less than a week! The most of them have taken the
Erie Branch, Steam Flying Machine, so that you will not see
them, or they you, unless the wind blows them very much out
of their course.

Smallwood went out of his way to taunt the most notable of the region's slave-catching constables. He name-checked Constable John Zell
and his associates, who had recently charged a Black Baltimorean named
Meade with organizing escapes—and possibly with being Sam Weller
himself. But at trial, Meade had been found not guilty. Smallwood
claimed he himself had been so brazen as to walk right past Zell's private
detective office with a fugitive, Richard Brown, previously the property
of John Waters, in tow:

And the result of [Meade's] acquittal has been to give a new
impulse to business. Our agents *were* becoming a *little*, very
little, too bold; and while we were diverted to see the poor
police officers, Zell, Ridgely, and Hays, make such a blunder
in their man, it seemed to show us the need of more boldness,
which is the best caution. So the other day, when I took Richard Brown to Baltimore, we went and laughed in their faces, as
one of them was reading Waters' advertisement. Poor puppies!
I have taken a *load*, at mid-day, right by their office, and the
lazy dogs didn't look up!

Did Smallwood really stroll up to Zell's office at 15 Mercer Street, a
few blocks north of Baltimore's Basin, accompanied by a wanted man
whose enslaver was offering a reward for his capture? Had he driven
a wagonful of fugitives past the constable's office one day at noon as a
lark? Perhaps these claims were pure invention, intended to send tremors
though the slave power, to make the slave-catching constables look over

their shoulders for their audacious adversary. Or perhaps Smallwood had indeed chosen to flaunt his invisibility as a free Black man, to deploy that superpower that allowed him to spy and eavesdrop on his white targets and opponents.

In either case, he was taking obvious pleasure in the pseudonymous safety from which he could call dangerous constables "dogs" and "poor puppies"—and inform them that they had missed the chance to grab Richard Brown, who Smallwood said was safe in the Canadian city of Kingston with relatives who had escaped earlier.

In the same letter to the *Patriot,* Smallwood recounted the brief stories of Brown and eight more of the people he had recently helped north. One of the fugitives, James Berry, had come all the way from Norfolk, Virginia, connecting with Smallwood after reaching Washington. Smallwood, with acid sarcasm, speculated that perhaps Berry had chosen to give up the advantages of enslavement because he had not read about them in the work of one of slavery's most prominent defenders, Thomas Roderick Dew, then president of William & Mary in Williamsburg, Virginia. Dew argued that love bound the slave to the master, with a relation comparable to that of child and parent.

"Alas! He could not read!" Smallwood wrote of Berry's failure to embrace Dew's glowing portrait of slavery. He didn't need to explain that it had been illegal for more than a decade to teach enslaved people in Virginia to read. Torrey added a parenthetical note to Smallwood's letter: Berry, too, had reached Canada.

Smallwood bragged about how, during his return from leading this group of people north, he had stopped by Harford County in northeast Maryland (which he, or the printer, spelled "Hartford")—and helped another four men escape! His account named names, as usual:

> One result of my visit has been several indications of *powers of locomotion* not before exercised. Charles Smith thought he had toiled for Thomas Tyers, of Hartford, for nothing, quite long enough. Bill Dagin had the same view of his relations to Wm.

Bell, of the same place. Their masters are pretty clever fellows, a little fierce, at times, especially Bell. But liberty is sweet. David Colmon, of the same place, thought proper to leave Wm. Pites; and left. Henry Guidon's service had no charms for Stephen Hall, without pay! *Steve* is a queer fellow. The way he rolled up his eyes, half tearful, half mirthful, when he crossed the old Mason and Dixon's line, was funny!

Smallwood claimed to have seen such emotional crossings from slave state to free state many times: "Oh, how many scenes of deep interest I have witnessed, on that spot! Last year a large company were so affected that they embraced and kissed the stone that marks the line of Pennsylvania, weeping over it and then shouting out for joy of heart!"

By a rough estimate, Smallwood and his friends might have helped three hundred people go north to freedom by this time. For months, with Torrey in Albany, Smallwood had worked in Washington largely on his own, with the occasional assistance of his wife and Torrey's sympathetic landlady, Mrs. Padgett. "I continued to defy detection, and sent them off in gangs; never less than a dozen," he would write in his memoir. But even as he projected an insouciant confidence, as if he might keep draining slaveholders' wealth for years to come, the reality was far bleaker. Even as he boasted about his invention, the underground railroad, he feared that his leading role in it might be nearing an end.

⊷══◉══⊷

By the time he was mocking John Zell and the slaveholders of Harford County in mid-1843, Thomas Smallwood's enemies were multiplying and closing in. There were the separate, substantial rewards on offer in both Washington and Baltimore for the unmasking of those who were assisting escapes. Slaveholders who had received gratis copies of the *Tocsin of Liberty* or *Albany Weekly Patriot* with a Sam Weller letter singling them out for mockery began to compare notes on who might be depriving them of their unpaid laborers. And the Albany connection was a key to the hunt for the real Sam Weller; Torrey had been well known in Washington and was now the editor of the newspaper recording the escapes, so anyone who knew of Smallwood and Torrey's close association might have directed their suspicions at the one still in Washington.

After months puzzling over just who might be their silver-tongued scourge, the cleverest of the police were beginning to keep a particular watch on the shoemaker and family man living in the southeast corner of Washington. As Smallwood later recalled:

> For several reasons the entire arrangement, management and setting off those gangs forward, I had to attend to myself, but it was not practicable for me to travel with them always, because suspicion had already pointed to me, and I could not be absent from Washington without its been known; therefore my absence at the times of the departure of those gangs might have led to my arrest, and an investigation, resulted in my conviction. Besides, I was the sole proprietor of the so-called underground railroad in that section, it having been started without the assistance of any earthly being save Torrey, myself, my wife, and the Lady with whom he boarded. Torrey having gone North the burden and responsibility of consequences rested entirely on me, therefore I had to watch every moment as with an eagle's eye.

Worse than white suspicions was the fact that some Black acquaintances whom Smallwood had trusted as allies had turned out to be traitors, in the pay of the slave power. He described his predicament in vivid prose: "I had been for some time, between two fires," Smallwood wrote, "my own color, on the one hand, through envy and for the sake of filthy lucre were trying to betray me; while on the other hand, the slaveholders were offering large rewards for the detection of the person or persons who were thus robbing them of their goods and chattels."

As the number of people who dealt directly with Smallwood grew, word of his clandestine operation naturally spread. Inevitably some spotted an opportunity. People acting as go-betweens would demand from enslaved people a large payment to connect them with Smallwood—and then, at the last moment, knowing the would-be escapees were desperate, demand still more money to arrange a meeting. Free Black people who posed as supporters would, for money or to curry favor, tip off a slaveholder or a constable to the whereabouts of people hiding out in anticipation of making a run.

It was unavoidable that the wealth and power of the slaveholders and slave catchers, and the poverty and vulnerability of most African Americans, would lead to some easy marks. Smallwood would later recount three cases of treachery that endangered or sacrificed some of those desperate to escape while putting Smallwood himself in grave danger.

In one case, Smallwood had recruited a Black neighbor named George Lee to hide fugitives in his "stable loft" and to guide escaping parties from Washington to the first "place of deposit" in or near Baltimore. For a while, Lee was a reliable partner. But then he saw an opportunity to exploit the frightened and desperate runaways, who in many cases had been scraping together savings for months before making their escape. "Lee turned out to be both swindler and traitor," Smallwood wrote, "for he went about among the slaves collecting money in my name from them, appropriating it to his own use."

Lee's greed then grew still more poisonous: by Smallwood's account, he essentially cashed in two men entrusted to his care, alerting slave catchers to their location in return for a payoff.

Smallwood accused another supposed Black ally, Benjamin Lanham, of a similar betrayal. Two men and a woman on the run had met Smallwood on a Saturday night, as he had directed, at an obscure spot on the shore of the Eastern Branch, the river that ran near Smallwood's home. But they had left behind a fourth person, another fugitive who was in extreme danger, and instead of arriving at 8 p.m., as Smallwood had directed, they reached the spot at midnight. It was two hours after the curfew for African Americans, making the passage through Washington hazardous, and too late to reach a Baltimore safe house. So Smallwood led them to Benjamin Lanham, who on multiple occasions had allowed people awaiting a trip north to hide in his house. The plan was to unite the three runaways with the desperate fourth fugitive and depart a few nights later.

But when the appointed time came, Smallwood discovered that the three fugitives were no longer at Lanham's house—they had been seized and delivered to the slave jail operated on the Mall by the capital's leading slave trader, William H. Williams. Such a disaster might have resulted from any number of lapses: a nosy neighbor, an indiscretion of one of the fugitives, an observant police patrolman. But as it happened, a woman had seen Lanham approach William H. Williams's house and converse with him through an open window—and had then confronted Lanham in church about this suspicious exchange. Her account left little doubt as to Lanham's role in consigning the three to an awful fate, most likely sale south.

For Smallwood, there was only one consolation from this disaster: the three people betrayed to the slave trader by Lanham "could not describe me to the slave catchers, for I was only with them in the dark." They knew his last name, he wrote, "yet as there were other Smallwoods in Washington, they could not find the guilty one, therefore I escaped the snare laid for me in that piece of treason."

The third case of treachery was the predictable result of an old feud. Abraham Cole was the minister whom Smallwood had denounced in public and later sued for defamation. But the lawsuit clearly had not deterred his longtime rival. Now that Smallwood was under suspicion, Cole and his friends targeted him again. "They would try to make it appear among the respectable portion of my own color, that I was a great traitor to my race, by circulating the most absurd falsehoods about me; while on the other hand, they would try underhandedly to point me out to the slaveholders as being the man who was aiding in the escape of their slaves," Smallwood wrote.

Of all the attacks Smallwood weathered, the accusation that he was somehow exploiting or betraying the enslaved clearly stung him the most. He was later at pains to defend his record, noting that he had spent his own money on his underground railroad activities and had certainly never profited. At times, he noted, he had a dozen or more fugitives from slavery hidden around Washington:

> The united rewards for them would amount to from six to eight hundred, and a thousand dollars. . . . But it is passing strange, and not be credited by any reasonable, just, and un-prejudiced person, that I should for a paltry sum of a few dollars or pounds become an enemy to my brethren for whom I have almost worn myself out, while those who have had the audacity to accuse me, (who have stood in the midst of dangers for my race, beset on every side by enemies,) stand off at a respectful distance, out of harm's way, and like cowardly curs bark at slaveholders, but do nothing more.

Smallwood's detractors often suggested that he must be rolling in money from white abolitionists. Certainly, the abolitionists would have done well to invest in what had become an effective pipeline out of slavery. But while Torrey may have gotten some help from Gerrit Smith or other northern allies during his months in Washington, it appears that Smallwood received no such support. He seems to have gotten the worst of both fantasy and reality: rumors of abolitionist money, "filthy lucre" in Smallwood's words, drew unscrupulous people who were quite ready to loot the escape operation for whatever they could get; but the actual expenses of travel north had to be scraped together from his own meager resources and those of the people he was trying to help.

Referring to one of the betrayers, George Lee, Smallwood wrote that Lee and others "thought that I was acting in what I was doing as agent for the abolitionists, hence for the purpose of supplanting me, they commenced a correspondence with my friend G. in Baltimore, who acted the same part there that I did in Washington," a reference to his ally Jacob Gibbs. Gibbs, he said, saw through the "underhanded piece of business" and ignored the interlopers. With pride, but a justified pride, Smallwood declared: "I was the establisher of that underground railroad" and "as independent of the Abolitionists in my operations as oil is of water, with one or two exceptions. And with regard to pecuniary aid afforded me by them it was not the amount of one farthing."

Smallwood's fury at the web of jealous and untrustworthy associates surrounding him was unmistakable. It was one thing to be in peril from slaveholders, slave traders, and their hired hands. But to be put in danger of failure, arrest, or worse by his fellow African Americans was, he felt, too galling.

⤞⟞◉⟝⤝

For a time, Smallwood "evaded all the snares that were set for me," taking additional precautions every time he organized an escape. He stopped accompanying most groups escaping north, delegating that task to others. He chose a new gathering spot in or around Washington for each departing group of fugitives and visited the day before to make sure the location was suitable. He asked that each fleeing adult travel separately to the departure point, ideally from different directions, to avoid stirring suspicions.

A curious document in the Washington archives makes clear how worried Smallwood had become. In October 1842, ten months after he had met Torrey and begun arranging escapes, Smallwood had persuaded his former enslaver, John Ferguson, to accompany him to the courthouse. There, in the clerk's office, Ferguson completed the official paperwork attesting to Smallwood's freedom: "John B. Ferguson, in consideration of five dollars, manumits, his Negro man Thomas Smallwood, who is forty two." The simple statement might seem puzzling at first, because by his own repeated and detailed testimony, Smallwood had completed the purchase of his freedom by 1830. At this point he had lived as a free resident of Washington for a dozen years, and on file in Prince George's

County was the 1815 manumission that promised Smallwood his freedom at the age of thirty. For years, the two men, who seemed to be mutually respectful neighbors, had not found it necessary to file in court a new legal document proving what they both knew to be true.

But by late 1842 things had changed. Smallwood was playing with fire. He risked his own freedom every time he left his neighborhood to guide a party to Baltimore or beyond. He might well have to prove his freedom to any suspicious white person, whether a constable, a bounty hunter, or merely a busybody. And so he seems to have decided that he needed an up-to-date document establishing his freedom, one he could carry every time he left home or when he possibly had to follow his own path north.

Through the first half of 1843 Smallwood kept up a steady succession of escapes despite his growing sense of danger. But finally he decided that his extra precautions were not enough:

> Seeing that through the treachery of some of my color I could be of no further service to my poor slave brethren, and that the cloud of treachery began to thicken, and get blacker and blacker over me, and that Washington was no longer a place of safety for me, I determined to seek a resting place in some other clime, and I was convinced that the place could only be found . . . to my satisfaction, in the British dominions, where the laws are equal, and know no difference between man and man on account of color.

He would follow the advice he had given to scores of others headed north: you will not be safe on the territory of the United States. In other words, he was headed for Canada.

⌖

On June 30, 1843, Thomas Smallwood left Washington, presumably traveling openly by train and boat with the protection of the manumission paper Ferguson had signed. He made stops in Philadelphia and Albany, mainly to make sure his abolitionist allies there did not believe any of the scurrilous claims that had been made by his enemies, and arrived in Toronto on July 4.

In 1852, Frederick Douglass would ask in a famous oration, "What, to the American slave, is your 4th of July?" Smallwood, landing on British territory nearly a decade earlier, pondered the same question, as he would recall in his memoir published in 1851, a year before Douglass's speech:

> How different were my feelings that day to what they would have been had I been in the States. There I would have been compelled painfully to witness as I had done for many years their hypocritical demonstrations in honor of a day, which they say, brought to them freedom; but I sorrowfully knew that it was in honor of a day that brought to me, and my race among them, the most degrading, tyrannical and soul-withering bondage that ever disgraced the world or a nation. But here, I was on Canada's free soil, and I may rejoice and give thanks to God in honor of that day, it being the day on which I first put my feet in a land of true freedom, and equal laws.

It was a reconnaissance trip, to see whether Toronto might be an accommodating home for Smallwood, his wife, their four children, and a fifth on the way. He liked what he saw, but after visiting several small Black communities in Canada West (now Ontario), he hurried home, even as he concluded it would not be home for much longer.

"I speedily returned to Washington," he wrote, "there to have another contest with slaveholders, and treacherous colored persons, and prepare to take leave of that mock metropolis of freedom, and sink of iniquity."

The same disposition is shown in the ordinary intercourse of white people with colored men and women, both bond and free. The *tone of command* is that which is almost always employed, in addressing them, no matter what the subject may be. To speak to them with respect, would be to *descend* to their level, in the view of the community. If the tones used are kind, they are still the indications of the kindness of an acknowledged superior, towards one accustomed to be treated as an inferior, for no other reason than their different color. The difference between the atmosphere of Washington and one of our northern cities, in this respect, strikes the mind at once, and with great force. And there is a degree of timidity, and a want of self-respect, apparent in the manners of a large part of the people of color, which very naturally results from this state of things; and which would soon disappear, as it has in northern cities, under a different course of treatment.—There are exceptions, it is true, and marked ones; but just sufficient to confirm the general truth of what I have said.

Yours for *equal rights*,
SAMIVEL WELLER, JR.

Thomas Smallwood, writing as Sam Weller, makes a serious comment in the *Albany Weekly Patriot* in 1843 about what would later be called racism. Having lived in slavery and then as a free Black man, Smallwood was an astute observer of both crude and subtle discrimination. [Courtesy of Boston Public Library]

11

A Fugitive from Justice

If Smallwood returned to Washington looking for "another contest with the slaveholders," he got one—and a dire contest with the police as well. In his absence of several weeks, the gossip mill had churned with suspicions about his role in escapes. "On arriving there, I learned that it was rumored about that I was the person that was getting away the slaves and that my visit to the North was to make arrangements to further that object," he recalled later. "I found it therefore necessary to make speedy arrangements for leaving."

Even as Smallwood worked on his plan to move his family to Toronto, the Sam Weller letters continued without interruption in the *Albany Weekly Patriot*. But no longer were there long lists of people who had fled and gleeful ridicule of their former enslavers. Now the letters grew more somber.

One passage illustrated Smallwood's dilemma as he drew more attention. He denounced a navy officer, a Captain Pendegrass, who had hired an enslaved woman from "the notorious C——s, of Maryland—notorious for their severity to their slaves"—almost certainly the Carroll family, one of the most prominent in the state. The woman had been separated from her children when she was sent by the family to the Navy Yard in Washington, where Pendegrass was stationed. On the advice of Mr. C "not to let her want for whipping," Smallwood wrote, Pendegrass regularly lashed the woman, evidently in public: "Is he not a fine specimen of a Naval Commander? WOMAN-WHIPPING IN THE NAVY-YARD AT WASHINGTON! How would it sound in London or Rome! Why, the arch Inquisitor would shake his sides for laughter, in scorn of these pretenders to republican freedom."

Smallwood's exposure of brutality and his public humiliation of the perpetrator by name, along with the broader point about the hypocrisy of American pretensions to be a land of the free, were vintage Sam Weller. But by writing in such detail about someone living just steps from his house, the man known as "Smallwood of the Yard" surely risked giving his enemies another clue as to the identity of the pseudonymous writer who was instigating escapes and tormenting the enslavers.

Though his focus had generally been on the plight of the enslaved, Smallwood now more often took up for his fellow free African Americans, in passages that underscored his decision to emigrate. Once he reported that while visiting Washington's city jail to witness the sale of a woman because her enslaver had run up debts, he saw a free Black man brought in and locked in a cell. He had no admiration for the man himself, whose face was bruised and whose clothes were soiled, "very evident marks of the drunken loafer species." But in his usual spy role, Smallwood found himself deeply disturbed by the conversation he overheard between constable and jailer: they made it clear that this free man was to be illegally stripped of his freedom and sold into bondage.

"He was committed to prison as a *runaway slave*," Smallwood recalled, a lawless outrage that captured the impaired citizenship of free Black people. "This is a sample of the petty legal oppressions to which the free colored man is occasionally exposed in this city." Treatment of Black residents, he said, "depended very much on the *caprice* of the constables," including their demands for payoffs that amounted to "barefaced highway robbery." Smallwood enlarged on this theme, clearly reflecting the disrespect he had personally experienced:

The same disposition is shown in the ordinary intercourse of white people with colored men or women, both bond and free.

> *The tone of command* is that which is almost always employed,
> in addressing them, no matter what the subject may be. To
> speak to them with respect, would be to *descend* to their level,
> in the view of the [white] community. If the tones used are
> kind, they are still the indications of the kindness of an ac-
> knowledged superior, towards one accustomed to be treated as
> an inferior, for no other reason than their different color.

Smallwood was a perceptive analyst of what would only later be
called racism. He was growing steadily less able to tolerate not only the
crimes of enslavement but the broader ideology of white supremacy that
underlay them. He was scathing about "this Metropolis of *free* and *christian* America; whose free institutions (!!) are so much admired," asking,
"Do Americans think that the rest of the world have not sense enough
to see and despise their hypocrisy?"

Signing off on another Weller dispatch, he expressed regret that
"business"—the business of escapes—forced him to pause in his writing. "I must even leave my pen, which is a matter of regret when I can
expose the knavery of the robbers and tyrants who rule this capital of
the nation," he wrote. "I do love to see them snarl as they walk about the
District, and note their wincing under my lashes." But he continued to
bear witness to the slave trade: "Why, a fortnight ago, last Tuesday, no
less than SIXTY HUMAN BEINGS were carried right by the *Capitol*
yard, to the slave ship. The MEN were chained in couples, and fastened
to a log chain, as is common in this region. The women walked by their
side. The little children were carried along in wagons."

For months, Smallwood had been conscious of the increasing attention he was getting from the police—particularly the Auxiliary Guard
that had been formed the previous year and that he had repeatedly lambasted, wearing his Sam Weller mask, as a corrupt tool of the slave power.
Now, in the fall of 1843, on the eve of his planned departure with his
family, as he gathered in his house one more group of prospective northern travelers, he suddenly found the house surrounded by the guard and
its leader, John Goddard.

According to what Smallwood later learned, a snitch had put him in danger: a man named James Williams had told his enslaver, a white butcher named Charles Miller, that Smallwood was about to lead a group to Canada, and Miller had tipped off the Auxiliary Guard. With the guard posted outside, a policeman Smallwood knew personally in the small world of Washington stepped inside. "Thomas," he said, "I have been instructed in consequence of information that you intend starting for Canada with some slaves to come and search your house."

Most of the ten or twelve people gathered in Smallwood's house had apparently not yet been missed by their enslavers; they were able to meet by taking advantage of the limited freedom of movement often permitted people in urban bondage. But one woman was in particular jeopardy, probably because she had been officially reported missing and presumed to have run away. "To get her out of the house unperceived was a matter of great importance," he wrote. As the policeman searched the house and Goddard and his crew kept watch outside, several of the women present somehow contrived to spirit her away. "That was speedily accomplished by some females, who took her through a back door into the garden, and concealed her in some corn." Even in the city, it seems, a backyard corn patch big enough to conceal a runaway was nothing unusual.

After the third search of the house, Smallwood recalled, "the black-guard Goddard came in and said, 'Smallwood, I understand you are going off to Canada and intend to take slaves with you.' He then proceeded to examine those in the house as to whether they were chattels or free negroes." But Goddard could not prove they were planning an escape and did not detain them. In fact, Smallwood later wrote with sardonic wit, the group had been "preparing to leave for Canada the next morning, and take a final leave of such beautiful scenes of republican freedom."

◦⟫⊙⟪◦

After this brush with disaster, Smallwood rescheduled his family's departure for October 3, 1843. But before they left Washington, there was some crucial paperwork to obtain, and Smallwood called on John Ferguson one more time. Ferguson, who a year earlier had signed the paper confirming Smallwood's manumission, once again went to the Washington courthouse, this time completing a Certificate of Freedom for the rest of the family—on the very day of their departure. "John B. Ferguson swears," said the document, "that Elizabeth Smallwood, who is about thirty-five years old, and her five children, Thomas Smallwood, who is about twelve, Catharine Smallwood, who is about ten, Susan Smallwood, who is about six, and William Smallwood, who is about five, and Celestine Smallwood, who is about one month old, were all born free."

Why had they chosen to collect the freedom certificate in the last hours before their departure? Was it a result of last-minute jitters, since Smallwood seems to have planned to depart without a freedom certificate until the visit from Goddard and the Auxiliary Guard? Perhaps, but any free African American traveling interstate knew it was critical to be able to prove one's freedom, especially on trains and ships.

Was it a mere matter of calendar, finding a time when Ferguson and the Smallwoods could meet at the courthouse? Did Ferguson procrastinate until the Smallwoods told him he could put off the paperwork no longer? Whatever the reason, they completed the courthouse visit, said goodbye to Ferguson, the reluctant enslaver who had played such an essential role in Smallwood's life, and headed for the wharves, where the steamship *Columbia* waited to take the family to Baltimore. The plan was for Elizabeth and the children to stay there and wait for Thomas, who would sell off the furniture in their Washington home and take the train north to meet them the next day.

But complications for Smallwood seemed to be multiplying—he couldn't even walk to the Potomac wharves without running into more trouble. On the way, he was "assailed" by two constables and a white man named Kennedy, whose ostensible purpose was to collect a debt of twenty-nine dollars incurred by Smallwood to bail a man out of jail. The note was not due for some time, but Smallwood decided to pay it off anyway to avoid trouble with the constables. He knew Kennedy posed a much larger danger: a relative of Smallwood's old betrayer George Lee lived with Kennedy, and Lee had revealed all he knew of Smallwood's operation to the relative, who Smallwood assumed had repeated it to Kennedy. Indeed, Kennedy urged the constables to arrest Smallwood, but they balked, saying they had no warrant for his arrest.

Smallwood saw his family off on the steamship but abandoned his plan to return home to sell off the furnishings, afraid that the police might now get a warrant and hunt him down. Nor did he dare take the train, or "the cars" in 1840s language, north to meet his family the next day, as he had planned.

"I doubted not that the constables were looking out for me; they doubtless having had knowledge of my original design to take the cars that morning," he wrote. Instead, after hiding out in Washington for the rest of the day and evening, he rose at 4 a.m., when the night watch went off duty but before the town awoke, and took off on foot "on a by-road for Baltimore," a trek of some forty miles. Thirteen hours later, at 5 p.m., he finally reached his wife and children in Baltimore, to the relief of Elizabeth, who had "undergone much uneasiness" when her husband did not arrive on the train as planned.

Here we get a rare and revealing glimpse of Elizabeth Anderson Smallwood, the laundress from Virginia who by Smallwood's account had continually assisted him in organizing escapes. In Baltimore, Elizabeth Smallwood learned that the paranoia of slaveholders had created a new obstacle for free African Americans traveling north. Previously, freedom papers like the ones she and her children had gotten from the courthouse in Washington were sufficient for most free Black travelers to board a train, steamboat, or stagecoach heading north. But some enslaved people had managed to make their escape using forged papers, and their enslavers had sued the railroad, boat, and stagecoach companies, demanding compensation for their losses. As a result, the railroad had added an onerous requirement for free Black passengers—that they "procure a responsible person or persons to enter bond to the amount of the value of the person or persons wishing to procure a passage," as Smallwood explained.

During her anxious day of waiting for her husband, while having to feed and look after five children aged one month to twelve years,

WASHINGTON, D.C. 1842

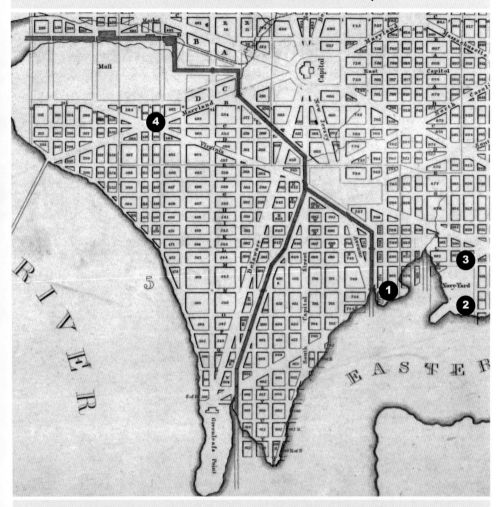

1. Home of Thomas Smallwood, Fourth and M Streets, Southeast
2. Navy Yard, the bustling center of Smallwood's neighborhood and shoe business
3. Home of the Reverend John B. Ferguson, Smallwood's enslaver, who sold him his freedom
4. Slave trader William H. Williams's slave jail, where Smallwood claimed he led Charles Dickens

SOURCE MAP: MAP OF THE CITY OF WASHINGTON, WM. M. MORRISON, 1840, LIBRARY OF CONGRESS

Thomas Smallwood lived near the Navy Yard, the large white building on the Eastern Branch of the Potomac River (now the Anacostia River) in the center of this 1833 print. On the hilltop is the U.S. Capitol; the White House is at far left. (PAINTED BY G. COOKE; ENGRAVED BY W.J. BENNETT; LIBRARY OF CONGRESS)

The U.S. Capitol during Smallwood and Torrey's time, before the addition of its modern dome. Built by enslaved laborers, it was the site of many battles over slavery. (1846 DAGUERREOTYPE BY JOHN PLUMBE, LIBRARY OF CONGRESS)

UNITED STATES SLAVE TRADE.

This antislavery print from 1830 depicts the slave trade in Washington—two traders holding whips, shackled captives about to be loaded aboard a ship, and the American flag and the Capitol in the background. (LIBRARY OF CONGRESS)

A SLAVE FATHER SOLD AWAY FROM HIS FAMILY

"A Slave Father Sold Away from His Family," illustration from an antislavery book, 1860. The trader is at right in dapper dress, speaking with a white woman who appears to be the slaveholder selling the man away from his distressed wife, children, and other relatives. (LIBRARY OF CONGRESS)

BALTIMORE 1842

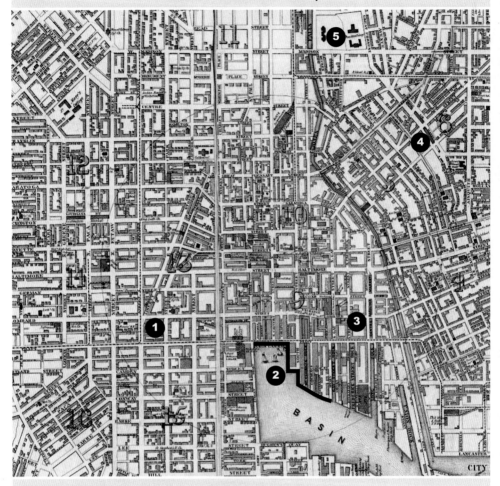

1. Slave trader Hope H. Slatter's office and slave jail
2. Docks along the north side of the Basin and harbor, from which ships carried thousands of enslaved people to New Orleans
3. Mansion of merchant Robert Gilmor, whose enslaved workers fled
4. Home of Jacob Gibbs, Thomas Smallwood's key Baltimore ally in aiding escapes
5. The Baltimore Jail and Maryland Penitentiary, where Charles Torrey was imprisoned

Baltimore's harbor, c. 1845. From these wharfs, Hope H. Slatter and other slave traders shipped thousands of people to the Deep South, often separating them from spouses, children, or parents. (DAGUERREOTYPE BY HENRY H. CLARK, MARYLAND CENTER FOR HISTORY AND CULTURE)

Baltimore Street and Market Place, Baltimore, c. 1845. Thomas Smallwood bragged of passing the Baltimore office of John Zell, constable and slave catcher, with runaways. He hid in the house of Jacob Gibbs before escaping to Canada. (DAGUERREOTYPE BY HENRY H. CLARK, MARYLAND CENTER FOR HISTORY AND CULTURE)

The former "slave jail" of Hope H. Slatter on Pratt Street near Baltimore's harbor, in a 1910 photograph. Slatter ran daily "Cash for Negroes!" newspaper ads and imprisoned people in these locked rooms until they could be shipped south. (MARYLAND CENTER FOR HISTORY AND CULTURE)

Hope H. Slatter's slave jail and "showroom" in New Orleans, at left, where thousands of people he purchased in the mid-Atlantic, delivered south by ship, were sold to cotton and sugar planters. (NOTARIAL ARCHIVES RESEARCH CENTER, NEW ORLEANS)

Slatter appears to have used a tunnel to move his enslaved captives between his private jail and Baltimore's harbor, to avoid unpleasant scenes with angry or distressed relatives who knew they might be parting with a loved one forever. The tunnel was described by an elderly African American, Rezin Williams, in 1937, and discovered the same year by utility workers digging beneath the streets. (BALTIMORE'S *EVENING SUN*, SEPTEMBER 18, 1937)

Susquehanna River, at the site of the long-gone bridge near Port Deposit, Maryland, that Smallwood crossed in his final escape to Canada. Many people he had helped to flee slavery avoided the exposed bridge and used a secret ferry operated by a sympathetic local man. (COURTESY OF SUSQUEHANNA STATE PARK)

Hope H. Slatter's grand tomb in Magnolia Cemetery in Mobile, Alabama, where the slave trader found a society that would accept him despite his longtime profession. (COURTESY OF THE AUTHOR)

above: The Toronto Necropolis, the old and verdant Canadian graveyard where Thomas Smallwood; his wife, Elizabeth; and other family members are buried. If there was ever a Smallwood gravestone, it disappeared beneath the grass-covered soil long ago. (COURTESY OF EDWARD RUDNICKI)

left: Charles Torrey's monument in Mount Auburn Cemetery in Cambridge, Massachusetts. Part of the inscription reads, "When the fetters shall be broken, And the SLAVE shall be a MAN." (COURTESY OF THE AUTHOR)

Elizabeth somehow managed to find a generous Baltimorean named Pittman—evidently Edward Pittman, who had a dry-goods business—willing to post bond in the amount of $2,000, an enormous sum that was the estimated value on the slave market of the seven members of the Smallwood family. Thomas Smallwood, who generally wrote little of his wife, made a point of praising her ingenuity on this occasion, writing that Elizabeth "had sufficient presence of mind to make arrangements to remove the only obstacle that lay in the way of our obtaining a speedy passage out of Baltimore."

They left Baltimore at 7 p.m. on a Thursday, and by noon on Saturday they were in Albany, for so long the northern hub of the escape network that Smallwood had constructed, where they were warmly welcomed by local activists.

"I shall ever hold in grateful remembrance, especially Messrs. Croker, Thomson and Latimore, of Albany, N.Y. I mention these, because of their unbounded benevolence to fugitives, falling in their way," Smallwood wrote.

From those three or from others whom Smallwood called "bright stars of benevolence" in Albany, he got offers to help him make a new home in the city. But Smallwood had now spent years urging people fleeing slavery not to stop until they reached Canada, and even if he and his family were not in danger from slave catchers, he took his own advice:

> Notwithstanding their kind offers to assist me in business, I declined to settle there. I pushed on for Canada, and arrived at Toronto, October 14, 1843, and settled in it, and I have never regretted one moment for having carried out my first intention, which was, inasmuch as I had to leave the metropolis of the United States, to seek freedom, from whose legislative halls freedom is proclaimed to all the world, except to the African race, I would seek it in no part of that inconsistent nation, because I was aware that there was no freedom for a colored person within its limits.

But if Smallwood thought he was at last through with the United States, the United States was not through with him. Even as he and Elizabeth began the complicated work of resettling their family in a new land, furnishing a household, and figuring out schooling, four Toronto men—Osburn Turner, James Woodland, Stephen Brown, and Levi Scott, all of whom had escaped slavery in Washington—approached him. Three of them had escaped with Smallwood's help, and now they pleaded with him to help their wives and children get away and join them.

Perhaps Smallwood agreed because he felt his work was incomplete as long as the families were separated. Whatever his considerations, by early November he had crossed back into the United States, where he spent three weeks visiting abolitionist circles in northern New York State to try to raise the funds necessary to pay the fares north. He grumbled at the stinginess of the donors, who gave him only forty dollars, but he reconnected again in Albany with Torrey, now preparing to wrap up his stint as editor of the *Albany Weekly Patriot,* and together they worked to arrange the four families' escape from Washington.

It could not have been a surprise to Elizabeth Smallwood that her husband was still asked for help. But what did she think when Smallwood, who had brought his family north with such trouble, readily agreed to go south again, potentially risking his freedom or his life? Perhaps she was herself so devoted to the cause that she urged him to try to unite the families of their new neighbors. Just as plausibly, she may have been distressed that he found himself unable to leave his dangerous calling behind. Thomas Smallwood does not record the reaction of this very devoted spouse when he left her and the children for yet another mission arranging escapes.

As Smallwood was raising the money to help the Toronto men bring their wives and children north, Torrey was on the verge of turning the deeply indebted *Patriot* over to a new owner. His wife, Mary, and their two children seem to have left Albany about this time, probably to return to her parents' house in Massachusetts. So Torrey, giving up his newspaper post and without his family, seems to have been eager to leave behind the annoyances of editing and chasing subscribers for payment to return once again to the escape business. Possibly against his better judgment—or simply because he could not resist dreaming and plotting once more with his old partner—Smallwood allowed Torrey to lure him into the slave south one last time. Torrey, he wrote, had "conceived the following scheme, that we should try and obtain a team and proceed to Washington, and bring away as many slaves as we could."

In other words, it was back to the operation they had started two years earlier—and never mind the fact that Washington was by now dangerous territory for both men. Together, the two took an overnight steamer from Albany to New York, traveled on to Philadelphia, and spent a night in Wilmington with an old friend and fervent abolitionist, Thomas Garrett. From there they traveled into Pennsylvania, where they obtained a wagon and a team of horses. In Baltimore, they stopped at the dock to meet the four families whose escape from Washington they had arranged—but only two showed up, the other two wives having "declined to come," for unexplained reasons. Smallwood and Torrey arranged for the two families to continue north to Toronto, and then turned to their new scheme.

Smallwood had recruited a Washington friend, John Bush, a free Black man who lived a few blocks from the Capitol, to help prepare a new large-scale escape. Bush had agreed to recruit people who wanted to make a run and to make available the barn beside his house as a gathering spot. So he and Torrey drove their wagon south from Baltimore, arriving that night at Bush's house. "We kept ourselves very close the next day," Smallwood recalled, "intending to start at night with our chattels, about fourteen in number." But as Smallwood worked in the barn late that day, November 24, 1843, adjusting the harness, and Torrey spoke with the nervous passengers, a sympathetic acquaintance burst in.

"Friend Smallwood, I see some white men standing out there on the hill side and they look like constables," the man said. Smallwood asked Torrey—whose white skin might offer at least some fleeting protection—to take a look. "He soon returned to me trembling, and saying they were constables and requested me to try and get the people out of the wagon," where ten of the would-be fugitives were already hiding.

> But he soon said to me, you can't, they are closing on us; therefore we had to make speed in making our own escape and leave the poor creatures to the mercy of the bloodhounds. After getting about a quarter of a mile from the place I heard the clanking of the chains, and shrieks of the poor souls, but we could afford them no help, they were in the claws of the lions.

The choice—abandoning the people they were assisting or staying to face certain capture—must have been excruciating. Smallwood would be haunted by the decision, but he and Torrey clearly felt they had no other option. In their frantic escape from the constables, the two men became separated and Smallwood turned down an offer from a friend he encountered to help him hide.

> I thanked him and declined his kind offer, and told him I would not stop until I reached Baltimore, for that while they would be ransacking Washington, thinking I was still there, I would be far away out of their reach. So I took leave of him just as the bell began to ring for ten o'clock, at which time all colored persons had to be in doors, and pushed forward for Baltimore, steering clear of every dwelling on the road by taking a circuitous route, fearing that the dogs might be roused, and that they might rouse the inmates, and I myself be attacked for a fugitive.

⋆⇒◦⇐⋆

Smallwood's account of his final flight north is almost cinematic, with details that urgency and terror had carved into his memory. The danger

he faced was all the greater because he had left his freedom papers—
that 1842 manumission signed by John Ferguson—at his new home in
Toronto, not expecting to travel south of the Mason-Dixon Line. If he
were captured now, he would surely face criminal charges, and if he fell
into the hands of unscrupulous slave catchers, he might even be sold
back into slavery and shipped south, thousands of miles from his family
in Toronto.

The bravado of Sam Weller, who had boasted of brazenly walking
and driving with fugitives past the offices of the notorious John Zell, was
gone now. Smallwood's identity was known, and the evidence against
him was irrefutable. He could not afford a misstep, and he understood
that whatever the hazards Torrey faced, his color made his own predicament worse. Indeed, as it turned out, Torrey did not even leave Washington; he stayed in part for a noble, if perhaps foolhardy, purpose: to
arrange a lawyer for John Bush.

> Mr. Torrey was not molested during his stay in Washington;
> being a white man they dared not publish him, or bring any
> charge against him, because they were not sure that they could
> sustain it; and it would only have subjected them to legal ac-
> tion. But with regard to myself it was different, I was a col-
> ored man, and so it made no difference; besides they had other
> charges against me which they could sustain.

Making his second desperate overnight trip on foot from Washington to Baltimore in the space of three months, Smallwood headed for
the East Street house of his friend Jacob Gibbs, the housepainter who
had been a critical link on the escape route north, arriving at eight the
next morning, a Saturday. Evidently the authorities had not connected
Gibbs to Smallwood, and so Smallwood "kept a close house," in his res-
onant words, while the two men waited for the searches following what
Smallwood called "the catastrophe" to lose steam. On Monday, after two
days in hiding, the men read a fulsome account of the thwarted escape
in *The Baltimore Sun*. The newspaper's Washington correspondent had

been briefed by John Goddard about the Auxiliary Guard's heroism in breaking up a large-scale escape, and the journalist, identified as "J. S. of Oldtown," repaid the favor in fawning prose.

Goddard had been tipped off that an escape was planned in the evening, J. S. wrote, and "that indefatigable officer, accompanied by a portion of our vigilant police officers," set up a watch on Bush's house. When they pounced, they found only a small Black boy in the house, so they decided to search the stable, where by the light of the lantern they found "a two horse spring wagon, with curtains closely buttoned down—the horses harnessed—a variety of bundles, parcels &c. all ready for the start; and, to cap the climax, *no less than four likely colored women, and two children, looking as innocent as lambs, quietly and comfortably sitting in the wagon!*"

By *The Sun*'s excited account, several Black men were grabbed as well, for a total of ten runaways—and another four more were not caught simply because they had not yet arrived at Bush's place. A "white man"— clearly Torrey—was permitted to "decamp," because the police officers outside the barn assumed in the darkness that he was another officer.

But Goddard had been tipped off about the role of Smallwood, with whom he had tangled several weeks before when would-be fugitives had gathered at Smallwood's house and one was hidden in the corn patch out back. Goddard informed the *Sun* correspondent exactly whom he believed to be the ringleader: "a negro fellow, named Thomas Smallwood" who had been living in Toronto "for some months past" had arrived in Washington with the horse and wagon on Thursday, the night before the escape attempt.

"He is yet at liberty," *The Sun* reported, which must have given Smallwood a smile as he read it somewhere in the recesses of Gibbs's house. After all of the escapes Smallwood had chronicled in the Albany newspapers, after all of his searing lampoons of the slaveholders and slave catchers, it was the first time his real name had been publicly associated with the underground railroad that he had helped shape and given a name.

It is known that a negro fellow, named Thomas Smallwood, who formerly lived here, but for some months past has resided in Toronto, Canada, arrived here, with the wagon and horses on Thursday night. He is yet at liberty. Bush's wife delivered up a bundle of letters, directed to slaves here, dated at Toronto, and signed by negroes who once lived here, but who have ran away, from time to time, and are now residents there. One of these letters (the latest) is dated 30th October last, and advises them to escape from this "land of bondage" and go there and join them "on Queen Victoria's lands."

Part of a report in *The Baltimore Sun,* November 27, 1843, about Thomas Smallwood and Charles Torrey's thwarted mass escape attempt. Smallwood had written on escapes for the Albany newspaper under his pseudonym for many months, but he had never before been named in the press in connection with flights from slavery. [Courtesy of American Antiquarian Society and Genealogy Bank]

The Sun's account, packed with information despite the proslavery bias, included one more poignant detail. Smallwood had brought with him from Toronto "a bundle of letters" written by people formerly enslaved in Washington and now living in freedom in Toronto, addressed to relatives and friends in the nation's capital. With families separated by hundreds of miles and worried about trusting the mail for fear of giving away new locations in Canada, Smallwood's courier service must have been a precious gift. But now these treasures, too, fell into the hands of the police.

Smallwood had given the letters to John Bush's wife to be distributed to the recipients, but she was now forced to turn them over to Goddard, who shared them with the reporter. "One of these letters (the latest) is dated 30th October last," *The Sun* reported, "and advises them to escape from this 'land of bondage' and go there and join them 'on Queen Victoria's lands.'"

By now Smallwood knew he, too, would have to make his final escape to Queen Victoria's lands. It was his home now, and staying in the south was no longer a possibility.

One memorable visitor interrupted his week in hiding. Charles Torrey made his way to Baltimore and visited Smallwood at Gibbs's house, delivering some money for the journey north—since Smallwood had previously turned over all the cash he had raised to Torrey. In his memoir, Smallwood does not dwell on the visit—he says merely that "Mr. Torrey arrived in Baltimore from Washington the succeeding week"—but it must have been an emotional meeting.

The unusual partnership of these two men, Black and white, the purchaser of his own freedom and the graduate of Andover and Yale, had proved most consequential. They must have compared notes on their failed mission and discussed what was behind the police ambush that had thwarted it. Smallwood, who would only speak highly of Torrey in the future, does not seem to have blamed his partner for proposing one more mission. They presumably discussed their plans, which would diverge; even Torrey must have understood that he should not press Smallwood to try again to organize escapes. They would not meet again.

⊷═◉═⊶

On Saturday night, December 2, a week after his arrival in Baltimore, Smallwood and Gibbs and an enslaved man who was ready to run—why waste one more chance to get someone to freedom?—headed north on foot. Smallwood noted the irony that he, a free man, was now forced to flee the slave power just as surely as the hundreds of enslaved people he had helped. He had put together the network of allies for those running north, and now he was to take advantage of it. "Friend G. had to accompany me, as he did fugitives from slavery, because I had been published as a fugitive from justice, and was liable to be taken and carried back to Washington, where I should be tried, and if convicted, sent to the Penitentiary for fourteen years," Smallwood wrote. He didn't explain how he calculated the precise sentence but, as he had made clear, capture might mean a fate even worse than prison: a return to slavery after thirteen years of freedom, permanent separation from his wife and children, and shipment to a brutal southern plantation—quite likely via Hope Slatter, whose jail was an easy walk from Gibbs's house.

The three men set out across the dark landscape north of Baltimore in the direction of Port Deposit, on the north side of the broad Susquehanna River. Gibbs knew the route better than Smallwood, and he had often enlisted the help of the woman named Turner, whose house was just short of the Port Deposit bridge, to hide fugitives until a boatman Smallwood identified only as "P." could row them across. They had generally avoided the bridge itself, which offered no cover and was an easy ambush point for lurking slave catchers. But Gibbs told Smallwood that Mrs. Turner had recently "turned traitress" and given up some fugitives to slave hunters.

> Therefore it was necessary to keep clear of her. In order to do this we thought to pass her house before day-light, so as not to be seen, but when we got opposite the house, to our surprise, who should be standing at the window looking down on us but the old dame herself; she being so used to friend G's movements, it was hard to delude her. We passed on, however, and crossed the bridge just at the rising of the sun, and went to friend P's, and there put up for the day.

But Mrs. Turner had evidently alerted the constables just downriver at the village of Havre de Grace, which Smallwood described as a "den of slave catchers." At 6 p.m., the constables suddenly appeared at the house of P., who ran the "secret ferry" that had carried so many fugitives across the Susquehanna. First, outside the house, they encountered the enslaved man accompanying Smallwood and Gibbs. "They then made a rush in the house, evidently in search of me," Smallwood wrote. Hearing the commotion, Smallwood slipped out a "secret door" built into one room while the constables were searching another room. Though mythical secret exits, tunnels, and hideaways in the lore of the underground railroad hugely outnumber actual ones, the border area

was certainly a likely zone for such contrivances. Smallwood wrote that
the door "had been put there for such purposes," and it may have saved
his freedom.

Smallwood, who had been distraught at having to abandon the fugitives gathered in John Bush's barn, now had to leave P., Gibbs, and the
runaway to try to fend off the constables. Though it was early in December, "considerable snow" covered the hill behind the house. Smallwood
first briefly hid in the brush and then started walking in the dark, though
he had only the vaguest idea where he was and which way he needed to
go. "I went on all night trudging through the snow, up hill and down hill,
over streams and through plains in a part of the country I knew nothing
of. My object, of course, was to reach Pennsylvania, and at about three
o'clock in the morning I thought I might be in that State," he recalled.
He spotted a house by the roadside and, despite the hour, decided to risk
knocking. He knew that asking the sleepy man who came to the door
whether he had reached Pennsylvania might flag him as a fugitive. So
instead he "inquired what county I was in, and if there were any colored
people living in that vicinity."

> The answer satisfied me that I was in that State, it also in-
> formed me that opposite there lived two colored families
> whose houses I could see through a little skirt of bush that in-
> tervened, so I bore away for them; passing by the first, I rapped
> at the door of the second, and after answering to the call, "who
> is that?" and telling my story, the door was opened and I re-
> ceived a hearty welcome. I was not long in the house before I
> let them know that I wanted something more than being let
> in, and warmed by two fires, one in a stove, and one in a chim-
> ney or fire place, between which I had snugged myself, for I
> had eaten nothing since the previous morning.

Smallwood reveled in the predawn reception from strangers; they were
African American strangers, after all, living near the border between slave

state and free, and the family of Ezekiel Clark, whose home it turned out to be, immediately embraced him as a friend. They warmed him and fed him, and by 9 a.m. he was on the road again, walking the fourteen miles to the nearest rail depot. By 9 p.m. he was in Philadelphia and safe from any pursuers—or so he thought.

Smallwood whiled away the next day listening to the debates at an antislavery convention. But then the local antislavery committee that was hosting him got an urgent message—"a dispatch from Mr. Torrey urging that I should leave immediately for other parts of the North; that the slaveholders were in hot pursuit of me."

After Goddard's discovery of the previous week, the slaveholders and slave catchers of Washington and Baltimore may finally have deduced the true identity of "Samivel Weller Jr.," who had spent two years robbing, mocking, and defying them. The constables who traveled to Albany and Troy in pursuit of fugitives would have been pleased to hop on a train to Philadelphia to capture such a prize. So Smallwood traveled onward, accompanied by the two women whose departure from Washington he had helped arrange and who were now heading north with their children to be reunited with their husbands in Toronto.

But Torrey had given Smallwood only six dollars of the modest stash of money they had collected for the escape, and it was not enough for train and boat fares for the whole party. They had to walk much of the long, cold way north. "So we travelled on slowly, getting a little here and there," Smallwood wrote. "Our means however, not be[ing] sufficient, I sold my watch in Buffalo to get them to Toronto." They arrived in the Canadian city two days before Christmas aboard a steamboat called the *Transit*—and managed only because the skipper, a man named Richardson, was an acquaintance of Smallwood and supported the antislavery cause.

"Capt. Richardson, according to his usual benevolence reduced the fare for us," Smallwood wrote. It was a small act of kindness at the end of an eventful and dangerous passage north. A month had passed since the police had surprised Smallwood and Torrey at Bush's barn.

⟞⟞⟞◎⟞⟞⟞

Smallwood's reunion in Toronto with Elizabeth and his children was surely a huge relief for all of them. He had, with care, courage, and luck, skirted the dangers of prison or death. But there was a dark coda to his and Torrey's aborted escape mission. Smallwood's reaction is not recorded, but he must have read about it in the *Albany Weekly Patriot*, which listed him in early 1844 as the newspaper's sales agent in Toronto, or in other abolitionist papers that reached him in Toronto.

It turned out that among the people planning to escape in the getaway foiled at John Bush's barn were a mother and two sons and two daughters, all enslaved by the United States Senate's assistant doorkeeper Robert Beale. By one account, the woman had decided to flee with her children because she believed Beale had been planning to sell her children away from her. And after their capture, Beale had indeed sold three of her children, leaving her with only her youngest child, an eight-year-old son. One of the daughters sold was twenty years old, at risk of sexual slavery. The *Patriot* reported the development under the headline "AN ASTONISHING ATROCITY."

A subsequent report in the same issue, by the abolitionist journalist Joshua Leavitt, said that "nearly all" of those captured in Bush's stable had been "punished for their love of liberty by being sold to the slave traders, to be sent to New-Orleans, and thence to the slaughter of the sugar plantations of Louisiana." Once again, the underground railroad and the slave trade proved deeply connected: the threat of being sold motivated attempts to escape, and failed escapes fed the trade.

Smallwood, now safely reunited with his wife and five children in Toronto, had particular reason to appreciate the agony of the families who were being separated. Such a disaster may also have confirmed his conclusion that he had become compromised. The job he had jokingly described as the general agent of all the branches of the National Underground Railroad, Steam Packet, Canal and Foot-it Company was over.

Along with its report on Robert Beale's actions, the *Patriot* included a preprinted petition "TO THE SENATE OF THE U.S." calling for the Senate to investigate whether Beale had indeed sold the children away from their mother and, if so, to fire him from his government post. How many readers took the trouble to clip, sign, and mail the petition is unknown. But whatever the number, the appeal had no effect. In 1845, Beale was promoted to doorkeeper of the Senate, a title that was later changed to sergeant at arms, a job he kept for eight years.

Six negroes were decoyed a few nights since fromr their master, Mr. Bushrod. Taylor, of Winchester, Virginia, by an individual named Charles T. Torrey.— The negroes was last seen in Philadelphia. Torrey, the abductor, passes himself off as a minister of the gospel.

A report from the *Baltimore American* reprinted in the proslavery *Easton Gazette,* from Maryland's Eastern Shore, January 6, 1844, naming Charles Torrey as the organizer of the Webb family's escape from Winchester, Virginia. Torrey's bold and reckless conduct led to his quick public identification. [Courtesy of American Antiquarian Society and Genealogy Bank]

12

***

Perhaps Reckless

Two weeks after he had fled John Bush's barn in Washington with Thomas Smallwood, Charles Turner Torrey checked into a hotel in Winchester, Virginia, seventy-five miles west of the nation's capital. He signed the register with a thinly disguised pseudonym: "C. Turner." He was on a new mission.

A remarkable woman named Emily Webb, a mother of thirteen children whose tangled life story captured many of the horrors of slavery, had approached Torrey in Philadelphia looking for help. Her mother had spent years being raped by her enslaver before being sold south; Emily was one of several children born as a result. She had married an enslaved man, John Webb, and eventually managed to purchase her own freedom with money earned as a laundress. But two of her sons had already been sold south. Now her husband and five more of their children belonged to a Winchester man named Bushrod Taylor, a former hotelkeeper who now earned part of his living as a slave trader, and Taylor was preparing to sell them south. Torrey agreed to help.

On the night of December 18, 1843, John Webb slipped away from Taylor's farm, carrying his youngest child and with the four others walking beside him. They met Torrey, who had rented a carriage and a team of horses, perhaps with the money left unspent after the disaster at Bush's barn. The group fled straight north to Chambersburg, Pennsylvania, a journey of twenty-three hours, "over more horrible roads than I *ever* had the misfortune to travel before in my life," as Torrey described it. They boarded a train from there to Philadelphia. Torrey learned later that two "pursuers" from Winchester, plus the sheriff of Hagerstown, Maryland, had arrived in Chambersburg just four hours after he, Webb, and the children had caught the train.

Though he had used a pseudonym at his Winchester hotel, his role was revealed in the press just days after the escape: "Six negroes were decoyed a few nights since from their master, Mr. Bushrod Taylor, of Winchester, Virginia, by an individual named Charles T. Torrey," reported the *Baltimore American,* in a brief item reprinted in many other newspapers. "Torrey, the abductor, passes himself off as a minister of the gospel."

If what Smallwood called "the catastrophe" at Bush's barn had shaken Torrey, or if Smallwood's final departure for Canada had left him discouraged, he showed no outward sign of it. Though Torrey was clearly in danger of arrest in Washington, he had stayed there for a few days while arranging for a lawyer to represent John Bush, who had been charged for allowing his barn to be used to stage an escape and released on $500 bail. Then, after visiting Smallwood in Baltimore at Jacob Gibbs's house, Torrey moved on to Philadelphia, where he stayed with James J. G. Bias, an African American physician, dentist, and antislavery activist. He immediately resumed writing for the *Patriot* in Albany—and plotting more escapes, still confident that if a sufficient number of enslaved people gained their freedom, stripping slaveholders of their wealth, the slave system might be undermined.

As Smallwood had noted, a white man could get away with a great deal more than a Black man in challenging the authorities. And Torrey had lost none of his ambition in imagining what his actions might accomplish. His admirable, and risky, dedication to John Bush's legal defense was more than just loyalty to an ally who had been arrested when Torrey and Smallwood had escaped. Torrey hoped Bush's lawyers would use his case to challenge "the very *existence* of slavery in the District of Columbia," a long-standing ambition of the antislavery movement. "Bush must not be allowed to suffer, especially when the great cause can be so much benefitted," Torrey wrote, appealing to abolitionists to donate to Bush's legal defense. "May I not urge on the friends of liberty the immediate appointment of a committee to take it in charge, raise funds, and carry on the suit?"

Torrey—not a lawyer, of course—laid out this aggressive, if vague, legal strategy in the first of a series of columns for the *Patriot* that he signed "By a Negro Stealer." His cover was not hard to see through; he had, after all, just stepped down as editor of the same newspaper, and any regular reader would know that the style and views of the "Negro Stealer" closely resembled Torrey's. (Once, in fact, the "Negro Stealer" wrote that while his name was withheld, "I have little fear but that you will recognize an old friend.") But whatever his concerns about being identified, Torrey had lost none of his militancy. He blamed the debacle at Bush's barn on three police informants, and addressed John Goddard, head of the Auxiliary Guard, with what amounted to a threat of vigilante violence: "This is to give notice to Capt. Goddard, of the Auxiliary Guard, that the three stool pigeons must be sent from Washington, sixty miles at least, on or before April 26, on peril of their *lives*."

He attacked the Auxiliary Guard as a band of former professional slave catchers and promised more dispatches from the "Negro Stealer" that he said "will be likely to make the slaveholders squirm." In effect, Torrey was trying to replicate the popular success of "Samivel Weller Jr.," now that Smallwood was out of the business.

But the confident tone of Torrey's writing, and his unquestionable daring in rescuing people from slavery, had a darker, more personal source. Writing in January 1844 to his old friend and patron Gerrit Smith, the wealthy New York State abolitionist, he briefly recounted his recent escapades, including the rough carriage journey with John Webb and his five children, who, he said, were now "safe at Niagara, Canada." He acknowledged that he had "narrowly escaped arrest" but vowed to keep on, venturing farther afield than he had during his partnership with Smallwood: "I am expecting soon to go for a man in Raleigh, N.C.; a woman in Staunton, Va; and a man in New Orleans, with some others."

Though Smith had famously called upon enslaved people to attempt to flee north, Torrey knew that he, like many abolitionists, worried about the dangers of aiding and engineering escapes. "Do you ask, 'Why waste your time so, and incur these risks?'" Torrey wrote, anticipating Smith's query. He discussed his motives briefly before reaching a painful and candid conclusion: "Private causes of personal misery render me—perhaps reckless. In toil and excitement the misery one cannot relieve, may be forgotten.... And, for a time to come, I shall relieve a few individual cases of suffering, while, I hope, I am not unfitting myself for duty to the whole cause."

What were the "private causes of personal misery"? Torrey was in debt, struggling financially as usual, and he had just been forced to turn over ownership of the newspaper to others. But he was almost certainly referring mainly to his marriage. Mary Torrey had been at his side for his year in Albany as editor of the *Tocsin* and *Patriot*. She had shared his political mission, serving as president of the Female Anti-Slavery Society, the women's auxiliary to the eastern New York abolitionist group, placing regular notices in the newspaper ("ATTENTION, LADIES!") inviting Albany women to meetings and fundraising events at one another's homes. But Mary and the children had not joined him during nearly a year he spent in Washington, and now, as he headed south again, they moved in once more with her parents in Medway, Massachusetts.

Torrey's biographer, E. Fuller Torrey, notes that their letters had revealed tensions in the marriage as early as 1841, when Charles had written, "Mary, can we not love one another with the freshness and purity, and tenderness of our first affection?" Fuller Torrey concludes that "by the autumn of 1843, the marriage had, for all intents and purposes, ended."

That may be an overstatement—Mary would prove strikingly loyal to her husband during the tribulations he would soon face—but there can be little doubt that Torrey had fallen short as a provider and repeatedly placed the antislavery cause ahead of his role as husband and father. His awareness of this failure, on top of his earlier flameouts as a teacher and preacher and his business woes as a newspaper proprietor, surely weighed him down. Though he could be scathing about those in the antislavery movement who advised him to be more "prudent," Torrey was willing to concede that it was personal despair that made him "perhaps reckless."

⋄⟫⟩◦⟨⟪⋄

The contrast with Smallwood was striking. Smallwood, more than a decade older than Torrey, had stuck far more closely to his own wife and children. He had taken many chances helping people escape, but he had a healthier sense of the limits of tolerable risk, and when the threats became too great, he had relocated beyond the reach of his many enemies. There were indications that he had wanted to keep writing from Canada for the *Patriot,* even as he carved out a new life in Toronto, but it was not to be.

In a brief but poignant item in the same issue of the *Patriot* carrying his first "Negro Stealer" report, Torrey used the newspaper to send what was in effect a private message to Smallwood in Toronto—a reminder of the slow and unreliable options for communication in 1844. "To T.S., *of Toronto,*" the item said, "Mr. T.B. *refuses* to act as your attorney in disposing of your goods, and has returned the power to me so *torn,* that it cannot be used to transfer it to any body else. Your coat, carpet bag, etc. will be sent the first opportunity.—C.T.T."

It is not hard to decipher the message: Smallwood had sent a signed power of attorney to Torrey with a request that he give it to a local lawyer so that he could sell the furniture and other goods the Smallwoods had been forced to abandon in their house in Washington. The lawyer had not only refused the request but evidently had torn up the power of attorney in a fit of pique. It is hard not to read into these bare facts a racial implication: the white lawyer, though presumably an acquaintance, was offended even to be asked to do a minor but important job for a Black man. Torrey, at least, was willing to ship to Smallwood the coat and suitcase he had left behind. But his use of the newspaper to send an unpleasant message seems impersonal and cold. Though he never said so, Torrey may have resented Smallwood's decision to put his own and his family's safety ahead of more escapes.

Far harsher was a notice in the *Patriot* some weeks later, evidently written by Edwin W. Goodwin, the newspaper veteran who had returned to the editor's post he had held before Torrey took it over, again addressing Smallwood through the *Patriot*:

> *Thomas Smallwood* is informed that we cannot publish his communication, as it involves facts that must be better substantiated than his appear to be. He requests us to publish his article immediately, and send him two copies of the paper containing it. We could not do it, as he has not given the place where he wrote it, or wishes it sent. And moreover we have great repugnance to complying with such directions where persons forget to pay postage.

It is hard to fully assess what appears to be a small-minded and tetchy outburst from Goodwin. Perhaps Smallwood, understandably fixated on the treachery that had forced him to leave the country, had written a screed naming the Black Washingtonians whom he believed had betrayed him and the cause of the enslaved and making unproven accusations that any editor might hesitate to publish. But Smallwood was not just any contributor. As Goodwin presumably knew from Torrey, he was the author of the dozens of dispatches that had appeared under the Sam Weller pen name, one of the paper's most popular features. Beyond his writing, he had risked everything to help engineer escapes, which Goodwin may well have known, since Smallwood's long-guarded anonymity had ended with the news reports of the fiasco at Bush's barn. To brush him off in so high-handed a manner seems unjustified and unfortunate. More significantly, Goodwin's rebuff may have cut off what could have been a stream of continuing contributions from Toronto by a brilliant writer with a proven knack for satire.

Shortly after Goodwin's rejection notice appeared, Smallwood's name disappeared from the list of the *Patriot*'s official agents, or sales representatives. Whether Goodwin had dropped Smallwood or Smallwood had dropped Goodwin is uncertain, but it was a severing of a literary and political relationship that had served both parties well.

⋄⇒◉⇐⋄

Despite his private confession of "personal misery" to Smith, Torrey kept sending to the *Patriot* his dispatches from the "Negro Stealer," often under the headline "Notes of Southern Travel." They were lively, often searing, even if they didn't have quite the trenchant wit and distinctive style of Smallwood's Sam Weller letters. (Twice Torrey's "Negro Stealer" reports were signed "Samivel Weller Jr.," perhaps because an editor wanted to keep alive the popular byline.) In February, as the "Negro Stealer," Torrey reported that an informant had told him that slaveholders and slave traders had offered the police (presumably in Baltimore or Washington or both) a new $1,000 reward for his capture. He reported that the Methodists in Baltimore, where Hope Slatter had tried to purchase respectability with his church pew, were turning more and more against slavery. He offered routine observations on passing landscapes, mountain views, rising train fares, and interesting towns he had visited in western Maryland and Virginia.

Torrey also carried on Smallwood's tradition of attacking the slaveholders, often focusing on the pattern of rape that had produced generations of biracial offspring. He singled out a wealthy planter living south of Baltimore named Tom W. (he later identified the man as Tom Withington), "a stout, fat man, with a shrewd, but sensual face," who by Torrey's account had "large families of children by four colored women, and other children by his own daughters," numbering about fifty children in all.

"Not many years since he shot a colored lover of one of the women, as the poor man was entering the window of her hut," Torrey wrote. "Yet this brute beast is a rich and quite 'respectable' man!"

A Baltimorean whom Torrey identified only as "Col. S—t" had two daughters by an enslaved woman, and then had more children by each of the daughters: "Not long since he sold the mother, daughters, and grandchildren, all, to the slave trader Hope H. Slatter, for the southern market." Such a case—of a white man selling his own progeny for cash—might strain credulity, Torrey recognized. But, as he knew, there was ample evidence of such conduct across the slave south. Such appalling behavior, he suggested, was merely a symptom of the moral degradation wreaked by slavery:

> Is the reader shocked at the enormity of such disclosures? Let him remember that these form a part, not the worst part, even, of the *every day life of slavery*. I say, it is not the worst part. The horrible corruption of thought and feeling, the cheapening of human virtue, the contempt of human affections and sufferings, the hard hearted cruelty to the victims, evinced in their daily trampling on their wishes, feelings and enjoyments; *these* indicate a corruption far more deep and deadly than the outward immoralities I have recited.

By April 1844, Torrey had moved his base from friends' houses in Philadelphia to a boardinghouse in Baltimore, invading slave country once more with the clear intent of organizing more escapes. Only a few of these were documented, but it appears Torrey worked boldly and relentlessly, often driving the wagon himself, as he had from Winchester. He displayed unquestionable courage, though not necessarily good judgment. Though he must have met Jacob Gibbs when he had visited Smallwood in Baltimore the previous December, he does not appear to have involved Gibbs or other Black collaborators in his new escape schemes. The reason is hard to fathom. Gibbs was a careful and experienced operator, and a white man reaching out to enslaved African Americans could attract unwanted public attention, either from enslavers or from passersby. But Torrey seems to have operated largely on his own.

His fresh immersion in the escape routes north from Baltimore prompted him to write knowingly about a gang of ruffians living just south of the Mason-Dixon Line who lived off the rewards for catching people escaping from slavery or by kidnapping free Black people and selling them into slavery. "A set of careless scoundrels whose chief business is man-hunting," Torrey called them, "and whose occasional amusements are counterfeiting, stealing sheep, stabbing, killing men, and debauchery in its lowest forms. These convenient tools of the refined, genteel slaveholders, are a scourge and terror to the neighborhood."

Local farmers and villagers were afraid to challenge the gang members for fear of violent retaliation, but Torrey named them: John Lyman, his brother Sampson Lyman (who Torrey said was then incarcerated at the Eastern Penitentiary in Philadelphia for counterfeiting), Cad Jones, and Jake Forward. Still, Torrey did not mistake these small-time criminals for the true villains. "In my opinion," he wrote, "the slaveholder is a much more despicable creature. He is the *principal* in all this knavery."

Shortly after he moved to Baltimore, a far bigger and busier city than Boston or Washington, Torrey had special reason to consider the endurance and reach of the slave power—the web of financial interest and political influence that profited from and protected human bondage. In his first weeks in the city, the Whig Party held its nominating convention, meeting in a downtown church and choosing as its presidential candidate Henry Clay of Kentucky, a slaveholder and colonizationist who had often expressed ambivalence about the system but had not seen fit to free those he enslaved. Three weeks later, the Democrats meeting a few blocks away nominated James K. Polk of Tennessee, the unapologetic enslaver who would borrow Slatter's carriage and quietly buy and sell people from the presidential mansion. Torrey's Liberty Party, which he had helped found, took an outspoken antislavery stance—and was dwarfed by the other two. If Torrey needed proof that proslavery forces had an iron grip on the nation's political class, he did not have to stray far from his boardinghouse to find it.

But Torrey believed that local popular opinion was trending in the right direction. "The mechanics of Baltimore, too, are much more hostile to slavery than they were a few years ago," he wrote. "They are rapidly growing in intelligence, and feeling the crushing influence of the slaveholding aristocracy." He was new to town, and his view may have been wishful thinking, but his sense that antislavery opinion was spreading may well have made him bolder in his opposition.

Living in Baltimore for the first time, Torrey also began to study more closely the slave traders, beginning with Slatter. In the Albany paper, he had often lambasted Slatter, but now he could actually watch his operation on Pratt Street up close. Remarking on how the banned African trade had given way to a thriving domestic trade, Torrey declared: "This is a great and glorious country of ours! She won't allow her people to buy and sell any but *her own citizens* under penalty of death!" (Though enforcement of the prohibition of the African trade was lackadaisical, the punishment for violating it could indeed be hanging.)

Torrey reported in the May 1, 1844, *Patriot* that an increase in cotton prices was producing a parallel increase in the demand for unpaid laborers, and then he sketched what he saw in Baltimore:

> There are now *three* large slave prisons in this city; Slatter's, Donovan's (formerly Woolfolk's), and Campbell's. They accommodate sundry other small dealers with prison room, at 25 cents a day for each victim. Hope H. Slatter, the most gentlemanly of his clan, has sent 400 to the New Orleans market, on his own account, since last October. This is about one third of the number *shipped* from the Port of Baltimore, in that period. Slatter sent 28 last week. He has five or six men out in the country to purchase slaves for him. These wolves prowl about the land, seeking whom they may devour. Their appearance strikes terror into the hearts of the helpless poor.

Torrey's numbers appear to be slightly high, if the official manifests of the slave shipments for the 1843–44 season are complete and accurate; they show five shipments carrying a total of 307 captives for Slatter between September 1843 and April 1844. But his understanding of Slatter's business methods—"most gentlemanly" is presumably a sardonic reference to his social pretensions—was right on target. On another occasion, an acquaintance reported to Torrey what he had witnessed on the streets of downtown Baltimore late one night, as Slatter or one of his competitors moved their human goods through the dark streets:

> A friend, a few nights ago, met nearly 30, in Camden street, handcuffed together, two and two, on their way to a slave pen, guarded by five armed villains. It was about 1 o'clock at night. Secrecy and darkness are necessary to keep the loathsome traffic from the eyes of the *white* mechanics of Baltimore.

Torrey evidently had seen Slatter—he had compared him to Raphael's depiction of Judas Iscariot. But he had never met Slatter in person. That would soon change.

✦═◐═✦

William Heckrotte operated a modest tavern at Charles and Camden Streets in downtown Baltimore, just steps from the Basin. He relied on enslaved labor to run the place. Somehow, Torrey connected with a woman enslaved by Heckrotte named Hannah Gooseberry, and together they devised an escape plan for Gooseberry and her teenage son and daughter, Stephen and Judea. To pluck these workers from Baltimore's crowded and busy center was a bold stroke, but one night in early June 1844 they made a successful escape, with Torrey again driving the wagon on the usual route, roughly following the course of today's Interstate 95 toward Pennsylvania and freedom.

Heckrotte placed a runaway ad the day after their disappearance in one of Baltimore's many newspapers, the *Republican & Daily Argus*, offering a substantial hundred-dollar reward for their return. Hannah was about forty, had "a pleasing countenance," and was a good cook and washerwoman, Heckrotte wrote; it was odd how often enslavers paid public tribute to the skills of those they enslaved only after the latter had fled. Stephen was skilled at opening and cooking oysters. Judea could read a little, and she and her mother both had new shoes and straw bonnets trimmed with black ribbon. The tavernkeeper, perhaps hoping to get word to the runaways that he would not sell them south if they came back, added an unusual note at the bottom of his ad: "If the Servants will return to their duty, they will not be punished in any manner, as I believe they were evil advised in taking the step they did. They were all three sober, honest servants."

The tavernkeeper was not the first slaveholder to affect hurt feelings when his unpaid workers decided they had had enough. But the escape was another success for Torrey, and evidently one of quite a number. In his "Negro Stealer" notes, he made clear he had ranged from Baltimore across Maryland and Virginia, sometimes farther, traveling by wagon or train. In his travels, he witnessed new, distressing elements of the slave system. In Leesburg, Virginia, he saw an unusual winter scene:

> Many of my readers are not aware, that Christmas and New Year week, the season of hilarity all over the south, the annual holyday for the slaves, is also the day of terror and anguish to multitudes. Their brief hour of freedom and gaiety, which they enter upon with the keenest zest, is followed by more heart-rending scenes than the seasons of severest toil. All over Maryland, Virginia, etc., there are large numbers of slaves whom their masters cannot profitably employ, who are therefore hired out, for the most they will bring, for the year. . . . [In Leesburg] there were 2 or 300 slaveholders and others in the village, to let or to hire slaves. There were many hundreds of slaves, of every sex, and shade of color. Some of them were cheerful, as if *any* change in their condition might be regarded as a relief—but the most of them looked anxious, suspicious and careworn. The families broken up at these hirings are often separated as effectually as death itself would divide them.

For the most part, Torrey did not detail his "Negro stealing," leaving it to his pseudonym to express the purpose of his southern travels. But there is every likelihood that he was recruiting and assisting people to run north during all of his meandering journeys. We know that he was lurking, chatting, taking notes, and meeting people in Frederick, Hagerstown, and Cumberland in western Maryland; at other times he traveled through Leesburg, Middleburg, and Winchester, Virginia. If he was despairing about his personal life, he seemed energized by the travel and hopeful that his efforts might be, slowly but surely, helping to unravel slavery.

⋯⊱◦⊰⋯

Among the outrages that caught Torrey's attention while he lived in Baltimore was the case of Benjamin Jones, a Black farmer in Bucks County, Pennsylvania, who more than a decade before had fled from his Maryland enslaver, William Anderson. Jones had settled in a Quaker community below Buckingham Mountain and become a respected neighbor, known locally as "Big Ben" for his height, nearly seven feet. Now Anderson had somehow learned of Jones's whereabouts, hired four men to accompany him, and headed north more than one hundred miles to capture Jones. They found him chopping wood near his house. Jones tried to defend himself with his axe, but the posse clubbed him into submission.

Over the protests of Jones's neighbors, they took him to Philadelphia, where they boarded a ship and sailed to Baltimore. They lodged him in Hope Slatter's jail and sent word to Jones's Quaker friends in Pennsylvania that they could buy his freedom for $700—or he would be shipped to New Orleans.

In a "Negro Stealer" dispatch in April 1844, a few weeks after Jones was captured, Torrey called Anderson "a smooth-faced, gray-headed Methodist devil from the neighborhood of Baltimore" and reported the case as one of a growing number of kidnappings in the border region. At first, for Torrey, it was just one more unspeakable injustice in an unending list. But a few weeks later, it got personal. Torrey heard from Jones's supporters that they were having trouble raising the money to free him and feared that he might be sent to New Orleans before they could meet

Slatter's price. Torrey, either at their request or on his own, decided he might be able to negotiate what amounted to a lower ransom for the Pennsylvanian.

Somehow Torrey talked himself into believing that the man he had publicly called "the great *Negro thief*" and "the shame of the whole man-stealing South," whom he had held up as a despicable symbol of the inhuman commerce in human beings, might listen to an appeal for benevolence from his avowed enemy. Torrey decided to visit Slatter's jail to talk to the man he had so many times attacked in print. The thirty-year-old former teacher, preacher, and editor strolled down to Pratt Street on his mission of mercy.

$100 REWARD.

RUNAWAY between 8 and 9 o'clock at night, June 4th, 1844, my THREE NEGROES, Hannah Goosbury, Judea Goosbury, and Stephen Goosbury. HANNAH, (mother of the above Negroes) is of pleasing countenance, first rate cook, washer, &c., is about 40 years old, very large and stout built; a tooth out in front, the small toes on both feet off, occasioned by frost when young. The two women have good clothes, calicoes, fancy and black, both alike. They all have new shoes. I believe straw bonnets, trimmed with black ribbon.

JUDEA, is about 18 to 19 years old, very stout, smooth skin, small mouth, and moves slow.

STEPHEN, is about 17 or 18 years old, the little finger off at the second joint, caused by play with a saw when small; his clothes as well as I recollect, are a casinet round-jacket and pantaloons, dark color, 2 striped shirts with some white ones also. He has a small scar under the left eye, caused by play, full round face, small mouth, and resembles Judea; he walks slovenly. He was brought up to house work, opening oysters, cooking them, &c.

I will give the above reward for the three Negroes, or in proportion for either of them, and pay all reasonable expenses if secured so I get them. They were bought from Mr. Sindle about 19 years ago.

WM. HECKROTTE,
corner of Charles and Camden sts.

N. B. If the Servants will return to their duty, they shall not be punished in any manner; as I believe they were evil advised in taking the step they did. They are all three sober, honest servants. Any person communicating this to them will do them a favor, and oblige me. Judea, can spell some, was taught by my children.   W. H.

je 5 2t*

Ad placed by Baltimore tavernkeeper William Heckrotte in the *Republican & Daily Argus* of June 5, 1844, after Charles Torrey helped three people he enslaved escape north. Heckrotte took a conciliatory stance, hoping to lure them back— possibly to be sold south, like many runaways. [Courtesy of Maryland State Archives]

13

Let the Strife Go On

In early June, Hope Slatter's slow season, a white stranger, slightly built but intense in manner, called on him at his office. Slatter had sent off his last captives of the spring in mid-April, twenty-nine people aboard the ship *Tippecanoe*. His agents were out trolling Maryland's rural counties for prospects, but their purchases would pick up only in late summer, after the harvest was in. Slatter, who was celebrating his fifty-fourth birthday that week, had been living in Baltimore for nearly a decade. His business was a fixture at the busy harbor, and he had achieved as great a degree of social acceptance as his money could buy. He had been married to his third wife, Emma, from a local Baltimore County family, for more than six years, and they'd had two children, in addition to his three surviving children from his previous marriages. He was an immensely successful businessman, and he was now the nation's leading symbol of the domestic traffic in human beings—admired by some, envied by others, and despised by many more.

It would have taken only moments for Slatter to understand that his visitor, twenty-three years younger, was in this last camp. If he caught the name, he might have recognized it. There had been the reward organized by Baltimore's slavery defenders, Slatter likely among them, for the capture of Charles Torrey the year before, and Torrey's signed articles from the *Tocsin* or the *Patriot* attacking the slave traders in general and Slatter in particular might have reached him. But whether or not he immediately understood who Torrey was, Slatter would hear him out. After all, he had tried to be courteous on numerous occasions to just such pious, moralistic types who wanted to tour his slave jail and flamboyantly express their dismay.

This man wanted to talk to Slatter about Ben Jones, the towering runaway who had been brought in two months earlier, his head battered and bloody, to lodge in Slatter's jail until his fate could be decided. Slatter, probably in consultation with William Anderson, Jones's former enslaver, had set the price to purchase Jones's freedom at $700—a reasonable amount for such a big man and capable worker. Jones's friends in Pennsylvania were trying to raise the money, and Slatter, showing an accommodating façade to Jones's Quaker neighbors, was willing to wait for the outcome. If they couldn't meet his price, Slatter would be happy to ship him to New Orleans, where he knew he could get far more than $700.

Now this meddling abolitionist wanted him to lower his price. Slatter talked politely to the young man—and saw absolutely no reason to bargain with him. If anything, the ardent abolitionist's visit suggested to him that the price had been set too low. If Jones's friends were this devoted to winning his freedom, they'd meet Slatter's price. But as he and Torrey sparred, Slatter began to focus on something else: this fellow seemed to fit the description of the Yankee who had inveigled away the slaves of Bushrod Taylor, his fellow slave trader down in Winchester, a hundred miles to the west. Though the traders were competitors, they faced the same enemies, and they shared tips and warnings. As soon as he got rid of this fellow—*What's your name again? Where can I reach you?*—Slatter would write to Taylor and pass on the name.

◦─➡ ⇐─◦

Like Smallwood, Torrey had impatiently dismissed the complaints of other abolitionists that direct action to free the enslaved was not "prudent." But by walking into the office of his sworn enemy and introducing himself, he was displaying a truly rash disregard for his own safety. Was he eager to confront the man he had so long bedeviled in print? Had his recent success in liberating the six Webbs and three tavern workers, among many others, made him overconfident? Or, as he had written in January, did "private causes of misery" make him reckless? He was separated, perhaps estranged, from his wife and children. And he knew the tuberculosis that had killed his parents and sister, and with which he was permanently infected, could flare up and threaten his life at any time.

Whatever his state of mind, Torrey's days of planning escapes came to an end the night of June 25, 1844, when Baltimore's most famous constable and slave catcher, John Zell, and Zell's associate Simeon Hays turned up at his boardinghouse with a warrant for his arrest for aiding the Webbs' escape from Winchester. Torrey was armed with two pistols, the authorities claimed—if true, a marker of the devout Christian's increasing willingness to threaten or use violence to pursue his goals. The arrest report in *The Baltimore Sun*, which was unfailingly friendly to Zell, oozed with hostility for Torrey:

> *Fugitive arrested*—A person not unknown to fame, having gained some notoriety at the slaveholders meetings in Annapolis, in 1842, and subsequently by some proceedings in Washington, named *Chas. T. Torrey*, sometimes known we believe, with the prefix of "Rev.", was arrested on Tuesday night by officers Hays, Zell & Co., as a fugitive from justice from the State of Virginia, where he stands charged with aiding and abetting the escape of six negroes.

The proslavery *Sun* implied that Torrey's clerical status might well be dubious, given his history of troublemaking on behalf of the enslaved. The report noted that when Torrey came before a magistrate, he was further charged with helping the mother and two teenagers enslaved by Baltimore tavernkeeper William Heckrotte to escape, and *The Sun* mentioned witnesses who had allegedly seen the four traveling through Harford County, north of Baltimore.

It didn't look good for the accused. Torrey had repeatedly lambasted the police in the newspaper as corrupt tools of the slave power, attacking John Zell and his private detective firm by name. Now it looked like Zell, and prosecutors in two states, had the goods on his role in two escapes. He was tossed into a decrepit cell with a half dozen others awaiting trial. He described the vile conditions in a colorful letter to his uncle, the Reverend William Torrey:

> I am confined in a room with the worst class of prisoners; one murderer, one counterfeiter, one receiver of stolen goods, and others charged with the most infamous crimes. For a week or two, vermin, of all sorts, abounded; lice, roaches, bed-bugs by thousands, fleas, weasels [presumably meaning weevils], red-ants and moths. However, in time, by patient effort, we have got quite rid of them.

In Massachusetts, Torrey's acquaintances traded news about his arrest, and his old friend Joshua Leavitt, the abolitionist journalist, wrote an appeal for donations to Torrey's defense. Leavitt wrote that Torrey lacked funds because he "had just commenced a promising business in Baltimore, in *the manufacture of starch*." It was the first and only indication that Torrey had pursued paid work after moving to Baltimore. It is possible that Torrey had considered entering Baltimore's thriving starch industry, perhaps with the goal of supporting his wife and children, and had mentioned it to Leavitt. But after his arrest, in many public and private defenses of his own character, Torrey himself appears never to have raised any such business scheme.

In his early letters from jail, Torrey seemed to veer between anxiety and defiance. He told his uncle in his letter that he had "very little desire to become a martyr." But in the next breath he made it obvious that the notion of sacrificing himself for his cause held some appeal to this devout man, steeped in the history of Christian heroes: "Did you ever hear of a Torrey that suffered martyrdom? I hope among our good old Puritan ancestors there were some who had the martyr spirit." In another letter, he suggested that with his arrest, he himself had become the battlefield on which the fate of slavery would be decided: "Now, I am made, in a manner I never dreamed of, the battle-ground between slavery and freedom. A battle-field is commonly torn up by the violence of the conflict.—But let the strife go on! Whether it be over my prison or over my grave."

Torrey, with characteristic passion and grandiosity, saw an opportunity in disaster. Friends paid for him to place a notice in *The Baltimore Sun*. "I AM NOT ON TRIAL," he assured readers, who must have been surprised to hear it. "No. thank God! Maryland and Virginia must go to trial before the tribunal of the civilized world." When he had been jailed in Annapolis, he had framed his disruption of the Slaveholders' Convention as a triumph and his *"pledge made in Annapolis jail"* to vanquish slavery as a vow worthy of the history books. Now he began to plot out in his mind a legal strategy that might leverage the new case against him to take down the entire slave system.

In July, a month after his arrest, he wrote a formal address to be read to a Liberty Party gathering planned in Salem, Massachusetts, laying out his thinking. He would challenge the "requisition," or extradition request, filed by Virginia's governor demanding that Maryland authorities hand him over for trial. With two states involved, he reasoned, the case would land at the Supreme Court. The requisition would be defeated because it had been sent without any evidence that he had committed the crime in question, Torrey postulated. And the court would rule further that trying to escape slavery is no crime, he said, so aiding such an escape could not be criminal—thus invalidating multiple statutes in both Maryland and Virginia. As his thinking careened into this imaginary future, Torrey cited the recent freeing of American hostages in North Africa:

> The State of Maryland, that voted its *thanks* and swords of honor to those who rescued a few of our countrymen from slavery in Tripoli, CANNOT, by any statute law, make it a *crime,* to help her *own native citizens out of slavery on her own soil.* The thing is absurd. Courts of equity cannot maintain it. Constitutional judges must laugh such a monumental folly out of court.

Once these laughing judges dispensed with the laws that banned escapes and prohibited anyone from assisting with escapes, Torrey predicted, "slavery cannot be maintained an hour in any of the border States." From there, he wrote, the doom of the slave power would spread like wildfire: "The very *agitation* of these mighty issues, in courts held in the bosom of the slave States, will topple down the whole crazy fabric of slavery." Torrey, sitting in his cell with the vermin and accused criminals, gave the system just two, maybe three, years to collapse following his projected triumph in the Supreme Court.

It was a tantalizing picture, described in such resounding language that a reader might get caught up in his inspiring fantasy. Torrey wrote to his wife around the same time to lay out his moral logic: "Shall a man be put into the Penitentiary for doing good?—For doing his plain duty to the poor and oppressed?—That is the real question at issue, and it is one that will shake down the whole edifice of Slavery." His rhetoric was powerful, and his cause was just. Yet as Torrey well knew in his more sober moments, many Americans had gone to prison for encouraging and aiding escapes—for doing good. "Constitutional judges" had already had multiple opportunities to issue crushing rulings against the "monumental folly" of slavery in a country that purported to stand for liberty. They had not done so.

In any case, the Maryland prosecutors had a simpler strategy to keep Torrey's case from getting anywhere near the Supreme Court. Though the escape from Heckrotte in Maryland had occurred months after the escape from Taylor in Virginia, they would try Torrey first in Maryland, avoiding the complication of disparate jurisdictions. The fabric of slavery would be safe.

⋅→═◦═←⋅

In an America deeply polarized over slavery and abolitionism, Torrey's arrest became national news, the reactions underscoring the chasm separating north and south. *The Picayune* of New Orleans, the largest receiving city in the domestic slave trade, took a grim pleasure in the development. "The *Rev.* Mr. Torrey," the newspaper wrote, with italics to undercut his title, was "most deservedly in prison, in Baltimore," having "deliberately meditated such gross injuries to Southern gentlemen. . . . We hope—and we are confident in our hope—that the people of Maryland will take proper care of Mr. Torrey."

In New England, newspapers published an appeal for donations for Torrey's defense from a committee of abolitionists, organized by the prominent New York antislavery activist Lewis Tappan. Torrey was accused of "aiding suffering fellow men in attempts to escape from cruel bondage," the appeal said, listing Torrey's past clerical posts in Massachusetts and congressman grandfather and urging support for his wife and children.

Despite the deep tensions inside the antislavery movement, even Torrey's longtime critics and rivals denounced his arrest and offered support. Most notable among them was William Lloyd Garrison, who said the arrest recalled his own brief jailing in Baltimore many years earlier:

> He is in great danger of being crushed, no matter how inno-
> cent he may be of the charges now preferred against him. . . .
> Mr. Torrey, as an avowed abolitionist, has just as good a chance
> of receiving a fair trial, whether in Baltimore or Richmond,
> as a lamb in the embrace of a wolf has of being set at liberty,
> without bodily harm.

Even as he offered sympathy and support, Garrison found it impossible not to recall Torrey's past vituperation against him in their battles over the tactics of abolitionism, when Torrey had dubbed him "William Lloyd Garrulous," editor of the "Lyingberator":

> Probably, of all the false friends who have lifted up their heels
> against me—of the host of enemies who have deliberately sought
> to destroy my influence in the anti slavery cause, by covertly

> assailing and misrepresenting my religious sentiments, no one
> has surpassed him in the venom or subtlety of his attacks. . . .
> But I care nothing for the past. He is now in distress and in
> prison, on a charge which, if it be true, is highly creditable to
> his courage and humanity.

Even if it was obviously untrue that he cared "nothing for the past," Garrison urged others to contribute to Torrey's defense and to spread the word about his plight. "Let all the anti-slavery journals speak out in thunder tones on this subject," he wrote.

Other antislavery activists recalled that Torrey had ignored their warnings about the danger he was in. The Black pastor and activist Daniel A. Payne of Philadelphia recounted that he "had repeatedly warned him not to come to Baltimore or Washington," writing to both Torrey and his frequent host in Philadelphia Dr. James J. G. Bias: "The warnings were unheeded. The idea of liberty consumed him." More troubling were the oblique criticisms of Torrey for neglecting his family that began to appear in the press. A report of the case in a leading abolitionist paper, *The Emancipator*, lauded Torrey as "a devoted Abolitionist, a man of education and of talents, and of unimpeached character." But just two columns away on the same page appeared a letter from a writer calling himself "Norfolk"—the name of the Massachusetts county where Torrey's wife and children were now staying with her parents—that raised questions about Torrey's judgment and about his priorities.

First, "Norfolk" attacked the whole notion of traveling to slave states to encourage people to flee slavery: it was "unwise and hurtful to the *general* cause of emancipation," though he added that Torrey "should not be judged too severely for a mere error of judgment." Then, the pseudonymous writer got more personal. "It is so evident to those acquainted with Mr. T., and especially with the circumstances of his family, that he has greatly mistook his calling," "Norfolk" wrote. He urged contributions to Torrey's defense "especially for the sake of an amiable wife and two children, who are now thrown upon the cold charity of the world for their support." Though he wrote indirectly, this person—clearly an acquaintance of Mary Torrey's family—implied that Torrey had neglected the support of his family in the pursuit of ill-advised adventures in the south.

The criticism stung Torrey. He was keenly aware of his shortcomings as a provider and family man, and these public hints from someone who favored the antislavery cause were galling. He soon deduced that "Norfolk" was a friend and neighbor of his wife's parents named Milton Metcalf Fisher, which suggested that Fisher was reflecting views Mary's parents had expressed of their wayward son-in-law. Months later, Torrey was still shaken by the public rebuke, writing to Fisher in a ten-page letter that the article "did me more injury than all the malice of my enemies could have done."

If Torrey believed Fisher's slighting references to him in the "Norfolk" letter reflected the views of his father-in-law and former teacher and mentor, the Reverend Jacob Ide, he was right. Fisher visited Ide and then wrote in a note to Torrey's old friend Amos Phelps that Ide was "deeply afflicted with the case of Mr. Torrey, yet not so much from the fact of his imprisonment as from the state & temper of his feelings toward him and Mrs. T." Fisher said Ide was distressed by what he considered Torrey's erratic behavior and worried about him and about Mary. "Mr. T is the strangest man I ever saw," Ide had told Fisher. Mary Torrey would later write in a letter that her husband was "partially insane upon some subjects."

The picture is of dedicated friends and sympathizers very concerned about Torrey's state of mind, and it raises a question that occurs to anyone who studies Torrey's life: Did he suffer from a serious mental illness? Certainly, his extreme ups and downs, his impulsiveness, and his grandiosity all suggest the possibility of bipolar disorder, in an era before psychiatric medications. E. Fuller Torrey, his biographer, a prominent psychiatrist, raises the possibility of "cerebral tuberculosis," in which the TB infection might have spread to Torrey's brain. But he concludes that "there is no evidence whatever that Charles Torrey was ever insane in a clinical sense."

What is notable is that Mary Torrey stood with her husband under the most difficult of circumstances. While trying to support her family by taking writing jobs that friends found for her and raising two children on her own, Mary wrote frequently to Charles, worked relentlessly to organize and support his defense, and managed to visit him in Baltimore, undertaking the long journey from Massachusetts. If she was exasperated at times, she was also loyal. Their correspondence, or the part that has been preserved, shows mutual affection and support, with Mary sending news about the children and family friends who plan to make a prison visit, and Charles making practical requests (an Italian dictionary) and expressing his love. Torrey told Mary that he was trying to devote the same hour of the evening to prayer as she habitually did, "so we can more literally 'meet together,' when we plead for the mercies we need, at the day's close. I try to think of you, and dear Charles and Mary, as kneeling with me, and pray to our Father as the God of the family covenant."

As if their relationship did not have enough to bear, Charles and Mary Torrey now faced an organized campaign to slander him, break his spirit, and perhaps poison future jurors against him. He had to refute rumors that Mary was seeking a divorce, and he saw the hand of his old enemies behind the falsehoods: "From the time of my arrest, the whole clique of slave traders, slave-catching police men, low slaveholders, and their abettors, including one or two of the prison officers, have made it their business to abuse and slander me and my friends, with the general object of preventing the existence, of at least the expression, of any personal or Christian sympathy for me."

Then the attacks got more specific. Torrey's kind Baltimore landlady and her daughters visited him almost daily "to give me a chance to breathe the fresh air, by walking a few moments in the prison yard." But these friendly visits were soon viciously distorted: the jail authorities banned the landlady and her daughters from the premises after a false allegation of "gross lewdness" was leveled against Torrey and the landlady. Torrey persuasively denied any sexual connection between them and said "the busiest of these agents of shame are a noted slave trader and two

police men," likely having in mind Slatter, Zell, and one of Zell's partners. Torrey was probably correct in his belief that the local proslavery
establishment had made the bogus accusation in an attempt to reduce
any chance that Torrey might be exonerated and return to the fight.

❖═◗◖═❖

They were not wrong to view Torrey as a formidable enemy. While in jail,
despite his desperate situation, Torrey continued to do what he could to
keep up his crusade against slavery and injustice. During the months he
was jailed and awaiting trial, he claimed to have arranged the escape of
fifteen more people from slavery, ten of whom were "rescued from the
clutches of slave traders"—not an implausible notion, since he seems to
have regularly talked with enslaved people who were temporarily jailed.
He presumably could advise them on escape routes and who might help
them on the way north. Until the warden forbade it, he preached to his
fellow inmates, listened to their stories, and sought to help them any way
he could.

Torrey claimed to have put an end to an old corrupt practice at the
Baltimore Jail: locking up a free Black person on baseless grounds, let-
ting the charges for their food and lodging accumulate, and then "selling
them for their jail fees"—in other words, selling them to Slatter or another trader to pay off the charges. His intervention with jail authorities
to stop the practice "incurred not a little of the wrath of the lower classes
of slaveholders, slave traders and their abettors," he wrote.

He also met a fifteen-year-old Black boy, born free, who had been
illegally enslaved and abused by a white man who then planned to sell
him to a slave trader. The boy ran away, got caught, and was jailed in
Baltimore. Torrey went to work to win his freedom (it is unclear whether
he succeeded). Like many educated people before and since who found
themselves in prison, Torrey felt he had new insight into the inequity and
corruption that saturated the legal system: "I have seen much, very much,
of the oppression of the poor, both white and colored, since I have been
a prisoner. I have seen thorough-paced knaves liberated, and innocent

men, because poor or simple-hearted, subjected to imprisonment and loss of property."

Still, after prosecutors made it clear they would start with the Maryland case, eliminating any likelihood that his case might go to the Supreme Court, Torrey gradually lost his optimism. On September 13, 1844, after nearly three months in jail, he attempted an escape, using saws and chisels smuggled into jail, evidently by his former landlady. He had made the mistake of confiding in his cellmates, and one of them—a slave trader named Dryer, jailed for counterfeiting—betrayed him to the authorities. Torrey was punished by being placed in leg irons, and his health swiftly deteriorated. Sleepless and feverish, he wrote apologetically to Mary: "I deemed it my duty to try *once* to escape out of the hands of my enemies." A week later, he wrote her again, with dire news: his tuberculosis had flared up again. "My old disorder, which so nearly killed me in 1835, had returned in all its force. My heart throbs constantly and painfully, and my head, and body, and limbs are never free from pain. The last nine nights, I have slept in all, less than fifteen hours."

Torrey had recovered some of his strength, at least temporarily, by the time his trial began in late November. The testimony demonstrated just how unwise he had been to try to organize escapes without the assistance of Smallwood or another Black collaborator. Charles Heckrotte, the son of tavernkeeper William Heckrotte, recalled that one night a few days before the three enslaved workers fled, he had seen "a white man standing at the gate of our yard, talking with Judah Gooseberry; the white man looked at me rather suspiciously, and went away."

Torrey had been spotted repeatedly as he drove the carriage north toward Pennsylvania with the three Gooseberrys aboard. Worse, it turned out that he had been seen on multiple occasions transporting other fugitives; it was memorable to see a white man driving Black passengers. Witnesses had also seen Torrey and the Gooseberrys stopping to eat crackers and sausage that were later traced to the tavern. Others found on the picnic spot a ribbon that Judea Gooseberry had been given to tie up her hair. The man who rented Torrey the carriage and team of horses on the day of the escape testified that he had brought them back several days later, the horses "very much fatigued." And so on.

John Zell, the constable and slave catcher, orchestrated the testimony of Torrey's cellmates, who claimed that he had confided to them details of his escape operation. Torrey, they said, had each group of freedom seekers meet at a house behind Baltimore's grand Green Mount Cemetery, where a trusted African American blacksmith known as "Old Nick" helped keep them out of sight until the time of departure.

Torrey contested the details, and it is certainly possible that the cellmates were rewarded by the authorities to invent or exaggerate Torrey's supposed confidences. But the case was overwhelming. A number of notables, including Thomas G. Pratt, a lawyer who had just won the race for Maryland governor by a mere 548 votes, turned up to hear the closing arguments. The lead prosecutor, George R. Richardson, urged the jurors to ignore the moral and political issues that gave the case its electric charge. "I shall not pretend to discuss the subject of slavery as it exists in the South," he said, "or the peculiar views and sentiments of an adverse character entertained by the people of the North."

Richardson seemed to have some concern that the jury might be swayed by sympathy for Mary Torrey, who had sat through the entire trial alongside her father, Jacob Ide—even the unsympathetic *Sun* called her steadfastness "another proof of the abiding constancy of woman's heart." Richardson urged jurors to separate such understandable emotions from the case at hand: "You can sympathize with her, gentlemen, you must; with all the anxiety of your minds you may feel and dwell upon the intense anguish which your verdict may inflict upon the wife, but you must render that verdict in conformity with the obligations of your oath."

Torrey's attorney, Reverdy Johnson, a silver-tongued lawyer who would five years later be appointed attorney general of the United States, had struggled diligently throughout the trial to raise doubts about the state's witnesses with persistent cross-examination. Now Johnson, who had refused to take a fee, produced what the *Baltimore Sun* reporter called a "magnificent" argument that held the crowded courtroom "spell

bound, in breathless silence." But even as he spoke in handsome paragraphs about slavery and Maryland history and Saul on the road to Da-
mascus, Johnson seemed to concede that the case was a lost cause. When
he appealed to the jurors to consider the plight of Mary and the children,
he declared that she faced "the probable adverse termination of this trial"
and the loss of her husband for "long and distressing years." The moment
would be revisited later by one of Torrey's most fervent supporters, who
said Johnson's "wrong and fatal admission" had given "the whole case
over into the hands of the prosecutors."

Whether a less conciliatory closing argument from Johnson might
have made a difference is dubious. It took the all-male jury one hour and
forty minutes to reach a verdict: guilty on all counts.

⋆⊶⫩⊷⋆

Paradoxically, the verdict seemed to give Torrey new energy: the next day
he sent a long letter to an abolitionist newspaper—at once a refutation
of the case against him, a general admission that he had indeed aided
escapes, and a call for prison reform. "Do you ask, 'Have you anything to
regret, in what you have done, whether for individual slaves, or the cause
of freedom?' No, from the bottom of my heart, NO," he wrote.

Perhaps responding to the critics who had faulted him for neglecting
his family, Torrey decided to write a book that might bring his family some
income. In just twelve days he completed a 256-page memoir of his childhood and spiritual development called *Home! Or, the Pilgrims' Faith Revived*, discussing plans for publication with Mary and his closest friends.
The intent was to capitalize on the trial publicity, as notations on the title
page made clear: "Written during his incarceration in Baltimore Jail, after his conviction and while awaiting—his sentence. . . . Published for the
benefit of his family." It would sell modestly, but Mary treasured the income. At his urging, she began collecting his letters for a planned volume
of correspondence, another potential source of revenue for the family.

In the midst of these efforts, Torrey returned to the courthouse and

HOME!

OR

THE PILGRIMS' FAITH REVIVED.

BY

CHARLES T. TORREY.

Written during his incarceration in Baltimore Jail, after his
conviction, and while awaiting—his sentence.

———

' Aye, call it holy ground,
The land whereon they trod ;
They left unstained what there they found,
Freedom to worship God.'

———

PUBLISHED FOR THE BENEFIT OF HIS FAMILY.

The title page of Charles Torrey's spiritual memoir, written in
prison in Baltimore in hopes of raising some money for the support of his wife and two children.

was sentenced to six years and three months in the Maryland Penitentiary. What followed was months of frantic efforts by Mary, her father,
and Torrey's many supporters to find some way to free him. They, and he,
were quite aware that his struggle with tuberculosis could not end well
in the cold and drafty prison cell, which measured four feet by eight feet.
Mary, with the encouragement of her parents, proposed seeking a pardon from the new Maryland governor, Thomas Pratt, who had attended
the last day of Torrey's trial. Her husband would vow to leave the state
of Maryland and never return; they could raise money to pay William

Heckrotte for the three people who had fled from him, trading compensation for a statement supporting, or at least not objecting to, Torrey's release. Mary enlisted Amos Phelps and other friends in the effort to arrange such a deal, displaying an impressive grasp of practical politics and dedication to her flawed and ailing husband.

Torrey, meanwhile, labored in the penitentiary's weaving shop when his health permitted, studied Italian and German, and read with interest a prison memoir by an Italian revolutionary. At his request, Mary obtained and sent him an Italian Bible. He received visitors, wrote letters, and regularly saw a prison doctor. But his physical decline could not be stopped.

In lucid and less painful moments, he sent Mary parenting advice: don't scold young Charles too much for his absentmindedness; use the winter to teach the children about insects and other creatures and then, in the spring, take them outside. "Childhood is the time to teach and enjoy all the branches of Natural History," Torrey wrote. "Let Grammar go, to be learned by reading and talking, and studied at maturer years." He expressed gratitude to friends, including Gerrit Smith, who had assured him that they would make sure his family had financial support. It would give him great satisfaction, he wrote to Mary, "to know that you and our children were protected and cared for by friends, able and pledged to provide for every want you would make known to them" and "that no dishonor attached to my name, in the minds of the great and good."

But at other times, Torrey's mood took a darker turn, one that seems to have frightened him:

> Very often, for three months past, I have been obliged to struggle to repress the impulse to utter insane ravings, and even wicked follies which my whole soul abhors. Most of the time I have very little control over my thoughts. If a painful idea takes possession of the mind, it is as if a rough iron was drawn over the brain, for whole hours, and even days at a time. These forms of mental suffering depend wholly on the degree of bodily pain I endure.

In February 1846, Mary sent a petition to Governor Pratt that was frank about her "beloved husband's" declining health. Charles Torrey had been adamant that she not misrepresent his views of slavery, and she walked a careful line. While Torrey may have broken the law, she wrote, his act "involves no moral guilt" but rather "sudden, rash and imprudent yielding to his sympathies." After more than eighteen months of incarceration, she wrote, "his health is failing—his mental faculties are impaired, and unless mercy is extended, he will die or become a maniac ere the term for which he is imprisoned shall have expired." A separate petition, signed by more than forty friends and supporters from Massachusetts, expressed regret for Torrey's actions and for his "mistaken views" and promised to, in effect, keep an eye on him should he be freed.

But Governor Pratt, who was the son of slaveholders and whose own son would fight for the Confederacy, took his time, clearly calculating the political damage that a pardon might do him. He may also have been delaying in hope that the prisoner's tuberculosis might save him a decision. Nearly three months later, with Torrey moved to the prison hospital and declining fast, Pratt finally granted the pardon, "on condition of him leaving this State, not returning thereto, and paying for the Slaves taken off by him." Torrey would pay $1,200 to the warden of the penitentiary, to be passed on to Heckrotte, the document said. All the details had been agreed, and Pratt signed the pardon with a flourish on May 9.

Word of the pardon reached the prison later the same day. It came too late. At three that afternoon, Torrey, in the words of a friendly newspaper writer, had been "freed from the prison, without the aid of the governor." He died in his penitentiary hospital bed at the age of thirty-two.

⋄⇒◉⇐⋄

Predictably, Torrey's death proved as divisive in the fractious abolitionist community as had his bold and reckless course in life. His funeral was first scheduled for Boston's Park Street Church, a bulwark of abolitionism where William Lloyd Garrison had given his first public speech against slavery. The funeral and its location were even printed in

Garrison's *Liberator*. Then, just two days before the event, permission to use the church was suddenly withdrawn. No one who knew the history of Torrey and Garrison's feuding doubted that Garrison was behind the decision.

The funeral was moved to Tremont Temple, a block away, and drew more than three thousand people, who heard the Reverend Joseph C. Lovejoy—brother of abolitionism's first martyr, the journalist Elijah Lovejoy—deliver a stem-winder of a sermon. "Torrey is no more!" Lovejoy declared: "The cruel murder of a righteous man, for acts of mercy, has been consummated by the slow torture of confinement in the prison of one of the sovereign States of Christian America." He argued that Torrey had broken only illegitimate laws protecting the morally bankrupt system of slavery and, instead, had followed God's law. The state had conspired with the slave power, Lovejoy said, to make sure his illness turned his sentence into a death penalty. But now, Lovejoy said, was the time to redirect the mourning into political action. "Slavery has murdered the young, vigorous, social, talented, and pious Torrey!" he declared. "Now, either shed no tear on that early grave, or write there the vow of Hannibal—eternal war against slavery!"

It was quite an event in the world of antislavery activism, with abolitionist papers everywhere excerpting the sermon and eulogizing the martyred hero. A boisterous meeting at Boston's Faneuil Hall after the funeral gave more speakers a chance to interpret the life that had been lost and use its example to rally supporters. Torrey, whose visits to Black churches in Washington had helped inspire his work, might have especially appreciated the tributes of African Americans honoring him and denouncing his foes. A gathering of "the colored people of Oberlin," Ohio, praised Torrey for "obeying the dictates which he believed reason and reason's God had given him" and becoming "a martyr to our cause." Governor Pratt, the group declared in its resolutions, "has shown himself guilty of a base servility to the demon of slavery."

Torrey had set an example for the radical wing of abolitionism, choosing direct action and putting his life on the line for the freedom of others. The poet John Greenleaf Whittier recalled those whose lives Torrey had indisputably changed, in simple and eloquent homage to his departed friend: "In the wild woods of Canada, around many a happy fireside and holy family altar, his name is on the lips of God's poor." A line in the remembrance published by *The New Jersey Freeman* sounded a defiant note, suggesting that his memory and model would invigorate the war against slavery.

"Mr. Torrey has gone to rest in peace beyond the reach of his persecutors," it said, "but they are not out of *his*; they are done with him, but he is not done with *them*."

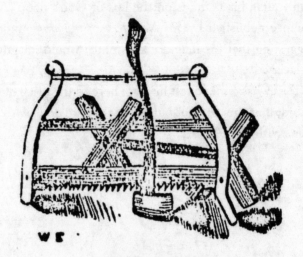

NOTICE.

THE _____ ed begs to inform the public generally, that he is prepared to furnish the following articles by Wholesale and Retail:

AXE HANDLES,
PICK AXE HANDLES,
ADZE HANDLES,
BUCK SAW FRAMES, and
SAW-HORSES, &c.,
Made in the best manner.
ALSO, BY RETAIL,
New BUCK SAWS, of the best quality, in complete order for service. Also, Axes ready Handled. Also, Handes put into Axes, and other Tools.
T. SMALLWOOD'S Saw Factory,
York Street, No. 88.

An 1859 ad in a Black-owned Toronto newspaper, *The Provincial Freeman*, for Thomas Smallwood's saw factory. The former Washington shoemaker had built a successful new business in his new Canadian home. [Image from ProQuest's Black Studies Center displayed with permission of ProQuest LLC]

14

Fly to Canada, and Begin Anew

The big, biracial crowd at Torrey's Boston funeral did not include Thomas Smallwood. He was still in danger of arrest on American soil in 1846, even in the northern states, and he was busy with his new life in Toronto. He and Elizabeth were raising two boys and two girls then between the ages of three and fifteen; their daughter Susan had died the previous year, at the age of ten, of what was called "worm fever," a parasitic illness. Despite that tragedy, and nearly three years after reaching Canada, he was operating a thriving business, manufacturing and sharpening saws, from his new house in the very center of Toronto.

It is clear, however, that Smallwood closely followed the American abolitionist press, which carried many accounts of Charles Torrey's imprisonment, trial, final illness, and death. Among the encomiums were some that cited a claim Torrey had made several times late in his life: that he had helped free some four hundred people from slavery. Defending his record to Milton Fisher, who had implied that he had neglected his wife and children, Torrey wrote: "Acting on the maxim of 'doing good as we have the opportunity,' I suppose I have freed about 400 who, otherwise, would have lived, and, most of them died, in slavery."

This total of four hundred people aided in escapes is plausible—if it includes everyone assisted in flight by the network Torrey helped establish, measured from the day Torrey met Smallwood to the end of

Torrey's prison days. It roughly fits with Smallwood's previous claim that they had helped free one hundred and fifty people from Washington alone between March and November 1842. It might well be exaggerated, and it is impossible to confirm. But given the energy and daring with which they pursued their goal, and their use of wagons and carriages to try to make every escape a mass escape, four hundred seems a reasonable estimate.

In the annals of major figures associated with the underground railroad, it would place their numerical achievement somewhere between those of two later and better-known figures, the courageous Harriet Tubman, who would personally help free about seventy people in repeated ventures south during the 1850s, and the indefatigable Philadelphia activist William Still. Still's biographer says he "personally interviewed and ascertained the needs of 995 runaway slaves" and gave practical help to most of them, though he generally did not help initiate escapes in the way that Smallwood, Torrey, and Tubman did.

The glaring problem with Torrey's statement—"I suppose I have freed about 400"—was the omission of any mention of Smallwood. At least half of the four hundred likely escaped during the more than fifteen months when Smallwood was operating solo in Washington and Torrey was either serving as editor of the *Tocsin* and *Patriot* in Albany or traveling in the north. Moreover, without Smallwood's crucial role in communicating with the enslaved and expanding operations to Baltimore by recruiting Jacob Gibbs, it is not clear that Torrey would have been able to organize most of the escapes in which he did play some role. Nor was the omission of Smallwood's name a onetime lapse. In his correspondence and published writings, at least those that survive, Torrey never once mentioned Smallwood's role in organizing escapes. In articles and statements, this may be forgivable—he knew that Smallwood was operating covertly in a very risky environment, addressing the public only via the pseudonym Sam Weller, whom Torrey did praise in the pages of the Albany newspaper. But by October 1844, when Torrey wrote to Milton Fisher from prison, Smallwood had been named in *The Baltimore Sun* after the fiasco at Bush's barn and had been safe in Canada for many months.

Torrey's failure to credit Smallwood would become part of a larger pattern. In an article about Torrey's death and his career, a Boston newspaper, *The Chronotype,* credited him with conceiving the underground railroad while locked up in the Annapolis jail: "It was, if we understand it, here that he formed a plan of operations which has been denominated the Underground Railroad, and by means of which 400 slaves are now rejoicing in freedom." In 1847, as part of the campaign to raise money to support Mary Torrey and the children, Joseph C. Lovejoy, who had preached at Torrey's funeral, compiled and published his *Memoir of Rev. Charles T. Torrey, Who Died in the Penitentiary of Maryland, Where He Was Confined for Showing Mercy to the Poor.* Not once in its 364 pages of journal entries, letters, and reminiscences did Smallwood's name appear.

Torrey was praised and eulogized as a historic figure and Christian martyr largely based on his role in aiding escapes. Smallwood, whose achievements were significantly greater, including assisting more escapes, writing the inimitable Sam Weller letters, and christening the underground railroad, gets not a single reference. Nor does the name "Smallwood" appear in the other contemporary book on the Albany escape route, *Memoir of Rev. Abel Brown,* published in 1849 by Brown's widow. Torrey rates a half dozen mentions.

The erasure of Smallwood, which would continue in many subsequent books on abolitionism and the underground railroad, surely reflects the oblivious or conscious racism of even the white Americans most progressive on racial matters at the time. It seems almost as if Torrey was so anxious to defend his own achievements that he could not bear to share the spotlight. But Smallwood, never one to shy away from complaining about perceived injustice to him, seems never to have expressed resentment at the slight. When he got around to writing his own memoir—surely in part to make sure his role was recorded for history—he wrote of Torrey only in the warmest terms: "that most excellent and whole-souled Abolitionist," "the beloved friend . . . who is now no more," "the good friend Torrey," and so on. He consistently credited Torrey as the spark that lit the fire that became the underground railroad, even as he made clear that he had long considered organizing escapes: "I, who had made it a matter of study for years, had by the assistance of the Lord and Mr. Torrey opened a way through which scores were successful in their attempt to escape from slavery." This magnanimity on Smallwood's part seems to have reflected a deep affection for and gratitude to Torrey. But perhaps he had also learned not to have high expectations of credit or praise from white people.

⋄⇒◉⇐⋄

It was August 1, 1854, and Toronto's Black community had been preparing for months to mark an anniversary: exactly twenty years before, under the terms of the Slavery Abolition Act passed by the British Parliament, Great Britain had officially emancipated the hundreds of thousands of people still enslaved across the far-flung British Empire. The politically and socially active from the city and outlying towns had risen early on that summer Tuesday to attend a 5 a.m. prayer meeting at Sayer Street Chapel, near the heart of Toronto's small Black community. Then, after waiting out a rain shower, they gathered for a formal procession led by Scott's Cornet Band and including members of the local Order of Odd Fellows in full masonic garb. After walking about a mile, they reached Browne's Wharf, on Lake Ontario, where they greeted a steamboat load of Black residents from the city of Hamilton, thirty-five miles away at the far western end of the lake. Then, with the crowd still growing, the man chosen as "President of the Day" made a speech. "Fellow subjects of this noble province, and citizens of Hamilton," Thomas Smallwood began his welcoming remarks:

> It is my pleasing duty, in behalf of a portion of the fellow citizens of Toronto, to welcome you, who have honored us this day with your presence, to partake of a festival in commemoration of one among the greatest events in British history, when that magnanimous nation swept the bonds from 800,000 bondsmen, and made them free.

It must have been a gratifying moment for the fifty-three-year-old Smallwood, who had made his home in Canada a decade earlier precisely because British authorities had made this historic decision. He and Elizabeth had suffered the death of another daughter, Catharine, at fourteen, of what was reported simply as "decline." But he had thrived in business, and with Elizabeth at his side he had seen his surviving daughter and two sons begin to make their way in the world. It was telling, in fact, that *The Provincial Freeman,* the local Black newspaper, had to identify the speaker as "Thomas Smallwood, Senr.," to distinguish him from his son, Thomas W. F. Smallwood, who at the age of twenty-three was already active in business and political circles.

But even on this day, when the *Freeman* would write that "a more orderly, harmonious, and better disposed body of persons never met together here," Smallwood Senior did not shy away from controversy:

> Though some narrow-minded individuals object, saying, because we did not achieve it [i.e., emancipation] ourselves, it is disgraceful for us to celebrate this day. I am assured by your presence here today, that I speak your sentiments, when I say that I envy not the narrowness of the mind, that can entertain such disloyal sentiments: so you are therefore heartily welcome to our hospitality.

The celebratory day, which continued with a service at Toronto's new Anglican cathedral and a dinner where Smallwood gave the major address, captured the new life he had built nearly five hundred miles north of Washington, D.C. He had become a leader in the civic life of the diverse and often fractious community of freeborn Black migrants and former fugitives from slavery that clustered in Toronto and a dozen other towns. And when he thought he was right, he never shrank from a dispute. At different times, he would be a principal player in battles over a church, a newspaper, and a famous settlement for the formerly enslaved.

When the Smallwoods arrived in Toronto in 1843, they settled in a fast-growing, working-class suburb of small cottages about a mile north of Lake Ontario. The neighborhood, which was first settled in the 1830s and by the turn of the century would become a notorious slum called simply "the Ward," attracted a mix of Black fugitives from American slavery, free Black people, new immigrants from Europe, and other strivers of modest means.

By the 1850s, there were an estimated thirty thousand Canadians of African descent, most of them in Nova Scotia and what would become the province of Ontario, first known as Upper Canada and later as Canada West. From at least the 1820s, African Americans fleeing slavery had begun to settle north of the border, joining those who had fought with the British during the Revolution and the War of 1812 and been rewarded with Canadian land. In the late 1820s, an African American machinist and activist in Baltimore named Hezekiah Grice printed up a map of Black settlements in Canada and sold it to aspiring emigrants. The argument that Smallwood invariably made to those he helped to head north—that they should not stop running until they reached Canada—found a significant audience, and the Black population continued to grow at least until the Civil War. There were Black schools and Black churches and a continuing debate about whether Black Canadians should try to integrate themselves into the larger community or build their own institutions.

Those who had hoped to escape racism were disappointed. Smallwood never ceased to hold up British Canada as hugely preferable to "that inconsistent nation," "the so-called land of liberty," as he called the United States, which simultaneously enslaved people and congratulated itself for its supposed love of freedom. But he acknowledged that white Canadians, especially as they began to see Black people not as temporary refugees but as permanent neighbors, were perfectly capable of expressing and acting on anti-Black racism. "Even here," he wrote, referring to Canada, "I have met a prejudice equal to any thing I ever experienced in the south." But unlike those in the United States, he added, Canadian laws generally upheld racial equality: "Thanks to the laws, it may go no further than verbal illustration!"

Smallwood appears never to have doubted his decision to move to Canada, even as many former fugitives eventually chose to return to the United States and settle in the north. Nor did he try to continue his underground railroad work, though he was generous in helping new arrivals. Once, in 1847, he was approached by a fellow activist with a request—and money to back it up—that he try to rescue some people enslaved in Kentucky. "I refused, because I had had enough of getting slaves off, at risk to my own freedom," Smallwood recalled. A year later, pressured again, he agreed to travel with a group to Cincinnati to assess the possibilities. They discovered that a recent unsuccessful attempt by a white abolitionist to liberate a hundred people from slavery in Kentucky "had so created so great an excitement and vigilance on the Kentucky side of the Ohio river" that they were advised to abandon their plan. It is unlikely that Smallwood ever again crossed the American border to arrange an escape.

⊷═◉═⊶

What prompted Smallwood to switch from his old trade of shoemaking to saw making is uncertain; perhaps he saw a bigger market for construction equipment in the dynamic setting of Canada's biggest city. In any case, he was listed in the 1846 Toronto city directory as "labourer"; by the next edition, in 1850, he was a "saw sharpener"; by 1856, he was a "sawmaker." He built a business that would last for decades.

"T. Smallwood's Saw Factory," according to his 1859 advertisement in *The Provincial Freeman*, offered wooden handles for axes and other tools for the wholesale market, suggesting that the business was of considerable size. The retail business sold axes and bucksaws—a type of bow saw with an H-shaped wooden handle—and provided repair services as well.

As his business grew, Smallwood quickly found a respected place in Black Canada's social and political life. He became active in the British and American Anti-Slavery Society, based in Toronto. By August 1847, when he had been in Canada for just four years, he was a leader at an unprecedented gathering of Black Canadians at Drummondville, east of

Montreal, joined by some who traveled from the United States. The purpose was to create a "central power, to which the self-emancipated slave might look for protection and assistance," particularly in view of evidence of mishandling of donations given for the support of new arrivals.

Smallwood, one of three delegates from Toronto, had long been a devout churchman and now identified himself as "Rev. Thomas Smallwood." As the convention went on, he faced off with Josiah Henson, who had been born into slavery in Maryland and would soon become famous as the supposed inspiration for the hero of Harriet Beecher Stowe's 1852 novel *Uncle Tom's Cabin*. Henson was a founder of the Dawn Settlement, a community of the formerly enslaved north of Lake Erie that had received large donations of money, clothing, and other goods that Smallwood believed Henson had misappropriated for his own use. (Smallwood would later accuse "a few designing persons" of seeking "to line their own pockets" by soliciting contributions to Dawn.)

After a debate, Smallwood won a vote 13 to 1, with only Henson in opposition, on a resolution: "That this Convention declares their belief that frauds have been practiced upon the People of Color in Canada, in regard to monies, clothing, and other articles, given by friends in the United States and elsewhere for our benefit." The next day the two kept up their decorous battle, each proposing a resolution denouncing the other. The convention seems to have set aside the personal squabble but clearly sided with Smallwood, criticizing the handling of donations and setting up a new oversight board.

Smallwood's willingness to rock the boat, even when it was awkward to do so, emerges again and again in surviving records. He sued *The Provincial Freeman*, in which he was an investor, in a financial dispute with its proprietors. He was the leader of one faction in a split of the congregation of the Colored Methodist Wesleyan Church of Toronto; his faction ultimately sought to unite with a white Wesleyan church. In the land of slavery, Smallwood argued, separation was necessary. But in Canada, he wrote, "It is our business to identify our interest with that of our white fellow citizens, and to form the most intimate relations with them of which our circumstances of life will admit."

A determination to tell his own story, refuting his detractors and preserving some important history, prompted him to write his only book. It had a stacked title that read like a marketing campaign: *A Narrative of Thomas Smallwood, (Coloured Man:) Giving an Account of His Birth—The Period He Was Held in Slavery—His Release—and Removal to Canada, etc. Together with an Account of the Underground Railroad. Written by Himself.* It appears that Smallwood financed a small printing in 1851; the book was "Printed for the Author by James Stephens," proprietor of a Toronto printshop.

Frederick Douglass had recently become famous with his first memoir, published in 1845, titled *Narrative of the Life of Frederick Douglass, An American Slave.* The underground railroad had become a much-discussed national phenomenon, and Smallwood had played the key role in naming it and had organized one of its major branches. He had been left out of the posthumous memoirs of Charles Torrey and Abel Brown. He was fifty. His oldest child, Thomas, was now an adult, and he may have wanted to record his life in far-off Washington for the benefit of his children.

His decision to become an author served some other purposes, too. He had earned his living with his hands, making shoes and saws, and he had written newspaper columns under a pseudonym, so he had never had a chance to display his surprising erudition to the public. And in the small, contentious world of Black activists he inhabited, he wanted to refute rumors his detractors had spread about him. "This little work," he wrote, "is wholly original, containing a simple narrative of unvarnished facts, interspersed with such comments as I conceived to be necessary." He said he wrote the memoir "to clear up my character, and do justice to humanity," and to counter the "slanders" that he immodestly says "great men" had often been subject to. He quoted Shakespeare twice to underscore the point—*The Comedy of Errors* and *Cymbeline*—and in fact seemed determined to bludgeon the reader with literary allusions: Milton, Samuel Johnson, Burns, Byron, Shelley, Wordsworth, Longfellow, and multiple books of the Bible are cited in just the first pages.

It is as if Smallwood was declaring up front: *I may have been born in slavery, but look at what I have made of myself!* He even included a six-stanza poem he had written in tribute to George Thompson, a British member of parliament who had been criticized in the United States for denouncing American slavery. (Smallwood's poem was later reprinted without attribution in London in a literary miscellany.)

Smallwood sought to preempt any claim from his adversaries that he was writing to cash in on his life story. "Let no one suppose that I have written this for the sake of pecuniary gain, such is not the case. . . . I have labored night and day at my calling, therefore I have no need of charity at the hands of any one." In fact, he asserted, he regularly gave financial help to the people steadily arriving in Canada after fleeing the slave catchers: "From the proceeds of honest toil I have given away many pounds." He claimed that just in the past fall and winter he had given fugitives more than six pounds—about $750 today. "This I am prepared to prove," he added, underscoring the combative political atmosphere in which he lived. (A few years later, in 1855, Smallwood was advertising in *The Provincial Freeman* on behalf of a newly arrived fugitive named Charles Fisher, seeking any news of Fisher's family members.)

Unlike Douglass and others who recounted in detail their suffering in slavery, Smallwood breezed over those first thirty years of his life—the promise of the book's subtitle ("*The Period He Was Held in Slavery*") was mostly advertising hype. There were no whippings described, no family separations, no long days of forced labor, though they all may have occurred. Instead, he seemed eager to leave behind the passivity of his early years and get to the action: his direct intervention to counter, disrupt, confuse, and mock the slaveholders of the Chesapeake, which takes up most of his sixty-three pages. He recalled that when word got out of his plan to assist escapes, "after a time they crowded upon me by scores," and he followed with many of the stories of escape recounted earlier in this book.

He appended one of his Sam Weller letters and explained: "I very much regret that I have not the manuscripts of the various articles which appeared in the Albany Patriot, over the signature of Sam. Weller, in

1842 and '43, to append to this narrative, in addition to the letter appended; but being so beset by the slave hunters before I left Washington, I was compelled to destroy them, for fear of detection."

In addition to recounting some of his exploits, Smallwood wrote more sweepingly about slavery, racism, and America than the newspaper format had allowed, and he did so with a prescience that is striking in retrospect. He played up loyalty to his new country, saying the British territory to the north had intrigued him for many years: "Long before I had purchased myself from my owner I had a desire to visit Canada." Now he felt vindicated, if also dismayed, that Congress had passed the Fugitive Slave Act of 1850, which strengthened the legal pressure on northerners to return people fleeing slavery to their enslavers. He had clearly followed the congressional debate closely. He attributed the slave power's victory to wealthy northerners who favored sending free Black people to Africa—his old enemies the colonizationists—and who, while not themselves enslaving anyone, depended upon and profited from the slave system:

> The success of the fugitive bill may be attributed mainly to the influence of Northern Colonizationists, for any one having any knowledge of that fraternity cannot but have observed that it is composed mostly of the great merchants, manufacturers, and aristocrats of the North, who suck their riches from the South off from the sweat and blood of the African race, with as little reason and humanity as the stall-fed hog sucks the swill that is poured into his manger.

With such American betrayers both north and south, Smallwood had clear advice: "I would say to every sober, industrious colored man, in the States, come to Canada, and you will get freedom, yea British freedom! which is the best national freedom in the world!" He was clear-sighted about the nature of white supremacy in America and how it infected even the abolitionists, the white people he knew best and who were most friendly to his cause and his people. He believed some abolitionists truly favored Black equality—but also that many others, while opposing slavery, had no interest in embracing African Americans as equals:

> I believe many of them had a fond, though vain hope; of seeing a day when the colored race in the United States would be admitted to equal rights with the whites; but I believe that national prejudice may be attributed to a very large portion of them. It is a part of the principles ingrafted in their national compact, and have been carried out to the present time, without abatement, that the African race should never ascend to an equality with the whites.

Smallwood was able, from the distance of Canada, to analyze racism with a certain scientific detachment as a disease of white people with little bearing on the actual capabilities of Black people. Consider his discussion of the Washington physician William Gunnell, whom Smallwood had relieved of his enslaved people. Smallwood wrote, using a phonetic spelling for the most pernicious racial epithet, that Gunnell "frequently boasted that a neger could not beat his time"—this is, flee fast enough not to be caught. But Smallwood calmly assured the husband of a woman he planned to free: "I told him that . . . by the assistance of the Lord, I would beat his time, though a neger, according to his sense of the word."

"According to his sense of the word"—the phrase rings with Smallwood's sense of self-worth, and his contempt for white people's resort to racist insults to falsely assert their superiority.

Not only were Americans largely champions of white supremacy; they had done their best to export it:

> Not content with inoculating the length and breadth of their own land, with that infernal principle, they have the audacity to attempt to insert it into foreign countries, and if Canada had not been an integral part of the glorious British empire, they would have succeeded in it to their utmost wishes. But

the Lord be thanked for the existence and maintenance of such a just and powerful nation;—she has triumphed, to the great annoyance of her enemies.

Smallwood had developed over many years the habit of assuming the worst about white Americans—with a few notable exceptions—and they had rarely proved him wrong. The reader feels that Smallwood would not have been surprised to learn that nearly two centuries after he purchased his freedom, despite tremendous change, the United States would still be struggling fitfully toward racial equity and justice.

⊷⟐⊶

If Smallwood was pleased with his decision to move to Canada and stay there, one reason may have been that his surviving children were thriving. Thomas, the elder son, had followed his father into the saw-making business and later worked as a bricklayer. But he also became an activist in his father's footsteps, and by 1863, when a committee of Black Torontonians gathered to draft the "Address to the Colored Citizens of Canada," on the progress of the Civil War in the United States, both father and son were among the seven members. Their statement welcomed Lincoln's Emancipation Proclamation while noting that it was incomplete, urged Canadians to support the Union cause, and offered fervent good wishes: "We extend our sympathy to President Lincoln in the prosecution of the great work for freedom. We trust that the Union armies will be strengthened and sustained, and that they will go on 'conquering and to conquer.'"

Later the same year, Smallwood gave an interview to an American physician, Samuel Gridley Howe, who was visiting Canada on behalf of the American Freedmen's Inquiry Commission, a wartime panel that was assessing the conditions of the formerly enslaved. It is a uniquely direct sample of Smallwood's voice from his new country, speaking far more personally than in his surviving formal speeches and letters to newspapers. The preserved part of Howe's interview is brief and consists mainly of

Smallwood, always politically involved, complaining about the poor advocacy for refugees from slavery by the Canadian branch of the British Conservative Party. But Smallwood, noting that he had been in Canada for two decades, also made a few personal remarks. Like many aging exiles, he sounded wistful about his old life:

> I have been in Canada 20 years the 14th of next month. I have made a good deal of money, and have lost a good deal. I lost $300 in a paper that was started here by colored men. I find the climate agreed with me, still I would rather go back to the old place, and intend to go back. Nothing but slavery and the wish to educate my children, in some part, brought me away from there. I lived in Washington, D.C., and the facilities at that time were not at all favorable to the education of colored children there. Our people are drawn on juries here. They have a right to the jury-box as well as any body else; but whether they get in it or not depends upon what kind of Government we have here.

Smallwood would never return to the United States. But his younger son, William Henry Smallwood, did go back after attending Canada's most prestigious secondary school, Upper Canada College, and then going on to university and law school. By 1870, at the age of twenty-nine and one generation removed from slavery, he would be part of the vanguard of Reconstruction in the south, practicing law in Jackson, Mississippi. According to a history of African Americans in Mississippi, William Smallwood "was recognized as the city's leading expert on leases, deeds, and contracts, an excellent penman, and an able auditor and bookkeeper" who "audited the books of some of the leading firms of the city, including one of the larger banks."

The Smallwoods' surviving daughter, Celestine, had opened a hairdressing business, one successful enough that she once had to publish in the newspaper a warning that another woman was posing as her to capitalize on her reputation.

Such achievements by their two sons and daughter must have been gratifying to Thomas and Elizabeth, justifying their hard work and sacrifices and giving them hope for the future. But alas, it was not to last. Smallwood would outlive all five of his children, an unusually tragic fate even in the nineteenth century. The eldest child, Thomas, died in Toronto in 1874 at the age of forty-three. Celestine died in 1878 at thirty-five, following her two sisters to the grave. William died in Jackson in 1883, at forty-three. How Smallwood weathered the loss of all his children can only be imagined. But if someone thought to send him the tiny notice of William's death in the Jackson newspaper, which came after the reactionary southern response to Reconstruction, it would only have underscored the loss to his family and to the United States:

> W.H. Smallwood, a popular colored citizen, of fine intellect, died here last Saturday, and was buried Sunday. He was a licensed attorney, and always did a good business. He was secretary of the Hope Fire Company, and belonged to the colored Benevolent Orders.

Correspondence of the Evening Journal.

HORRORS OF SLAVERY!

WASHINGTON, April 22, 1848.

Friend Weed—Last evening, in passing the railroad depot, I saw quite a large number of colored persons gathered round one of the cars, and from manifestations of grief among some of them, I was induced to draw near and ascertain the cause. I found in the car towards which they were so eagerly gazing, *fifty colored persons*, some of whom were nearly as white as myself. A large majority of the number were those who attempted to gain their liberty last week, in the schooner Pearl. About half of them were females, a few of whom had but a slight tinge of African blood in their veins; they were finely formed and beautiful. The men were ironed together, and the whole group looked sad and dejected. At each end of the car stood a ruffian-looking guard, with large canes in their hands. In the middle of the car stood the notorious slave-dealer of Baltimore, who is a member of the Methodist Church, in good and regular standing. He had purchased the men and women around him, and was taking his departure for Georgia. While observing this old grey headed dealer in the bodies and souls of men, the chaplain of the senate—a Methodist brother—entered the car, and took his brother Methodist by the hand, chatted with him for a short time, and seemed to view the heart-rending scene before him with as little concern as he would look upon cattle! I know not whether he came with a view to sanctify the act, or pronounce the parting blessing; but this I do know, that he justifies slavery. A

Part of a published letter from John I. Slingerland, congressman from New York, describing his encounter with Hope Slatter at the Washington train depot as Slatter prepared to transport to Baltimore fifty people caught trying to escape on the *Pearl*. [Courtesy of American Antiquarian Society and Genealogy Bank]

15

Resident Capitalist

Hope Slatter had helped vanquish Charles Torrey. He had earned a fortune from the slave trade. But he had not won the unqualified respect he thought he was due as a successful businessman. He had a bit of a national reputation, but not necessarily one he wanted—whenever abolitionists wanted to name a villain of the traffic in human beings, they seemed to choose him. He turned fifty-five years old in 1845, and after a decade living and working in Baltimore, he knew that his quest for social status—full acceptance by the city's wealthy elite—had fallen short.

The disagreeable lawsuits, often picked up by the press, weren't helping. Lucy Crawford said her enslaver had agreed to let her buy her freedom but then sold her to Slatter instead. Robert Trunnell said he was a free person of color, but Slatter had him jailed in Washington and claimed to own him. The teenage boy named Shadrack, being shipped by Slatter to his purchaser in Saint Louis, slipped across to another boat, introduced himself as "Jim Thornton," and disappeared. Anne Coale and her three children were to be held in trust until her legal owner became an adult, but the trustee took them to Slatter and sold them. Win or lose, the cases were endless, complicated, and invariably made Slatter look heartless, unscrupulous, or criminal.

It was perhaps a sign of his weariness with his contentious trade, and an excess of cash, that led Slatter into bigger and bigger wagers on the outcome of political races. The newspapers sometimes picked up on his bets, notably when he won "a large sum" betting on James Polk for the presidency in 1844. That success evidently encouraged Slatter to wager four years later on Lewis Cass, the Michigan senator who won the Democratic Party nomination for president and was running against the Whig war hero Zachary Taylor. The *New-York Tribune* reported that "the Baltimore negro-trader" had come to Washington with the goal of placing the huge sum of $25,000 in bets on Cass. When Taylor won the presidency, Slatter seems to have had no trouble covering his losses.

One day in 1845, when a local preacher called on Slatter, he found the trader ruminating on his future. It's doubtful that the trader was thinking of Charles Torrey, then growing steadily sicker in his prison cell, but for whatever reason he was pondering a change. He told the Reverend John S. Mitchell, agent of the Maryland State Bible Society, that "he intended to close up and quit his business, *seek his soul's salvation,* and join the church of his fathers," by Mitchell's account. Despite his purchase of a pew in Baltimore's elegant new Methodist church, Slatter had never taken the step of trying to officially join the church, a process that might have subjected him to unwanted scrutiny and have possibly ended in rejection. Now he seemed to be wrestling with leaving his business behind and belatedly turning his attention to spiritual matters, or at least to the repair of his shabby reputation.

Slatter may have been putting on a show of piety for the minister. But his impulse to move on seems to have been real, if premature. It would be three more years before Slatter followed up on this inclination to leave the business of purchasing and selling human beings. His most spectacular and notorious episode as a slave trader still lay ahead, and it would begin with a man many viewed as Torrey's successor in Washington.

❧⟶⊙⟵❧

Even as Charles Torrey sat awaiting trial in the Baltimore jail, tuberculosis gradually eroding his strength, the *Albany Weekly Patriot* decided to dispatch a new correspondent to Washington. The editors had not forgotten Torrey, whom they praised in print as a victim of men like Slatter: "Poor Torrey! Our heart bleeds for him." While there were decent people in the slave south, the editors declared, they were by and large "cowards" who did not dare speak up against the tyrants who ran the slave system: "One SLAVE DRIVER or MANSTEALER like Hope H. Slatter will over awe the Christianity of a whole city."

Still, the news didn't stop. The *Patriot* editors called their new man in Washington, William L. Chaplin, a "gentleman widely known for his ability and thorough love of democratic principles." Chaplin was a lawyer and temperance advocate who had come to the antislavery cause later than Torrey, though Torrey was seventeen years younger. But Chaplin had embraced abolitionism with total commitment. He had traveled in the same circles as Torrey in Massachusetts and New York for years and was regularly mentioned in the *Tocsin of Liberty* and the *Patriot*. Now, Chaplin seemed quite deliberately to retrace Torrey's path in Washington. Like Torrey, Chaplin arrived in the city as a congressional correspondent. Like Torrey, he attended Black churches and heard the terrible stories of families split and parents, children, and spouses sold south. And like Torrey, he soon turned his energies to aiding escapes. But one of his first schemes was breathtaking, going far beyond the wagonloads of Smallwood and Torrey.

In 1848, with the help of an old friend of Smallwood from the Navy Yard, the now-free African American blacksmith Daniel Bell, and aided by money from Torrey's friend and patron Gerrit Smith, Chaplin arranged for a ship to carry away from Washington some seventy-five enslaved people, including Daniel Bell's wife, eight children, and two grandchildren. Some of the seventy-five knew they were shortly to be sold south, and many of the rest feared that if they failed to escape soon, they, too, could end up in a distant cotton field. Chaplin engaged a sympathetic captain, Daniel Drayton, who had the use of a fifty-four-ton schooner called the *Pearl*. It was a fraction of the size of Slatter's New Orleans–bound slave ships, but it was seaworthy enough for the plan Chaplin, Bell, and their coconspirators cooked up: sail from the Washington docks on a spring night, follow the Potomac River to the Chesapeake Bay, round the corner north, and sail to the Maryland port of Frenchtown at the top of the bay, where the fugitives would be taken to Pennsylvania and new lives in freedom.

It was a bold scheme, and not entirely crazy. On a Saturday night in mid-April—always a favored night for escapes, since enslaved people often had time off on Sundays and might not immediately be missed—they managed to gather about seventy-five men, women, and children and load them into the *Pearl* at a Potomac wharf without setting off any immediate alarms, a considerable achievement. But the vagaries of the weather proved devastating. Winds were slack, and the tide turned against them, forcing them to anchor in the river for the night. Early the next morning, Drayton and the crew sailed on, but soon word of the mass escape was racing around Washington, as slaveholders met at church or for social outings and expressed puzzlement about their missing servants. Then a Black man named Judson Diggs, who had helped carry a woman's luggage to the ship but had not received the twenty-five cents he demanded, told the baffled enslavers about the extraordinary escape vehicle.

By Sunday evening, some of the aggrieved slaveholders had hired a steamboat, the *Salem,* to try to chase down the *Pearl.* The ship and its fugitive cargo might have been able to sprint north up the bay and outpace the pursuers, but now the winds rose to a dangerous level, and the crew had to anchor for the night near Point Lookout, where the Potomac enters the Chesapeake. In the early hours of Monday morning, while the exhausted crew and fugitives slept, they were surprised by the posse of slaveholders and hired hands aboard the *Salem*. One lifted a hatch, held a lantern on the faces of the Black runaways below, and, as many subsequent accounts would have it, shouted a racial slur in triumph, reasserting the enslaved status of people who had dared to dream of freedom.

⋆⇒◉⇐⋆

Chaplin and his accomplices, with the kind of imagination familiar from Torrey's earlier flights of fancy, had speculated that the sudden disappearance of scores of people aboard the *Pearl* might prove a lethal blow to the status of slavery in Washington. Now that theory would not be tested. But the capture of the *Pearl* and its passengers set off turmoil in the nation's capital, as angry slaveholders and their supporters faced off repeatedly with abolitionists and city officials over the fate of the captives, temporarily lodged in the city jail. As always, the enslavers had to make a calculation: If their drivers, housekeepers, gardeners, and nannies were so determined to escape that they had joined this wild conspiracy, could they ever be trusted again to stay at their unpaid jobs? And as so often happened, most decided the answer was no.

One of them sent word to Baltimore to the presiding potentate of the region's slave trade. Hope Slatter learned that he might have landed a prize greater than any before, even in his long career: dozens of men, women, and children, ready to be sold south for big profits at his New Orleans showroom. A correspondent of the *New-York Commercial Advertiser* commented cynically on the way the *Pearl*'s fugitives were eyed by the traders: "Prominent among the arrivals of dealers in men and women who have been attracted by the scent of prey, is Mr. Hope H. Slatter of Baltimore, distinguished through all the South as the great negro buyer." The Baltimore correspondent of *The New York Herald* also heard about the arrival in the capital of "the great slave dealer of this city" and gave readers some context: "He sends thousands of captured runaways" to New Orleans "yearly, and has made an immense fortune at the business."

When Slatter reached Washington to investigate the opportunities, he found the capital in an uproar over the *Pearl*. A mob of white men roamed the streets, provoked by the effrontery of the Black people who had tried to escape—and especially by the white abolitionist types they blamed for stirring up trouble. Eyewitnesses claimed that the mob included a number of slave traders, Slatter among them.

Among its first targets was Gamaliel Bailey, a physician who had started an antislavery newspaper, *The National Era*, the previous year. There was a tense standoff between the leaders of the mob, who were determined to destroy the press, and Bailey, who politely explained the principle of press freedom. The newspaper was saved only by the timely arrival of none other than police captain John Goddard, who had helped drive Thomas Smallwood from the city. Though Goddard and his Auxiliary Guard had so often done the dirty work of the slaveholders, this time they saw their duty in preventing violence and vandalism.

Slatter was again part of the throng the next day at the city jail, where the *Pearl*'s fugitives were being held along with Daniel Drayton, the ship's captain. The crowd discovered that two abolitionists were already at the jail to comfort the inmates: Joshua Giddings, the Ohio congressman who had been an ally of Torrey and Smallwood, and Edward S. Hamlin, an antislavery editor, lawyer, and former Ohio congressman. This discovery of their enemies was an unexpected boon for the marauding defenders of slavery, and the crowd erupted in curses and threats.

A jailer told Giddings and Hamlin that if they tried to leave through the mob, he could not guarantee their safety. But they made their way through the crowd anyway, and only later did an eyewitness tell Giddings that they had been in real danger, the congressman said in a statement to Congress the next day. The witness had stood in the crowd and heard the shouted threats, including "the proposition made by individuals to lay violent hands upon me as I came out of the prison—one of whom, he informed me, was a Mr. Slatter, a slave-dealer from Baltimore, whom he states to have been active in instigating others to acts of violence." Later in his statement, Giddings said that "the infamous" Slatter "headed the mob at the jail."

It was an unusual venture into the rough-and-tumble of street politics for the slave trader, who was generally so sensitive about his reputation. Giddings was not an unbiased witness, but there is little reason to doubt that Slatter was in the mob—after all, his lucrative prize was inside the jail—or that he would have been infuriated by the meddling congressman. Within a week of the *Pearl*'s capture, in any event, Slatter had managed to purchase about fifty of the runaways from their enslavers. Without the omnibuses he used in Baltimore, he shackled them in a coffle—a line of chained captives, a regular spectacle in Washington—and marched them to the railroad depot. Among those who saw the miserable captives staggering to the train was a first-term congressman from Illinois who had moved the previous year into the abolitionists' boardinghouse, Mrs. Sprigg's, where he found himself a moderate on the slavery issue by comparison with his housemates.

Abraham Lincoln was likely hearing Giddings's account of the unfolding drama of the *Pearl* and the aftermath of the failed escape around the dinner table each night. That drama culminated at Washington's rail station, where Slatter, on the largest and most public stage of his life, left an indelible impression.

Giddings, evidently repeating what he heard from eyewitnesses, gave a memorable description to his congressional colleagues of the people who flocked to the train to say farewell to family members they expected never to see again:

> The scene at the depot is represented as one which would have disgraced the city of Algiers or Tunis. Wives bidding adieu to their husbands, mothers in an agony of despair, unable to bid farewell to their daughters; little boys and girls weeping amid the general distress, scarcely knowing the cause of their grief. Sighs, and groans, and tears, and unutterable agony characterized a scene at which the heart sickens, and from which humanity shrinks with horror. Over such a scene that fiend in human shape, Slatter, presided, assisted by some three or four associates in depravity, each armed with pistols, Bowie-knife, and club.

A New York congressman, John I. Slingerland, happened upon the scene at the rail station and found himself horrified and fascinated: an entire railcar was filled with the "sad and dejected" captives, he wrote, and "in the middle of the car stood the notorious slave dealer of Baltimore." But what truly shocked Slingerland was another person who suddenly appeared:

> While observing this old grey headed dealer in the bodies and souls of men, the Chaplain of the Senate—a Methodist brother—entered the car, and took his brother Methodist by

the hand, chatted with him for a short time, and seemed to
view the heart-rending scene before him with as little concern
as he would look upon cattle!

The Senate chaplain, Henry Slicer, deeply embarrassed by Slingerland's description, which was reprinted in many northern newspapers,
would protest Slingerland's interpretation as a distortion. But he would
not deny his acquaintance with Slatter or his failure to object to the mass
deportation. The encounter seemed to underscore the cozy relationship
between the slave trader and the politically powerful and the way Washington's elite hardly noticed even the most heartless displays of the commerce in human beings.

Slingerland would record one more scene at the depot that summed
up the cruelty of Slatter and the slave trade, and the desperate position of
those whose loved ones were about to disappear forever:

> A husband, in the meridian of life, begged to see the partner
> of his bosom. He protested that she was free—that she had
> free papers, and was torn away from him, and shut up in the
> jail. He clambered up to one of the windows of the car to see
> his wife, and, as she was reaching forward her hand to him,
> the black hearted Slave Dealer ordered him down. He did not
> obey. The husband and wife, with tears streaming down their
> cheeks, besought him to let them speak to each other. But no;
> he was knocked down from the car and ordered away!

Perhaps this terrible spectacle and the coverage it received were enough
for Slatter. Perhaps the rowdiness of the mob was too much for this aging
man, who was approaching sixty. Maybe the casual identification of Slatter as a "double-distilled devil" in abolitionist newspapers like *The Liberator* was growing tiresome. But by July 1848, two months after he had

disposed of the *Pearl* refugees, Slatter had sold the business to a smaller competitor, the brothers Bernard and Walter Campbell.

"Persons having slaves to sell will hereafter find us located at the extensive establishment formerly owned by Hope H. Slatter," said the Campbell brothers' new ads. "We have purchased his entire possessions on Pratt Street No. 244, at which place all who have slaves to sell will be sure to get the highest price." Slatter's name evidently stood for reliability among slaveholders just as it stood for perfidy among abolitionists, and the Campbells appended to their notices Slatter's endorsement: "Having retired from the business, I would cheerfully recommend my friends and customers to call at my old establishment to obtain the highest prices for their slaves.—Hope H. Slatter."

Slatter left no diary, and no personal correspondence survives. So his next steps, as recorded in public records, are subject to interpretation. But it appears that he took some time in his search for a new life and a new reputation. In October 1848, Slatter was still in Baltimore and *The Sun* announced that he had purchased a mansion in the prestigious Mount Vernon neighborhood for $20,000 (about $600,000 today) and an impressive additional $8,000 ($240,000) for the furnishings. "The lot is 36 feet front by 160 deep, and is one of the most delightful houses in this city," the newspaper wrote, choosing not to mention the source of the purchaser's money. Was Slatter simply trying to turn a quick profit on a desirable property, or was he considering staying in Baltimore, hoping the memory of his slave trading would fade? Possibly the latter; it seems odd to buy a large house in the city he was preparing to leave.

But if he was considering staying in Baltimore, he seems to have changed his mind for the house was quickly put back on the market. Soon Slatter appeared in Richmond, according to a couple who had met him in Baltimore and now called on him in Virginia's capital. Slatter, wrote Robert and Sarah Lindsey in their diary, was "residing in Richmond, having purchased a beautiful residence, and endeavoring to gain the respect and attention of the citizens, so as to be admitted to their society."

But Slatter's relentless quest to escape the taint of the trade was not successful, the Lindseys wrote in one of the most penetrating comments by contemporaries on the subject. Slatter's efforts, they wrote,

> appeared to be all in vain. Although slaveholders themselves, and feeling no objections to buy or sell slaves for their own use and convenience, yet, strange as it may seem, they stand aloof from the man who makes it his business to traffic in them, and look down upon him as it were with abhorrence. And we understand it is the case throughout all the slave states. Although the slaveholders unhesitatingly deal with these traders when their convenience requires it, yet they will not associate with them, scarcely live in the same neighborhood, nor even allow them to worship with them at the same altar. This is one of the anomalies in human nature which it is difficult to solve, at least for those who are not participators in the system, and are disposed to consider the slaveholder and the slave-dealer as standing on one common platform.

It seemed a crucial insight into human nature: even those who claimed to own human beings and occasionally to buy and sell them needed someone to look down on and consider their moral inferior. Slave traders like Slatter served the purpose beautifully. He had outlasted Thomas Smallwood and Charles Torrey; he had amassed a considerable fortune; but to his lasting frustration, he could not quite shed the shame that clung to his money like an unpleasant smell.

That was perhaps why, just months after he had purchased the "beautiful residence" in Richmond, Slatter moved on again. For his next try at respectability he took his wife and children away from the mid-Atlantic to Alabama, to a city on the same Gulf Coast as New Orleans and one almost as involved in the domestic slave trade: Mobile.

Perhaps in this major hub for the cotton industry, Slatter calculated that he had the greatest chance of leaving opprobrium behind. He seems to have given up the large-scale purchase and resale of people; the Mobile newspapers carried none of the ads seeking to buy and sell "likely Negroes" that had been the foundation of his business in Baltimore and New Orleans for so many years. He certainly made no moral break with the institution of slavery—in fact, shortly after arriving in Mobile he advertised a new sideline, apparently something he had arranged in Richmond: renting out enslaved laborers on a significant scale. "TO HIRE," said his notice in the *Mobile Daily Advertiser.* "Seventy young able-bodied NEGRO MEN, from Virginia, by the month. I would prefer their going upon steamboats or cotton presses," the facilities used to compress raw cotton into bales for transport. "Also, a few choice house servants."

He would continue for the rest of his life to enslave a half dozen or more people to serve his family, who soon moved into a handsome rented mansion on Government Street in downtown Mobile. The house had such lovely ironwork that it would later be photographed for a national architectural survey. His wealth and slave owning fit comfortably into white Mobile society.

But his new trade, which he carried out from a separate office a few blocks from the house, was in real estate, not people. Slatter went on an extraordinary buying spree, putting much of his slave-trade fortune into the purchase of some of Mobile's major buildings. He bought, among other properties, the city's sole theater, a major bank (a "beautiful edifice," one of the local papers called it, reporting Slatter's acquisition), the post office, the telegraph office, and two large houses downtown, near the theater. He also got involved in several insurance companies, a natural adjunct to the commercial real estate business. Owning buildings undoubtedly proved less complicated, litigious, and "notorious"—the word that had long been attached to his name in northern newspapers—than buying and selling human beings.

He had found a new life in a more accepting place. But it was not to last for long. In 1853, not quite five years after the family had settled in Mobile, a yellow fever epidemic raged along the Gulf Coast. The worst toll was in New Orleans, where Slatter had done his grim business for so long, and where more than eight thousand succumbed. But in Mobile, too, enough people were dying each day that the local papers had no space for more than a line or two even for the wealthiest and most prominent of the deceased. The *Mobile Daily Advertiser* of September 16, 1853, reported a lengthy list of "Interments in the City Grave Yards" and noted just a few of the more interesting among the thirty new yellow fever deaths in Mobile that day—a nun from the Sisters of Charity, the nineteen-month-old youngest son of a city couple, and one more:

> On the morning of the 15th inst., of yellow fever, in the 64th year of his age, Hope H. Slatter, of Clinton, Ga., formerly a resident of Baltimore, Md., but for the last four years a citizen of this place. Baltimore and Georgia papers please copy.

The next day *The Picayune* of New Orleans ran a more poetic and personal dispatch from its Mobile correspondent:

> Notwithstanding the favorable weather of the past few days, the epidemic still marches along with giant strides, leveling alike the old and young, the poor laborer and the wealthy merchant. Hope H. Slatter, Esq., as I advised you by telegraph, died on Thursday morning. In him, Mobile loses a man she can ill spare—a resident capitalist, and a liberal one, too. You are perhaps aware he owned the theatre, the old bank, &c., and was a director of several insurance companies.

If only Slatter could have returned from the grave to read it. "Resident capitalist"! "A liberal one"! "A man she can ill spare"! Not so much as a whisper of the slave trade—and in the newspaper of the city where Slatter had sold thousands of people. By the time yellow fever killed him, it seems, he had successfully completed the laundering of his reputation and removed the stench of the trade—except, perhaps, in one ironic respect. Yellow fever had first traveled to the New World aboard the slave ships from Africa. This accidental import of the international slave traders had now cut short the prosperous semiretirement of one of the tycoons of the domestic slave trade.

If the southern papers were delicate about Slatter's past—remarkably, the Baltimore papers did not even report his death—the same cannot be said about the abolitionist press, which could not resist taking one last shot at this mogul of the slave trade and the damage he had done to so many. Several ran substantial stories recounting, and condemning, Slatter's career, including some from Baltimoreans who had watched him work. One, who signed his column only "Looker-On in Baltimore," wrote that he had once stood on a Baltimore wharf and seen Slatter aboard a ship, trying to calm the people he was shipping away from their families. He compared Slatter to a Dickens character who had become a byword for hypocrisy: "Slatter was standing upon deck, smiling most blandly— most Pecksniffianly upon every one as he passed, and saying to the anguished girls, 'never mind, Molly, you'll find another husband, better than the one you have left.'" This eulogist believed Slatter fully appreciated the moral costs of his profession. "Slatter knew he was engaged in a bad business," Looker-On wrote. "A gentleman once remarked to him, 'Your business must be very profitable.' 'One ought to be well paid to engage in such business,' was the reply."

◄═◯═►

At sixty-three, Slatter was no longer a young man, and the epidemic was sweeping away many people, but his death was sudden and unexpected nonetheless. He had never written a will. His brother Shadrack was appointed the administrator of his estate, which was initially valued at about $120,000—an impressive $3.6 million today—earned on the bodies of people shipped away from all they had known and of hundreds of families torn apart. Shadrack and Hope's widow, Emma, took on the job of operating Slatter's real estate business, collecting the rent and seeing to the management of the major buildings he owned, paying and collecting debts he had left behind, and covering legal bills for the attorneys handling Slatter's outstanding lawsuits.

Emma Slatter, just thirty-six when her much-older husband died, saw to the erection of a grand, gleaming white, rectangular block of a tomb—

among the largest in Mobile's Magnolia Cemetery—topped by funerary sculptures and surrounded by a wrought-iron fence painted gold. "FAM-ILY TOMB of Hope H. Slatter" was carved into the stone. Three years later, Emma would remarry a man much closer to her own age, Alexander Beaufort Meek, a poet, lawyer, and former Alabama attorney general. She would have a falling-out with Shadrack, and the two would battle for years over Hope's estate.

One perhaps telling legacy of the late slave trader was the fate of his son and namesake, Hope H. Slatter Jr. Not long after his father's death, Hope Jr. came to Washington to attend Georgetown College, later Georgetown University, which some years earlier had been saved from financial collapse by the sale south of 272 people enslaved on Jesuit plantations in Maryland. Hope Jr. went on to serve as a second lieutenant in the Confederate army and later settled in Washington. In 1873, he was charged with stabbing another man to death in a drunken brawl at Washington's Schützenfest, an annual shooting competition and beer bash. One sympathetic newspaper reporter described the defendant as "a handsome young fellow of about 23 years"—he was actually thirty-one—and seemed to suggest that the circumstances mitigated his guilt: "As is generally the case, women and wine were the cause of the murder." The case received national coverage; a Cleveland paper noted that "Slatter, who is wealthy, is said to be backed by a portion of the Alabama, Georgia, and New Orleans delegations in Congress." He was convicted by a jury of first-degree murder, despite the well-paid efforts of four prominent lawyers, two from Alabama and two from Washington, to argue that it was a case of justified self-defense.

But that was not the end of it. Before he could be sentenced, Slatter unexpectedly won a new trial on vague grounds, pleaded guilty to manslaughter, and was sentenced to four years in a federal penitentiary. Young Slatter's powerful friends immediately appealed to President Ulysses Grant for clemency, and a year later Grant agreed to give Slatter a pardon on the condition that he testify about corruption in Washington. The case in which Slatter was to testify was, amazingly, his own. The assistant United States attorney who handled the murder case was charged with accepting a $15,000 bribe not to oppose Slatter's motion for a new trial, and one of Slatter's attorneys was accused of handing over the bribe. The source of the bribe money was not disclosed, but clearly it came from Slatter himself or his family and friends. So, to sum up: Hope Slatter Jr. killed a man; a jury convicted him of first-degree murder; but he served less than three years in prison—because he paid a bribe, and then agreed to testify about the bribe he had paid. It was a generous deal.

It is interesting to note that at the time Hope Slatter's son was embroiled in the murder and bribery cases, Thomas Smallwood's son William, roughly the same age, was a respected and successful attorney in Mississippi. It is not hard to imagine what might have happened to a Black man at the time had he fatally stabbed a man and then tried to bribe his way out of prison. But the well-connected Hope Slatter Jr., buoyed by his father's wealth from human trafficking, was to have a brighter future. Indeed, the old slave trader might well have been proud of his son's resilience. A decade after Slatter Jr. was released from prison, he was named the chief of police in Mobile.

DEAR EDITOR—I wish to inquire for my mother, brother and sister. Mother lived in Baltimore, Maryland, on South two doors from Sawsberry street. When I left, she was living with James Jone, a merchant tailor. I belonged to Jacob Graving Stein at that time. Her name name is Eliza Johnson. My brother and sister were brought to Louisiana by a negro trader named Slater. Brother's name is Andrew Johnson; sister's, Mary Johnson, and mine was Charley Johnson. I left Baltimore in 1844. Any information of them will be thankfully received. Address me at Greenwood, Leflore Co., Miss.   CHARLEY STRONG.

One of hundreds of so-called lost friends ads placed by Black families after the Civil War to try to locate relatives lost to the domestic slave trade. Many of the ads named Slatter, whose name was sometimes a crucial clue in tracking parents, children, spouses, or siblings. [Courtesy of Historic New Orleans Collection]

Epilogue

NO BREEZE COMES

July 27, 1863

At 4 p.m. on a baking Baltimore day, Colonel William Birney of the United States Army arrived with two other officers at Slatter's old slave jail on Pratt Street. It was late July, three weeks after the Battle of Gettysburg, a turning point in the titanic conflagration that had grown out of the irresolvable conflict over slavery. Exhausted Union troops were everywhere around the city. But Birney was on a special mission: to recruit African American men for the United States Colored Troops, who would now bolster the Union effort. His first move would be to liberate the city's slave jails.

Birney, in his midforties, had led a peripatetic life: practicing law in Cincinnati, serving as a professor of English in France, publishing a newspaper in Philadelphia. In his Union army service, he had been wounded twice and praised for his courage and tenacity, and he would soon be promoted to brigadier general. But he may have been especially well suited by family history for the task the war served up for him now. His father, James Birney, was a Kentucky-born plantation owner who in his forties had liberated his enslaved workforce, denounced slavery, and become one of the nation's leading abolitionists. The elder Birney was a friend of Charles Torrey and had twice run for president as the nominee of the Liberty Party that Torrey had helped start. Now, on this summer day in Baltimore, the younger Birney, long devoted to the abolitionist cause, found himself face-to-face with the brutal commerce that was slavery's foundation. Slatter had been dead for a decade, but the Campbells had kept the Pratt Street business going, regularly shipping people from the city's wharves.

Now, deep into the Civil War, the Baltimore slave jails had become grim savings banks for enslavers, preserving the cash value of people whom slaveholders believed might flee in the chaos and uncertainty. Congress had ended the slave trade in Washington in 1850 and abolished slavery in the capital in April 1862. Then, in January 1863, President Lincoln had signed the Emancipation Proclamation, but because it was, as he put it, a limited "war measure for suppressing said rebellion," it freed the enslaved only in the states in rebellion. Because Maryland was one of four slaveholding states that had not seceded, slavery was still legal within its borders—as it also was in New Orleans, because that city was under Union control.

Birney's official report, in blunt and arresting language, described one patch of hell the slave trade had created. He mistakenly called it "Camlin's slave-pen" instead of Campbell's, but his powers of observation and description did not fail him as he detailed the compound of cells and brick walls surrounding the central yard. He set the scene as if he knew he was writing for history:

> In this yard no shrub or tree grows—no flower or blade of grass can be seen. Here the midday sun pours down its scorching rays, and no breeze comes to temper the summer heat. A few benches, a hydrant, numerous wash-tubs and clothes-lines, covered with drying clothes, were all it contained.
>
> In this place I found twenty-six men, one boy, twenty-nine women, and three infants. Sixteen of the men were shackled together by couples, at the ankles, by heavy irons, and one had his legs chained together by ingeniously contrived locks

connected by chains suspended to his waist. I sent for a blacksmith and had the shackles and chains removed.

Birney listed the names of the men and women he was freeing, noting their enslavers and where they had lived, and adding the reason they
were locked up: in almost every case, "disloyalty," or fear that they might
run away. It was an odd word, in the midst of a war of armed disloyalty
to the nation by Confederate forces defending the institution of slavery,
to apply to the very victims of that institution. But clearly it meant the
slaveholders no longer believed they could trust the captives to continue
to serve them, so they had turned them over to Campbell's jail, perhaps
in the deluded hope of selling them in another border state or in some
postwar future. Some had been inmates only a matter of days, but others
had been jailed for many months. Birney's report included the last inven-
tory for a business that had operated for decades:

> Chas. Dorry, belongs to Thomas Worthington, Baltimore
> county, imprisoned 16 days, disloyalty.
> Wm. Simms, Nancy Counter, Prince Georges county, 17
> months, disloyalty.
> Samuel Davis, Wm H. Cleggett, Prince Georges county, 4
> months, disloyalty. Mr. C. is said to have two sons in the Rebel
> army.
> John F. Toodles, James Mulligan, Prince Georges county,
> 18 months, disloyalty. This man has been confined in all about
> three years.

On went the roll, listing nearly every county around Baltimore and
Washington and giving full names for all the captives—not just the first
names slaveholders had so often preferred as a mark of subordination. The
document paired the enslaved and their enslavers for the last time. One of
those in Campbell's pen, James Walker, jailed for sixteen months, was "a
boy of 14." Another man, locked up for fifteen months, was, remarkably,
named Abraham Lincoln.

Accused of disloyalty, the male prisoners were now invited, somewhat coerced by their circumstances, to pledge a new kind of loyalty—and instantly win their freedom:

> These all expressed their desire to enlist in the service of the
> United States and were conducted to the recruiting office on
> Camden street, to be examined by the surgeon.

The women's future was less certain. A few had babies or young children with them:

> Lenah Harrod, Dr. S. Makel, Georgetown, 15 months. Rachel
> Harrod (6 years old) . . .
>   Susan Collins, Hammond Doucey, Ellicott's Mills, 24
> months, disloyalty. Willie, child of Susan (4 months old; born
> in prison) . . .
>   Louisa Foster, John Talbot, Baltimore county, 23 months,
> disloyalty. Philip Foster, 2 years old, been in prison 23 months
> of his young life.

Birney sent the report to his commander, Lieutenant Colonel William H. Cheesebrough, assistant adjutant general, explaining that most of the prisoners had been enslaved by "Rebels or Rebel sympathizers" or had been moved from Washington to evade the ban on slavery there. "These unfortunates were all liberated in accordance with your orders," Birney wrote. He and his men then moved on to the remaining slave jails in Baltimore, freeing everyone they found incarcerated inside. Slavery would remain legal in Maryland for another sixteen months, but after so many years and so much suffering the slave trade in Baltimore had come to an end.

Some northern newspapers found room amid all the reports of battles and troop movements to reprint Birney's report in part or in full; he knew the newspaper business and may have made sure that editors, along with his commander, got timely copies. The editors of one New York paper understood that the eyewitness report documented the very terrors that the Union army was trying to vanquish. "A Baltimore Slave Pen," read the headline. "Horrors of the Barbarous Institution—A Sickening Sight to Behold—Specimen of the Rebel Cause." The editors added: "The following official report needs no comment. The facts it states speak for themselves."

⊶⟹◉⟸⊷

Hope Slatter's legacy was evident by the time Birney arrived in Baltimore: thousands more sold south by his successors and imitators, more generations torn apart, more Chesapeake-born Americans tossed into the maw of the cotton and sugar industries. For at least three decades after the Civil War, the lasting human consequences of the slave trade could be read in the advertisements placed in newspapers, especially those published by and for African Americans, by people seeking to find relatives they had lost to the trade. The ads are one more wrenching measure of the suffering the slave trade inflicted on families. As the historian Heather Andrea Williams discovered in her study of these "lost friends" ads, the efforts at reunion faced enormous obstacles and often failed.

One irony of the search was that the identity of a slave trader was often a crucial clue, so the name of an engineer of the separation could become an instrument of reconnection. Naturally, many of the ads named Slatter, a notorious and thus memorable figure among enslaved people. In 1878, Rosanna Patterson of Baltimore County asked readers to help her find "my mother, who was sold by Mr. Wilkins to a lady in Baltimore, named Phillips, and by her to Mr. Slatter, and from him to New Orleans." In 1880, Charley Strong of Greenwood, Mississippi, appealed to anyone who might know of "my mother, brother, and sister." She knew only the last address in Baltimore of her mother's enslaver, and also that "my brother and sister were brought to Louisiana by a negro trader named Slatter." In 1892, nearly forty years after Slatter's death, a woman he had sold in her childhood was still desperately searching for her family:

Mr. Editor: I wish to inquire for my relatives. My parents were
Hannah and Joseph Walker. . . . We have been parted ever
since I was seven years old. I was sold from Mrs. Eliza Devall
to a Negro trader named Slatter. Address, Emeline Edwards,
370 Second street, New Orleans, La.

⋅—◉═◎═◉—⋅

Before the first shots of the Civil War, the brief but fierce flame lit by
Smallwood and Torrey had burned on in multiple ways. They had mod-
eled a militant, daring mode of battling slavery that other activists had
adopted for nearly two decades afterward—though Torrey's reckless
style and Smallwood's greater pragmatism led to separate legacies. William Chaplin, who had organized the *Pearl* escape attempt, saw himself
as carrying on the work that Torrey had begun—and soon enough he,
like Torrey, was arrested and jailed, after a brazen escape attempt by
carriage from Washington of two brothers owned by Georgia congressmen. They were waylaid north of the city by a posse led by Smallwood's
old foe, the constable and slave catcher John Goddard, who captured
Chaplin after a shoot-out. Abolitionists had apparently learned a lesson from Torrey's death behind bars, and Gerrit Smith and other supporters donated a huge sum—$25,000—to bail Chaplin out of jail. He
skipped bail and returned to New York, where he led a quieter life until
his death in 1871.

Perhaps the most important successor to Torrey was John Brown, another protégé and financial beneficiary of Gerrit Smith, who hoped to
spark an armed revolt by men enslaved on Virginia plantations, starting
with an attack on the federal armory in Harpers Ferry in 1859. Brown,
like Torrey, was an intensely religious figure driven by grandiose dreams;
both justified violence and welcomed martyrdom for the cause to which
they had devoted their lives. But Brown's scheme, as Frederick Douglass
had warned, was utterly unrealistic. The raid collapsed in a matter of
hours. Like Torrey, Brown spent his weeks in jail in a prolific sprint of

letter writing in support of the campaign against human bondage. Then he was hanged, joining Torrey as a celebrated martyr to the antislavery cause.

Smallwood's most direct heir may have been Jacob Gibbs, the Black housepainter who had been Smallwood's reliable partner in Baltimore. Gibbs moved to New York City and became a linchpin of the underground railroad in that metropolis, helping hundreds of people on the way north. In 1857, he signed a private letter "Ex-agent of the underground railroad," adding "this title is a secret between us." He died a decade later.

The underground railroad that Smallwood had named kept spreading and operating, giving a fast start or a night's refuge or a meal and directions to thousands who found the courage and opportunity to flee north. Though he was far from the first engineer of organized escapes, Smallwood had set an example of covert operations that many would emulate, though usually with a more cautious approach to publicity than Smallwood's inimitable Sam Weller letters.

Smallwood, and especially Torrey, had entertained the tantalizing notion that escape operations like theirs, like waves eroding the foundation of an oceanside fortress, might quickly undermine the institution of slavery. That did not happen. But the flight from slavery that they and many others encouraged and organized became a major cause of the secession crisis. It took a war of unimaginable scale and brutality to finally put an end to the legalized human bondage on which so much of America's wealth had been built. Charles Torrey's son and namesake fought for the Union; Hope Slatter's son and namesake fought for the Confederacy.

Perhaps Smallwood and Torrey's most important achievement could be seen in the men, women, and children walking the streets and pursuing their lives in freedom in Upstate New York, New England, and the Black Canadian communities that clustered around Lake Ontario and Lake Erie. Families who narrowly escaped sale south, who might otherwise have been advertising for lost relatives, had for decades been getting educations, working for wages, and raising children and grandchildren in freedom.

It was more than a year after Birney's visit to Baltimore, in November 1864, that Maryland finally, and reluctantly, gave up slavery, in the same election that returned Abraham Lincoln to the White House. It wasn't easy. The proslavery legislators who had controlled Maryland for so many years had essentially booby-trapped the state constitution with an 1836 amendment declaring that slavery could be abolished only by a unanimous vote by both the House of Delegates and the Senate—a practical impossibility. So abolition required the adoption of a new state constitution, hammered out at a constitutional convention amid the dislocations of wartime Maryland and then ratified by popular vote.

Passions ran high, especially in rural counties where unpaid labor was still the backbone of the economy. The *St. Mary's Gazette,* in southern Maryland, complained bitterly about the pro-constitution vote expected in Baltimore City, without which, the newspaper declared, "our old Constitution would then have been preserved, and our ancient institutions protected. As it is, we are doomed to be an outraged, plundered and disenfranchised people." It was quite clear which "ancient institution" the writer wanted to preserve, and quite breathtaking that he would portray the enslavers, not those they enslaved, as the Marylanders who were "plundered and disenfranchised."

The newspapers tracked the votes as they came in from one county after another, with fifteen rural counties voting against the constitution and just five in favor, and only the big pro-constitution majority in Baltimore City nearly evening up the score. The *Baltimore American* reported that the civilian vote left a margin of 319 statewide against adopting the new constitution. But just as the northern army was saving the republic, its soldiers in Maryland were voting to turn the tide on emancipation in the state: by the *Baltimore American*'s count, the troops' votes had pushed the pro-constitution total to a statewide margin of 54 in favor. On the same day, *The Baltimore Sun,* far more friendly to slavery, gave a different count: a margin of 435 votes *against* the constitution.

Baltimore American.

MONDAY, OCTOBER 31, 1864.

MARYLAND FREE.

Slavery Forever Abolished.

Ploclamation of Gov. Bradford.

The New Constitution Adopted.

THE SOLDIERS' VOTES.

Opinion of the Governor

Headlines in the *Baltimore American* marking the end of slavery in Maryland some twenty-two months after Lincoln signed the Emancipation Proclamation. Only the votes of Union soldiers put the referendum approving a new constitution over the top in the deeply divided state. [Courtesy of American Antiquarian Society and Genealogy Bank]

After some skirmishing in court, on October 29, 1864, the official count was declared to be 30,174 for the constitution and 29,799 against it—a margin of 375 in favor, just over half of 1 percent of the total vote of nearly 60,000. Maryland had again shown its colors as a deeply divided border state. The newspapers were subdued, giving little space to the momentous emancipation of the 80,000 people officially counted in Maryland as enslaved—though many, perhaps half, had already fled their enslavers during the war. The celebrations of Maryland's belated abolition of slavery seemed to be larger and more boisterous in Philadelphia than in Baltimore, though Baltimore's unionist mayor did order a five-hundred-gun salute at sunrise, noon, and sunset, and church bells were rung. Two weeks after the vote became official, African Americans gathered in a discreet Baltimore location—inside a Howard Street meeting hall where they would not risk attacks from disgruntled whites. There were addresses, musical performances, and the singing of a new "Freedom Song" composed for the occasion:

> *Sing, sing, oh can't you sing,*
> *Lord, we offer praise unto Thee,*
> *Let Thy goodness as a fountain,*
> *Resound from hills and mountain,*
> *Old Maryland, my native home, is free.*

⋯⟝⟞⋯

In Toronto, Thomas Smallwood must have followed the belated good news from Maryland with some joy, but also with the skepticism that had guided his entire adult life. He had outlived Torrey. He had outlived Slatter. He would outlive all his children and his wife, Elizabeth, who died in Toronto in 1876, when she was sixty-five and he was seventy-five. He would live to be eighty-two, dying on May 10, 1883, of "old age," according to the official record. A few of the Canadian papers took parsimonious note, reporting only that "Thomas Smallwood, who was at one time a slave, died yesterday." His personal self-emancipation a half century before, his role in liberating so many others, his writings—all went without notice. He was buried in the Toronto Necropolis, the major downtown cemetery, the next day.

His lifelong doubt that the United States would ever grant political or social equality to African Americans—expressed as antic humor in the Sam Weller letters and as somber condemnation in his memoir—would prove prescient. He had noted in his memoir the ritual disempowerment of African Americans in the United States, both enslaved and free, displaying a grim confidence that such inequity would prove lasting. "In a word," he wrote, "the oath of a colored person is not allowed against a white person in any matter whatever; on the other hand, it only requires the oath of the meanest white person in that country, unsupported with any other evidence, to dispossess the most respectable colored person of all he or she has."

He had noted that many Black men had fought in the American Revolution—and been repaid with status that even in the north did not rise to second-class citizenship: "It is true, the colored people have as good a right to live in the United States, and enjoy the fat of the land, as their oppressors, but 'might overcomes right,' where tyrants rule. Did not our fathers fight side by side with their fathers, against the sires of the best friends they now have, to win that independence they now so much boast of? Yes they did! And the only reward they received is a refusal on their part to permit them to enjoy a share of the freedom they had so nobly helped them to gain, and to oppress their children down to the last turn of the screw."

Referring perhaps not just to the enslaved but to semi-free Americans like he had been, he had declared flatly: "Now then I will give my opinion of the United States, caring not who may demur thereto, nor what may be said thereof. In the first place, I premise that the people of the United States will never voluntarily grant the African race among them freedom."

If in his last years Smallwood was closely following the legal and civic career of his son William in Reconstruction Mississippi, he may have begun to see an exciting glimmer of hope—that perhaps a man born in slavery, as William had been, might seriously aspire to equality and acceptance in the American south. But by 1883, when William died so young, Thomas Smallwood would surely have understood the vicious counterrevolution that was well underway, as white southerners grabbed back political power and wielded it mercilessly to obliterate Black progress. He might have been crushed, but he would not have been surprised.

Today, Hope Slatter's big white block of a tomb in Mobile with its sculptures and wrought-iron fence still seems a blunt statement of wealth and power. Charles Torrey's memorial monument in Mount Auburn Cemetery in Cambridge, Massachusetts, is an elegant and moving tribute, with a gravestone declaring him a "Martyr for Liberty" and an obelisk that includes both his bust sculpted in bronze and his life story carved in marble.

Thomas Smallwood's grave in Toronto, by contrast, evokes the neglect he experienced even in Canadian exile. It is an apt symbol of his virtual erasure from the records of abolitionism by white contemporaries and the scant attention he has received from historians in the century and a half since his death. If there ever were Smallwood gravestones in section 1, plot 125, of the Toronto Necropolis, where records show Thomas and several family members were interred, they have sunk over a century beneath the lush green grass.

Nor is there any memorial to Smallwood in Washington, where he did his pathbreaking work. One wonders what the author of the Samivel Weller letters, a clear-eyed witness to the crimes of slavery and the tragedies of race in America, might say of this absence, and of his native country's agonizing, fitful, and incomplete struggle toward justice.

Appendix

THOMAS SMALLWOOD'S SAM WELLER LETTERS: A SELECTION

The letters signed by "Samivel Weller Jr." in Albany's abolitionist newspaper are an arresting collection, using a slashing humor to assert the nobility and intellectual superiority of the enslaved while finding endless ways to denigrate their enslavers. They are also a rare running account of escapes, discussing the terrors of slavery, the clever ruses used to get away, and the motives and aspirations of those setting out for freedom.

Despite the fact that they were signed with a pseudonym, there is no doubt that nearly all of the letters signed by "Samivel Weller Jr." were written by Thomas Smallwood, who noted his authorship at the end of his memoir (*A Narrative of Thomas Smallwood*, pp. 60–61). It is possible that Charles Torrey had a hand in the first few letters, written from Washington when Torrey was still living there and working closely with Smallwood. After Smallwood moved to Toronto and his writing for the Albany paper came to an end, Torrey published a few letters using the Sam Weller pseudonym, but their content and style are quite distinct from Smallwood's, and their authorship is clear.

Reading Smallwood's letters nearly two centuries later takes a bit of practice. Their style is sometimes arch and indirect, and they are very much written to frustrate and annoy the slaveholders. Some begin with the slaveholders' runaway ads, playing on the ads' omissions and euphemisms. The letters' underlying joke is often to reveal that this "Sam Weller," whoever he is, knows a great deal more than any stranger should about the people who fled and the people who claimed to own them. He knows about slaveholders' sexual exploitation and physical abuse; he knows details about how and when people escaped; he knows and quotes what the runaways said after departing and where they settled. Smallwood hints that there is a secret, organized effort to help people flee, one that is invisible but operating close at hand. To that invisible organization he gives the name "underground railroad."

Transcribed below are seven of Thomas Smallwood's eighteen letters to the *Tocsin of Liberty* and *Albany Weekly Patriot*, with the goal of making them easily accessible for the first time. This selection samples the range of his satirical and somber styles and includes many highlights discussed in this book—the first use of "underground railroad" (August 10, 1842), the claim to have met Charles Dickens (April 27, 1843), and a surprisingly modern discussion of how racism works (June 22, 1843). The original copies of the newspapers, containing all the Weller letters, were microfilmed and digitized by the Boston Public Library at the request of the author and are now available online at digitalcommonwealth.org.

Tocsin of Liberty, August 10, 1842

[In this letter, Smallwood reprints three runaway ads from the Washington, D.C., newspapers and dissects them, flaunting his inside knowledge of the people who fled and their frustrated enslavers, including "widders" (widows). To lampoon slaveholders and police, he introduces the absurd notion that the escapes must use an "underground railroad" or "steam balloon," since the befuddled former owners cannot otherwise explain these overnight disappearances.]

For the Tocsin

Business in Washington, D.C.

> RAN AWAY from the subscriber, residing on East Capitol street, Washington city, on the night of Monday, the 11th instant, my servant man ROBERT BARNS, aged about twenty-five years, 5 feet 9 inches high, and rather stout, large eyes, with a scar above one of them, fine teeth, ears bored, bushy head, and of a swarthy copper color, and an open, pleasant countenance. He had on when he left home, a blue cloth coat with velvet collar, and gilt buttons, nearly new, black vest, and cravat, light drilling pantaloons and boots, and took with him other summer clothing, and a silver watch. He went off in company with three other negro men, one of whom has since been taken.
>
> When apprehended and brought home I will pay the following reward for him: If taken in the District of Columbia, or either of the adjoining counties, $30; if taken in any other part of Maryland, $50; and if taken beyond the limits of that State, $100.
>
> A.M. Harrington.

The subscriber is extremely sorry for *Miss* A.M. Harrington's loss. Mr. Barns *has* "an open pleasant countenance," is a fine manly fellow, and you ought not to have served him so! Woman! I charge you before your maker with *robbing* that young man! aye, of keeping him in ignorance, so that he could not read the word of God. You even demanded of him an account of his *presents*, and generally took them from him! Why you're worse than the *widder* I told about some time ago, though she was a shark sure enough, and the way she *did* swear when she found Mr. Carroll was missing, was a caution to the 4th commandment. Verry sorry a lady has no more government over her tongue! sorry to contradict a lady but can't help it. Your friend *did not* leave in that company, and not one of his company has been taken, or ever will be. And news from the district shows that Mr. Fuller's man, who was taken up at Williamsport, departed to *parts unknown* three days after, and has not since been heard of by his tyrant. By the way, Mr. Azariah Fuller stands a smart chance of hearing some *black facts* about his history told, that won't read quite so well among his New England acquaintances!

Here's another fact.

> $100 REWARD—*Ran away from the subscriber, living in Washington county, D. C., on the 18th ultimo a negro man named HENRY HAWKINS, about twenty-seven or twenty-eight years of age, supposed to be five feet high eight or ten inches high, rather inclined to be copper-colored, broad forehead, thin visage and front teeth very much decayed. Had on when he left a pair of course, brown linen pantaloons, a light mixed cloth round jacket, a new cotton shirt, and an old fur hat, and took with him a carpet bag containing a dark frock coat, a pair of drab pantaloons, and a pair of fine boots. When spoken to he has a pleasant countenance. I will give for the above described slave $50 if taken in the District of Columbia and $100 if taken in any of the States, and secured in jail so that I get him again.*
>
> *He formerly belonged to Mr. Alexander Talburt living on 7th street, has a free wife on the corner of 10th and H streets, Washington, and a mother at the Navy Yard by the name of Sarah Brown.*
>
> THOS. A. SCOTT

Pretty accurate description Mr. Scott! only quite exact as to the clothing—Poor fellow, he *couldn't* take all the clothing you speak of, from his haste! I half suspect you describe so much clothing merely to give northern people the idea that you *clothed him well,* when *you know* that he had to buy for himself, and that it was *your cruelty* to him, that made him disappear by that same "under ground rail-road" or steam balloon, about which one of your city constables was swearing so bitterly a few weeks ago when complaining, that the "d——d rascals" got off so, and that no *trace* of them could be found! Very true!

Mr. Scott! Will you inform the editor of the Tocsin, how *Mr. Hawkins'* mother should be called Sarah *Brown,* with no second marriage. I know you are too good a man to allow that "amalgamation" or any *sich* thing, takes place in your city. Take care sir! It is true his boots are "fine," but I am quite sure *you* didn't buy them for him, and you are quite mistaken about the "carpet bag." He could get it to the depot of the subterranean railroad, without notice. By the way! Just to show you how great *fools* your constables are, I will add for your *instruction and consolation,* that Mr. Hawkins was one evening, some time after he fled, in *Dr. Hall's room* in the *medical college*, standing behind the door, when the puppies wanted to come in, but couldn't 'cause the "Doctor didn't allow folks to come into his room when he wasn't there." Narrow escape, wasn't it! The way Henry laughed when he told it, showed his *want of teeth* about which your advertisement speaks, and for which such a *humane* man as you ought to be able to account in a man so young, or you will be grievously suspected of knocking them out.

> *$5 REWARD—Ran away on the night of the 22nd inst., from the residence of the subscriber, corner of 11th and L streets, Washington, D.C., negro boy Henry (commonly called Henry Clay). He is about ten years of age, is a light copper color, and has tolerably straight black hair. Had on when he left a pair of dark cloth pantaloons, light striped roundabout and a straw hat. When last heard of he was on board of one of the long boats employed in bringing wood from Dumfries and other places in Virginia to this city; the name of the boat was supposed to be Henry Clay. The above reward will be given upon his being delivered to me, free of cost, at the place above mentioned.*
>
> *MARTHA D. ALLEN*

Mrs. Allen! Mrs. Martha D. Allen, corner of 11th and L streets, I'm ashamed of you! "HENRY CLAY" run off, and you only offer five dollars for him! Oh! I see; it is the young one! Allow me to note a few points in your very entertaining advertisement.

1. "Negro." Why you say he is of "a light copper color"! Had you said "nearly white, long face, high narrow forehead," it would have suited quite as well.
2. Will you tell us *why* he is "commonly called Henry Clay," of all the Henry's in the world? Is it from the general understanding about his FRATERNITY?

How does the idea correspond with the "tolerably straight black hair," and the other features of resemblance to his namesake! Why, exactly! But remember madam, I advise you to drop no *hints* on this subject, as it might hurt Mr. Clay's political prospects, and wound the feelings of his "whig *abolition*" friends, if you are not very careful what you say. For consider, my sweet woman, that it is now, *in fact*, seven or eight years since Mr. Clay sowed his wild oats, and can't *you suppose*, (merely *suppose*,) that it is ten or eleven, and that this was the *last wild oats* he sowed!? I beseech you, be prudent! One thing more.

I am very much afraid you won't see young master Clay again. Nay, I fear you will be thought *miserly*, and in fact, *no good whig*, for offering only a paltry five dollars for one who bears such an honored name, and who has so good a right to bear it too! Mrs. Allen! Mrs. Allen, sweet Martha, (you used to be sweet when you was 20 years younger,) think what evil construction may, nay must, be put upon your conduct!

One word to your northern readers—Please Mr. Editor to suggest to them the propriety of raising a fund to defray the cost of *advertising* fugitives. It costs so much, and so little is got by it, that the poor poverty stricken slave-holders are getting unable to bear it. Perhaps it is on that account, and perhaps it is to throw some fugitives off their guard, that several owners recently have refrained from advertising their missing property.

By the way, your printers, Mr. Editor, made as many queer blunders in printing my last piece, as Mr. Boz Dickens did in printing my, and my father's memoirs.—One who didn't know us might think we want up to speakin and writin good English, or American either. So pray do tell 'em to be careful, and do send the three advertisers a copy of your paper, containing this piece of mine, and enclose your bills for printing to their address in Washington, for all these "business advertisements" come from the National Intelligencer.

Yours and Mrs. Allen's
Very humble servant,
SAM WELLER.
All along shore, Liberty day Aug. 1 '42.

Tocsin of Liberty, **August 24, 1842**
[Here Smallwood uses six more runaway ads to scold and ridicule the enslavers: their refusal to recognize the last names of the people they enslave; the biracial children they have fathered; their brutal exploitation of "two legged property." He shows off his erudition (Ovid's *Metamorphoses*) and his inside knowledge of Washington (Mrs. Sprigg's abolitionist boarders) and gleefully declares his recently christened underground railroad a state secret.]
For the Tocsin of Liberty
Runaway Property

Mr. Tocsin,—
My information from the capital warrants me in saying, that my comments on the *two legged property converted into humanity*, greatly disturb those gentle loving spirits, ycleped slave holders. Somehow, these modern metamorphoses, more strange than any that Ovid ever knew or sung, become more and more frequent every day. I cut from a single number of the National Intelligencer, (which is the slave trader's and man-hunters' principal advertising sheet in that region,) a whole column of notices of walking property walked off! I subjoin a portion of them with appropriate comments.

> *"$100 REWARD—Ran away from the subscriber's residence, near Upper Marlboro', Prince George's County, Maryland, about the 20th of April last, my negro woman MATILDA, aged about 35 years; about 5 feet 1 or 2*

inches high, generally called by the servants MATILDA BOWIE; a likely mulatto, with a very bushy head, which she keeps tied up with a handkerchief, and has a scar behind one of her ears, occasioned by a bile. Her clothing cannot be described, as she had a variety.

"I will give $50 reward if taken in this State or District of Columbia, or $100 if taken out of the State or District, and delivered to me.

W. BOWIE BROOKE."

"The servants" are correct! A lady in Washington assured my informant that this "mulatto" girl has a *good right* to the name of Bowie; and so have *some of her children*, unless they *prefer* that of Brooke. The lady referred to, declared that she was rejoiced at Matilda's escape, for she had been very *brutally* used by her owner.

The stupidity of some slaveholders is very great. They advertise people a month after they are missing, when 24 hours is ample time for a shrewd slave to escape. For example, Mr. George H. Gardiner of Pleasant Hill P.O. Charles co. Md. advertises his dear friend and servant, "Henry, who calls himself Henry Edelen," as having run away on the 7th of July, in the Intelligencer for July 27.

The "yellow fellow," as Mr. G. calls him, is doubtless out of harm's way, long ago. Pray what should he "call himself," Mr. Gardiner? Do you mean to insinuate that his proper name is Henry GARDINER. Mark it! *I* don't mean to insinuate any such thing; Not I! It may be that your phrase is only part of that despicable system by which slaveholders are led to deny to their victims a *family name*, as if their family relations were not to be acknowledged even in words. Mr. Gardiner, I'm *afeard* your $50 will hardly make Henry Edelen into plain Henry again.—The same general marks of folly appertain to the advertisement of the "*negro* boy Hensen," who is of a "*light copper color*," by Mr. Wm. T. Berry of Upper Marlborough, Prince George's co. Md. Ran away May 19th, advertised June 28th.—*Hope* the $100 offered, and the "*light* copper color," are not indications of paternal feelings in the advertiser! Ungrateful child, to leave his dear papa!

So too, Mr. G. Combs of Washington, D.C. is too late in advertising. Austin probably thought that a man 54 or 5 years old, was old enough to visit his wife without asking leave any longer. A man of that age, "a little bent" from hard service, is hardly worth your $40; so that your kind feelings toward an aged servant, Mr. G. Combs, must account for your care of him.

"$100 REWARD.—On the 5th instant, my servant JACOB, a slave for life, left home with the avowed intention of going to Loudoun county, Virginia, to harvest.—I gave him a pass for that purpose. I now have reason to believe that he has made off, perhaps to Pennsylvania. He is very tall, from three to four inches above six feet high; not heavy built, but good size, and very active in his movements; black; very pleasant countenance when spoken to, regular features and good teeth. I do not recollect any particular marks about him. Is about 22 or 23 years of age, very intelligent, and a

good deal of cunning. It is useless to describe his clothing, as he has no doubt procured new clothes, having without doubt a good supply of money.—He may have forged free papers, or procured the free papers of some of his free acquaintances.

"I will give $50 for his apprehension in the State of Maryland, or $100 if taken in Pennsylvania, so that I may get him again.

"JOHN HARRY.
"Georgetown, D.C."

"P.S. I wish to hire by the year, a servant to supply the place of the above.

J.H."

Well, John Harry, I must say your P.S. shows your good sense; you have more than your neighbors give you credit for! I hope you will hire a *free* man. You have your *soft spot*, or you would not have trusted to the "avowed intention" of a shrewd fellow like Jake, who knew the way to the "underground rail-road."—Sorry I can't give you more information about him.

Out of sympathy with dear "Brother Lee," I add the following, as his *sister Martha* is willing that he should know that she is well, and "hopes these few lines will find him in the enjoyment of the same blessins." A friend of mine happened to be in Baltimore the night your handsome sister left. She *scorns* the word "absconded." No such thing! She went openly in the public vehicle as a member of your very respectable family ought to go. So take back your shabby word about one so dear to you, and so popular, as the following description shows.

"$100 REWARD.—Ran away from the residence of the subscriber, during his absence from the city, a light mulatto slave woman, named MARTHA, aged about 26 years. She is above the ordinary size and inclined rather to be tall; has black eyes, and straight black hair. When spoken to appears to be indifferent and moody in her manner of replying; is quite likely, and had a large circle of acquaintances among her own color. [Which color is that Mr. Lee?—Ed. Tocsin.] She was seen here on Monday afternoon last, and must have absconded on that night or the following morning. She carried a variety of clothing, and was much addicted to dress and company.

"She has no doubt made for the north or Pennsylvania, with some free or runaway negro fellow. Her mother and family reside in Washington, and she sometimes calls herself Martha Lee, having been raised in the family.[!!] The above reward will be given for her apprehension and delivery in Baltimore.

Z. COLLINS LEE."

Subjoined are advertisements of *four* persons who seem to have left Washington the same night.

A friend informs me that *eight* left together in one way; and several more left by a vessel for Boston, about the same time!

> "*$100 REWARD.—Ran away on the night of the sixth of this month, my slave man, by name ISAAC DORSEY, aged about 28 years. The said slave has an indelible mark on the left side of the head, on or about the temple, caused by a burn; his ears are pierced by ear-rings. He is about five feet nine or ten inches high; his clothing cannot be described; he is civil when spoken to. The above slave has a father living in Montgomery county. He is also well acquainted in Fredericktown and county.*
>
> *"At the same time a slave named JOSEPH LEE, the property of Mr. Griffith Coombe, about 22 years of age, 5 feet 8 or 10 inches high, neither stout nor thin.—He was dressed in a blue frock coat, and linen pantaloons; is accustomed to the care of horses; is civil when spoken to. The last named slave has probably accompanied the first. And the above reward will be given if they are brought to Washington city and lodged in jail; that is, if they are taken out of the District of Columbia or Montgomery county; if taken in Frederick, all of the above reward, and if nearer in proportion.*
>
> *"JAMES G. COOMBE"*

These Messrs. Coombe are northern men, with robber, alias southern principles. The son, James G. is a physician. I should just like to ask him *if* he didn't feel *particularly* sheepish when *he met Dr. May* south east of the capitol a few days ago, when his contemptible trick of using a poor woman as an instrument (an unconscious one,) to find out how Dorsey and Lee escaped, failed of success?

I hope he won't take any offence at my bluntness! I would just hint to him, by way of caution, that the secret of the "underground rail-road," has never been communicated to any but the PRESIDENT and his CABINET: so that a few constables and an ignorant woman who knew nothing about it, won't help him very much!

I am very sorry to add that Mr. Shaw is *mistaken* as to David's clothing. Moreover, he is respectfully informed that *Liberty* has had the wonderful effect of *curing* David's impediment in his speech!—Mr. Shaw will find it hard even to recognize his voice again. And if Mr. Thomas Talburt does not wish to have a full length portrait of himself, drawn in *nature's* own dark colors, he had better send the Editor of the Tocsin some money for Woodland, instead of trying to get him back again!

> "*$50 REWARD.—Ran away, on Saturday evening, the 6th instant, from the subscriber, living near the Navy Yard, Washington, my negro man who calls himself JAMES WOODLAND. Said Woodland is about 35 years of age, of a copper color, about five feet ten inches high, good countenance and speaks free; has a scar on one side of his nose, and a scar on his forehead near the hair; a lump on the back of his neck, supposed to be occasioned by*

a sprain, as he has been employed in the Navy yard. He had on a black fur hat, linen roundabout, white shirt, and gray pantaloons. He took with him a new grass linen roundabout, a blue frock coat, and a pair of boots. It is believed that he has a free pass, and is making his way to a free state.

"*I will give twenty-five dollars if taken in the District or State of Maryland, and the above reward if taken in any other State, and secured so that I get him again.*

THOMAS TALBURT."

"*$100 REWARD.—Ran away from the subscriber, on Saturday night last, the 6th instant, residing in the outside on the farm called Brentwood, owned by Mrs. C. Pierson, about two miles north of the Capitol, a negro man named DAVID HAMILTON, about 21 years of age, six feet high, rather dark complexion, had a down look, and stammers when spoken to, and a large scar over the left eye, from a scald when young, which is very conspicuous. When he left had on coarse linen pants and cloth coat. I will give the above reward if taken over forty miles from the District; if within forty miles of the District, I will give fifty dollars; and if within the District fifteen dollars—if secured in some way that I can get him.*

JAMES A. SHAW."

[We cannot tell but some of the above chattels of the "peculiar institution" were among those of the "grand shipment of humanity," a few days ago, made up of *eighteen bales*, labelled by their own Creator, and destined to the free north beyond Ontario. We hope Sam will notify the proprietor of the Washington Hotel, Washington, D.C., that Henson Hutt was well when we saw him last, and that he may expect to hear from him in a few days from her Majesty's dominions. He is a fine smart young man. Henry Jefferson, from Washington, wished me to say to his master, he was well and thought he could take care of himself.—Ed. Tocsin]

My news from Washington warrants me in laughing at Mr. Azariah Fuller and his sons a little. The great blockheads cannot yet account for the mysterious disappearance of their man! Let me explain it to you, sweet sirs! When you sent him down the avenue on that errand, it is true, you thought you watched him very close; but there were many people in the street at the time, and, though he was in his shirt sleeves, your eyes might fail to fix on him, just at the particular moment when he slipped into the door of the apothecary's shop on the corner of 11th street, and out of the other, that opens on the back street! How he went to another city and then sent for money to help him on, and escaped to Canada, it don't just now suit my purposes to tell you.

☛ But, allow me to assure you, that no abolitionist who is or has been in Washington, helped him off. And if I hear of any more complaints of your son and a constable making impertinent visits and inquiries about Mr. Leavitt and others, at Mrs. Sprigg's, on Capitol Hill, I will make your name stink in New England as it does in Washington, for a slave-trader!—So please be careful! So no more at present from your faithful friend,

Sam Weller,
late of England.
(See my life and dad's by Boz.)

Tocsin of Liberty, **September 7, 1842**
[Smallwood's newspaper has apologized for some of his brazen earlier columns, and he pauses to note the paradox of making "fun" out of the dark deeds of slaveholders, who—in a turnabout—are "writhing" under his "lash." He pretends outrage that someone has mixed him up with the "obscure abolitionist" Charles Torrey. He scoffs at the business proposition of a Mississippi planter seeking to purchase an enslaved workforce with an ad in Washington.]
Business at the Capital.

> *"TWO HUNDRED NEGROES WANTED.—The subscriber has a plantation, with a sufficiency of land attached, (in the most compact form, viz: embraced in a point between two streams) for 200 or 250 hands. The land is equal in quality of soil, timber and water, and secure against overflow, to any alluvial lands in the state, convenient to the Mississippi river, and contains extensive improvements, such as Grist Mill, Saw Mill, and Gin: a large quantity of land cleared and partially cleared, so that by the second year two thousand bales of four hundred pounds each can be made, if it be a good crop year, and more than a thousand the first year. I will enter into bond for the deficiency. There are near 400 acres of the tract, a very small—a very unusually small portion of which is not tillable.*
>
> *My object is to form a copartnership with some one or two gentlemen, who will furnish the above number of hands, and I own one-third and they two-thirds; or a small number, and I own half. I have lived near seven years upon the place.—It has the best well of water I have seen, and is as healthy as any of the alluvial lands of the state, It is supposed to lay in the very centre of the cotton region on the Louisiana side of the Mississippi, 40 miles north of Natchez. The mortality among the black adults in the neighborhood, I think, for the last six years, has not exceeded one or two percent, per annum. Communications directed to me at New Carthage, Louisiana, will be attended to.*
>
> *J. BUTLER."*

Albeit, I come not from a *judicious county*, (my father and I being both of us, as Mr. Boz Dickens has shown, rather rough and homespun characters.) I even I, Samivel Weller, junior, will endeavor to comment on sundry matters in the newspapers, in a *werry* modest and sensible way, for the *benefit of those* who are concerned!

☛ Let the judicious readers, (I grant they are so,) who took offence at my levities, please to remark one thing, viz: that I *had a purpose* in those articles, beyond the mere *fun* of it: the "fun" of commenting on atrocities at which the Pit might well blush!—"fun" indeed!

☛ Nevertheless, a sure and tried friend in Washington, declares that the end is already, in some measure answered. The slaveholders are writhing under the affliction of the lash! Some are ashamed to continue to advertise: some avoid it altogether. The Mr. Azariah Fuller alluded to in a former paper, has put himself to considerable trouble to interfere with the comfort of one of my *old and intimate friends*, the Rev. C.T. Torrey, threatening him with beating, a mob, and sundry other minor evils, because he mistook Mr. Torrey for me, even me, Sam Weller, jr! The ignorant blunderhead! Is not *my* name carried to the world's end? Am I to be confounded with an obscure abolitionist, and *he* to be persecuted for my misdeeds! Mr. Torrey will probably tell his own story. It will be a rich "*devil-opement*" as Mrs. Child says, of the character of a "northern man with southern principles," in the small way.—Meanwhile, lest Mr. Torrey should be troubled again by these hyenas on my account, I beg you to assure them, that he and Samivel Weller, jr. are very, *very* different persons in their habits, views, feelings, characters, homes, names, looks, and every thing else! And farther, that while Mr. Torrey will, as heretofore, be occupied with more important matters, I, Samivel Weller, jr. will continue to SCOFF at, *annoy*, and *expose* the slaveholders, and their crooked ways, to their perfect mystification and great pain, during weeks and months to come! The ignoramuses! to think to catch *such* a weasel as I, asleep.

But it is time to turn to my first picture of the "peculiar institution," so very peculiar that it can't bear to be spoken of, much less laughed at.

Queer fellow, this Mr. Butler! In the city of WASHINGTON, the Nation's capital, he issues his *piratical* proposition, to any other wholesale plunderer of his species, to join with him in depriving 200 human beings of all their earnings on *shares*.

The mortality of "adult" negroes is only "one or two per cent. per annum"! Indeed! Fine healthy country that! Let us calculate the profits of the investment a little!

OUTLAY—200 negroes at $500, $100,000; as the tools are on hand, and the land ready; we will add nothing to the expenses for these items.

Interest on the amount so invested, (say $20,000,) at 6 per cent, $1,200 a year.—Interest on the purchasing of negroes, at 6 per cent, $6,000 a year. Loss by death 2 per cent, $2,000 a year. Food and other supplies for the plantation, at $20 a head for negroes, $4,000 a year; do. For three white families, (including the overseer's) at $2,000 each, $6,000.

Now count it up.

Interest on land,	$1,200
Interest on "negroes,"	6,000
DEATH,	2,000
Supplies,	4,000
Families,	6,000
	$19,200

So much, therefore, is to be wrung out of these poor children of sorrow, before any profit accrues from his investment.—Look at the

INCOME.—Crop 1,000 bales 1st year, 400 pounds each, short staple cotton, at an average price of 8 cents, comes to $32,000. Deduct for waste, expense of getting to market, and exchange, or cost of getting returns in *kind* as the plantation may require, say 1 cent a pound, equal to $4,000. This leaves the clear income at $28,000, and the clear profit on the investment at $9,000. This is very little more than 7½ per cent interest on the mere capital invested—not a very good promise to speculators. If I had made all the deductions truth would warrant from the profit, and all the just additions to the expenses, the clear income would turn out to be considerably *less* than 6 per cent, to say nothing of extraordinary casualties, failures of crops, fluctuations of prices, *runaway chattels* turning into MEN, (not uncommon even in Mississippi!) and other things that cannot be very well estimated. I'm afraid Johnny Butler won't have many offers!

N.B. He says nothing of the mortality among *children*, or the prevention of "breeding," and other evils by over-work, nor of the gradual wear and tear "of the adults."

> "$100 REWARD.—*Ran away from the subscriber, on Sunday night, the 24th instant, a negro man named PETER MATTHEWS. He is about 27 years of age and about 5 feet 10 inches high, of a mulatto color, of good form, and generally very well looking; polite when spoken to, and speaks in a low tone of voice; hair black, and when he left bushy on the sides of his head. Peter is a good dining room servant, and carriage driver, in which capacity he has for the last five years been employed. He chews tobacco, and his teeth are not very good.*
>
> *He took with him a good assortment of clothing; such as recollected, are as follows: A green frock cloth coat, yellow buttons; a black cloth coat; gambroon and other pantaloons, light colored; and light colored vests, &c. with a black hat; fur cap (brown.)*
>
> *I will give fifty dollars if the above negro be taken in the State of Maryland, and confined so that I will get him again, or one hundred dollars if taken in any other state, so that I can get him again; and thirty dollars if taken within the District of Columbia.*
>
> JAMES LARNED,
> Washington, D.C."

Peter, the graceless scoundrel! when his loving master got him back a few weeks ago, and went to such an expense about him, wouldn't stay at home, after all! So one day he passed to Canada by the "under-ground rail-road." The way Mr. James Larned *did* swear when he went into the Bank of Washington to get the $100 to pay for catching him, fully proved his need of better instruction in the ten commandments! Peter was caught only four miles from the Pennsylvania line! He won't be caught again so easily!

Bad habit, that of chewing tobacco! I hope now that Peter is out of your grasp, Mr. Clerk, he will reform in that particular. You should have saved your $100 for Peter's use, after he got to Canada!

☞ RETRIBUTION. Among the slaves recently escaped from Washington city to Canada, is a fine "boy," belonging to the man who *went down to Annapolis last winter, to stir up the mob against the Rev. C. T. Torrey.* Eh, mister? I reckon you had better stay at home, and mind your own business, the next time; and perhaps you will have less to answer for, and suffer less in your pockets, too!

I will close by an item of *law.* The sale, I believe, did not take place, the debt being paid. But it shows how things *might* be done!

> *MARSHALL'S SALE.—In virtue of a writ of fieri facias issued from the Clerk's Office of the Circuit Court of the District of Columbia for the county of Washington and to me directed, I expose at public sale, for cash on the 11th day of this month, at 11 o'clock, A.M. before the jail door of said county, one NEGRO MAN named William, aged between 35 and 40 years, levied upon as the property of one J. Brooke, and sold to satisfy judicials No 107 to November term 1841, in favor of Richard M. Warring.*
>
> "*ALEXANDER HUNTER,*
> "*Marshall District Columbia.*"

Yours judiciously,
SAM WELLER

Tocsin of Liberty, **November 3, 1842**
[Smallwood congratulates Torrey, now the *Tocsin's* editor, for leaving Washington and insists that "Sam Weller" is neither Torrey nor Abel Brown. He offers faux sympathy for the "Patriarchs" whose workers keep fleeing north, including a physician, a butcher, and the bureaucrat in charge of public gardens, and rails at another for claiming he has no idea why they left him. He tells the story of James Burgess and threatens to expose a slaveholder if Burgess's wife is not freed.]
More Fleeing from Happiness.
Washington, D.C., Oct. 22d, 1842.

Mr. Editor.—My father and I are very glad to see you safe out of the hands of the Philistines! I should have sent a letter to your paper before, but I have been waiting to get some particular facts which I now send you. By the way, I want you to assure the good people in Albany, and thereabouts, that Samivel Weller, jr., and Abel Brown are neither kith, kin, nor acquaintance. And the date of my letter will assure Mister Fuller that *you* and I are very different people. Strange that he ever mistook a yankee for me! How I laughed when his son Ned came home from Boston, Albany and elsewhere, with a flea in his ear, just as wise about that "boy Henson," as he was before he spent so much money in the chase. Why couldn't he believe my letter that said Henson was in Canada? I rather reckon he must look me up before he gets the real state of the case; for I'm an *old settler*, here; and I know the *rich man* in whose stable Henson was hid, the day he left, till after dark. He don't live a thousand miles from F street! I hope you will expose Mr. A. Fuller's treatment of you. What business had he to threaten and swagger at you, swearing like a pirate: and to give you 12 hours to leave the city, or he and some *gentlemen*, forsooth, would *force* you out! [I have concluded to spare Mr. Fuller, vile as his conduct was, out of regard to his family and friends. Ed. Tocsin.] Give it to him, strong! There's a peck of trouble among the Patriarchs, in this city, since you left. I want to comfort the dear souls a little, by assuring them that their absent friends have all reached Canada, in safety, having been seen in Toronto, and some of them have written back to me, in this city, that their relations might be assured of their health and good prospects.

It was *wery* cruel, *wery*, in Peter Matthews to run off to Canada, after his sweet, swearing master had paid $100 for catching him only 6 weeks before! Poor James Larned! Why did you listen to your tender hearted wife? Had you sold him when he first come back, your money would have been safe. But alas, there is no hope for you! Peter is in Toronto. He loved a certain bright eyed Sophy Jackson even better than his dear master; and Sophy you know, left Washington a year ago, on the grand tour! If you are really rich enough to pay the second cool hundred out of your salary as Clerk, it would only be fair to send it to Peter. For he lost nearly that when he jumped into the water, from the bridge, where your man-hunters headed him off, on his first attempt to get to Canada, by way of Frederick. Will you do it?

Surely Job's trials were nothing to those of poor NOTLEY MADDOX. I will copy his last advertisement from the Intelligencer. I wonder the editor did not condole with him!

> "RUNAWAYS—*One thousand and fifty dollars reward.—I have not heard from mine, as advertised in the National Intelligencer during September past. In addition to those therein described and named, my young lad called HANSON, and sometimes FRANK, left me on the night of the 26th ultimo. He is a mulatto, rather dark, about 20 years old, common size, moderate intellect; took away a black cloth coat, other clothing not recollected. He has been often sent to the Washington market with vegetables. I have now five males and one female that have now left me without cause known to me.*
>
> *For their arrest and confinement in any jail so that I can get them again, I will give two hundred dollars each for the men, if taken in a free State; and fifty for the woman; or one half, no matter where taken. Forged certificates of freedom, with good imitations of official seals, are common.*
>
> "NOTLEY MADDOX
> "Near Washington, D.C."

Notley is mistaken about the "official seals." They are all good ones, for God gave them, in stamping MANHOOD on the brow of his poor slaves. He is a booby to advertise the slaves who went to Canada years ago. Hanson, the "young lad" of "20 years old," happens to think himself a man! and so he went to the Springs, and sprung over to Canada! and "SAM," alias, Mr. Samuel Johnson, has been there these two months. A witty fellow, Sam is! I don't wonder, Mr. Maddox, that you mourn $200 worth of tears and sighs for his company. He would force a smile on the granite face of the "old man of the mountain," that I saw once, in the Franconia Notch, up in New Hampshire! I *must* say, Notley Maddox, if you insult the nation again, by pretending that your six slaves left you "without any cause known to you," that I shall be obliged to expose your *cruelty* to them; your robbing them of liberty and property, was quite bad enough. But it hurts my feelings to write about your violent temper, and tyrannical conduct and it *might hurt* yours to have it known! You may make yourself easy about Frank. He went to Canada, direct.

Mr. JAMES MAHER, the public gardener, must regret to lose the company of Margaret Myers, and I don't doubt he does—But Uncle Sam pays him so much money for nothing, that he can afford the pecuniary loss, very well. Doubtless, Mr. Maher's conscience has never been *quite* easy, since he killed that slave in his barn with the piece of old cart tire. Let him remember that a *white witness still lives, who was not present at his trial.* I don't wonder Margaret wanted to leave him, if all I have heard of his conduct to poor laboring *white* people is true! Why does this man never employ an AMERICAN laborer on the public grounds? Perhaps they would [not] submit so quietly to his hard conditions!

DR. WM. H. GUNNELL, down there by the wharf, is a 'cute one, sure enough. How many times have I heard him boast that "no nigger could ever get away from him!" Ah, you're not so wise as you thought for; *or* Mrs. Tilly could never have taken her child out of your very bed room! On reflection, don't you think it was cruel, Dr. Gunnell, to make that little child, only five years old, lie on your chamber floor, and keep awake to tend your own *white* baby, while you and your wife slept? Don't you think it was wrong to treat that Christian mother as a mere "breeding wench" and refuse her husband for *months* together, all access to her society? If you have a mind to confess your wrong to Mrs. Tilly, and pay DENNIS SHAW his wages, and make his double and twisted eyes sparkle, I will give you a letter to them, on application at the office of the "underground railroad."

JAMES BURGESS and his sister Eliza, (and her child) wish to assure their tender hearted mistress that they are well and happy in Queen Vic's dominions. Perhaps her son-in-law, Mr. Francis Markoe, can comfort her widowed heart; if not, I don't know who can. James, before he left, wished me to write a few things about his story for some northern paper. Be it known, then, that James has been cook in the U.S. Navy Yard, in this city, for eight years. He was enlisted contrary to law, as the officers of the yard well knew. His mistress received $18 a month for his services, and never allowed him *one cent* of it for his own. True, the regulations of the Navy Yard compelled her to keep him well clothed. His mistress went to the Warrenton Spring this summer, and authorized James to receive his last three months wages, which fell due in her absence. James very naturally thought that the best use he could make of his earnings was to take a trip to Saratoga with his dear sister, for their health, and when they were *so near* Canada, they doubtless found it pleasant to cross the line, just to see a few old acquaintances. That sister of his well deserves his care and love, for she was a second mother to him in his childhood. He will pay her by watching over her fatherless child.

How James' whole frame quivered when he told me the story of his wife's being whipped on her naked back with the rawhide in his presence! She is nearly 25 years old, and at 25 is entitled to beg her liberty. Her tyrant master, Mr. F——g M———-, lives just off from the old road to Bladensburg, in Maryland. James could never go see his wife except on Sundays. One Sunday in order to aggravate his feelings, the old tyrant chose to tie up his wife to a tree to flog her, just as James got there. James saw four or five blows inflicted, but he could bear no more. He cut her loose, and when the master undertook to punish him for it, James gave the old tyrant a sound beating, and fled. The next morning the woman whipper came to the Navy Yard in a great rage, and demanded that James should be severely punished. The Lieutenant of the yard was disposed to gratify him, but James claimed a trial by court martial, utterly denying that he had violated any rule of the service; for he was absent on leave, and was out of the district. The officer scolded; but he knew that the *enlistment of a slave*, contrary to law, might cost him his commission, if the matter came to trial, so James was let off with a reprimand. If the old woman-whipper don't let his wife go to Canada next summer, I will expose him, *by name*, if I remain in Washington, as I expect to; for it's a satisfaction I cannot forego to show up the deeds of darkness in our capital. How the wounded do flutter! They are great ninnies to suppose that such abolitionists as yourself and Leavitt would run any risk to ship off their slaves, when you are doing so much more in other ways to put down slavery. I can tell them better. Why, there's a rich lawyer in this city, a slaveholder, who does a deed of mercy in that way at times. Pro-slavery members of Congress do it often out of mere humanity. Besides, a shrewd slave has wit enough at any time to get round a lazy, mole-eyed slaveholder. Even the Fullers lost so much of their Yankee 'cuteness by becoming slaveholders, that HENSON disappeared from before their face and eyes in the middle of the afternoon, when three of them were watching him!

☞ Now I wish all these gentry to take notice that their slaves get off just as fast now, while all the abolitionists they suspected of aiding them are absent, as they did last Spring, when they were here. ☞ And another thing. ☞ Here am I, SAMUEL WELLER, jun., still in the city to scourge and mock at them, and defy all their puny efforts to discover me, or the "underground railroad."

Perhaps Mr. PHILIP OTTERBACK, one of our principal butchers, a German by birth, is "chief mourner" after the long procession of runaways. It was a cool $600 out of his pocket to lose Edward Brooks, "my negro man Ned Brooks," as his advertisements in the papers call him. I presume Ned, being a capital butcher, thought it became an enterprising young man, like him, to set up for himself, and as he wanted a woman to *try out the fat* for him, who could he take better than his charming little wife? Mrs. Brooks wishes to be remembered to Mr. D.C. Croft, whose kindness, and that of the family, she gratefully speaks of in her letter. She would not have left them, but for her husband's sake, and she thanks them for not advertising her: it would have hurt her feelings to have her name put in the papers in such a way.

But Mr. Philip Otterback, doubtless, mourns the loss of his darling Betsey Williams, far more than that of Ned Brooks. People *do* say that Philip loved Betsey a little better than Mrs. Otterback altogether approved of. Betsey is a noble girl. Bought, when a child, for a *certain purpose*, and trained up under his eye, it was provoking to find her virtue so stern as to repel her master with scorn. Nay, to jump out of her chamber window when the intruder kicked in the door! Happily, the vigilance of a wife and son will sometimes prevent the evil intended by the head of the family. If Mr. Otterback ever becomes a widower, and will come to Toronto a courting in an honorable way, perhaps Betsey will relent. It was sad to see how dejected he looked in the market for weeks after it. Perhaps he can spare a few tears by way of sympathy with Mrs. McKune and her son-in-law, the Hon. Virgil Maxcy, late Minister to Holland, on the loss of George and John Turner, two as fine fellows as ever lived; too white, by many shades, to pass for "niggers" any where but in a slaveholding city. When Canada is a free Republic they will be her boldest soldiers.

But I must cease for the present, or I shall not have room in my letter for a few little incidents worth naming.

The other day I was at the Rail Road Depot, when Dr. Gunnell, with Patten, the constable, (a mean fellow,) were there. Some one said to Gunnell—

"Why Doctor, I thought you and DENNIS were like brothers! They say he's left you!"

The Doctor replied, "If Dennis should come back to-morrow I would trust him to the Bank with $1000, as soon as any one." Patten, pointing over to Mrs.——'s, said, "It was that fellow over yonder, that helped him off," (mentioning your name!*) "I've had a warrant out against him for a fortnight, but could never catch him. I sent —— to Mrs——'s after him.—That d—d old b—h was as guilty as he."

The poor manstealers and their watchdogs are greatly at a loss to know how their victims escape. At times they watch the Rail Road, with eagle eyes.—But men and women *do* go off in the cars before the faces of Suit, Thorn and other wretches like them, very often. "Their eyes are holden," as a slave said once, "so that they see the poor fugitive."

At other times they reckon their victims escape in coaches or wagons. Then they imagine they go by water, which is often the case. All this shows that they would give a *plum* to know where the under-ground Rail Road begins! That name was given to it by constables ZELL of Baltimore.

Have you forgotten a certain Walter W. W. Bowie, who made two very violent and vulgar speeches in the great Slaveholders' Convention at Annapolis last winter; and who helped get up the mob against you? A few days ago he sold to one of our city traders SEVEN slaves—two men, two women and three well grown lads, all for $1300 only! Less than $186, a piece! Five years ago they were worth $5000. Some one asked him why he sold them? He replied, "niggers were running away so fast he meant to have something for his, while he could get it!" Gunnell and Otterback have both declared they never meant to have any more slaves! "Sour grapes," I reckon. An attempt was made, recently, to find out the way a certain slave escaped by intercepting the correspondence of our colored people. But the upright delivering clerk, Mr. TREE would not listen to it at all. He deserves credit for it.

I must close my letter without paying my respects to the large number who have recently been afflicted by the loss of their beloved servants! The conductor of the "U.G.R. Road" tells me that over 20 have gone, this month! You may depend on hearing from them, through me, as soon as I learn of their reaching the other end of their journey!

Yours, in hatred of slavery,
SAMUEL WELLER, Jr.

P.S. My father writes me that Boz DICKENS, in his new work on America, abuses this country shockingly. I'm sorry we let him write our Biography. For this is a glorious land after all, if the curse of slavery could be removed. Pa says, the way Boz shows up the slaveholders is a caution to snakes! What a capital subject for him to show up, in a novel! How MEAN he'd make the robbers of the poor look! Slaveholders are worse than Ralph Nickleby, or even the old Jew, in Oliver Twist!

Yours, SAM
*I call on Patten for an explanation.—I never avoided him or any one. I passed him daily, the last fortnight I was in the city. I believe his talk of the warrant was a coward's bravado over an absent man.

ED. TOCSIN

Albany Weekly Patriot, **April 27, 1843**
[In this dispatch, Smallwood complains of a slaveholding British consul who might try to recover two people he had enslaved, now in Canada, by accusing them of a crime—taking the clothes they were wearing! He claims to have led the visiting Charles Dickens to see a slave trader's jail. He rattles off nine other enslavers and purports to pass on messages from the people they formerly enslaved. And he urges slaveholders to free and pay wages to their workers.]
WASHINGTON, D.C., April 17, 1843

Mr. PRINTER:
Sometime you remembered our friend, Lord Palmerston, issued a circular, requiring all British consuls, in slaveholding countries, to cease to hold slaves. I very much wish that the attention of the British Government could be turned to some of their functionaries in this country.

There is John McTavish, Esq., the consul at Baltimore, Md., who married the slaves of Richard Caton, Esq., (with the incumbrance of his daughter, attached). He is a slaveholder, and no very gentle one, either, as his fugitive slaves have more than once testified. There was a *woman* who fled from his lash, last spring, a year since. And in the fall, John Miniski, a fine looking young man, who got tired of working for nothing, for one of Queen Victoria's servants. A Scotchman and a Yankee make hard masters! Their own energy makes them exact as much labor *without any proper motive to industry*, as they are accustomed to see performed where labor is well paid for. Now, why is this Mr. Tavish to be permitted to trample on the requirements of his Sovereign? *Perhaps*, as a special favor to *his* aristocratic American relatives, the "10th article" might be stretched, so as to recover John and Elizabeth, under the plea of "felony," in wearing off *some clothes*, instead of fleeing *in puris naturabilus*!

(You never heard how I learned Latin, did you? One day Boz Dickens and I were walking down to see Williams' *Slave Pen*, right in front of the President's House. Boz, after turning up his nose, in his very curious way, at the flag, on the Capitol, began to quote some Latin stuff about hypocrisy and republican despotism, as he said. And I thought I would learn it, to use *in cursing slavery with*! And it comes very convenient, sometimes, when I'm at a slave auction, or looking at a whipping, or visiting the slaves, in connection with our operations, to vent my feelings in a language the woman-whippers don't understand! A surly slave-catcher actually took off his hat to me, when I denounced him as a *"monstrum horrendum."* I suppose he thought me some great one!) Leaving Mr. Tavish I will pay a passing tribute to some other worthies.

1. There is Charles Carroll, of Howard District, Md., whose relative, "Sam Castle," desires to be remembered to him. He forgives him his countless stripes, in view of the fact that the *last one* has been laid on.

2. Wm. Jones assures Mr. Crumpton Gantt, of Huntington, that his fame, as a tyrant, shall *not* be spread as widely as it deserves!

3. When I was last at Baltimore, I found my old friend Henry Hylon, mourning because he hadn't heard of his faithful Henry Lucas. But I *now* assure him that Henry is perfectly well and happy.

4. You remember the interest Reverdy Johnson, Esq., of Baltimore, took, last winter, to help you out of the clutches of the slaveholding convention. Lewis Jackson says he is a very kind master, and that he never would have left him, if *Mrs.* Johnson had been blessed with an *angel's temper*! Slavery does make *women, who imbibe its spirit*, into very fiends!

5. Tom Berry, of Prince George's county, Md., renowned for his cruelty to his poor victims, can hardly expect John Allen to forgive him, at present; while the scars on his back remain so bright and fresh! Oh, he's a terrible tyrant!

6. The Widders *is* desperate! There is Widder Henrietta Dawson, who drove

her faithful Isaac Johnson to flee. And Widder Ann Page, (quite another thing from the image of beauty, life and joy, Will Shakespeare imaged, in the Merry Wives of Windsor,) of Cambridge, Md., who compelled James Wright to seek, in Canada, that home she denied to his patriotism, in this, his native land! Then Widder Eliza Jones must mourn that her "boy, Bennett," is no longer willing to work for nothing. And Mrs. Washington, of New Orleans, may cry her pretty eyes out! but she will never see her Chas. Williams again! He loved to travel; his organ of locality was large; he had heard of Toronto, Canada, and wanted to visit it!

7. Wm. H. Edes, of Georgetown, who keeps the Feed Store, and would not let you have a horse, last summer, because you was a stranger, in pursuit of a lost child, may consider himself punished by the loss of William Martin.

8. Finally, I must condole, once more, with that much afflicted man, Notley Maddox. Just before cold weather, Washington Bell left him; and then, *old* Henson, his *last* male slave, a man of 55 years of age, had the cruelty to leave his "dear, old, grey-haired master, to die alone." Even his smart fop of a son couldn't catch the old fellow, though he went to Baltimore on purpose. I set by his side, in the cars, as he returned; and the way he *did swear*, was a caution to MEMBERS OF CONGRESS! The old man has *hired* two white laborers, for his farm. Don't he regret, now, that he hadn't sense enough to emancipate *seven* as good men as Maryland holds, who had grown up with him and his children, and were used to the farm and his ways, and *hire* them? If old Notley has a spark of manliness about him, if he is not afraid his grey head will yet go down to the grave in sorrow, let him emancipate the three daughters of Henson, and the innocent children of the oldest girl, and so cease to be a slaveholder! I have much regard for Notley. I have known him long; and I pray that he may be led to do it.

Yours, in hatred of Republican slavery,
SAMIVEL WELLER, JR.

Albany Weekly Patriot, **June 15, 1843**

[Smallwood, in his guise as Sam Weller, gives himself an impressive title as the agent of not just the underground railroad but all other means of escape as well. He records multiple escapes; boasts of daring to drive runaways past the offices of John Zell, a Baltimore constable; and wishes Torrey ("Mr. Printer") could have tasted the spring peas in Washington's Gadsby's restaurant. And he brags about bribing police officers from the city's new Auxiliary Guard.]

WASHINGTON CORRESPONDENCE.
WASHINGTON CITY, June 6, 1843.

Mr. Printer,—Here I am, back to my post, as general agent of all the branches of the National Underground Railroad, Steam Packet, Canal and Foot-it Company.

Business begins to be *very* brisk. I have sent off no less than nine passengers, from this city, within a week! The most of them have taken the Erie Branch, Steam Flying Machine, so that you will not see them, or they you, unless the wind blows them very much out of their course. The nefarious attempt to swear a poor colored man, named Meade, of Baltimore, into prison, on pretense that he was in my employ, did not succeed, as you know. And the result of his acquittal has been to give a new impulse to business. Our agents *were* becoming a *little*, very little, too bold; and, while we were diverted to see the poor police officers, Zell, Ridgely and Hays, make such a blunder in their man, it seemed to show us the need of more boldness, which is the best caution. So the other day, when I took Richard Brown to Baltimore, we went and laughed in their faces, as one of them was reading Waters' advertisement. Poor puppies! I have taken a *load*, at mid-day, right by their office, and the lazy dogs didn't look up! You remember JOHN WATERS' place, near the Columbia College, on the road we often walked, when we were discussing the "affairs of the nation!" 'Tis a beautiful, shady spot. And Waters isn't *half* so bad as he might be!—But Dick,—I mean Mr. Richard Brown,—preferred Kingston, in Canada, where he has relatives, to all the charms of the Farm.

The day after he left, we passed along the *goods* of James Berry, who thought that Mr. JOSEPH CHAPMAN, of Norfolk, Va., had no better title to his services than Gray had to those of Latimer! Poor, benighted fellow! He had never read the convincing arguments of Rev. Mr. DEW,—(alas! He could not read!)—so that it is not so much to be wondered at. So he took the new steamer to New York, and sent on his goods to my care. I learn that there is not much doing in the Human Cattle Market, of Norfolk, just now.—There have been but few sent to New Orleans, this spring, compared with former exports. Prices very low. The sensation caused by the Latimer case has not yet subsided. James' friend (my agent,) writes me that James and Latimer were old acquaintances; and Latimer will be glad to learn from you, of James' safety. [He is in Canada.—ED. PAT.]

On my return home from the North, I stopped a day or two in the upper part of Maryland. One result of my visit has been several indications of *powers of locomotion* never before exercised. Charles Smith thought he had toiled for THOMAS AYERS, of Hartford, for nothing, quite long enough. Bill Dagin had the same view of his relations to WM. BELL, of the same places. Their masters are pretty clever fellows, a little fierce, at times, especially Bell. But liberty is sweet. David Colmon, of the same place, thought proper to leave WM. PITES; and Mr. HENRY GUIDON'S service had no charms for Stephen Hall, without pay! *Steve* is a queer fellow. The way he rolled up his eyes, half tearful, half mirthful, when he crossed the old Mason and Dixon's line, was funny!

Oh, how many scenes of deep interest I have witnessed, on that spot! Last year a large company were so affected that they embraced and kissed the stone that marks the line of Pennsylvania, weeping over it, and then shouting out for joy of heart!

Stephen Perkins wanted me to send his love to JAMES CHAMBERLAIN, of Easton. And his wife, Lydia, wished to be remembered to CHARLOTTE EVANSON, and to say, that not all the love she *might* have borne her as an equal *free* woman, could persuade her that it was right to suffer her unborn infant to become a slave to a woman not much whiter than its mother!

WATSON SWAN, of Baltimore, will not hereafter be troubled to distinguish his boy John Thomas, from other *white* young men, when he passes them in the street. Even according to Southern notions, Swan was doing a *black* deed, to enslave a worthy young man quite as white as himself. But my time is as occupied with the cares growing out of the great extension of my business, that I must postpone further notices of individuals, for the present.

The weather, here, is very warm; and the supply of vegetables in the market abundant. I wish I could send you some of Gadsby's green peas, on which I luxuriated yesterday. Do come on and make us a visit, Mr. Printer!

By the way, the slaveholders this season, have advertised the fugitives but very little, in the political papers. They are trying them hard at handbills, and fees to the Auxiliary Guard and the Police. But we have *bought up* a few of the *Guard*, and you know we always despised the regular police as a set of poor tools!

Yours, respectfully,
SAMIVEL WELLER, JR.

Albany Weekly Patriot, **June 22, 1843**
[Smallwood lambastes an officer at the nearby Navy Yard for whipping an enslaved woman. He describes overhearing at Washington's city jail a plot to sell a free Black man by falsely claiming he is enslaved. This episode prompts him to complain of the atrocious treatment of free African Americans, particularly by policemen exploiting the 10 p.m. curfew for all Black people. He adds a sober passage analyzing racism and ends with an unusual sign-off: "Yours for equal rights."]

WASHINGTON CORRESPONDENCE.
For the Albany Weekly Patriot.
WASHINGTON, D.C., June 14, 1843.

MR. EDITOR:
I have various odds and ends to put together today—some old, some new.

I believe you remember the introduction I gave you, one day, to Capt. Pendegrass, of the Navy? He is a son-in-law of that fine old soldier, Com. Barron. But he is as unlike him, in every respect as possible. I have a rod for his back. He is from Pennsylvania, but he must need ape the manners of the place, and hire a slave, in his family. So he hired one from one of the notorious C——s, of Maryland—notorious for their severity to their slaves. She is a mother of three or four children, from whom she is separated, to wait on the wife and children of this Pennsylvanian. C——told him "not to let her want for whipping." Accordingly, Mr. P. bares, as it were, the bones of the poor woman. Is he not a fine specimen of a Naval Commander? WOMAN-WHIPPING IN THE NAVY-YARD AT WASHINGTON! How would it sound in London, or Rome! Why, the arch Inquisitor would shake his sides for laughter, in scorn of these pretenders to republican freedom!

Let me advert once more to some slighter details. A few months ago, I went up to the old jail to witness the sale of a woman at auction, for debt. It did not take place, as the master concluded to pay his debt, and reclaim the victim.

While I was standing in the entry of the jail, a constable brought in a dark negro man—his face bruised and his clothes soiled—bearing very evident marks of the drunken loafer species; though he was sober enough at that time. He was a free boy, and not detected in the violation of any law. Why, then, was he imprisoned?

The jailor and constable talked the matter over, in my hearing, and their explanations amounted to this: He was committed to prison as a *runaway slave*. The constable, with a becoming wink and smile, added, "Why, if he don't turn out to be so, we must let him go, at the time."

Meanwhile, the fees of the constable, jailor, and District Marshall, (for maintenance,) are secure, from the Treasury of the United States! And as the freeman whose rights are trampled on is a friendless stranger, and one whose bad habits deprive him of public sympathy, no one is concerned to interfere.

This is a sample of the petty legal oppressions to which the free colored man is occasionally exposed to in this city. The oppression under the 10 o'clock law, of the City Corporation, by which all free colored persons who are out later than that hour are liable to be arrested, put in the watch-house till morning, and then fined $5, or less, at the discretion of the Magistrates, I have often noticed. That the Corporation has no power to pass such a law, I need not stop to show.

In one instance, last fall, a servant of Daniel Webster's was thus dealt with; but Webster had no idea of submitting to the petty ordinance, and sent his lawyer, Mr. Hall, to contest its validity. The Magistrate thought it best to free the servant, without exacting the fine!

But with the colored man or woman who lacks so powerful a protector, the case is otherwise; and the lawless ordinance is sometimes enjoined, with every circumstance of oppression.

An active City Magistrate told me to-day, that the enforcement depended very much on the *caprice* of the constables! If one of these worthies did not make quite so much as his pockets required, in the *more honorable* part of his duty, he would watch his chance to pounce on some helpless colored people that were out late, perhaps on their return from church, or a visit to their friends; and either put them in the lockup and have them fined, or let off for a private payment to the *constable*, of a *part of the fine*! That such barefaced highway robbery is perpetrated, I have no doubt. It is impossible for the colored man to prevent it, or get redress, as his color is a bar to his evidence against the white constable; and the laws of the United States, or city ordinances, that Congress sanctions by *not* revoking them, will bear the oppressor out in his iniquity.

The ordinance, it is true, was not generally enforced, *till reward was established*:

but the very caprice in regard to its enforcement, made its action the more oppressive. No constable would think of enforcing it against any of the more wealthy and well-known people of color. So that those who are commonly the sufferers, are the most helpless of their class.—This is the true instinct of lawless power, to bind the heaviest burdens on those who are least able to bear it. It is the *meanness of slave holding chivalry*.

The same disposition is shown in the ordinary intercourse of white people with colored men and women, both bond and free. The *tone of command* is that which is almost always employed, in addressing them, no matter what the subject may be. To speak to them with respect, would be to *descend* to their level, in the view of the community. If the tones used are kind, they are still the indications of the kindness of an acknowledged superior, towards one accustomed to be treated as an inferior, for no other reason than their different color. The difference between the atmosphere of Washington, and one of our northern cities, in this respect, strikes the mind at once, and with great force. And there is a degree of timidity, and a want of self-respect, apparent in the manners of a large part of the people of color, which very naturally results from this state of things: and which would soon disappear, as it has in northern cities, under a different course of treatment.—There are exceptions, it is true, and marked ones; but just sufficient to confirm the general truth of what I have said.

Yours for *equal rights*,
SAMIVEL WELLER, JR.

Acknowledgments

This book has its origins in my discovery, some years after our move to Baltimore in 1983, that around the same Inner Harbor where we pushed our children in strollers and went to Orioles games, the domestic slave trade had once thrived. Where we applauded street unicyclists and earnest saxophonists, people had been torn from their families, shackled in private jails, and forced aboard ships that carried them to southern plantations many hundreds of miles from all they'd ever known. I found that, like me, most of my friends did not know that a million people had been forcibly moved south in the five decades before the Civil War. I wrote about that history for *The Baltimore Sun,* and a decade later a historic marker to those sold south from Baltimore was erected. It was planted, however, not in direct view of the tourists and locals thronging the waterfront but in front of the Reginald F. Lewis Museum of Maryland African American History & Culture a few blocks away. Even as overdue attention was paid to local history, the old American tradition of averting our eyes from harsh truth was honored.

When I mentioned to my brother that I was working on this book, he instantly responded with affectionate brotherly sarcasm, "That's great—it's about time we learned what a white guy thinks about these things." He had a point. I try to approach the topic of racial slavery with humility and an awareness of my limited perspective. But I also bring to it a long-standing belief that "Black history" has sometimes been a way for white Americans to avoid looking squarely at their own past. Black Americans did not own themselves, sell themselves, rape themselves, or ship themselves south. Slavery was an institution of the white power structure, the "slave power," as it was memorably called two centuries ago. To try to separate the history of Black Americans from the history of white Americans seems impossible if truth telling is the goal.

At this moment, it seems especially important for white people to read and think and write about the crimes of slavery carried out by the ancestors of many of us. The idea that some state legislatures have recently proposed laws to protect white children from feeling discomfort over the history of race in America is beyond parody. It is very much of a piece with the Maryland law under which in 1857 a free African American, Daniel Green, was sentenced to ten years in prison for mere possession of *Uncle Tom's Cabin,* the bestselling novel exposing the cruelty of slaveholders and slave traders.

Any writer of history stands on a foundation of knowledge built up over decades. When I first began to write about the domestic slave trade in Baltimore more than twenty years ago, I relied on the work of Ralph Clayton, a pioneer in the field, and especially his 2002 book *Cash for Blood: The Baltimore to New Orleans Domestic Slave Trade,* which I have consulted repeatedly in working on this book. I first explored the life of Charles Torrey in E. Fuller Torrey's judicious biography, *The Martyrdom of Abolitionist Charles Torrey* (2013), and I learned a great deal about Torrey, Smallwood, and the borderlands from Stanley Harrold's work, especially his 2000 article "On the Borders of Slavery and Race: Charles T. Torrey and the Underground Railroad" and his 2003 book, *Subversives: Antislavery Community in Washington, D.C., 1828–1865.* Both Harrold, whose quotations from Smallwood's Sam Weller letters sparked my interest in them, and Fuller Torrey were generous with research advice. I should also mention the invaluable work of Tom Calarco, a tireless chronicler of the underground railroad and one of the few to recognize Smallwood's contributions, notably in his *People of the Underground Railroad.*

Many other scholars answered queries and pointed me to the right places in the archives. I am grateful to Jennie K. Williams, who has done heroic work in compiling the records of the voyages of the domestic slave trade; Ed Papenfuse, a force of nature, who advised me when I was starting my research and helped me navigate the Maryland State Archives; William G. Thomas, who knows a great deal about slavery in and around Washington; Joshua Rothman, who gave me excellent advice before a research visit to New Orleans, including steering me to the walking tour of the slave trade he helped produce; Matthew Furrow, who transcribed Thomas Smallwood's interview with Samuel Gridley Howe; Karolyn Smardz Frost, chronicler of the underground railroad at the Canadian end; and Guylaine Petrin, who gave invaluable advice on Toronto research and dug up crucial records of Thomas Smallwood's family. I appreciated the work of the few scholars who have analyzed Smallwood's memoir, including Sandrine Ferré-Rode, Nele Sawallisch, and Richard Almonte.

Archivists and librarians are the unsung but crucial partners of anyone writing about the distant past. I owe a particular debt to the staff of the Boston Public Library, especially Chris Glass, who became my advocate in hunting down copies of the *Tocsin of Liberty* and *Albany Weekly Patriot* in a warehouse and making them available for the first time; Thomas Smallwood's extraordinary letters are now available online at digitalcommonwealth.org as a result. Russell Hill of the National Archives and Records Administration went the extra mile in digitizing and sending me documents when COVID-19 closed the archives. Thanks also to Chris Haley, Owen Lourie, and the staff of the Maryland State Archives; Liza Duncan and her colleagues at the New York State Library; Lee Grady of the Wisconsin Historical Society; William McCarthy of the Congregational Library; Brianne Barrett, American Antiquarian Society; David Armenti, Micah Connor, and Leslie Eames, Maryland Center for History and Culture; Rob Schoeberlein, Baltimore City Archives; Susan G. Pearl, Prince George's County Historical Society; the staff of the Historical Society of Baltimore County; Matt Benz, Ohio History Connection; Maya Davis, Riversdale House Museum; Julie O'Connor, Friends of Albany History; Elizabeth Allen, Notarial Archives Research Center, New Orleans; Paul McCardell, *The Baltimore Sun*; Jennifer Navarre and Heather Green, Historic New Orleans Collection; Chuck Torrey (a distant relative of Charles Torrey) and museum supervolunteer Michelle Cooke, History Museum of Mobile, Alabama; and the staffs of Magnolia Cemetery (in Mobile), Mount Auburn Cemetery (in Cambridge, Massachusetts), and the Toronto Necropolis.

My friends and family have helped in endless ways. Steve Luxenberg did a forensic reading of my first draft, caught many errors, and gave valuable advice at every phase. Richard Bell of the University of Maryland brought his comprehensive knowledge of American slavery and sharp authorial eye to a draft. Michael A. Fletcher, my old *Baltimore Sun* pal and one of the nation's finest writers on the intricacies of race, gave the book a perceptive and appreciative read. Douglas M. Birch advised on Baltimore history and offered valuable editing suggestions. Helene Cooper read the proofs while roaming the world as a Pentagon correspondent and gave me encouragement and edits. Bob Cronan offered generous advice on maps. Many friends offered advice and support, including Bill Zorzi, Milton Leitenberg, Wick Sloane, Ed Donnellan, Amy Davis, Nancy Goldring, Chuck Lacy, Robert Ruby, and Michael Hill. Tom Piazza gave a warm welcome and writerly encouragement in New Orleans. Francie Weeks and Suse Shane took the time to mark up the very rough first draft. Martha Shane and Nathan Shane gave crucial advice on later drafts. Laura Shane and Nick Murray provided cheerleading and crucial entertainment in the person of our first grandchild.

My agents, Larry Weissman and Sascha Alper, were a great help in shaping my book proposal. My editor at Celadon Books, Bill Hamilton, an old friend from *The New York Times,* was a good-natured and encouraging companion along the way. He made every chapter better. Thanks, too, to Randi Kramer and the rest of the team at Celadon and Macmillan. This book would never have happened without the steadfast encouragement of my wife, Francie Weeks, who helped with research on our trips to New Orleans, Mobile, and Toronto, and made my project hers as well.

Scott Shane

Notes

A few technical matters: I have sometimes preserved the original spellings, capitalization, and punctuation from nineteenth-century writings to give their flavor, but generally I have corrected printer's errors and regularized the misspellings of names, such as the common "Torry" for the correct "Torrey." I quote archaic words like "colored" and "Negro" and racial slurs in a few instances—including Smallwood's interesting phonetic rendering of the N-word as "neger"—in order not to obfuscate language common in the 1840s. I generally follow the contemporary practice of avoiding labeling people as "slaves," which suggests a permanent condition that inexplicably befell them, and preferring "enslaved," which more accurately suggests a condition that was forced upon them by others. As this story shows, that condition was by no means always permanent.

Prologue

1   **"Morning arrived, and with it a terrible uproar":** This quote and those that follow are from Thomas Smallwood, *A Narrative of Thomas Smallwood, (Coloured Man:) Giving an Account of His Birth—The Period He Was Held in Slavery—His Release—and Removal to Canada, etc. Together With an Account of the Underground Railroad. Written by Himself,* Toronto, 1851, p. 14. Available at https://docsouth.unc.edu/neh/smallwood/smallwood.html, pp. 21–24.

3   **"More Fleeing from Happiness," it read:** *Tocsin of Liberty,* Nov. 3, 1842.

4   **first to use in print: "under ground rail-road":** See the detailed discussion of the earliest uses of "underground railroad" in chapter 7.

5   **"general agent of all the branches":** *Albany Weekly Patriot,* June 15, 1843.

6   **the paperwork for his latest shipment south:** "Slave Ship Manifests filed at New Orleans, 1807–1860," preserved by the National Archives at archives.gov and also available via Ancestry.com.

7   **"I frequently had lots of slaves concealed":** Smallwood, *Narrative,* p. 24.

1. The Most Inhuman System That Ever Blackened the Pages of History

9   **"They were amazed at the fact":** Smallwood, *Narrative,* p. 14. Available at https://docsouth.unc.edu/neh/smallwood/smallwood.html. I have generally Americanized British spellings, except in book titles, but for the record, as an enthusiastic Canadian in later life, Smallwood diligently used "coloured" and "neighbours."

10   **Smallwood was born on February 22, 1801:** Smallwood, *Narrative*, p. 13. There is no reason
to doubt the year Smallwood gives for his own birth, but his enslaver, John Bell Ferguson,
would say in manumission papers filed on February 2, 1815, that Smallwood was then fifteen years old. If Smallwood's date is accurate, he would have been only thirteen at the time
of the 1815 filing. Also, the deed of manumission sets the date of his emancipation as his
thirtieth birthday, which it lists as February 12, 1830, not February 22, 1831, as would be
the case using Smallwood's date. That suggests that Smallwood may have been inadvertently
freed at age twenty-eight, ahead of the intended age of thirty. None of the details matter
greatly, but it is surely possible that Smallwood deliberately failed to correct Ferguson's error,
accelerating the date of his freedom by more than a year. Slaveholders were often careless or
deliberately negligent about recording the birthdates of the enslaved, so Smallwood's failure
to fix Ferguson's error may have been his tiny blow against the overwhelming injustice of
enslavement.

11   **"Who can calculate the amount of suffering":** Smallwood, *Narrative*, p. 52.

11   **Ferguson may have intended his deed of manumission:** The deed of manumission, filed in
Prince George's County, is available online through Maryland's very complicated land records
database at https://mdlandrec.net/main/. Also available at the site is a similar deed of manumission for Smallwood's younger sister, Kitty, filed on April 22, 1811, and promising that she
would be freed when she turned twenty-five years old on May 4, 1828.

14   **Black troops recruited from among thousands:** Jonathan D. Sutherland, *African Americans
at War: An Encyclopedia,* 2004, vol. 1, pp. 151–52.

14   **"A great number of negroes":** An Old Sub [George Gleig], "Recollections of the Expedition
to the Chesapeake, and Against New Orleans, in the Years 1814–1815," *United Service Journal
and Naval and Military Magazine,* 1840, part 2, pp. 27–28, via the Internet Archive.

15   **An enslaved woman from Bladensburg named Anna Williams:** Anna, or Ann, Williams's
story is told in many places, never more reliably than in William G. Thomas III, *A Question of
Freedom: The Families Who Challenged Slavery from the Nation's Founding to the Civil War,* 2020,
pp. 195–200. The great early Washington, D.C., site called O Say Can You See is especially
useful in linking to historical documents: https://earlywashingtondc.org/people/per.000831. It
includes a twelve-minute animated film as well: https://earlywashingtondc.org/stories/anna.

15   **When an antislavery activist heard the terrible story:** Jesse Torrey, *A Portraiture of Domestic
Slavery, in the United States,* 1817, p. 42ff., with a haunting etching of Williams's leap; available
via the Internet Archive.

16   **John Ferguson and his family had moved:** John B. Ferguson appears as a "clerk at the lumber
yard" on Smallwood's Wharf (owned by Smallwood's neighbor the former Washington mayor
Samuel N. Smallwood) on the Eastern Branch in Washington in an 1822 city directory transcribed here: http://www.theusgenweb.org/dcgenweb/geography/dc_people_1822.shtml.

16   **Ferguson would become a respected figure:** Ferguson's activities are documented in many
official notices and advertisements in Washington newspapers, including the *Daily National
Intelligencer* and *The Daily Globe.*

16   **"But for my advancement from two syllables":** Smallwood, *Narrative,* p. 14.

17   **From McLeod's school advertisements:** See, for instance, *The Washington Gazette,* Mar. 29,
1822; *Daily National Journal,* Jan. 18, 1827.

17   **none other than the vice president of the United States:** *Daily National Intelligencer,* June 20,
1838.

17   **"Columbian Academy—The subscriber informs the public":** *Daily National Intelligencer,*
Aug. 10, 1838.

18   **"A Gentleman, a graduate of a respectable University":** *Daily National Intelligencer,* Apr. 1,
1822.

19   **"If my memory be not at fault":** Smallwood, *Narrative,* pp. 14–15.

19   **James E. Brown was training:** For more on James E. Brown, see Gregory Bond's excellent
two-part article in *Pharmacy in History,* "Love Him and Let Him Go," vol. 60, no. 3, 2018, pp.
77–88, and no. 4, pp. 124–41.

20   **Samuel Ford McGill:** Susan Green, "Grit and Determination," *Dartmouth Medicine,* Spring 2020.

20   **A pamphlet published by the American Colonization Society:** "A FEW FACTS RE-SPECTING THE AMERICAN COLONIZATION SOCIETY, AND THE COLONY AT LIBERIA," available online from the Library of Congress.

21   **"I was grievously deceived":** Smallwood, *Narrative,* p. 15. The original reads "draining off the free colored population"; I take "off" to be a misprint for "of."

22   **a public meeting of African Americans in Washington in April 1831:** *The Philadelphia Inquirer,* May 6, 1831, p. 2.

22   **a gathering of opponents took an even tougher stand:** The language of resolution passed by meetings of African Americans in Baltimore and elsewhere is recorded in *Annual Report Presented to the Massachusetts Anti-Slavery Society by Its Board of Managers,* 1833, p. 36ff.

22   **a sensational pamphlet published in 1829:** The full title was *Walker's Appeal, in Four Articles; Together with a Preamble, to the Coloured Citizens of the World, but in Particular, and Very Expressly, to Those of the United States of America.* Available online at https://docsouth.unc.edu/nc/walker/walker.html.

23   **"I determined to do something in the matter":** Smallwood, *Narrative,* p. 16.

24   **While the marriage was officially recorded:** "District of Columbia Marriages, 1811–1950," database compiled from Washington, D.C., records, available at familysearch.org.

24   **Smallwood in his memoir dates their union:** Smallwood, *Narrative,* p. 13.

24   **surviving records do not show him directly employed:** I am grateful to the historian John G. Sharp, who has chronicled the Navy Yard and its African American workers in great detail, for this fact.

24   **"looks like a small piece of country":** Charles Dickens, *American Notes for General Circulation,* 1842, chapter 8.

25   **"It is sometimes called the City of Magnificent Distances":** Dickens, *American Notes,* chapter 8.

25   **Smallwood's Washington City had only 23,364 people:** "Population of the 100 Largest Urban Places: 1840," U.S. Bureau of the Census, 1998. The detailed breakdown is in the bureau's "Compendium of the Sixth Census."

25   **Smallwood lived in 1834:** E. A. Cohen, *Full Directory for Washington City, Georgetown and Alexandria.*

26   **Samuel N. Smallwood:** Allen C. Clark, "Samuel Nicholls Smallwood, Merchant and Mayor," *Records of the Columbia Historical Society,* Washington, D.C., 1926, vol. 28, pp. 23–61.

26   **His first job after arriving in Washington in 1795:** "The First Mayors of Washington, D.C.," pamphlet published by the Association for the Preservation of Historic Congressional Cemetery, p. 3.

26   **draconian requirements on the growing free Black population:** *The Washington Gazette,* May 3, 1821.

27   **called the neighborhood "the Island":** John W. Cromwell, "The First Negro Churches in the District of Columbia," *The Journal of Negro History,* vol. 7, no. 1, Jan. 1922, p. 83.

27   **probably first at Ebenezer Methodist Episcopal Church:** The only record I have found connecting Smallwood to Ebenezer is the class roll mentioned below. But given John Ferguson's membership, the biracial nature of the church, and its proximity to Smallwood's home, it seems likely that he attended services there for a time.

27   **a class register at Ebenezer for 1836:** Thanks to historian John Sharp for sharing this church document, which also notes that one member of "Class No. 16" was "expelled for immorality."

27   **helped lead his own exodus from the church:** William Martain Ferguson, *Methodism in Washington, District of Columbia,* 1892, p. 58.

28   **"wher snacht away from me and sold":** Michael Shiner diary entry quoted in Chris Myers Asch and George Derek Musgrove, *Chocolate City: A History of Race and Democracy in the Nation's Capital,* 2017, p. 61. For more on this episode, see also Thomas, *A Question of Freedom,* pp. 246–48.

28 **Another Navy Yard worker:** Daniel Bell's freedom suit is recounted in Thomas, *A Question of Freedom*, pp. 240–52.

28 **The so-called Snow Riot:** The story of Beverly Snow and the riot that chased him from Washington is vividly told by Jefferson Morley in *Snow-Storm in August: Washington City, Francis Scott Key, and the Forgotten Race Riot of 1835*, 2012.

29 **prosecution of a white physician named Reuben Crandall:** The prosecution of Crandall is recounted in detail in Morley, *Snow-Storm in August*.

29 **Smallwood had been a founder:** The church dispute played out in ads the two sides took out in the newspapers, notably *The Baltimore Sun*, Jan. 20, Feb. 24, Mar. 1, Mar. 22, and July 2, 1842.

30 **That December Smallwood filed suit:** Smallwood vs. Coale (the spelling varies in the lawsuit), Imparlance case no. 89, filed Dec. 13, 1841, at the National Archives, Washington, D.C.

30 **"the most inhuman system that ever blackened the pages of history":** Smallwood, *Narrative*, p. 48.

2. Until No Slave Should Be Found in Our Land

33 **He heard how the death of a Maryland slaveholder:** Charles Torrey in *The Friend of Man*, Feb. 22, 1842, reprinted from *Emancipator and Free American*.

34 **"I could not help weeping":** Torrey letter to *The Emancipator*, Feb. 4, 1842.

34 **"After listening to the history of their career":** Torrey in *The New-York Evangelist*, Feb. 23, 1842.

34 **Torrey had moved to Thomas Smallwood's Washington:** For a perceptive account of Torrey's arrival in Washington (and indeed his whole life), see the biography by his distant cousin, E. Fuller Torrey, *The Martyrdom of Abolitionist Charles Torrey*, 2013, p. 70ff.

35 **"I have not enjoyed the 'communion of saints'":** J. C. Lovejoy, *Memoir of Rev. Charles T. Torrey, Who Died in the Penitentiary of Maryland, Where He Was Confined, for Showing Mercy to the Poor*, 1847, p. 89.

36 **It was the first such gathering in Maryland:** The details of the meeting are taken largely from Torrey's own reporting in *The New-York Evangelist* and *The Emancipator*, as noted above.

37 **Torrey duly took notes:** Torrey's detailed account of his adventures is in *The New-York Evangelist*, Feb. 23, 1842.

39 **"GREAT EXCITEMENT," said the headline:** *Boston Daily Mail*, Jan. 17, 1842.

39 **"Arrest of an Abolitionist Reporter":** *Newark Daily Advertiser*, Jan. 17, 1842.

39 **"In my childhood, when about seven years old":** Charles T. Torrey, *Home! Or, the Pilgrims' Faith Revived*, 1845, pp. 131–32.

40 **Scituate, a fishing, shipbuilding, and farming town:** Chief Justice Cushing Chapter, Daughters of the American Revolution, *Old Scituate*, 1921. Torrey's ancestors are mentioned throughout this book of essays.

40 **his grandfather Charles Turner Jr.:** *Biographical Directory of the U.S. Congress*, searchable online.

41 **He kept a journal that largely survives:** Torrey's journal is extensively excerpted in Lovejoy, *Memoir*, and the passages quoted are from its early chapters.

43 **By late 1836, Torrey, twenty-two, was writing to Mary Ide:** Lovejoy, *Memoir*, p. 33.

43 **one called him a "miserable preacher":** Fuller Torrey, *Martyrdom*, p. 43.

44 **a plan for a vocational college for African Americans:** James Brewer Stewart, "The New Haven Negro College and the Meanings of Race in New England, 1776–1870," *The New England Quarterly* 76, no. 3 (Sept. 2003), pp. 323–55.

44 **he had served as president of the Andover Anti-Slavery Society:** Fuller Torrey, *Martyrdom*, p. 34.

44 **Torrey wrote to Phelps to report on shifting public opinion:** Torrey letter to Phelps, July 2, 1835, Boston Public Library, available at Internet Archive. The senior professor, whom Torrey calls "Dr. W.," is almost certainly Leonard Woods, the seminary's longtime chair of Christian theology.

45   **Garrison had first drawn public attention in 1830**: Henry Mayer, *All on Fire: William Lloyd Garrison and the Abolition of Slavery*, 1998, pp. 85–94.

45   **"Mr. Garrison! do you"**: Wendall Phillips Garrison and Francis Jackson Garrison, *William Lloyd Garrison, 1805–1879: The Story of His Life Told by His Children*, vol. 2, p. 273.

46   **The resulting rift in the Massachusetts Anti-Slavery Society**: Fuller Torrey, *Martyrdom*, pp. 1–19.

46   **"We must force them on the horrors of perfectionism"**: Torrey letter to Phelps, Mar. 21, 1839, Boston Public Library, available at Internet Archive.

46   **"I know how hard it is to my own spirit to keep still"**: Torrey letter to Phelps, Mar. 30, 1839, Boston Public Library, available at Internet Archive.

46   **"improvement of the free people of color"**: Fuller Torrey, *Martyrdom*, p. 52.

47   **"I am so much in debt"**: Torrey letter to Phelps, July 22, 1839, Boston Public Library, available at Internet Archive.

48   **"A few symptoms of mobocracy"**: Torrey letter to Phelps, Aug. 3, 1839, Boston Public Library, available at Internet Archive.

48   **delegates voted to create the Liberty Party**: Fuller Torrey, *Martyrdom*, pp. 57–60.

48   **Garrison ridiculed the gathering as "April Fools"**: Fuller Torrey, *Martyrdom*, p. 59.

48   **Torrey even bought a parcel of land in Maine**: Fuller Torrey, *Martyrdom*, p. 64.

49   **the moving plight of a man named John Torrance**: The *Boston Daily Mail* account of the case was reprinted in *The Liberator*, June 11, 1841, from which many of the details of Torrance's story are taken.

50   **A letter to *The Boston Morning Post* complained**: *The Boston Morning Post*, June 11, 1841.

50   **a scathing public letter from Torrey**: Torrey's letter was published in the Boston *Free American* and reprinted in *The New Bedford Register*, June 23, 1841.

51   ***The Cecil Whig*, northeast of Baltimore, complained**: *The Cecil Whig*, Jan. 22, 1842.

52   **"There is little doubt that the Torrey case"**: *The Georgetown Advocate*, Jan. 25, 1842.

52   **"I had heard of his arrest and trial at Annapolis"**: Smallwood, *Narrative*, p. 18.

3. That Mock Metropolis of Freedom

56   **"the highest toned, the purest, best organization of society"**: James Henry Hammond, "Remarks of Mr. Hammond, of South Carolina, on the Question of Receiving Petitions for the Abolition of Slavery in the District of Columbia," delivered in the House of Representatives, Feb. 1, 1836; pamphlet available on Internet Archive.

56   **"this everlasting dingdong"**: Mayer, *All on Fire*, p. 259.

56   **"An Address to the Slaves of the United States of America"**: Smith's address was reprinted in many abolitionist newspapers, including Garrison's *Liberator*, Feb. 11, 1842. Garrison recognized the significance of the speech, and in the same issue even took note of Torrey's jailing in Annapolis, publishing the proposals of the Maryland slaveholders' convention.

58   **Given that the value of an average enslaved worker**: This observation (for 1850) comes from a fascinating paper on the value of enslaved people: Samuel H. Williamson and Louis P. Cain, "Measuring Slavery in 2020 Dollars," on the *Measuring Worth* blog at https://measuringworth .com/slavery.php.

58   **"It is extremely hazardous to undertake to do any thing"**: Smallwood, *Narrative*, p. 17.

59   **"that most excellent and whole-souled Abolitionist"**: Smallwood, *Narrative*, p. 18.

59   **"that mock metropolis of freedom"**: Smallwood, *Narrative*, p. 33.

60   **Just a few weeks earlier, on December 8, 1841**: Torrey letter to John White, speaker of the House, Dec. 8, 1841, in the Congregational Library and Archives, Boston.

61   **the House Speaker, John D. White**: See *The Washington Post*'s compilation of members of Congress who had enslaved people, Jan. 10, 2022.

61   **"At our first interview he informed me of a scheme"**: Smallwood, *Narrative*, p. 18.

61   **George Edmund Badger, then forty-six**: *Biographical Directory of the U.S. Congress*, available online.

62 **a sort of taxi driver, named Leonard Grimes:** National Park Service, "Leonard Grimes," https://www.nps.gov/people/leonard-grimes.htm; Hilary Russell, *The Operation of the Underground Railroad in Washington, D.C., c. 1800–1860,* Historical Society of Washington, D.C., and the National Park Service, 2001, p. 186.

62 **a maximum penalty of six years in prison:** Maryland State Archives, https://msa.maryland .gov/megafile/msa/speccol/sc4800/sc4872/003183/html/m3183-0615.html.

62 **the father of the enslaved family, Waller Freeman:** For details of this case, see *Tocsin of Liberty,* May 4, 1842, where the report by Abel Brown lists the price for Freeman's wife and children as $1,800, not the $1,500 reported by Smallwood and others; for an example of the fundraising involved, see "Waller Freeman and Mr. Badger" in *Signal of Liberty,* the newspaper of the Michigan State Anti-Slavery Society, Nov. 28, 1842.

63 **"But they should also remember that justice has two sides":** Smallwood, *Narrative,* p. 19.

4. The Flesh-Mongers

67 **"CASH FOR NEGROES," the headline declared:** Slatter's ads are everywhere in the Maryland newspapers. The one quoted here can be found in *The Baltimore Sun,* July 9, 1838.

68 **incongruously named Hope for a Methodist preacher:** The circuit-riding preacher was Hopewell Hull, sometimes called Hope, who was active when Slatter's devout mother was naming her son and is sometimes credited with bringing methodism to Georgia. See The Hulls of Georgia, a genealogy site: http://thehullsofgeorgia.com/getperson.php?personID =I0421&tree=Main.

68 **taking the crown from Franklin & Armfield:** For more on Franklin & Armfield, see Joshua D. Rothman's superb 2021 book on the firm, *The Ledger and the Chain: How Domestic Slave Traders Shaped America*. Rothman writes that Franklin & Armfield was out of the active trading business by 1837, just as Slatter was stepping up his Baltimore operation (p. 253).

68 **"a tall, well-formed and good-looking man":** *National Anti-Slavery Standard,* Nov. 16, 1843. The visitor to Slatter's jail signed his published letter only with his initials, "S.D.H."

68 **he had started in the business with $4,000:** *Bangor Daily Whig and Courier,* Aug. 22, 1855.

68 **John Greenleaf Whittier, the abolitionist poet, visited Slatter's jail:** Joseph Sturge, *A Visit to the United States in 1841,* American edition, 1842, pp. 45–49; available at https://www.loc .gov/resource/lhbtn.00392.

69 **Ethan A. Andrews, a professor:** E. A. Andrews, *Slavery and the Domestic Slave-Trade in the United States,* 1836, pp. 77–80.

69 **one million enslaved African Americans were forcibly moved:** This round number has long been a rough consensus among scholars for the number of people sold south or forced to go south with their enslavers, though the total has long been debated. See Steven Deyle, *Carry Me Back: The Domestic Slave Trade in American Life,* 2005, appendix A, p. 283, which describes the debate and offers an estimate of "at least 875,000"; and Richard Bell, "The Great Jugular Vein of Slavery: New Histories of the Domestic Slave Trade," *History Compass,* 2013, pp. 1150–64. Bell notes that the number of enslaved people sold locally adds another million, for a total of two million sales, many of which separated families.

70 **families would place newspaper notices seeking lost relatives:** Heather Andrea Williams's *Help Me to Find My People: The African American Search for Family Lost in Slavery* is a moving book-length account of such desperate attempts to find relatives lost to the slave trade.

70 **the African slave trade would not be tampered with for twenty years:** United States Constitution, Article 1, Section 9: "The Migration or Importation of such Persons as any of the States now existing shall think proper to admit, shall not be prohibited by the Congress prior to the Year one thousand eight hundred and eight, but a Tax or duty may be imposed on such Importation, not exceeding ten dollars for each Person."

70 **"They abolished the external or African slave trade, in 1808":** Smallwood, *Narrative,* p. 52.

70 **"Tobacco, as our staple, is our all":** Maryland State Archives and the University of Maryland, *A Guide to the History of Slavery in Maryland,* 2007, p. 7.

70 **the soil in many places was growing exhausted:** Joyce Appleby, "Commercial Farming and the 'Agrarian Myth' in the Early Republic," *The Journal of American History,* Mar. 1982, pp. 833–49.

71 **from 73,000 bales in 1800 to 2.1 million five decades later:** *Federal Reserve Bulletin,* May 1923, p. 567, available at https://fraser.stlouisfed.org/files/docs/publications/FRB/pages /1920-1924/26396_1920-1924.pdf.

71 **An 1840 report on the transatlantic slave trade:** Ralph Clayton, "Baltimore's African Slave Trade Connection," *Baltimore Chronicle,* April 4, 2002.

72 **Frederick Douglass would explain:** Frederick Douglass, *My Bondage and My Freedom,* appendix, 1855, p. 412. Douglass refers to Louis McLane, the senior American diplomat in London at the time, who lived in Baltimore and served as president of the Baltimore and Ohio Railroad.

73 **A Methodist preacher traveling in Maryland:** John Dixon Long, son of a Maryland slave owner, *Pictures of Slavery in Church and State,* 1857, p. 198, available at https://docsouth.unc .edu/neh/long/long.html.

73 **a group of people who had fled Maryland:** *Tocsin of Liberty,* Dec. 22, 1842.

74 **James Watkins, who was born into slavery:** James Watkins, *Struggles for Freedom; or The Life of James Watkins,* 1860, pp. 16–17, available at https://docsouth.unc.edu/neh/watkins/watkins.html.

74 **The world Hope Slatter had been born into:** The details of Hope Slatter's early life are scattered in court records, newspaper notices, and genealogies, including some inaccuracies and contradictions.

74 **"She was a member of the Methodist E. Church":** A photo of her grave marker by Rich Dohm is on the indispensable Find a Grave site: https://www.findagrave.com/memorial /35450331/nancy-slatter.

75 **local real estate transactions:** *Georgia Journal,* of Milledgeville, Georgia, Nov. 27, 1821, and Nov. 11, 1823.

75 **In 1825, he was offering a toast:** *The Augusta Chronicle,* Sept. 10, 1825.

75 **By 1826, Slatter was serving as the sheriff:** *Georgia Journal,* June 5, 1827.

75 **a factory making cotton gins:** William Lamar Cawthon Jr., "None So Perfect as Clinton," available at http://www.oldclinton.org/wp-content/uploads/None-so-Perfect-as-Clinton.pdf.

75 **a tavern in Fayetteville, North Carolina:** *Fayetteville Weekly Observer,* Nov. 2, 1831.

75 **rented a house for a year in Charleston:** *Charleston Courier,* Feb. 20, 1834.

75 **by 1837 he had applied to Baltimore authorities:** Ralph Clayton, *Slavery, Slaveholding, and the Free Black Population of Antebellum Baltimore,* 1993, p. 31. See also the City Commissioners' notice in *Baltimore American and Commercial Daily Advertiser,* Feb. 9, 1837.

75 **he married a Baltimore woman, Emma Clackner:** Maryland State Archives, marriage no. 231, July 10, 1838.

76 **a report from the local grand jury:** "Presentment of the Grand Jury of Baltimore," July 1810, available at https://earlywashingtondc.org/doc/oscys.supp.0002.001.

77 **C. H. Bacon's circus, boasting of "astonishing feats":** *Baltimore American and Commercial Daily Advertiser,* Dec. 16, 1837.

77 **When "Wild Beasts and Birds" were on display:** *Baltimore American and Commercial Daily Advertiser,* Jan. 17, 1835.

77 **one in five Baltimoreans was Black in 1840:** See Seth Rockman, *Scraping By: Wage Labor, Slavery, and Survival in Early Baltimore,* 2009, p. 27; Christopher Phillips, *Freedom's Port: The African American Community of Baltimore, 1790–1860,* table 2, 1997, p. 27.

77 **negotiating the difficult middle ground:** See Barbara Jeanne Fields's pathbreaking *Slavery and Freedom on the Middle Ground: Maryland During the Nineteenth Century,* 1985, and Martha S. Jones's *Birthright Citizens: A History of Race and Rights in Antebellum America,* 2018, which is packed with human stories dug from archival records.

77 **Slatter and his family occupied a brick house:** Slatter's premises are described by several visitors, notably Oliver Johnson in *The Liberator,* Nov. 19, 1841, and Henry Stockbridge Sr., "Baltimore in 1846," written in 1875 and published in *Maryland Historical Magazine,* vol. 6, no. 1, March 1911, pp. 21–32.

77   **"hot as a little hell":** Stockbridge, "Baltimore in 1846."

77   **When a tax inspector visited Slatter's home:** Tax inspection record, Baltimore City Archives
      via Maryland State Archives, undated but on a reel labeled 1841–1846; available at http://
      mdhistory.msa.maryland.gov/bca_brg4/bca001610/html/brg4_bca1610-0086.html.

78   **"The flesh-mongers gather up their victims":** Douglass, *My Bondage and My Freedom*,
      p. 448.

79   **one of fifteen relatives sold south during his childhood:** Richard Bell, *Stolen: Five Free Boys
      Kidnapped into Slavery & Their Astonishing Odyssey Home*, 2019, p. 53.

79   **And Douglass himself, like many rebellious:** For instance, Douglass's enslaver, Thomas Auld,
      told Douglass he was considering "sending me to Alabama with a friend of his." Douglass
      shrewdly understood that this supposed friend was "an invention" intended to soften the blow
      of a sale to a slave trader. See Frederick Douglass, *The Life and Times of Frederick Douglass*,
      1881, p. 174.

79   **a 444-ton ship called the *Tippecanoe* left Baltimore:** The description of Slatter's shipping
      voyages comes from "Slave Ship Manifests filed at New Orleans, 1807–1860," preserved
      by the National Archives and introduced here: https://www.archives.gov/research/african
      -americans/slave-ship-manifests.html. They are also available via Ancestry.com.

79   **historian Jennie K. Williams has found:** Jennie K. Williams, "*Trouble the Water*: The Balti-
      more to New Orleans Coastwise Slave Trade, 1820–1860," *Slavery & Abolition* 41, no. 2 (Sept.
      9, 2019).

80   **An enslaved woman named Ruthy:** Notarial Archives, New Orleans, records of notary Paul
      Bertus, Jan. 22, 1842, vol. 3, act 11.

80   **A few months later, Shadrack sold James Cook:** Notarial Archives, New Orleans, records of
      notary C. Pollack, April 8, 1842, vol. 65, act 58.

82   **"a *daily traffic* in the persons of men, women, and children":** Torrey letter to the Essex
      County Abolitionists, July 1844, reprinted in Lovejoy, *Memoir*, p. 132.

82   **Joseph Sturge, the British Quaker who visited Slatter:** Sturge, *A Visit to the United States in
      1841*, p. 47.

83   **"Gentlemen, I suppose this looks strange to you":** *Liberator*, Oct. 20, 1843, reprinted from
      Bangor Gazette.

83   **built by wealthy Methodists "to gratify the aristocracy":** *Green-Mountain Freeman*, Mar. 7, 1845.

83   **"a slave trader here is regarded":** *Green-Mountain Freeman*, June 28, 1844.

84   **A popular singing group, the Hutchinsons:** David Ewen, *All the Years of American Popular
      Music*, 1977, pp. 66–67.

84   **"Today, 4th of November, we saw in an Alms-house":** Tocqueville's Baltimore stop came in
      1831, before Slatter's arrival, and the slave trader in question was most likely Austin Woolfolk.
      Alexis de Tocqueville, *Journey to America*, translated by George Lawrence, edited by Jacob
      Peter Mayer, 1960, pp. 159–60.

84   **Charles Dickens, on his American tour:** Dickens, *American Notes*, p. 692.

85   **"In the negro car belonging to the train":** Dickens, *American Notes*, p. 712.

85   **an acolyte of William Lloyd Garrison named Oliver Johnson:** Johnson's account of his visit
      to Slatter's jail was printed in *The Liberator*, Nov. 19, 1841.

5. Slavery's Borderland

89   **an abolitionist firebrand named Benjamin Lundy:** Merton L. Dillon, *Benjamin Lundy and
      the Struggle for Negro Freedom*, 1966.

89   **In 1826, an enslaved man named William Bowser:** Dillon, *Benjamin Lundy and the Struggle
      for Negro Freedom*, pp. 118–20; Benjamin Lundy and Thomas Earle, *The Life, Travels and Opin-
      ions of Benjamin Lundy*, 1847, pp. 206–9.

90   **Judge Nicholas Brice declared that "he had never seen a case":** *The Philadelphia Inquirer*,
      Apr. 11, 1827.

90   **once faced down a pistol-packing Woolfolk:** Sturge, *A Visit to the United States in 1841*, p. 10.

91   **Brice would serve as chief judge of Baltimore's criminal court:** *The Baltimore Sun,* "Maryland Heraldry: Brice Family, Of Annapolis," Jan. 13, 1907.

92   **ten to twenty years on any free Black person:** Ellis Lewis, *An Abridgement of the Criminal Laws of the United States,* 1848, p. 511.

92   **Another law prohibited Black people from joining:** Lewis, *An Abridgement of the Criminal Laws of the United States,* p. 511.

92   **a curfew was imposed in 1838:** Phillips, *Freedom's Port,* p. 194.

92   **By 1840, census takers counted only sixty-four enslaved people:** Bureau of the Census, Compendium of the Sixth Census, p. 24.

92   **Smallwood called the proximity of the border the "foundation":** Smallwood, *Narrative,* p. 20.

93   **a Supreme Court ruling handed down on March 1, 1842:** Prigg v. Pennsylvania, 41 U.S. 539 (1842).

94   **"within the very shadow of the Capitol!":** Solomon Northup, *Twelve Years a Slave,* 1853, pp. 42–43.

94   **The historian Richard Bell, who wrote a riveting account:** Bell, *Stolen,* p. 4.

94   **He was so "tormented with the liability of losing my liberty":** Douglass, *My Bondage and My Freedom,* p. 364.

95   **the Delaware-based gang led by a woman named Patty Cannon:** Bell, *Stolen,* p. 64ff.

95   **In 1840, *The Sun* reported on a free boy named Brinkley:** *The Baltimore Sun,* Jan. 31, 1840.

95   **Torrey recounted a particularly devious kidnapping ring:** *Albany Weekly Patriot,* Apr. 24, 1844 (Torrey under the pseudonym "The Negro Stealer").

95   **a free Black man he knew named Henry Chubb:** Smallwood, *Narrative,* p. 62.

96   **17,967 free Black residents:** Rockman, *Scraping By,* p. 27.

96   **schoolmaster, and political leader named William Watkins:** Bettye J. Gardner, "William Watkins: Antebellum Black Teacher and Anti-Slavery Writer," *Negro History Bulletin,* Sept./Oct. 1976, pp. 623–25.

96   **Watkins had approached James Carroll:** Phillips, *Freedom's Port,* p. 48. On James Carroll, see https://history.house.gov/People/Listing/C/CARROLL,-James-(C000188)/.

96   **part of an effort "to make us miserable here":** Bettye J. Gardner, "Opposition to Emigration, a Selected Letter of William Watkins (The Colored Baltimorean)," *The Journal of Negro History,* Summer 1982, pp. 155–58.

97   **An 1839 notice in *The Baltimore Clipper:*** *The Baltimore Clipper,* Nov. 12, 1839.

97   **In 1840, the brig *Porpoise* sailed:** *The Baltimore Sun,* Apr. 14, 1840.

97   **Jacob R. Gibbs worked as a housepainter and whitewasher:** See *Matchett's Baltimore Directory* for 1833 and 1842 under "Gibbs, Jacob."

97   **he sent three letters to acquaintances:** *The Baltimore Sun,* Aug. 20, 1840.

97   **Gibbs had taken the trouble to apply:** On the significance of the travel permits, see Jones, *Birthright Citizens,* p. 61.

97   **Gibbs was back in Baltimore by December 1840:** Baltimore, Maryland, U.S., Passenger Lists, 1820–1964, Oct.–Dec. 1840, p. 583, via Ancestry.com.

98   **"A vicious circle developed as slaveholders sold slaves south":** Stanley Harrold, *Border War: Fighting over Slavery Before the Civil War,* 2010, p. 10.

98   **"The fear of being sold South had more influence":** Benjamin Drew, *A North-Side View of Slavery,* 1856, p. 29.

98   **For George Ross, who fled Hagerstown in western Maryland:** John W. Blassingame, ed., *Slave Testimony: Two Centuries of Letters, Speeches, Interviews, and Autobiographies,* 1977, p. 405.

6. Safe from the Fangs of Robert Gilmor

101   **"The birth of her first child":** *Tocsin of Liberty,* Dec. 22, 1842.

101   **At sixty-eight, Robert Gilmor Jr. was one of Baltimore's wealthiest:** Some sources confuse two different Robert Gilmors of greater Baltimore, an uncle and his nephew, both at times called Robert Gilmor II or Jr. The enslaver of Elizabeth Castle was Robert Gilmor II (1774–1848), a

merchant and wine importer who lived on Water Street near the harbor. He was a son of the original Robert Gilmor, 1748–1822, a Scottish immigrant who founded the family firm. With another son of the founder, William, he took over the business, which was then called Robert Gilmor & Sons. The confusion comes because William's son was another Robert (1808–75), the nephew of the enslaver of Elizabeth Castle. He lived north of Baltimore and was noted locally for building a gothic castle that he named Glen Ellen in honor of his wife.

102   **he was worth an estimated $600,000:** Janine M. Yorimoto, "'To Draw Pleasure and Instruction': Robert Gilmor Jr. and Collecting the Early Republic," master's thesis, William & Mary, 2013, p. 16, available through the college website. The thesis has extensive information on Gilmor's collections.

102   **He caused a sensation:** *Baltimore American and Commercial Daily Advertiser,* Jan. 10, 1840.

102   **"a merchant whose books are without a blot":** *Baltimore American and Commercial Daily Advertiser,* May 20, 1843.

102   **"This of course renders negroes valuable":** Robert Gilmor, *Journal of Southern Travel,* 1806–7, https://digital.library.sc.edu/collections/robert-gilmor-travel-account-1806-1807/.

103   **Robert Gilmor's mansion on Water Street:** *Matchett's Baltimore Directory,* 1831, entry for "Gilmor, Robert."

103   **Jacob Gibbs, the housepainter:** See Smallwood, *Narrative,* references to "Friend G.," pp. 28, 30, 31, 40, 41. Gibbs later moved to New York City, where he was known for assisting people fleeing slavery.

104   **Torrey had traveled to Albany in April 1842:** C. S. Brown, *Memoir of Rev. Abel Brown by His Companion,* 1849, p. 151. This memoir, compiled by Abel Brown's widow, Catharine S. Brown, after his death, is the main source for the details of Brown's life that follow. A very useful edition of the memoir, with notes and index, was published in 2006 by one of the most prolific chroniclers of the underground railroad in New York, Tom Calarco.

104   **"*Please also inform* Robert Gilmore, of Baltimore":** *Tocsin of Liberty,* June 15, 1842. The name was regularly misspelled Gilmore, with a final *e*.

105   **The story of the Douglass brothers:** This account of the Douglass brothers' escape from slavery comes from Seth Gates's Dec. 5, 1848, letter to Joshua Giddings, at the Ohio History Connection archive in Columbus, Ohio; Thomas Smallwood's "Sam Weller" letter in *Tocsin of Liberty,* Dec. 1, 1842, and "Proceedings of the Annual Meeting of the Albany Vigilance Committee," Abel Brown, secretary, *Tocsin of Liberty,* Dec. 22, 1842.

106   **"He went to Smallwood of the Navy Yard":** Seth M. Gates to Joshua R. Giddings, Dec. 5, 1848, collection of the Ohio History Connection, Columbus, Ohio. The quotations in the following two paragraphs are from the same letter.

106   **The "boarders at Mrs. Sprigg's":** *Tocsin of Liberty,* Dec. 1, 1842.

107   **the city's 10 p.m. curfew for African Americans:** This curfew was imposed in 1831. See "An Act Relating to Free Negroes and Slaves," Laws of Maryland Online, vol. 141, p. 1068, Maryland State Archives, available at https://msa.maryland.gov/megafile/msa/speccol/sc2900 /sc2908/000001/000141/html/am141--1068.html.

107   **"we had two places of deposit":** Smallwood, *Narrative,* p. 20.

108   **Smallwood and Gibbs had recruited a woman named Turner:** Smallwood, *Narrative,* p. 41.

108   **"our passengers generally travelled in two nights":** Smallwood, *Narrative,* p. 20.

109   **he was born in Massachusetts three years before Torrey:** Again, the details of Abel Brown's life are from Brown, *Memoir of Rev. Abel Brown.*

109   **"living, burning eloquence":** *Albany Weekly Patriot,* March 16, 1843.

110   **"I would be greatly annoyed when with great danger":** Smallwood, *Narrative,* pp. 43–44.

111   **"taking an undue amount of money from them":** Smallwood, *Narrative,* p. 20.

111   **Elizabeth Castle, the seamstress, made it safely to Canada:** See Abel Brown's letter dated Nov. 20, 1842, in *Tocsin of Liberty,* Dec. 15, 1842, and the report on Castle and her companions in *Tocsin of Liberty,* Dec. 22, 1842.

113   **Smallwood later claimed that between March and November:** *Tocsin of Liberty,* Dec. 8, 1842. Writing with his usual pen name of Sam Weller, in a dispatch dated November 19,

Smallwood said that "since March last" Washington had lost enslaved people worth $75,000 at $500 apiece, or 150.

114 **Abel Brown had stated in a public talk:** *Tocsin of Liberty,* Aug. 17, 1842.

114 **Hope Slatter shipped some 208 people south:** This total comes from adding the number of enslaved people listed on each of the official manifests Slatter filed for the four shiploads he sent south in 1842. See "Slave Ship Manifests filed at New Orleans, 1807–1860," preserved by the National Archives and also available via Ancestry.com.

114 **By October, he had settled in Albany:** E. Fuller Torrey, Charles Torrey's biographer, concludes that Charles Torrey moved from Washington to Albany in October (*Martyrdom,* p. 104). But he had actually left Washington in August, when he led a large number of people as far as Troy, New York, as recounted in this book's prologue, and he almost certainly did not return south afterward. Torrey's note to Smallwood said that he was leaving Troy for Lynn, Massachusetts, an abolitionist hotbed where young Frederick Douglass had recently moved. And he almost certainly would have continued on from Lynn to Medway, Massachusetts, about fifty miles away, where his wife and children were living with her parents. On September 12, he was in Hudson, New York, where he filed a piece on a Supreme Court case for *Tocsin of Liberty*'s September 21 issue. So it seems that Torrey never returned to Washington before starting work in Albany, where he was first listed as editor in the Oct. 19, 1842, issue of *Tocsin of Liberty.*

7. The Laughingstock Letters

117 **"It was your cruelty to him that made him disappear":** *Tocsin of Liberty,* Aug. 10, 1842.

117 **the first time anyone had used the term "underground railroad" in print:** Two oft-repeated claims for the origin of the term "underground railroad" place it in 1831 or 1839. In 1831, the story goes, a Kentucky slaveholder, baffled by the flight of a man he enslaved (sometimes named as Tice Davids), exclaimed that he must have escaped by a "railroad under the ground" or a "road under the ground." But the claim seems to date to William M. Mitchell's 1860 book, *The Underground Railroad,* published nearly three decades later, and appears to be folklore, with details varying in every retelling. In 1839, according to a competing story, an article in a Washington, D.C., newspaper described an enslaved man captured trying to flee who, under torture, confessed that people were escaping by an underground railroad stretching all the way to Boston. But the story seems to come from Eber Pettit's 1879 book, *Sketches in the History of the Underground Railroad,* where Pettit recounts the supposed forty-year-old article "as close as I can from memory." So it appears to be a reconstruction of a newspaper account recalled from decades earlier, and newspaper databases include no article from 1839 resembling Pettit's account. I searched for "underground railroad" (and variants such as "under ground rail road") in two large newspaper archives including hundreds of nineteenth-century American publications, Newspapers.com and GenealogyBank.com. In the GenealogyBank.com collection, the phrase first appeared in *The Evening Post* of New York City on Sept. 23, 1842: the article in question was a reprint of a *Tocsin of Liberty* article published on Sept. 21, 1842. In Newspapers .com, the first use of the phrase was in a reprint of the same *Tocsin* article in a Vermont newspaper, *Vermont Telegraph,* Oct. 5, 1842. In GenealogyBank.com, the phrase without spaces, "underground railroad," appears 51,870 times; the first nine uses are all reprints from the *Tocsin of Liberty* and *Albany Weekly Patriot.* In Newspapers.com, the phrase appears 237,666 times; the first two uses, and the only two before 1844, are clips from the *Tocsin.* All evidence suggests that the metaphor originated in the Chesapeake region in 1842, perhaps in a frustrated outburst from John Zell, as Smallwood wrote. Smallwood clearly introduced the phrase to readers and popularized its use, and it came into widespread use in newspapers over the next year or so as shorthand for escapes from slavery, especially organized escapes with the help of sympathizers. I am grateful to historian Richard Bell of the University of Maryland for sharing his research on the early uses of "underground railroad."

118 **Smallwood credited John Zell:** "That name was given to it by constable ZELL of Baltimore," Smallwood (writing as "Sam Weller") wrote in the Nov. 3, 1842, issue of the *Tocsin of Liberty.*

118 **an Alexandria newspaper that year advertised a twenty-five-cent pamphlet:** *The Alexandria Gazette,* June 6, 1842.

119 **"I hope he won't take any offense at my bluntness!":** *Tocsin of Liberty,* Aug. 24, 1842.

119 **"to apply at the office of the underground railroad":** *Tocsin of Liberty,* Nov. 3, 1842.

119 **"Here am I, Samuel Weller, jun., still in the city":** *Tocsin of Liberty,* Nov. 3, 1842.

119 **"Sam invented and constructed the 'underground railroad'":** *Tocsin of Liberty,* Oct. 12, 1842.

119 **Joshua Giddings, the Ohio congressman:** Letter from Joshua Giddings to his son, Joseph Addison Giddings, dated Aug. 13, 1842; original at the Ohio History Connection archives in Columbus, Ohio.

120 **how the "walking property walked off":** *Tocsin of Liberty,* Aug. 24, 1842.

120 **"The poor manstealers and their watchdogs":** *Tocsin of Liberty,* Nov. 3, 1842.

121 **soon became a publishing phenomenon:** Nina Martyris, "The Sam Weller Bump," *The Paris Review,* Apr. 14, 2015, https://www.theparisreview.org/blog/2015/04/14/the-sam-weller-bump/.

122 **"You never heard how I learned Latin, did you?":** *Albany Weekly Patriot,* Apr. 27, 1843.

123 **President John Tyler (a slaveholder, like twelve of the first eighteen presidents):** The slave-holding dozen were George Washington, Thomas Jefferson, James Madison, James Monroe, Andrew Jackson, Martin Van Buren, William Henry Harrison, John Tyler, James K. Polk, Zachary Taylor, Andrew Johnson, and Ulysses S. Grant. See Evan Andrews, "How Many U.S. Presidents Owned Enslaved People?," History.com, July 19, 2017, https://www.history.com/news/how-many-u-s-presidents-owned-slaves.

123 **"the fifteen hundred or two thousand people present":** *The Georgetown Advocate,* March 26, 1842.

123 *Tocsin of Liberty,* **which would merge:** Torrey, whose job as the top editor did not change, explained in the first issue of the *Albany Weekly Patriot,* dated January 19, 1843, that the name change was prompted by the *Tocsin*'s merger with another paper, *The American Citizen,* and a desire not to have to choose between *Tocsin* and *Citizen* in naming the combined paper.

124 **would no long carry ads for "quack medicines":** *Albany Weekly Patriot,* Jan. 26, 1843.

124 **"Your Editor and Printers** *can't* **work without prompt payment":** *Albany Weekly Patriot,* Feb. 9, 1843.

124 **An abject apology under the heading "Sam Weller":** *Tocsin of Liberty,* Aug. 17, 1842.

125 **"you soft headed man-thief":** *Tocsin of Liberty,* July 27, 1842.

125 **he had noted that an enslaved boy named Henry Clay:** *Tocsin of Liberty,* Aug. 10, 1842.

125 **"Don't fail to read what SAM says":** *Tocsin of Liberty,* Dec. 15, 1842. The phrase "a liberty paper" refers to a newspaper that supports the Liberty Party.

125 **"'Sir,' said an old man, to one of the publishers":** *Tocsin of Liberty,* Dec. 15, 1842.

126 **Peter Matthews, a twenty-seven-year-old man:** The escape of Peter Matthews (and Sophy Jackson) is discussed by Smallwood in two Sam Weller letters, published Sept. 7 and Nov. 3, 1842.

128 **When Martha Lee fled Zaccheus Collins Lee:** *Tocsin of Liberty,* Aug. 24, 1842.

128 **"Besides, a shrewd slave has** *wit enough at any time*"**:** *Tocsin of Liberty,* Nov. 3, 1842.

128 **"The great blockheads cannot yet account":** *Tocsin of Liberty,* Aug. 24, 1842.

129 **When "John, who calls himself John More":** *Albany Weekly Patriot,* Apr. 27, 1843.

129 **"There's a peck of trouble among the Patriarchs":** *Tocsin of Liberty,* Nov. 3, 1842.

129 **"I have now five males and one female":** *Tocsin of Liberty,* Nov. 3, 1842.

130 **"Mr. James Maher, the public gardener":** *Tocsin of Liberty,* Nov. 3, 1842. Smallwood later referred to Maher, though not by name, in his 1851 memoir: "One of his slaves I had the pleasure to deprive him of and she is now in this city," a reference to Toronto (Smallwood, *Narrative,* p. 47).

130 *The Georgetown Advocate,* **took "Sam Weller" to task:** *Albany Weekly Patriot,* May 18, 1843.

130 **"Lawrence Paine begs leave to say to Esq. Fendall":** *Tocsin of Liberty,* Dec. 1, 1842.

131 **"How many times I've heard him boast":** *Tocsin of Liberty,* Nov. 3, 1842.

131 **"Recently, Dr. Wm. H. Gunnell received a copy":** *Tocsin of Liberty,* Dec. 15, 1842.

132 **When a butcher named Philip Otterback:** *Tocsin of Liberty,* Nov. 3, 1842.

132 **When the ten-year-old boy named Henry Clay:** *Tocsin of Liberty,* Aug. 10, 1842.

132   **Smallwood would write that the sexual exploitation:** Smallwood, *Narrative,* pp. 58–59.
133   **he printed a report of a talk by Lewis Clark:** *Tocsin of Liberty,* Nov. 3, 1842.
133   **"I have never approved of the very public manner":** Douglass, *Narrative,* p. 101.
134   **"Those letters were a great annoyance":** Smallwood, *Narrative,* pp. 60–61.
134   **"Samivel Weller wishes to say to the Friend of Man":** *Tocsin of Liberty,* July 27, 1842.
134   **threatening Charles Torrey with "beating":** *Tocsin of Liberty,* Sept. 7, 1842.
136   **In Albany, a letter arrived from Baltimore:** *Albany Weekly Patriot,* June 22, 1843.
136   **Smallwood wrote, the aggrieved slaveholders:** Smallwood, *Narrative,* p. 24.
136   **offered a bounty for three of the people:** *Albany Weekly Patriot,* April 27, 1843.

8. That Vile Wretch Slatter

139   **A February 1842 report for the *Tocsin of Liberty*:** *Tocsin of Liberty,* Feb. 23, 1842.
139   **Torrey called Slatter "the great slave trader of Baltimore":** *Tocsin of Liberty,* Nov. 3, 1842.
140   **telling a friend that Slatter resembled Judas Iscariot:** *Bangor Daily Whig & Courier,* Aug. 22, 1855.
140   **"His pride is that he always requires and gives 'good titles'":** *Tocsin of Liberty,* Nov. 3, 1842.
140   **Bowditch, roundly attacked "this vile wretch Slatter":** *The Liberator,* Feb. 24, 1843.
140   **"The great *Negro thief,* Hope H. Slatter":** *Albany Weekly Patriot,* Apr. 27, 1843.
141   **"Such occurrences are by no means unusual here":** Torrey letter to J. W. Alden, Nov. 21, 1844, reprinted in Lovejoy, *Memoir,* p. 166.
141   **"TO THE FEELING AND HUMANE COMMUNITY":** Ad in *The Sun,* Nov. 12, 1842.
142   **Richard Bradford's choir:** Ad in *The Sun,* Feb. 22, 1843.
142   **Slatter used a horse-drawn omnibus:** *National Anti-Slavery Standard,* Jan. 28, 1847.
142   **In 1937, Baltimore utility workers digging:** *The Baltimore Evening Sun,* Sept. 18, 1937.
142   **Rezin Williams, interviewed in Baltimore:** *Born in Slavery: Slave Narratives from the Federal Writers' Project, 1936 to 1938,* vol. 8, Maryland, pp. 9–10 (also marked pp. 76–77 in the volume), available via the Library of Congress.
143   **the Runaway Docket of the Baltimore City Jail:** Baltimore City and County Jail (Runaway Docket), 1836–1850, Maryland State Archives.
144   **A Philadelphia abolitionist visiting in 1843:** S.D.H., "Visit to a Slave Prison," *National Anti-Slavery Standard,* Nov. 16, 1843.
145   **An unsympathetic northerner who toured Slatter's jail:** *Green-Mountain Freeman,* June 28, 1844.
146   **he won a bet on the 1840 Pennsylvania governor's race:** *The Sun,* Mar. 2, 1840.
146   **When the mangled body of a man Slatter enslaved:** *The Baltimore Clipper,* Sept. 8, 1840.
146   **Slatter got a little public notice when he bought the Repository:** *The Sun,* Nov. 13, 1841.
146   **Slatter's "establishment," in *The Sun*'s polite locution:** *The Sun,* June 4, 1842.
146   **he advertised for "a genteel female of middle age":** *Baltimore American and Commercial Daily Advertiser,* Nov. 24, 1842.
146   **In the spring of 1844, a front wheel of his carriage:** *The Sun,* May 11, 1844.
146   **he was spotted assaulting a Black woman:** *The Baltimore Clipper,* Oct. 27, 1840.
147   **Charles Stafford was enslaved in Delaware:** *The Baltimore Clipper,* July 11, 1840.
147   **a young woman named Charlotte Jane Strother was sold to Slatter:** The Strother case (sometimes spelled Strowther) got extensive coverage, notably in two articles in *The Baltimore Saturday Visiter,* Apr. 13 and 20, 1844. See also *The Sun,* Oct. 28, 1843, and Mar. 16, 1844; *Christian Reflector,* Nov. 15, 1843; and *National Anti-Slavery Standard,* Nov. 16, 1843.
148   **She was described in one story as "an exceedingly bright mulatto":** *Christian Reflector,* Nov. 15, 1843.
148   **in another as "*white,* or so nearly so that she would pass for *white*":** *Pennsylvania Telegraph,* Jan. 6, 1844.
148   **"N.B. I wish particularly to purchase several seamstresses":** *Baltimore Republican and*

Commercial Advertiser, Feb. 2, 1835, cited in Frederic Bancroft, *Slave Trading in the Old South,* 1931, pp. 37–38.

149 **"Do you wonder why the trader did not have them display their needle-work":** Bancroft, *Slave Trading,* p. 130.

149 **a fourteen-year-old girl named Mary Ellen Brooks:** The full record of the case, *White v. Slatter,* is in the Historical Archives of the Supreme Court of Louisiana, docket 943, available online. Valuable discussions of Brooks's case can be found in Walter Johnson, *Soul by Soul: Life Inside the Antebellum Slave Market,* 1999, pp. 115, 126, 155; and Alexandra J. Finley, *An Intimate Economy: Enslaved Women, Work, and America's Domestic Slave Trade,* 2020, pp. 23–27.

149 **Slatter sent her to New Orleans in February 1847:** Manifest for the Feb. 16, 1847, arrival in New Orleans of the ship *Zoe,* "Slave Ship Manifests filed at New Orleans, 1807–1860," National Archives, via Ancestry.com.

150 **President James K. Polk stopped in Baltimore:** *Daily National Intelligencer,* June 23, 1847.

150 **While serving in the White House, he bought additional slaves:** Lina Mann, "The Enslaved Households of President James K. Polk," White House Historical Association, https://www.whitehousehistory.org/the-enslaved-households-of-james-k-polk.

9. Very Vigilant Officers!

153 **On June 4, 1842, Abel Brown, the antislavery preacher:** Brown, *Memoir,* p. 118.

153 **The "wretched constable" sent to retrieve:** Brown, *Memoir,* p. 121.

154 **In Washington in 1808, for instance:** Richard Sylvester, compiler, *District of Columbia Police: A Retrospect of the Police Organizations of the Cities of Washington and Georgetown and the District of Columbia,* 1894, pp. 23–24.

154 **In 1818, Washington authorities approved the payment:** Sylvester, *District of Columbia Police,* p. 24.

154 **In Baltimore, the mayor's delineated duties:** *Matchett's Baltimore Directory,* 1835–36, p. 13.

154 **An 1831 court document in the Maryland State Archives:** Certificate for Patrolling, Alison F. Beale, 1831, http://guide.msa.maryland.gov/pages/item.aspx?ID=C1187-1-34.

155 **An invoice given to the state of Maryland:** Account of Constable Daniel R. Dyer, 1842–43, http://guide.msa.maryland.gov/pages/item.aspx?ID=C1187-1-51.

155 **Torrey reported in the Albany paper an unusual account:** *Albany Weekly Patriot,* July 20, 1843.

156 **crowds of disappointed Harrison supporters:** This and other details on the Auxiliary Guard are from Sylvester, *District of Columbia Police,* pp. 27–30.

156 **the man they called "His Accidency":** "John Tyler," The White House, https://www.whitehouse.gov/about-the-white-house/presidents/john-tyler/.

157 **Smallwood called the Guard "infamous":** *Tocsin of Liberty,* Dec. 15, 1842 (Smallwood's "Samivel Weller jr." letter is dated Nov. 15, 1842).

158 **Eight months later, Smallwood renewed his attack:** *Albany Weekly Patriot,* June 29, 1843.

159 **"Doubtless our friend, Samuel Weller jr. was correct":** *Albany Weekly Patriot,* Apr. 20, 1843.

159 **"We have *bought up* a few of the *Guard,*" Smallwood wrote:** *Albany Weekly Patriot,* June 15, 1843.

159 **Torrey also asserted that nearly the entire guard:** "Notes of a Negro Stealer," *Albany Weekly Patriot,* Feb. 7, 1844.

159 **On a November morning in 1840, James Ducket:** The story of James Ducket and John Robinson was reported in multiple newspaper articles, including *The Baltimore Sun,* Dec. 7, 1840, and Feb. 18, 1841; *Baltimore American and Commercial Daily Advertiser,* Dec. 8, 1840; and *The Baltimore Clipper,* Feb. 18 and March 1, 1841. His transport south by Hope Slatter aboard the ship *Ewarkee,* arriving in New Orleans on March 4, 1841, is recorded in the "Slave Ship Manifests filed at New Orleans, 1807–1860," National Archives (also available at An-

cestry.com). The name Ducket is also spelled Duckit and Duckett in various documents and newspaper accounts.

160 **Torrey found that Baltimore police officers:** Torrey letter to J. W. Alden, Nov. 21, 1844, reprinted in Lovejoy, *Memoir,* p. 167.

161 **Zell's grandfather, a Pennsylvania slaveholder:** "ZELL (UZILLE, ZIELIE, ZIELE) FAMILY GENEALOGY," prepared by T. W. Pietsch III, available at https://docplayer.net /46168999-Zell-uzille-zielie-ziele-family-genealogy.html.

161 **he followed other family members into the grocery business:** Successive editions of *Matchett's Baltimore Directory* trace John Zell's years running a grocery store and subsequently working as a police officer and private investigator. The Baltimore newspapers carried many legal notices related to his insolvency.

162 **Zell was charged criminally with taking fifty dollars:** *The Baltimore Sun,* Mar. 29, 1841.

162 **Madison Jeffers, wrote a blistering letter:** *The Baltimore Clipper,* Mar. 31, 1841.

162 **Zell's energetic pursuit of fugitives sometimes strayed:** See Milt Diggins, *Stealing Freedom Along the Mason-Dixon Line: Thomas McCreary, the Notorious Slave Catcher from Maryland,* 2016, pp. 28–29.

162 **In late 1842, the annual report of the Albany Vigilance Committee:** *Tocsin of Liberty,* Dec. 22, 1842.

10. Between Two Fires

165 **"Mr. Printer—Here I am, back to my post":** *Albany Weekly Patriot,* June 15, 1843, also the source of the next several quotations. (Note that the Richard Brown whom Smallwood boasted of helping to escape from Washington in 1843 was not the same man as the Richard Brown mentioned in chapter 8, who had been caught trying to flee his Baltimore enslaver and jailed the previous year.)

166 **Zell's office at 15 Mercer Street:** The named personnel in Zell's private detective firm shifted, but for years it was at 15 Mercer Street. That is the address given for Hays, Zell, Ridgely & Cook in John Murphy, printer and publisher, *The Baltimore Directory, for 1845.*

167 **Thomas Roderick Dew, then president of William & Mary:** For a sample of Dew's work championing slavery, see his *Review of the Debate in the Virginia Legislature of 1831 and 1832,* 1832.

168 **"I continued to defy detection, and sent them off in gangs":** Smallwood, *Narrative,* p. 24.

169 **"For several reasons the entire arrangement":** Smallwood, *Narrative,* p. 25.

169 **"I had been for some time, between two fires":** Smallwood, *Narrative,* p. 32.

170 **Smallwood would later recount three cases of treachery:** Smallwood, *Narrative,* pp. 25–32. Smallwood's accounts of treachery are so involved that they are hard to sort out 180 years later, but they have a ring of authenticity. He spelled the last name of Benjamin Lanham, the second of the "betrayers," as "Lannum," but other records confirm the man himself spelled it "Lanham."

171 **the three people betrayed to the slave trader by Lanham:** Smallwood, *Narrative,* pp. 31–32.

172 **"The united rewards for them would amount to from six to eight hundred":** Smallwood, *Narrative,* p. 16.

172 **"filthy lucre" in Smallwood's words:** This phrase and the quotations that follow are from Smallwood, *Narrative,* p. 28.

173 **Smallwood "evaded all the snares that were set for me":** Smallwood, *Narrative,* p. 32.

173 **A curious document in the Washington archives:** Registration No. 2036, Recorded 14 October 1842, Slave Manumissions, Record Group 21, Entry 30, p. 442, National Archives. I am grateful to the late Dorothy Provine, who included this manumission in her compilation, *District of Columbia Free Negro Registers, 1821–1861,* 1996, p. 439.

174 **"Seeing that through the treachery of some of my color":** Smallwood, *Narrative,* p. 32.

175 **In 1852, Frederick Douglass would ask in a famous oration:** For background and context on Douglass's widely reprinted speech, see the 2020 essay by Arlene Balkansky of the Library of Congress: https://blogs.loc.gov/headlinesandheroes/2020/07/what-to-the-american-slave-is-your-4th-of-july/.

175 **"I speedily returned to Washington":** Smallwood, *Narrative,* p. 33.

11. A Fugitive from Justice

177 **Sam Weller letters continued without interruption:** A careful analysis of the last of the "Sam Weller" letters shows that he was their author, even in the tumultuous period between July and December 1843, when he traveled twice to Toronto and returned south before finally settling there after his third journey. See the introduction to the selection of Smallwood's letters in the appendix of this book.

177 **He denounced a navy officer:** *Albany Weekly Patriot,* June 22, 1843.

178 **visiting Washington's city jail to witness the sale:** *Albany Weekly Patriot,* June 22, 1843.

179 **"this Metropolis of *free* and *christian* America":** *Albany Weekly Patriot,* June 29, 1843.

179 **"I must even leave my pen":** *Albany Weekly Patriot,* Aug. 22, 1843.

179 **"no less than SIXTY HUMAN BEINGS":** *Albany Weekly Patriot,* Sept. 12, 1843.

179 **as he gathered in his house one more group:** Smallwood, *Narrative,* pp. 33–34.

181 **"John B. Ferguson swears," said the document:** Registration no. 2125, filed 3 Oct. 1843, Slave Manumissions, Record Group 21, p. 486. This freedom document was also transcribed in Provine, *District of Columbia,* p. 458.

181 **On the way, he was "assailed" by two constables:** Smallwood, *Narrative,* pp. 34–35.

182 **a rare and revealing glimpse of Elizabeth Anderson Smallwood:** Smallwood, *Narrative,* pp. 35–36.

183 **a generous Baltimorean named Pittman:** Smallwood spells the name "Pitman," with one *t,* but the dry-goods merchant Edward Pittman appears to be the only person by that name who might be a benefactor. Smallwood does not explain whether Elizabeth Smallwood knew Pittman from some earlier encounter or whether they met for the first time that day and she explained the family's predicament.

183 **"I shall ever hold in grateful remembrance":** Smallwood, *Narrative,* p. 36.

184 **Even as he and Elizabeth began the complicated work:** Smallwood, *Narrative,* p. 36.

184 **Torrey was on the verge of turning the deeply indebted *Patriot*:** The transaction was recorded in *Albany Weekly Patriot,* Jan. 2, 1844.

185 **Torrey, he wrote, had "conceived the following scheme":** Smallwood, *Narrative,* pp. 37–38.

185 **Smallwood had recruited a Washington friend, John Bush:** The account of the failed escape and its aftermath, including Smallwood's stay in Baltimore and his run north, is in Smallwood, *Narrative,* pp. 37–43.

187 **the East Street house of his friend Jacob Gibbs:** *Matchett's Baltimore Directory* for 1842, listed "Gibbs Jacob R., painter, East st s of Douglass."

187 **a fulsome account of the thwarted escape in *The Baltimore Sun*:** *The Baltimore Sun,* Nov. 27, 1843.

190 **Torrey made his way to Baltimore and visited Smallwood:** Smallwood, *Narrative,* p. 40; also see footnote, p. 42.

194 **the woman had decided to flee with her children:** This detail and the claim that the twenty-year-old daughter had been "sold for a harlot" are in Torrey's dispatch under the notation "By a Negro Stealer," *Albany Weekly Patriot,* Feb. 7, 1844.

194 **"AN ASTONISHING ATROCITY":** *Albany Weekly Patriot,* Jan. 2, 1844.

195 **In 1845, Beale was promoted to doorkeeper of the Senate:** "About the Sergeant at Arms," United States Senate, https://www.senate.gov/about/officers-staff/sergeant-at-arms/sergeants-at-arms.htm.

12. Perhaps Reckless

197 **He signed the register with a thinly disguised pseudonym:** This detail would come out in testimony at Torrey's subsequent trial. See Lovejoy, *Memoir,* p. 126.

197 **A remarkable woman named Emily Webb:** Webb's story and that of her husband, John, are captured in separate depositions included in full in Lovejoy, *Memoir,* pp. 106–24.

198 **"over more horrible roads than I *ever* had the misfortune to travel":** *Albany Weekly Patriot,* Mar. 6, 1844.

198 **"Six negroes were decoyed a few nights since":** Many newspapers reprinted the item published in the *Baltimore American,* including Boston's *Daily Evening Transcript* on Jan. 1, 1844, under the headline "A Rev Abductor."

198 **he had stayed there for a few days:** Smallwood, *Narrative,* p. 39.

198 **Torrey hoped Bush's lawyers would use his case:** *Albany Weekly Patriot,* Feb. 7, 1844.

199 **Once, in fact, the "Negro Stealer" wrote:** *Albany Weekly Patriot,* Mar. 13, 1844.

199 **Writing in January 1844 to his old friend:** Torrey letter to Smith, sent from Philadelphia, Jan. 23, 1844; original in the Syracuse University Libraries.

200 **serving as president of the Female Anti-Slavery Society:** See, for instance, the notice in the *Albany Weekly Patriot,* June 22, 1843.

200 **Torrey's biographer, E. Fuller Torrey, notes that their letters:** Fuller Torrey, *Martyrdom,* p. 120.

201 **In a brief but poignant item in the same issue:** *Albany Weekly Patriot,* Feb. 7, 1844.

202 **Far harsher was a notice in the *Patriot*:** *Albany Weekly Patriot,* Apr. 10, 1844.

202 **Smallwood's name disappeared from the list:** Smallwood was listed as an agent based in Toronto through the April 17, 1844, issue.

203 **Twice Torrey's "Negro Stealer" reports were signed "Samivel Weller Jr.":** *Albany Weekly Patriot,* May 1 and 29, 1844.

203 **Torrey reported that an informant had told him:** *Albany Weekly Patriot,* Feb. 14, 1844.

203 **He reported that the Methodists in Baltimore:** *Albany Weekly Patriot,* Feb. 21, 1844.

203 **a wealthy planter living south of Baltimore named Tom W.:** *Albany Weekly Patriot,* Mar. 6, 1844.

204 **His fresh immersion in the escape routes north:** *Albany Weekly Patriot,* May 1, 1844.

205 **In his first weeks in the city, the Whig Party:** J. Thomas Scharf, *History of Baltimore City and County, from the Earliest Period to the Present Day,* 1881, p. 122.

205 **"The mechanics of Baltimore, too, are much more hostile to slavery":** *Albany Weekly Patriot,* May 1, 1844.

206 **"This is a great and glorious country of ours!":** *Albany Weekly Patriot,* May 1, 1844.

206 **Torrey's numbers appear to be slightly high:** According to the ship manifests Slatter was required to file, he sent captives south in 1843 on Sept. 30 (seventy-three), Nov. 1 (eighty-eight), and Dec. 23 (sixty-nine), and in 1844 on March 9 (forty-eight) and April 15 (twenty-nine), for a total of 307. "Slave Ship Manifests Filed at New Orleans, 1807–1860," National Archives (also available at Ancestry.com).

206 **On another occasion, an acquaintance reported to Torrey:** *Albany Weekly Patriot,* May 22, 1844.

207 **William Heckrotte operated a modest tavern:** *Matchett's Baltimore Directory,* 1842. Heckrotte apparently called his tavern the Fountain Inn, but it is not to be confused with an older, larger, and more distinguished hotel by the same name, located a few blocks away on Light Street, where George Washington and many other notables had stayed.

207 **Heckrotte placed a runaway ad:** *Republican & Daily Argus,* June 5, 1844. Heckrotte's ad spelled the family's last name Goosbury; other sources spell it Gooseberry, which I have adopted here.

208 **"Many of my readers are not aware, that Christmas":** *Albany Weekly Patriot,* Mar. 13, 1844.

209 **the case of Benjamin Jones:** *Albany Weekly Patriot,* Apr. 24, 1844. Other details of Jones's story are recounted by Carl Lavo in "The Story of Big Ben," at http://buckscountyadventures .org/the-story-of-big-ben/.

13. Let the Strife Go On

215 **Torrey was armed with two pistols:** Fuller Torrey, *Martyrdom,* p. 126, citing *Pennsylvania Freeman,* June 6, 1844.

215 **The arrest report in *The Baltimore Sun*:** *The Baltimore Sun,* June 27, 1844.

216 **He described the vile conditions:** Lovejoy, *Memoir,* p. 127.

216 **"a promising business in Baltimore, in *the manufacture of starch*":** *Massachusetts Spy,* July 3, 1844.

216 **In another letter, he suggested that with his arrest:** Lovejoy, *Memoir,* pp. 138–39.

217 **"I AM NOT ON TRIAL," he assured readers:** "To the Public," *The Baltimore Sun,* Aug. 30, 1844.

217 **In July, a month after his arrest, he wrote a formal address:** Lovejoy, *Memoir,* pp. 130–39.

218 **Torrey wrote to his wife around the same time:** Lovejoy, *Memoir,* p. 128.

218 **The *Picayune* of New Orleans, the largest receiving city:** *The Picayune,* Sept. 26, 1844.

219 **In New England, newspapers published an appeal:** *Green-Mountain Freeman,* Sept. 27, 1844.

219 **Most notable among them was William Lloyd Garrison:** *The Liberator,* July 26, 1844.

220 **Daniel A. Payne of Philadelphia recounted:** Bishop Daniel Alexander Payne, *Recollections of Seventy Years,* 1888, p. 98.

220 **A report of the case in a leading abolitionist paper:** *Emancipator and Weekly Chronicle,* July 17, 1844.

221 **Months later, Torrey was still shaken by the public rebuke:** Torrey letter to Milton M. Fisher, Nov. 16, 1844, Massachusetts Historical Society at masshist.org.

221 **in a note to Torrey's old friend Amos Phelps:** Milton M. Fisher letter to Amos A. Phelps, July 23, 1844, Boston Public Library, available at digitalcommonwealth.org.

221 **Mary Torrey would later write in a letter:** Mary Ide Torrey letter to Amos A. Phelps, Sept. 15, 1846, Boston Public Library via digitalcommonwealth.org.

221 **E. Fuller Torrey, his biographer, a prominent psychiatrist:** Fuller Torrey, *Martyrdom,* pp. 139, 193.

222 **Torrey told Mary that he was trying to devote:** Lovejoy, *Memoir,* p. 224.

222 **"From the time of my arrest, the whole clique of slave traders":** Lovejoy, *Memoir,* p. 154.

222 **"the busiest of these agents of shame are a noted slave trader":** Lovejoy, *Memoir,* p. 156.

223 **he claimed to have arranged the escape of fifteen:** Charles Torrey to Milton M. Fisher, Nov. 16, 1844, Massachusetts Historical Society at masshist.org.

223 **Torrey claimed to have put an end:** Lovejoy, *Memoir,* p. 130.

223 **He also met a fifteen-year-old Black boy, born free:** Lovejoy, *Memoir,* p. 129.

224 **he attempted an escape:** Lovejoy, *Memoir,* p. 148.

224 **Sleepless and feverish, he wrote apologetically:** Lovejoy, *Memoir,* pp. 149–50.

224 **Charles Heckrotte, the son of tavernkeeper William Heckrotte:** Lovejoy, *Memoir,* p. 174. Newspaper accounts of the trial spell the Gooseberry daughter's name "Judah"; Heckrotte's runaway ad spelled it "Judea." Except as noted, quotations from the trial testimony are from *The Sun*'s account as reprinted by Lovejoy, *Memoir,* pp. 173–202.

225 **John Zell, the constable and slave catcher, orchestrated:** *The Baltimore American and Commercial Daily Advertiser,* Dec. 1, 1844.

225 **"I shall not pretend to discuss the subject of slavery":** *The Baltimore Sun,* Dec. 3, 1844.

225 **even the unsympathetic *Sun* called her steadfastness:** *The Baltimore Sun,* Nov. 12, 1844.

225 **Now Johnson, who had refused to take a fee:** Lovejoy, *Memoir,* p. 164.

226 **Johnson's "wrong and fatal admission":** The language is from Joseph C. Lovejoy's sermon at Torrey's funeral, included in Lovejoy, *Memoir,* p. 303.

226 **the next day he sent a long letter:** Lovejoy, *Memoir,* p. 206.

226 **In just twelve days he completed a 256-page memoir:** Lovejoy, *Memoir,* p. 214.

227 **was sentenced to six years and three months:** *Baltimore Saturday Visiter,* Jan. 4, 1845.

227 **the cold and drafty prison cell:** Lovejoy, *Memoir,* p. 217.

227 **Mary, with the encouragement of her parents:** See a sample of her brainstorming in a letter, Mary Ide Torrey to Amos A. Phelps, Sept. 5, 1845.

228 **he sent Mary parenting advice:** Lovejoy, *Memoir,* p. 270.

228 **It would give him great satisfaction:** Lovejoy, *Memoir,* p. 268.

228 **"Very often, for three months past, I have been obliged":** Lovejoy, *Memoir,* p. 267.

229 **In February 1846, Mary sent a petition:** *Baltimore Saturday Visiter,* Feb. 21, 1846.

229 **Pratt finally granted the pardon:** Maryland State Archives, Secretary of State, Pardon Record for the Rev. Charles T. Torrey, May 9, 1846, MSA S1108.

229 **At three that afternoon, Torrey, in the words:** *Baltimore Saturday Visiter,* May 16, 1846.

229 **Predictably, Torrey's death proved as divisive:** See Fuller Torrey, *Martyrdom,* pp. 159–61.

230 **"Torrey is no more!" Lovejoy declared:** Lovejoy, *Memoir,* p. 300.

230 **A gathering of "the colored people of Oberlin":** Lovejoy, *Memoir,* pp. 322–23.

230 **The poet John Greenleaf Whittier recalled:** Lovejoy, *Memoir,* p. 322.

231 **A line in the remembrance published by *The New Jersey Freeman*:** Lovejoy, *Memoir,* p. 329.

14. Fly to Canada, and Begin Anew

233 **their daughter Susan had died the previous year:** Toronto Trust Cemeteries 1826–1989, Potter's Field Cemetery, vol. 1, 1826–1850, line 2133, "Susan Smallwood," via familysearch .org. I am grateful to Guylaine Petrin for tracking down the death records for the Smallwood children.

233 **"I suppose I have freed about 400":** Charles Torrey letter to Milton M. Fisher, Nov. 16, 1844, Massachusetts Historical Society.

234 **Still's biographer says:** William C. Kashatus, *William Still: The Underground Railroad and the Angel at Philadelphia,* 2021.

235 **In an article about Torrey's death and his career:** Reprint of *Chronotype* article in *Baltimore Saturday Visiter,* May 23, 1846.

235 **The erasure of Smallwood, which would continue:** In 1969, when the distinguished African American historian Benjamin Quarles wrote his classic book *Black Abolitionists,* he did not mention Smallwood. Among many more recent, excellent books on escape networks that fail to credit Smallwood are Eric Foner's 2015 *Gateway to Freedom: The Hidden History of the Underground Railroad* and Damian Alan Pargas's 2022 *Freedom Seekers: Fugitive Slaves in North America, 1800–1860.* Others accord him a sentence or a paragraph in passing.

235 **"I, who had made it a matter of study for years":** Smallwood, *Narrative,* p. 28.

236 **the man chosen as "President of the Day" made a speech:** *The Provincial Freeman,* Aug. 5, 1854.

238 **working-class suburb of small cottages:** John Lorinc, "The Black Community in St. John's Ward," 2017, https://www.toronto.ca/explore-enjoy/history-art-culture/black-history-month /the-black-community-in-st-johns-ward/.

238 **an estimated thirty thousand Canadians of African descent:** Sandrine Ferré-Rode, "A Black Voice from the 'Other North': Thomas Smallwood's Canadian Narrative (1851)," *Revue française d'études américaines,* Mar. 2013, p. 24.

238 **activist in Baltimore named Hezekiah Grice:** Robin W. Winks, *The Blacks in Canada: A History,* 1971, p. 156.

238 **"that inconsistent nation," "the so-called land of liberty":** Smallwood, *Narrative,* pp. 36, viii.

238 **"I have met a prejudice equal to any thing I ever experienced":** Smallwood, *Narrative,* p. vii.

239 **"I refused, because I had had enough of getting slaves off":** Smallwood, *Narrative,* p. 57.

239 **he was listed in the 1846 Toronto city directory:** The listings for Smallwood's saw business are in

Toronto city directories, digitized at the Toronto Public Library, https://www.torontopubliclibrary.ca/history-genealogy/lh-digital-city-directories.jsp.

239 **"T. Smallwood's Saw Factory," according to his 1859 advertisement:** *The Provincial Freeman,* June 18, 1859.

239 **he was a leader at an unprecedented gathering:** "Report of the Convention of the Coloured Population, Held at Drummondville, Aug. 1847," pamphlet, available from the Colored Conventions Project at https://omeka.coloredconventions.org/items/show/451.

240 **Smallwood would later accuse "a few designing persons":** Smallwood, *Narrative,* p. 37.

240 **He sued *The Provincial Freeman*:** M.A.S.C. [Mary Ann Shadd Cary], "To the Patrons of the Freeman," *The Provincial Freeman,* Nov. 25, 1856. See also the introduction by Richard Almonte to the Mercury Press edition of Smallwood's *Narrative,* 2000, pp. 11–12.

240 **He was the leader of one faction in a split:** Letter from Isaac D. Shadd, *The Provincial Freeman,* June 20, 1857; see also C. Peter Ripley, ed., *The Black Abolitionist Papers,* vol. 2, p. 375, footnote 6.

241 **"This little work," he wrote:** Smallwood, *Narrative,* pp. vii–viii.

242 **Smallwood's poem was later reprinted:** James Torrington Spencer Lidstone, ed., *The Londoniad,* 1856, p. 108.

242 **"Let no one suppose that I have written this":** Smallwood, *Narrative,* p. 12.

242 **A few years later, in 1855, Smallwood was advertising:** *The Provincial Freeman,* Mar. 10, 1855.

242 **"after a time they crowded upon me by scores":** Smallwood, *Narrative,* p. 17.

242 **"I very much regret that I have not the manuscripts":** Smallwood, *Narrative,* p. 56.

243 **"Long before I had purchased myself from my owner":** Smallwood, *Narrative,* p. vi.

243 **"The success of the fugitive bill may be attributed":** Smallwood, *Narrative,* p. 17.

243 **"I would say to every sober, industrious colored man":** Smallwood, *Narrative,* p. 44.

244 **"I believe many of them had a fond, though vain hope":** Smallwood, *Narrative,* p. 45.

244 **Gunnell "frequently boasted that a neger":** Smallwood, *Narrative,* p. 23.

244 **"Not content with inoculating the length and breadth":** Smallwood, *Narrative,* p. 45.

245 **by 1863, when a committee of Black Torontonians gathered:** "Address by a Committee of Toronto Blacks," *Anglo-African,* Apr. 21, 1863, in Ripley, *The Black Abolitionist Papers,* vol. 2, p. 513.

245 **Later the same year, Smallwood gave an interview:** Testimony of Thomas Smallwood (Wood Worker), Toronto, Sept. 5, 1863, file no. 10, Canadian Testimony, Manuscripts of the American Freedmen's Inquiry Commission, U.S Department of War, Letters Received by the Office of the Adjutant General, Main Series, 1861–1870, National Archives via https://www.fold3.com/image/300487679. Thanks to Matthew Furrow for his transcriptions of this collection of letters and for his article, "Samuel Gridley Howe, the Black Population of Canada West, and the Racial Ideology of the 'Blueprint for Radical Reconstruction,'" *The Journal of American History,* vol. 97, no. 2, Sept. 2010, pp. 344–70.

246 **William Henry Smallwood, did go back:** Adrienne Shadd, Afua Cooper, and Karolyn Smardz Frost, *The Underground Railroad: Next Stop, Toronto!,* 2009, p. 49.

246 **According to a history of African Americans in Mississippi:** Vernon Lane Wharton, *The Negro in Mississippi, 1865–1890,* 1947, p. 129.

247 **"W.H. Smallwood, a popular colored citizen":** *State Ledger,* Apr. 21, 1883.

15. Resident Capitalist

249 **Lucy Crawford said her enslaver had agreed:** Negro Lucy Crawford vs. Hope H. Slatter, transcript of Baltimore City Court Proceedings, March 23, 1848, MSA SC 4239–26–16, Maryland State Archives.

249 **Robert Trunnell said he was a free person of color:** Robert Trunnell vs. Hope H. Slatter, Petition for Freedom, Circuit Court for the District of Columbia, Jan. 3, 1842, Record Group 21, National Archives.

249 **The teenage boy named Shadrack:** Slatter v. Holton, 19 La. 39 (1841), Louisiana Supreme Court, available at https://cite.case.law/la/19/39/.

249 **Anne Coale and her three children:** Laura L. B. Hutchins against Martha B. Fowler and Hope H. Slatter, Baltimore City Court, Chancery Papers, MSA SC 4239–5–118, Maryland State Archives.

250 **"the Baltimore negro-trader" had come to Washington:** *New-York Tribune* report, reprinted in *Huron Reflector,* Oct. 24, 1848.

250 **One day in 1845, when a local preacher called on Slatter:** *Green-Mountain Freeman,* Mar. 7, 1845.

251 **"Poor Torrey! Our heart bleeds for him":** *Albany Weekly Patriot,* Oct. 2, 1844.

251 **Chaplin arranged for a ship:** On the escape attempt aboard the *Pearl* and its aftermath, see Mary Kay Ricks, *Escape on the* Pearl*: The Heroic Bid for Freedom on the Underground Railroad,* 2007; Josephine F. Pacheco, *The* Pearl*: A Failed Slave Escape on the Potomac,* 2005; Daniel Drayton's memoir, *Personal Memoir of Daniel Drayton,* 1854; and John H. Paynter, "The Fugitives of The Pearl," *The Journal of Negro History,* vol. 1, no. 3, July 1916, pp. 243–60.

252 **Then a Black man named Judson Diggs:** Harriet Beecher Stowe, *A Key to Uncle Tom's Cabin,* 1853, p. 159.

253 **"Prominent among the arrivals of dealers in men and women":** *New-York Commercial Advertiser,* quoted in *Boston Recorder,* Apr. 28, 1848.

253 **The Baltimore correspondent of *The New York Herald* also heard:** *The New York Herald,* Apr. 23, 1848.

253 **Eyewitnesses claimed that the mob included:** The primary witness of Slatter's activities whose recollections survive was Joshua Giddings. See his statement to Congress, *Appendix to the Congressional Globe,* 1848, pp. 519–21.

254 **"the proposition made by individuals to lay violent hands":** "Privileges of Member of Congress—Mr. Giddings," *Appendix to the Congressional Globe,* 1848, pp. 519–21.

254 **Among those who saw the miserable captives:** *The Evening Star* (Washington, D.C.), Feb. 12, 1928.

255 **"The scene at the depot is represented":** Giddings, "Privileges of Member of Congress—Mr. Giddings," p. 520.

255 **an entire railcar was filled with the "sad and dejected" captives:** Slingerland's letter was printed in many newspapers, including *Buffalo Commercial Advertiser,* April 28, 1848.

256 **the casual identification of Slatter as a "double-distilled devil":** *The Liberator,* June 2, 1848.

257 **"Persons having slaves to sell will hereafter find us":** See, for instance, the ad in *Port Tobacco Times, and Charles County Advertiser,* July 27, 1848.

257 **The Sun announced that he had purchased a mansion:** *The Baltimore Sun,* Oct. 2, 1848.

257 **Soon Slatter appeared in Richmond:** Robert Lindsey and Sarah Crosland Lindsey, *Travels of Robert and Sarah Lindsey,* 1886, p. 31.

259 **"TO HIRE," said his notice in the *Mobile Daily Advertiser*:** *Mobile Daily Advertiser,* quoted in *The Liberator,* Jan. 18, 1850.

259 **The house had such lovely ironwork:** Slatter's rented house at 250 Government Street in Mobile is gone, replaced by a parking lot. But the handsome ironwork can be glimpsed in an old photo in the Historic American Buildings Survey of the Library of Congress, available at https://www.loc.gov/item/al0477/.

259 **Slatter went on an extraordinary buying spree:** Slatter's holdings are recorded in newspaper stories and in his extensive probate file at the Mobile County Courthouse, which has also been digitized and posted on Ancestry.com.

259 **a major bank:** *Mobile Daily Advertiser,* Sept. 7, 1850.

260 **thirty new yellow fever deaths in Mobile that day:** *The Autauga Citizen,* Sept. 22, 1853.

260 **"On the morning of the 15th":** *Mobile Daily Advertiser,* Sept. 16, 1853.

260 **"Notwithstanding the favorable weather":** *The Picayune,* Sept. 17, 1853.

260 **Yellow fever had first traveled to the New World:** Andrea Prinzi, "History of Yellow Fever in

the U.S.," American Society for Microbiology, May 17, 2021. Thanks to Dr. Ralph Hruban for sharing this bit of medical history.

261 **One, who signed his column only "Looker-On in Baltimore":** *The Commonwealth* (Boston), reprinted in *Herald of Freedom*, Nov. 4, 1853.

261 **His brother Shadrack was appointed the administrator:** Hope H. Slatter's probate file at the Mobile County Courthouse, also posted on Ancestry.com, lists his property and gives a fairly detailed account of his family's life over the next several years, including his widow's remarriage and her battles with Shadrack Slatter.

262 **Hope Jr. came to Washington to attend Georgetown College:** Hope H. Slatter's probate file lists the tuition payments for Georgetown College.

262 **Georgetown University, which some years earlier:** Rachel L. Swarns, "272 Slaves Were Sold to Save Georgetown. What Does It Owe Their Descendants?," *The New York Times*, Apr. 16, 2016.

262 **Hope Jr. went on to serve as a second lieutenant in the Confederate army:** President Andrew Johnson's Pardon of H. H. Slatter, Nov. 13, 1865, National Archives, record group 21, file unit 8021: United States v. H. H. Slatter.

262 **One sympathetic newspaper reporter described the defendant:** *The Cecil Whig*, Oct. 18, 1873.

262 **a Cleveland paper noted that "Slatter, who is wealthy":** *The Cleveland Leader*, Feb. 5, 1874.

262 **Before he could be sentenced, Slatter unexpectedly won a new trial:** *New Orleans Republican*, Apr. 9, 1875.

262 **a year later Grant agreed to give Slatter a pardon:** *The Evening Star* (Washington, D.C.), May 20, 1879.

262 **The assistant United States attorney who handled the murder case:** *Albany Evening Journal*, June 17, 1876.

263 **A decade after Slatter Jr. was released from prison:** *Mobile Police Department History*, 1902, digital archives of the Mobile Public Library, p. 91. The reference to Slatter does not give the exact dates of his service as police chief but says it was under Mayor Joseph Rich, who served from 1888 to 1894.

Epilogue

265 **At 4 p.m. on a baking Baltimore day, Colonel William Birney:** Several versions of Birney's report on the liberation of the slave jails were published in newspapers. For the most complete accounts, see *The Philadelphia Inquirer*, July 31, 1863, or *New-York Semi-Weekly Tribune*, July 31, 1863. *The Baltimore Sun*, July 28, 1863, had a local news report on both the freeing of the slave jails and Birney's recruitment for the United States Colored Troops.

265 **Birney, in his midforties:** This summary of Birney's life comes from ads for his law practice and news reports in multiple newspapers. See, for instance, the legal ad in Boston's *Emancipator and Republican*, Oct. 12, 1843; the report on his professorship in France in *Cleveland Plain Dealer*, Nov. 29, 1848; his founding of the newspaper *Philadelphia Merchant* in *The Portage Sentinel* of Ravenna, Ohio, Jan. 19, 1853.

266 **"In this yard no shrub or tree grows":** *The Philadelphia Inquirer*, July 31, 1863.

269 **"A Baltimore Slave Pen," read the headline:** *New-York Semi-Weekly Tribune*, July 31, 1863.

269 **As the historian Heather Andrea Williams discovered:** Williams, *Help Me*.

269 **Naturally, many of the ads named Slatter:** The ads quoted are from a collection of more than twenty-five hundred "lost friends" ads collected by the Historic New Orleans Collection that were published between 1879 and 1900 in *Southwestern Christian Advocate*, a local newspaper. The ads consistently misspell Slatter as "Slater," but the context makes clear that he is the slave trader involved, and I have substituted the correct spelling. See https://www.hnoc.org/database/lost-friends/.

270 **William Chaplin, who had organized the *Pearl* escape attempt:** *Weekly National Intelligencer*,

Aug. 17, 1850. See also Stanley Harrold, *Subversives: Antislavery Community in Washington, D.C., 1828–1865,* pp. 154–63.

271 **Gibbs moved to New York City:** Colored Conventions Project, "Jacob R. Gibbs," https://coloredconventions.org/black-mobility/delegates/jacob-r-gibbs/.

271 **In 1857, he signed a private letter:** Jacob R. Gibbs letter to Timothy B. Hudson, Oct. 18, 1857, in *The Black Abolitionist Papers, 1830–1865,* available via ProQuest.

271 **Charles Torrey's son and namesake fought for the Union:** Fuller Torrey, *Martyrdom,* p. 181.

271 **Hope Slatter's son and namesake fought for the Confederacy:** Pardon Application of Hope H. Slatter to President Andrew Johnson, Oct. 17, 1865, National Archives.

272 **booby-trapped the state constitution:** Maryland State Archives, "The Maryland Constitution of 1851," https://msa.maryland.gov/megafile/msa/speccol/sc2900/sc2908/000001/000631/html/am631--20.html.

272 **The *St. Mary's Gazette,* in southern Maryland, complained:** *St. Mary's Gazette,* reprinted in *Baltimore American,* Oct. 25, 1864.

272 **The newspapers tracked the votes:** *The Baltimore Sun,* Oct. 18, 1864.

272 **The *Baltimore American* reported that the civilian vote:** *Baltimore American,* Oct. 21, 1864.

272 **On the same day, *The Baltimore Sun*:** *The Baltimore Sun,* Oct. 21, 1864.

273 **the official count was declared to be 30,174 for the constitution:** Maryland State Archives, "The Maryland Constitution of 1864," https://msa.maryland.gov/megafile/msa/speccol/sc2900/sc2908/000001/000667/html/am667--95.html.

273 **The celebrations of Maryland's belated abolition of slavery:** *The Baltimore Sun,* Nov. 2, 1864.

274 **Two weeks after the vote became official, African Americans gathered:** "Freedom, Jubilee: Liberty," poster announcing Nov. 15, 1864, "Demonstration of the Celebration of the Emancipation," Library Company of Philadelphia, https://digital.librarycompany.org/islandora/object/Islandora%3A6264.

274 **He would live to be eighty-two, dying on May 10, 1883, of "old age":** Toronto Necropolis death records, 1883, via familysearch.org.

274 **A few of the Canadian papers took parsimonious note:** For example, *Winnipeg Free Press,* May 12, 1883.

274 **"In a word," he wrote, "the oath":** Smallwood, *Narrative,* p. 51.

275 **"Now then I will give my opinion":** Smallwood, *Narrative,* p. 48.

276 **If there ever were Smallwood gravestones:** Cemetery officials told the author they were unsure whether there were ever Smallwood family gravestones, but by the time of a complete survey in the 1980s no Smallwood markers were visible.

Index

About the Author

Scott Shane was a reporter for fifteen years at the *New York Times*, where he was twice a member of teams that won Pulitzer Prizes, and before that, for twenty-one years at the *Baltimore Sun*. His two previous books are *Dismantling Utopia*, a firsthand account of the collapse of the Soviet Union, and *Objective Troy*, the story of an American terrorist killed in a drone strike on orders of President Obama. In 2019–20, he was a fellow at the SNF Agora Institute at Johns Hopkins University, where he has taught courses on media and on the Russian attack on the 2016 American presidential election.

CELADON
BOOKS

Founded in 2017, Celadon Books, a division of
Macmillan Publishers, publishes a highly curated list
of twenty to twenty-five new titles a year. The list of
both fiction and nonfiction is eclectic and focuses
on publishing commercial and literary books and
discovering and nurturing talent.